ROCK

ROCK
MUSIC,
CULTURE,
AND BUSINESS

Joseph G. Schloss
New York University

Larry Starr
University of Washington

Christopher Waterman
University of California, Los Angeles

NEW YORK   OXFORD
OXFORD UNIVERSITY PRESS

Oxford University Press, Inc., publishes works that further Oxford University's
objective of excellence in research, scholarship, and education.

Oxford New York
Auckland   Cape Town   Dar es Salaam   Hong Kong   Karachi
Kuala Lumpur   Madrid   Melbourne   Mexico City   Nairobi
New Delhi   Shanghai   Taipei   Toronto

With offices in
Argentina   Austria   Brazil   Chile   Czech Republic   France   Greece
Guatemala   Hungary   Italy   Japan Poland   Portugal   Singapore
South Korea   Switzerland   Thailand   Turkey   Ukraine   Vietnam

For titles covered by Section 112 of the US Higher Education Opportunity Act,
please visit www.oup.com/us/he for the latest information about
pricing and alternate formats.

Published by Oxford University Press, Inc.
198 Madison Avenue, New York, New York 10016
http://www.oup.com

Oxford is a registered trademark of Oxford University Press

Library of Congress Cataloging-in-Publication Data

Schloss, Joseph Glenn.
   Rock : music, culture, and business / Joseph Schloss, Larry Starr, Christopher Waterman.
      p. cm.
   Includes bibliographical references and index.
   ISBN 978-0-19-975836-4
1. Rock music—History and criticism.   2. Popular music—Social aspects—United States.   I. Starr, Larry.   II. Waterman, Christopher Alan,
1954–   III. Title.
   ML3534.S356 2012
   781.6609—dc23   2011035706

Cover photo: Joan Jett and the Blackhearts on stage in 2011. Jett first came to prominence in the late seventies
as a member of the all-female hard rock band the Runaways, whose story is chronicled in the documentary *Edge-
play: A Film About the Runaways* (2004), and the feature film *The Runaways* (2010). After the group broke up in
1979, she formed her own band, Joan Jett and the Blackhearts, and became an MTV staple in the eighties with
such hits as "I Love Rock 'n' Roll," and "Crimson and Clover." Joan Jett achieved a third peak of popularity in
the nineties as a role model and mentor to many alternative musicians, and she remains active to this day.

Printing number: 9 8 7 6 5 4 3 2 1

Printed in the United States of America
on acid-free paper

CONTENTS

LIST OF LISTENING GUIDES

PREFACE

This book offers a fresh and comprehensive account of the rock era in American popular music, exploring "rock" as a cultural, social, and economic phenomenon as well as a musical sound and style. Drawing on the strengths of their best-selling *American Popular Music: From Minstrelsy to MP3*, authors Larry Starr and Christopher Waterman have joined forces with Joseph Schloss to create a book that is thoroughly new in conception, organization, and tone, and deeply original in content. Though some material has been adapted from the Starr/Waterman book, this volume consists primarily of new information, analysis, and perspectives.

We intend this book to serve a number of purposes. It may be used as a text for introductory college-level courses on rock, obviously, as it assumes a mature and literate reader but not one who necessarily has any specific background in music or in this particular area of musical study. These same assumptions will also make this book useful to the general reader who wishes a broad-based introduction to our subject. In addition, this volume will serve the interests of specialists—musicians, graduate students, teachers, and scholars—who need a comprehensive one-volume overview, or review, of the topic. We have kept this wide potential audience constantly in mind as we strove to keep our book accessible and inviting, while always reflecting our own deep involvement in the music and in contemporary scholarly issues surrounding it.

What distinguishes our book from others in its rapidly growing field is that it combines two perspectives not often found in the same place: the study of cultural, social, and economic history, on one hand; and the detailed study of musical style on the other. More to the point, we emphasize the influence that these two aspects of rock history have had on *each other*. One of the guiding principles of our approach is that these factors have interacted so continuously and profoundly over the course of rock history that it is actually impossible to understand the development of either aspect without studying the other. An added benefit of taking such an approach is that it raises a wide variety of fresh issues and questions that can be addressed from many possible points of view, depending on the instructor's preference.

A brief word concerning methodology: We have sought to limit the use of specialized terms, to employ them only when clearly necessary, and to define them as they arise naturally in the course of study. The most important and frequently employed of these terms appear in **boldface** when they first occur in the text, and are also given extensive definitions in the glossary at the end of the book. (The glossary is reserved for terms that recur throughout the book and that would not be defined adequately for our purposes in a standard college dictionary. This means that terms like "producer," which has a special meaning in popular music, will be found in the glossary, along with other expected terms such as "blues" and "syncopation.") A particularly original feature of this book follows directly from this approach: Rather than presenting any separate, abstract coverage of basic musical terminology (melody, chords, rhythm, and so forth) such as may be found in many introductory music texts, we have incorporated the introduction and definition of these musical elements directly into the first sustained discussion of specific recordings (see "Three Big Hits of the Pre–Rock 'n' Roll Period") in our Chapter 1. This methodology assures that the evolving historical discussion, the development of listening skills, and the understanding of essential terms all proceed together as aspects of an integrated discourse. Significant terms that are relevant only to a limited section of material are defined in context and may also be located by using the book's index.

As may be surmised from the preceding paragraph, our analyses of recordings are integrated directly into the text at the points where they become relevant to the developing narrative. This approach seemed to us both logical and functional. Listening charts are used to represent and summarize, in outline form, the most important elements of many recordings that are discussed in some detail in the text. The fact that we are dealing here to an overwhelming extent with songs—texted music—has enabled us to treat musical issues with some sophistication without having to employ actual musical notation, since lyrics may be used as points of specific orientation in the musical discussions. This keeps the focus on listening, and opens the musical analyses to the widest possible audience of readers without compromising depth of treatment.

Boxes are used occasionally in this book to provide further insight and information on significant individuals, recordings, and topics in cases where such material—albeit useful—would interrupt the flow of narrative. Important names are underlined throughout the book.

We would like to thank our families, who put up with a great deal as our work underwent its extensive development. We extend our gratitude to Janet M. Beatty, executive editor at Oxford University Press, and to her gifted associates Nichole LeFebvre and Shelby Peak. We owe a substantial debt to the many readers who offered extensive and helpful comments on our work in its various stages, including

Mark Adam, Acadia University

Steve Davis, Lone Star College–Kingwood

John Ellis, State University of New York at Potsdam

Howard Goldstein, Auburn University

Frank Gunderson, Florida State University

Clarence Hines, University of North Florida

Morten Kristiansen, Xavier University

Laura Lohman, California State University, Fullerton

Michael Morrison, Purdue University

Gary Pritchard, Cerritos College

Will Redman, Towson University

W. Anthony Sheppard, Williams College

Tony Steve, Jacksonville University

Dean Suzuki, San Francisco State University

Patrick Warfield, University of Maryland

We also owe a debt of gratitude to the folks at Joel Whitburn's Record Research for their series of books containing *Billboard* chart data. We could readily go on, like those CD inserts thanking everybody from the Almighty on down, but there's a story waiting to be told, and we'd best get on with it. If there's anybody out there we neglected to thank, let us know, and hope for a second edition so that we can do it next time!

Joseph Schloss
Larry Starr
Christopher Waterman

INTRODUCTION

A textbook about rock music may seem like a paradox. A textbook is reflective, analytical, and mature. Rock is wild, rebellious, aggressive, and loud. A textbook is about bringing order to chaos. Rock is about bringing chaos to order. A textbook is about thinking; rock is about feeling.

But thinking and feeling do not have to be mutually exclusive. Understanding a phenomenon can help you experience it more fully and help you connect it more directly to your own life. Sometimes thinking about something can even be a *way* of experiencing it. In fact, the idea of rock as a kind of spontaneous burst of raw energy that refuses to be bound by the rules of culture is *itself* a cultural construct that has much in common with romanticist impulses in other art forms.

In reality, rock, like all expressive arts, is the result of decisions made by specific people in particular times and places, each of whom tried to make the best use of available resources to accomplish their personal goals. What were they trying to accomplish (and why)? What cultural and material resources were available to them? Why did they choose certain options and reject others? And how did they find themselves in those situations in the first place?

In this book we address these questions by focusing on three interwoven threads of rock history: the evolution of its specific *musical* characteristics, the growth of its *cultural* principles, and the development of its approach to the *business* of popular music. More importantly, we focus on the *interactions among* these three factors. At every stage of rock's development, the complex relationship of music, culture, and business has profoundly shaped both the options that people had and the choices they made.

On a musical level, we explore the forms, styles, and techniques that have been associated with rock music at each point in its history. We view these musical characteristics not as rules that have been set in stone, but as tools created by musicians to achieve their artistic and social goals. This, in turn, can tell us much about the goals themselves as well as the logic of the musicians' strategies; moreover, a close analysis of rock's musical principles can show us the way both of these things have changed over time.

In looking at the cultural aspects of rock, we use the term "culture" in the broadest possible sense to include such things as historical and social context, the identities of individuals and groups, relationships between individuals and groups, technological developments, ideologies, and demographic issues including race, class, and gender. Each of these factors has shaped rock music profoundly.

The final thread of our discussion is business. When viewing rock as an art, there is a natural tendency to view the economic aspects of its production as marginal, and even—in certain circumstances—as parasitic. Our position is that, for better or worse, rock has always been a profession as much as it has been an art, and to ignore that fact is to distort the actual experience of those who have participated in it. This is not to say that the economic imperatives that have influenced rock have always—or even primarily—been positive, only that they are essential to understanding the decisions that artists have made throughout the course of rock's history.

We believe that this approach has several advantages, the first of which is simple accuracy. Almost all of the changes that have driven the evolution of rock were the result of the interplay among music, culture, and business, rather than any one of them in isolation. Another advantage is consistency. As the text moves chronologically through the history of rock, it systematically discusses these key elements in each subgenre and historical era. This, we feel, provides an analysis of each subgenre that is simultaneously reflective of its unique characteristics and fundamentally consistent with the others. Treating rock as a set of relationships also allows us to look critically at the ways different groups—both mainstream and marginal—have navigated and renegotiated these relationships to serve their own agendas. It also enables us to look at the influence of rock—as a concept—on musicians in other genres. Finally, looking at rock as a set of relationships makes apparent the organic connections between recent developments in the music industry and rock's earliest manifestations. Though much has changed between rock's earliest years and the present, the nature of the larger relationships that drive it has remained surprisingly consistent over the last half-century.

Taking such an approach naturally leads us to focus more on movements and issues and less on individuals. Although we do discuss the most prominent figures in rock history, our intention here is not primarily to recapitulate the careers of the "greatest" rock musicians of different eras. Musical quality is obviously a subjective phenomenon and can only be judged within the context of a specific set of expectations, and our goal is to discuss the development of those expectations themselves. For that reason, we have chosen to discuss artists primarily on the basis of their overall significance to the rock culture of their eras, as representatives of movements, subgenres and trends.

Underlying our exploration of rock music—its history and evolution, its styles, movements, and attitudes—are deeper questions about music itself, its cultural importance, social significance, and psychological impacts. Why do people make and listen to music? What do they want from it, and what does it give them? These questions take us beyond the central concern of classic aesthetic theory, the creation and appreciation of "beauty for beauty's sake." People value music for many reasons, including a desire for beauty, but also a great deal more: They use music to escape from the rigors of the work week, to celebrate important events in their lives, to help them make money, war, and love. In order to understand the cultural significance of rock, we must examine both the music—its tones and textures, rhythms and forms—and the broader patterns of social identity that have shaped Americans' tastes and values.

MUSIC AND IDENTITY

None of us is born knowing exactly who we are—we all *learn* to be human in particular ways, and music is one important medium through which we formulate and express our identity. Think back to the very first song you remember hearing as a child, when you were, say, five years old. Odds are you heard it at home, or maybe in a car, or (depending on your age) over a transistor radio or a portable CD player at the beach. The person playing it may have been one of your parents, or an older brother or sister. These are often the people who influence our early musical values, and it is they whose values we sometimes emphatically reject later in life. In elementary school, other kids begin to influence our taste, a development closely connected with the ways in which we form social groups based on gender, age, and other factors (boys versus girls, fifth graders versus first graders, cool kids versus nerds).

As we move into adolescence, music also enters our private lives, providing comfort and continuity during emotional crises and offering us the opportunity to fantasize about romance and rebellion. Music provides images of gender identity, culturally specific ways of being masculine and feminine. Ethnicity and race—including notions of how to act authentically "white" or "black" or "Latino"— are also powerfully represented in music.

As you grow older, a song or a singer's voice may suddenly transport you back to a specific moment and place in your life, sometimes many decades earlier. Like all human beings, we make stories out of our lives, and music plays an important role in bringing these narratives to life. Some songs—for example, Van Morrison's "Brown Eyed Girl" (1967); Don McLean's paean to rock 'n' roll history, "American Pie" (1971); John Cougar Mellencamp's "Jack and Diane" (1982), with its rueful refrain, "Oh yeah, life goes on, long after the thrill of living is gone"; and "Back in the Day" (2003), Missy Elliott's foray into hip-hop nostalgia—are really *about* memory and the mixed feelings of warmth and loss that accompany a retrospective view of our own lives. Such personal narratives are important to developing a sense of who we are and where we belong in the world. At the same time, music can also help us understand others. At its best, music can bring us to a deeper understanding of the many cultures that have come together to make up American society. At its worst, it can promote simplistic or reductive views of culture. Sometimes it does both at the same time.

One way that music in America has historically promoted a simplistic view of culture is by creating or reinforcing *stereotypes*, convenient ways of organizing people into categories. It is easy to find examples of stereotyping in this history: the common portrayal in song lyrics and music videos of women as sexual objects, and the association of men with violence; the image of African American men as playboys and gangsters; the stereotype of southern white musicians as illiterate, backwoods "rednecks"; the association of songs about money with supposedly Jewish musical characteristics; and the caricatures of Asian and Latin American people found in many "novelty songs" from the 1920s through the 1960s.

In order to understand the history of rock music in particular it is important to be critically aware of the long, complicated history of white fascination with black music—and of the complex and ever-evolving relationship between black and white musicians, and between African American and European American musical traditions. Many metaphors have been used to describe this relationship—homage, borrowing, syncretism, crossover, exchange, exploitation, rip-off—but none of them adequately captures the shifting, sometimes tensely ambivalent and sometimes joyously synergistic relationship between these two great musical streams, and the cultures that gave them birth.

Segregation, as both a cultural force and a practical reality, profoundly affected rock 'n' roll in its early years. Courtesy of Library of Congress.

The role of *race and ethnicity* in American music must be situated within a broader context. The very fact that Americans speak of "black" and "white" music as though these were self-evident, well-defined entities stems from a particular history of racial segregation—and in particular from the so-called Jim Crow laws designed during the early twentieth century to prevent racial commingling in the American South. This way of classifying human beings into racial categories is not universal and in fact differs substantially from perceptions of human diversity in many other parts of the world.

The history of rock music presents many examples of performers whose music in fact challenged racial stereotypes, who didn't "sound like they were supposed to." Indeed, much of the music that we discuss in this book does not admit easily of straightforward racial or ethnic classification. Although Elvis Presley was a white man born in the Deep South under the regime of official racial segregation, it is hard to know how to definitively "segregate" the music on his two-sided hit "Don't Be Cruel"/"Hound Dog" (1956), the only record ever to top the pop, country and western, and rhythm & blues charts at the same time. Ray Charles's country and western twang on "I Can't Stop Loving You" (1962), as well as the wildly eclectic juxtaposition of funk, rock, and European synth-pop in early hip-hop samples; the recorded work of Jimi Hendrix, the seminal African American rock guitarist whose records never sold particularly well in the black community; and that of the equally talented Duane Allman, a white guitarist raised in the Deep South who was a key player on classic soul music recordings by Aretha Franklin and Wilson Pickett, all challenge the idea that the history of American music can be understood along strictly racial lines.

This is not to say that racism is no longer a factor in American culture or in the production and marketing of music. Even if race is more a social fiction than a biological fact, it is a fiction that has taken on a powerful life of its own, helping some people to achieve their goals and radically disadvantaging others. If we accept the statement that "music has no color"—an assertion made in full sincerity by many musicians of all colors—we nonetheless cannot escape the fact that racial stereotypes arguably carry just as much force in contemporary popular culture (say, in many gangsta rap videos and in songs promulgated by white-supremacist rock groups on the Internet) as they did when white performers first artificially darkened their skins, or "blacked up," for a nineteenth-century minstrel show.[1]

One of the most significant ways that race and ethnicity have influenced the history of rock involves not its production at all, but the demographics of its audience. As we will discuss, arguments about who is—and who *should*

---

1. For more detailed information on the minstrel tradition, and other genres of popular music that lie outside the scope of this book, see *American Popular Music: From Minstrelsy to MP3*, by Starr and Waterman (third edition, 2010).

be—listening to rock are fundamental to its very existence. Rock music has traditionally been viewed as a genre with a primarily white, middle-class audience. In many cases this has been true. In some cases, it has been false. Often, it has become a self-fulfilling prophecy. In every case, however, this perception has influenced the music in complex and far-reaching ways.

Sexuality and gender are other aspects of identity that are central to the history of American music in general, and rock music in particular. A large proportion of American popular music has been concerned, in one way or another, with relationships between men and women. This polyphonic public conversation has represented many voices, attitudes, and viewpoints: for example, the male bravado of Muddy Waters's urban blues song "Hoochie Coochie Man" (1954); the mature resignation of singer-songwriter Carole King's "It's Too Late" (1971); the Freudian angst of Prince's "When Doves Cry" (1984); and the hip moralizing of Lauryn Hill's "Doo-Wop (That Thing)" (1998), a didactic song that urges both men and women to clean up their acts. We are sure that you could come up with many examples of this theme from the music you follow most closely. Suffice it for now to say that the history of rock music is also a history of popular attitudes toward romance, love, and sex.

Since so much popular music deals with love and sex, it is not surprising that public authorities of various sorts have been concerned to monitor representations of sexuality. We will encounter many examples of censorship in the history of rock music—for example, the 1954 cover version of Big Joe Turner's "Shake, Rattle and Roll" by Bill Haley and the Comets, which cleaned up risqué aspects of the original lyrics, or the production of "childproofed" versions of hip-hop and alternative rock hits, with the offensive references "bleeped" out. One area of particular concern has been the expression of perspectives on love that deviate from the normative views expressed by political and religious authorities. For example, the depiction of non-heterosexual relationships has been treated gingerly by the entertainment industry. However, the fact that homosexual and bisexual relationships have rarely been represented explicitly in popular music did not hinder the success of the Village People's disco hits "YMCA" and "In the Navy" (Numbers 2 and 3 on the charts, respectively, in 1979). These songs, which can be interpreted on one level as a defiantly out-of-the-closet celebration of gay popular culture, function on another level to reaffirm gay stereotypes, conveyed onstage and in music videos by the band's adornment in campy costumes—the cowboy, the construction worker, the sailor, the leather-clad biker, the Indian chief, and so on. (The question of what the Navy thought it was doing when it sought to use the song "In the Navy" for a recruitment campaign, or what millions of straight Americans think they're up to when they mime the song "YMCA" at sporting events, raises a number of interesting issues that we cannot probe here.) It must be noted that a number of prominent rock stars—including Little Richard, David Bowie, Prince, and Madonna—have fashioned personas that seem purposefully to *blur* public perceptions of their sexual orientation. In regard to sexuality, as with other dimensions of social identity, music seems particularly well suited to carrying multiple meanings, depending in substantial measure upon who is doing the listening.

Beyond sexuality, much rock music is concerned—directly or indirectly—with the concept of gender itself, and particularly with the performance of masculinity. What does it mean to "be a man"? To what extent—and in what ways—is being masculine synonymous with being a rocker? How have women and men in different times and places negotiated these expectations? A large part of many rock artists' appeal has been their ability and willingness to perform alternative visions of masculinity and femininity. Artists such as the Beatles, Janis Joplin, Patti Smith, and Kurt Cobain all challenged the conventional wisdom of their eras about how men and women should present themselves.

Although Americans, unlike the English, are often characterized as being oblivious to *class distinctions,* the expression of working-class, middle-class and upper-class identities and experiences runs right through the history of

Contrasting rock identities: **Lady Gaga** (accepting an award at the 2010 MTV Video Music Awards) and **Justin Bieber** (accepting an award at the 2011 MTV Movie Awards); (l) photo by Kevin Mazur/WireImage/Getty Images; (r) photo by Scott Gries/MTV/PictureGroup) via AP IMAGES.

American popular music. However, class identity has often bubbled just below the sleek surfaces of rock music. In Chuck Berry's "Maybellene" (1955), the protagonist's automotive pursuit of a young woman is given a distinctive flavor by the distinction between his working-class V-8 Ford and the girl's more expensive Cadillac Coupe de Ville. (The use of a French name—always a marker of elite culture—drives the point home, we might say.) The Crystals' 1962 hit "Uptown" sketches the social geography of New York City, tracing the daily path of a young man who works "downtown," where he "don't get no breaks," and comes home every evening to his lover's "uptown" tenement, where he feels like a "king." Although Americans do not tend to wear their class affiliations on their sleeves, rock music is full of references to wealth, poverty, and the effect of economic matters on the human heart.

Generational identity has, perhaps naturally, been a constant theme in an industry that relies to a great degree on the exploitation and creation of new styles, or at least the appearance of novelty. Popular music has played a major role in creating youth cultures and in shaping Americans' conceptions of adolescence. Beginning in the early twentieth century and continuing through the rock 'n' roll era and the myriad youth movements and fads that have followed in its wake, generational identity has been crucial to the workings of the American music industry and to the identity formations of musicians and audiences. The music industry now draws a broad distinction between kids in the twelve-to-sixteen age bracket—the patrons of teenybopper acts like Miley Cyrus and Justin Bieber—and young adults in the seventeen- to twenty-five-year-old range, whom the industry relies on to download millions upon millions of rock, rap, and alternative music tracks. The history of rock music provides us with a unique window onto changing conceptions of adolescence, ranging from the mild rebellion of the Beach Boys' "Fun, Fun, Fun" (1964) to the Beastie Boys' rowdy party anthem "(You Gotta) Fight for Your Right (to Party)" (1987) and Nirvana's sardonic, depression-tinged "Smells Like Teen Spirit" (1991). It is no exaggeration to say that rock music has been one of the main cultural forms through which Americans have learned how to "act their age."

WHAT IS ROCK?

The preceding issues of identity are fundamental to the very definition of rock, and thus to the organization of this book. The question of what is or isn't rock music is one that has had many different answers at many different times. Often, it has even had different answers at the *same* time. Rather than create a strict boundary between rock and other musical genres, we view rock as a continuously evolving set of relationships among musical expectations, cultural values, and business practices that developed in a particular time and place. The extent to which these relationships can be altered before they should no longer be considered "rock" is a subjective question, and one that we take on a case-by-case basis.

We have even chosen to include musical styles that are sometimes not considered rock at all if we feel they have a significant association—positive or negative—with the core set of rock relationships. For example, we discuss disco music in spite of the fact that it is almost never considered a form of rock precisely *because* it served as a foil to the rock culture of its era. In its time, disco was viewed as a significant threat to the future of rock music, and much rock music of that era was specifically conceived as a response to that threat. We discuss reggae music because many Jamaican artists of the seventies (especially Bob Marley) consciously modeled their approach on that of their rock contemporaries.

It is also important to note that at some points in its history, rock music has been the dominant form of popular music in the United States, while at other times rock has stood in direct opposition to the popular musical trends of the day. The blurry and ever-shifting line between "rock" and "pop" is itself an important aspect of the history of the genre, and one that we deal with as such.

A NOTE ON THE TERMS "ROCK 'N' ROLL" AND "ROCK"

The musical form we discuss in this book was initially known as "rock 'n' roll." This term applied from the mid-1950s to the late 1960s. As the music matured in the late sixties, the term "rock" began to be used to refer not only to the genre but to the entire culture associated with it, including a growing sense of its own history. For this reason, we use the term "rock" as a general term for the entire genre and its cultural associations, and the term "rock 'n' roll" to refer more specifically to the music that was made during the first fifteen or so years of the "rock" era.

1

THE PREHISTORY OF
ROCK 'N' ROLL

Rock 'n' roll was both distinctive from, and dependent on, the musical styles and popular cultural movements that preceded it, and it is important that we gain some sense of the historical factors that contributed to its emergence in the mid-1950s. While the rise of rock 'n' roll is widely recognized as a rebellion against the restrictive American culture of the 1950s, it was equally a rebellion against the business practices of the popular music industry at that time. Before rock 'n' roll, popular music was dominated by a centralized industry that excluded many artists, musical styles, and economic approaches that did not conform to its strict expectations. Rock 'n' roll, by contrast, embraced the outsider status of these excluded genres (such as rhythm and blues, country and western, and some forms of Latin music) and ultimately helped to bring them into the mainstream.

In this chapter, we discuss the roots of the mainstream music industry in the United States, the musical systems that competed with it, how their general approaches differed, and how these conflicts set the stage for the birth of rock 'n' roll. It is natural in retrospect to see the self-appointed guardians of the pre-rock era as hysterically overreacting to the perceived threat posed by the rise of rock 'n' roll. But—for better or worse—rock 'n' roll really *was* a threat to the existing order. To understand why, we must first take a look at the system that rock 'n' roll so fundamentally challenged.

POPULAR MUSIC BEFORE THE RISE OF ROCK 'N' ROLL

The fact that the modern music industry began more than a century ago as an outgrowth of the printing and publishing industries is an accident of history that continues to influence popular music to the present day. In the nineteenth century, before mass media and mass-produced recordings became commonplace, there were two primary ways that people enjoyed popular music: attending live performances by professional musicians, and performing the music themselves at home. Home music performance was encouraged by the growing perception in the nineteenth century that owning a piano—and displaying it proudly in one's home—demonstrated cultural sophistication and upward mobility. The popularity of amateur home performance (echoed in the modern era by karaoke and video games such as *Guitar Hero* and *Rock Band*) presented a new business opportunity: sheet music.

Sheet music was simply printed notation of popular songs, designed to be played by an amateur musician on a piano at home. Since sheet music was a form of mass-produced printed material, it is not surprising that its production would be handled by the same industry that produced books, magazines, and newspapers. The social, cultural, and—ultimately—legal expectations for sheet music sales were naturally based on those of books as well. Like authors, songwriters had a relatively straightforward relationship with publishing companies: The publisher would essentially purchase the song from the songwriter, and then print, distribute, and advertise it. Payments were usually made in the form of *royalties*—a percentage of total profits from the sheet music's sales. Since most of the songs that were published at that time were composed by two-person professional songwriting teams, in which one partner composed the music and the other wrote the lyrics, it was common practice to split the royalties evenly between the two contributors. Although the way music is composed has changed drastically in the one-hundred-plus years since this practice was established, this division (50/50, lyrics and music) is still commonplace.

In the twentieth and twenty-first centuries, as recordings, radio, television, and the Internet overtook sheet music as the preferred methods for the distribution of popular music, one might have expected the music industry to create new business models to fit them. This, for the most part, did not happen; the rules for sheet music were simply adjusted to fit each new situation. The result has been an industry that is substantially skewed to favor the interests of songwriters over those of performers. The ways that different rock artists and movements have dealt with that situation—in some cases accommodating themselves to it, in others rebelling against it—continues to be one of the largest influences on the development of the music to the present day. In fact, it could be argued that rock 'n' roll itself actually began as an attempt to destroy this system, known at the time as Tin Pan Alley.

At the dawn of the modern music industry in the late nineteenth century, publishers bought popular songs from their authors and sold the sheet music to the public. Publishing companies would then encourage as many artists as possible to perform their songs and thereby popularize them. Under this system, live performances were essentially viewed as advertisements for sheet music.

By the early twentieth century, publishers had streamlined the process: Rather than wait for songwriters to approach them and negotiate a price for each song individually, they began to sign the songwriters to exclusive contracts that covered all of their output. Songwriting essentially became an office job. In fact, so many songwriters were housed in offices on New York's West 28th Street that the sound of their many pianos playing at the same time was said to resemble the clatter of tin pans in a busy kitchen, an observation that led to the street being nicknamed "Tin Pan Alley." That term soon came to represent the entire popular music industry. This term can also be seen as comparing songwriters to chefs in a busy restaurant, trying to quickly "cook up" songs that would appeal to impatient customers—a description of the Tin Pan Alley approach that is relatively accurate.

Unlike the rock system that would replace it, the Tin Pan Alley system was based on a strict separation between the jobs of *songwriter* and *performer*. It was extremely rare for one person to fulfill both of these roles, not only because they were viewed as different kinds of talent, but also because they operated in different worlds. Songwriters were associated with publishing companies and wrote songs intended to appeal to the widest possible range of singers, in order to maximize publishing profits. Singers chose from the songs that were available (often influenced by bribes, threats, and other forms of influence on the part of publishers) and made their income from live performance. They were expected to present the broadest available variety of songs to appeal to the widest possible audience. Audiences, for their part, generally expected a working artist to perform a selection of popular hits of the day, which meant that most artists were drawing from the same repertoire of songs. In such an environment, artists who wrote their own songs would be viewed as cripplingly limited. They would be, in essence, restricting their repertoire to the work of a single songwriter (themselves), and would likely be seen much like a restaurant that only served one dish! In contrast to this perspective, rock presented the practice of writing one's own songs not as a limitation, but as an indicator of sincerity and a deep personal connection to the music. By changing this perception, rock would essentially change the entire economic structure of popular music.

One of the stylistic foundations of Tin Pan Alley was a distinctive four-part song form, the so-called AABA form. The structure of such songs includes four sections of equal length, in the musical pattern:

$$A \quad A \quad B \quad A$$

Later in this chapter we examine a specific example of this form, the song "Love and Marriage." Other AABA songs with which you may be familiar include "I Got Rhythm," composed by George and Ira Gershwin in 1930; and "Over the Rainbow," composed by Harold Arlen and E. Y. Harburg, familiar from the 1939 MGM film *The Wizard of Oz*. Over the course of many years, such song forms became the basis of listening habits; in those days, just as today, audiences were conditioned to hearing particular musical forms. **Composers**, singers, and **arrangers**—the individuals who bore responsibility for creating a musical environment (including choice of instrumental accompaniment, the pacing of the performance, and so on) that would match a given singer's vocal strengths to a particular song—became adept at fulfilling these expectations while introducing just enough unexpected variation to keep the listener's attention. The attractiveness of a popular song, and of its rendering on a particular recording, had much to do with achieving a balance between predictability and novelty. Although a lot of mediocre music was produced by Tin Pan Alley composers, the best songwriters were able to work creatively within the structural limitations of standard popular song forms.

It is important to recognize that this balance between predictability and novelty was not only intended to appeal to listeners as music lovers, it was also intended to appeal to them as consumers. Songs were commercial products, and from a business standpoint a good song was a profitable one. A considerable asset of AABA songs is that they were also extremely efficient to create. After all, a songwriter only had to create two short, contrasting, sections (A and B)—lasting a few seconds each—and the *form itself* converted them into a full-length song. Similarly, once everyone understood how it worked, AABA form also made it very easy to teach the songs to professional musicians in a matter of minutes. This is a perfect example of the way a song's form can reflect the social and economic environment in which its creators are working. AABA form was designed to be emotionally attractive to the widest possible audience, easy to produce (like a car, each piece fits together in a predetermined matrix), easy to *re*-produce (among musicians), and easy to perform and thus advertise. The fact that rock 'n' roll often (though not entirely) rejected the AABA form thus also indicates a rejection of the business strategies that made this form so important in the first place.

Most hit records of the decade leading up to the emergence of rock 'n' roll (1945–1955) were romantic Tin Pan Alley–style songs, backed by string orchestras and performed by *crooners*—sweet-voiced singers like Frank Sinatra, Perry Como, and Nat "King" Cole, who used the microphone to create a sense of intimacy. The sentimentality of these songs can be gleaned from their titles: "Prisoner of Love" and "(I Love You) For Sentimental Reasons" (1946), "My Darling, My Darling" and "You're Breaking My Heart" (1949), "Cry" (1951), "No Other Love" and "You You You" (1953), all Number 1 pop hits. These romantic recordings were interspersed on the popularity charts with catchy, lighthearted novelty songs, including Number 1 hits such as "Woody Woodpecker" (Kay Kyser, 1948), "I Saw Mommy Kissing Santa Claus" (Jimmy Boyd, 1952), and "The Doggie in the Window" (Patti Page, 1953).

The roots of this musical conservatism are not difficult to pinpoint. Although there was a brief depression just after the Second World War, the national economy expanded rapidly during the postwar decade, fueled by the lifting of wartime restrictions on the production of consumer goods, the increased availability of jobs in the industrial and service sectors of the economy, and the G.I. Bill, which provided educational and job opportunities for returning servicemen. After the uncertainty and personal sacrifice of the war years, many people simply wanted to settle down, raise a family, and focus on building their own futures. For millions of Americans who had served in the armed forces, or had come to the city in search of work during the war, or whose immigrant parents and grandparents had fled poverty earlier in the century, this represented

Nat "King" Cole (at the piano in an early 1940s recording session). Used by permission of the University of Missouri–Kansas City Libraries, Special Collections Department.

the first opportunity to buy a home. If we also take into account the underlying uncertainties and tensions of the postwar era—including the threat of nuclear war and the Cold War conflicts in Europe and Asia—it makes perfect sense that many new members of the American middle class preferred popular music that focused on romantic sentiments and helped to create a comforting sound environment in the home. In a sense, the "hi-fi" record player and the television set had come to replace the piano as symbols of middle-class domesticity.

The economics of the music industry also played a role in the conservativism of much mainstream pop music produced in the years preceding rock 'n' roll. During the postwar decade we see clearly for the first time a phenomenon that has helped to shape the development of popular music in the United States ever since: a constant tug-of-war between the music business's efforts to predict (and control) the public's consumption of music and the periodic eruption of new musical fads, usually based in youth culture. In general, the center of the music business—like many other sectors of corporate America—became increasingly routinized after the Second World War. Recorded music had become a product, sold in units, and listeners were consumers.

Teenagers study the offerings on a jukebox, 1957. Courtesy of Library of Congress.

The medium of radio played a critical role in the promotion of popular records of the era. The idea of *Top 40 radio programming*—another attempt to control the uncertainty of the marketplace—was developed in the early 1950s by Todd Storz, a **disc jockey** in Omaha, Nebraska. Storz observed teenagers dropping coins in jukeboxes and noticed that they tended to play certain songs repeatedly. He applied this idea to radio programming, selecting a list of forty top hits, which he played over and over. The idea spread quickly, and within a few years many radio stations were playing the same set of songs.

As popular music increasingly appeared on radio broadcasts and recordings, publishers rushed to find ways to apply the rules that had been created for sheet music to these new endeavors. *Licensing and copyright agencies* such as *ASCAP* (*The American Society of Composers, Authors, and Publishers*) and *BMI* (*Broadcast Music, Incorporated*) were established to control the flow of profits from the sale, broadcasting, and live performance of popular music. ASCAP was founded in 1914 in an attempt to force all business establishments that featured live music to pay royalties for the public use of music. By the 1920s almost all leading publishing houses and composers belonged to ASCAP, and by 1939 ASCAP had licensed around 90 percent of mainstream pop songs.

As profits from radio broadcasts rose, ASCAP turned up the legal pressure on the radio networks (ABC, CBS, NBC, and Dumont) to turn over a larger portion of their revenues. In 1940 the radio networks counterattacked by forming BMI, a rival licensing agency specifically designed to challenge

ASCAP's monopoly. While BMI was not initially expected to survive for long, its "open door" policy allowed songwriters working outside of mainstream pop to claim royalties from the use of their songs on the broadcast media, including radio and, increasingly, television. This gave a boost to musicians working in the idioms of country and western and rhythm & blues, genres which had largely been ignored by ASCAP and which rose in economic importance during and after World War II. It also led to these genres being played increasingly on the radio by broadcasters who wished to resist the control that ASCAP held over popular music, thus introducing rhythm & blues and country and western music to new audiences who would soon become the first rock 'n' roll fans.

Of all the new electronic technologies of the postwar era, television exerted the most profound influence on American culture. The development of television broadcasting, foreseen by science fiction writers of the nineteenth century, started in earnest in the 1920s. In 1946 it was estimated that Americans owned six thousand television sets; this figure shot up to three million in 1948, then twelve million in 1951. For better or worse, by the early 1950s television had become the central focus of leisure time in millions of American households.

Television's massive success rested on its ability to fuse the forms and functions of previous media, including radio, the record player, and cinema. Like Hollywood film, television was a multiple medium, combining sound and moving images. Like radios and record players, the TV set could be brought into the family parlor (now called a "living room") and incorporated into the daily round of domestic life. TV quickly became the main outlet for corporate advertising, and by 1952 the four big networks—ABC, CBS, NBC, and Dumont—began to turn significant profits. TV broadcasters used a great deal of recorded and live music, and there can be no doubt that the new medium was perceived initially by the record industry as a threat: In 1949 retail sales of records fell drastically, while sales of television sets increased by some 400 percent. By the mid-1950s, however, television had become the most important medium for launching new performers and recordings, and established stars such as Perry Como, Nat "King" Cole, Tommy Dorsey, and Jackie Gleason hosted their own weekly variety shows.

Meanwhile, the entertainment industry in general was growing rapidly after the war, and in 1947 record companies achieved retail sales of over $214 million, finally surpassing the previous peak, established back in 1921, more than a quarter of a century earlier. This growth was supported by the booming postwar economy and by a corresponding increase in the disposable income of many American families. In particular, record companies began for the first time to target young people, many of whom had more pocket money to spend on records than ever before. During World War II the demand for workers in military-related industries meant that many teenagers took on adult responsibilities, working for wages while continuing to attend high school. The idea that teenagers had the right to earn a salary of their own led after the war to the widespread practice of a weekly allowance in return for doing the household chores. Many young adults spent a considerable portion of their income on films, jukeboxes, and records. A survey of record retailers conducted in 1949 estimated that people under twenty-one constituted fully one-third of the total record-buying population of the United States, a great increase from previous eras. Nonetheless, the music produced by the largest record companies was still mainly aimed at an older audience.

THE SOUTHERN ROOTS OF ROCK 'N' ROLL

In discussing the role of record companies, also known as "labels," it is common to divide them into two categories: *major labels* and *independent labels*. Although these terms are not always consistently applied, the term "major label" generally refers to a large record company with substantial resources that works with artists in diverse genres, while the term "independent label" or "indie" refers to a smaller, lower-budget record company that tends to specialize in a single genre. As we have indicated, the major record companies of the postwar period—RCA Victor, Columbia, Decca, and Capitol Records—experienced considerable growth. At the same time, however, musical genres regarded as marginal by the industry came to influence even more strongly the musical taste of middle-class white Americans. Back in the 1920s, both the major record companies of the day and smaller upstart firms had begun to market recordings of musicians from the American South, performing music that drew upon a variety of rural folk sources ultimately derived from ancestral traditions in Europe and Africa. The market for this music was broadly segregated by race, the recordings of white artists often being classified as "hillbilly music," and recordings of black artists as "race music." By the 1940s the pattern of racial segregation persisted, but the categories had been renamed, respectively, "country and western music" (often simply called "country") and "rhythm & blues" ("R&B").

During the Second World War millions of people migrated from the rural South in search of employment in defense-related industries. Cities such as Chicago; Detroit; Pittsburgh; New York; Washington, D.C.; Nashville; Atlanta; and Los Angeles were all home to large populations of transplanted southerners, whose musical tastes were doubly shaped by their experience of rural traditions and by the desire to forge new, urbanized identities (and thereby distance themselves from the stereotyped image of the "hick" or "rube"). This migrant population greatly expanded the target audience for southern-derived music, providing a steady source of support for the urban honky-tonks, juke joints, and lounges where country and western and rhythm & blues groups played.

The rise of small independent record labels during and just after the war provided an outlet for performers who were ignored by the major record companies. The development of portable tape recorders made record **producers** and studio owners out of entrepreneurs who could not previously have afforded the equipment necessary to produce master recordings. Each company was centered on one or two individuals, who located talent, oversaw the recording process, and handled publicity, distribution, and a variety of other tasks. These label owners worked the system in as many ways as time, energy, and ingenuity allowed. They paid radio DJs **payola** (bribes) to promote their records, visited nightclubs to find new talent, hustled copies of their records to local record store owners, and occasionally attempted to interest a major label in a particular recording or an artist that they felt could become a mainstream star.

Most "indie" label owners worked a particular piece of musical and geographical territory. However, they also had dreams of the huge financial success that would accrue to the label that found a way to cross country and R&B records over to the pop music charts. The middle-class white audience for this music, and the big record companies' and radio networks' interest in it, were growing—but the competition was fiercer than ever. By 1951 there were more than one hundred independent labels slugging it out for a piece of the R&B market, and few of them lasted more than a few months.

Indie owners often put their names down for composer credits on songs they recorded and thereby often earned more royalties from a given song than the actual composer or performer! One of the reasons this was possible was that young artists generally did not understand the value of publishing rights, so they were often willing to sign them away for the promise of success. As we noted earlier, songwriting credits are the backbone of the music industry. The *performer* may make a profit from live concerts, the sales of their recording, or the use of their recording in a film or commercial. But the *songwriter* makes a profit from all of those things, *plus* any time the song is played on the radio, television, in a store or entertainment venue, as part of a corporate presentation, if the lyrics are quoted in a book (including this one!) or on a poster, or if another artist records the song or even samples it—essentially any time the song is used for any commercial purpose. Although they are rarely glamorous, arguments over publishing rights have driven some of the most important developments in rock history, as we shall see.

Radio also played a crucial role in the popularization of rhythm & blues and country music. There was a substantial increase in the number of radio stations catering specially to transplanted southerners, some capable of saturating the entire country's airwaves, others low-wattage affairs with a broadcasting radius of only a few miles. The country music radio business was booming in the late 1940s and early 1950s, with new shows coming on the air in all of America's major cities and on hundreds of small stations that sprouted in rural areas. During the war a number of white disc jockeys began to mix black popular music in with their usual diet of pop records, and 1949 saw the inauguration of the first radio station dedicated exclusively to playing music for a black audience—WDIA in Memphis, Tennessee, featuring the popular blues musician and disc jockey B.B. King. (Although this station catered to a predominantly black audience in the Mississippi Delta area, it was in fact owned by white businessmen.) It is also important to remember that there is really no way to know for certain who was listening to which radio stations at that time. After all, once the music went out over the airwaves, it could be heard by anyone with a radio. The assumption that American listeners adhered to a strict racial segregation in their musical preferences turned out not to be nearly

Elvis Presley & B.B. King backstage at a WDIA 1956 fundraiser. Photo by Ernest Withers.

as true as the music industry had assumed. This misperception would open the door for rock 'n' roll to emerge later in the 1950s.

PRE–ROCK 'N' ROLL RHYTHM & BLUES

Although the trade magazine *Billboard* adopted a new designation in 1949 for what had formerly been called "race records," in some ways the commercial logic underlying the category hadn't really changed much since the 1920s and 1930s. Like the older term, "rhythm & blues" described music performed almost exclusively by black artists and produced in the main (at least at first) for sale to African American audiences. R&B, as the genre came to be known, was a loose cluster of styles, rooted in southern folk traditions and shaped by the experience of returning military personnel and hundreds of thousands of black Americans who had migrated to urban centers such as New York, Chicago, Detroit, and Los Angeles during and just after the war. The top R&B recordings of the late 1940s and early 1950s included the music of "jump bands," various styles of urban **blues** (see Glossary), and gospel-influenced vocal harmony groups, along with love songs performed by black crooners.

Jump band music, the first commercially successful category of rhythm & blues, flourished during and just after World War II. The style grew directly out of big band swing music, the dominant style of American popular music from 1935 through 1945, and is the source of rock 'n' roll's strongest links to that earlier era. During the war, as shortages made it more difficult to maintain a lucrative touring schedule, the leaders of the big bands that played swing music were forced to downsize. They formed smaller combos, generally made up of a rhythm section (bass, piano, drums, and sometimes guitar) and one or more horn players. These jump bands specialized in hard-swinging party music, spiced with humorous lyrics and wild stage performances.

The most successful jump band was the Tympany Five, led by Louis Jordan (1908–75), an Arkansas-born saxophone player and singer who began making recordings for Decca Records in 1939. Jordan was tremendously popular with black listeners and, like black crooner Nat "King" Cole, was able to build an extensive white audience during and after the war. But Jordan himself regarded Cole as being in "another field"—the pop field. Although Cole enjoyed greater financial success, in the end Jordan had a bigger impact on the future of popular music, inspiring a number of the first rock 'n' roll artists. As the rock 'n' roll pioneer Chuck Berry put it, "I identify myself with Louis Jordan more than any other artist" (Shaw 1986: 64). James Brown, the godfather of soul music, was once asked if Louis Jordan had been an influence on him: "He was everything," Brown replied (Chilton 1994: 126).

"Choo Choo Ch'Boogie," which we examine in greater detail later in this chapter, exemplifies key elements of the jump band style of R&B. The song was cowritten by Milt Gabler, Jordan's producer, and two country and western musicians who worked at a radio station in New York City. (Eight years later

Muddy Waters (McKinley Morganfield) performing, about 1950. Photo by Tom Copi/Michael Ochs Archives/Getty Images.

Gabler was to produce the first hit record of the rock 'n' roll era, Bill Haley's "Rock Around the Clock.") The title "Choo Choo Ch'Boogie" draws a parallel between the motion of a railroad train—a metaphor of mobility and change long established in both country music and the blues—and the rocking rhythm of *boogie-woogie*, a style of piano music which originated in black communities in the Southwest during the 1920s and triggered a national craze during the 1930s. Boogie-woogie provided an important link between rhythm & blues and country music during the postwar period, a connection that was to prove important in the formation of rock 'n' roll. (See the discussion of boogie-woogie in Chapter 3.)

The song's lyric (see the Listening Chart included in the later discussion) describes a situation that would have been familiar to many Americans, particularly to ex-GIs returning to the United States during the postwar economic downturn of 1946, when jobs were temporarily scarce and the future seemed uncertain. The song brings back a character from the Great Depression era, the poor but honest hobo, hopping freight trains and traveling from city to city in search of work. The protagonist arrives home, weary of riding in the back of an army truck, and heads for the railroad station. His initial optimism is tempered as he searches the employment notices in the newspaper and realizes that he does not have the technical skills for the few positions that are open. (African American listeners may have interpreted the line "the only job that's open needs a man with a knack" as a comment on the employment practices of the many businesses that favored white over black veterans.) Despite his misfortune, however, our hero remains cheerful, and the lyric ends with an idyllic description of life in a shack by the railroad track.

The career of <u>Muddy Waters (McKinley Morganfield)</u> (1915–83) exemplifies the development of a very different urban blues tradition of the postwar era, *Chicago Blues*. Chicago was the terminus of the Illinois Central railroad line, which ran up through the Midwest from the Mississippi Delta. Chicago's black neighborhoods grew particularly rapidly during the 1940s, as millions of rural migrants came north in search of employment in the city's industrial plants, railroad shops, and slaughterhouses. The South Side's nightclubs were the center of a lively black music scene, and the musical taste of black Chicagoans, many of them recent migrants from the Deep South, tended toward styles closely linked to African American folk traditions but also reflective of their new, urban orientation.

Waters was "discovered" in the Mississippi Delta by the folk music scholars John Work and Alan Lomax, who recorded him in 1941 for the Library of Congress. In 1943 he moved to Chicago and found work in a paper mill while continuing to work as a musician at nightclubs and parties. In response to the noisy crowds, and to the demand for dance music, Waters soon switched from the acoustic to the electric guitar (1944) and eventually expanded his group to include a second electric guitar, piano, bass, amplified harmonica ("blues harp"), and drum set. During the late 1940s and early 1950s he was the most popular blues musician in Chicago, with a sizable following among black listeners nationwide.

Like many of the great Mississippi guitarists, Waters used his guitar to create a rock-steady, churning rhythm, interspersed with blues licks, which were counterpoised with his voice in a kind of musical conversation. The electric guitar, which could be used to create long sustained notes that sounded like screaming or crying, was the perfect tool for updating the Mississippi blues guitar tradition. Waters's singing style—rough, growling, moaning, and intensely emotional—was also rooted in the Delta blues. And the songs he sang were based on themes long central to the tradition: on the one hand, loneliness, frustration, and misfortune ("I Feel Like Going Home" and "Still a Fool"), and on the other, independence and sexual braggadocio ("Just Make Love to Me" and "Mannish Boy").

"Hoochie Coochie Man," composed by <u>Willie Dixon</u> (1915–92), Chess Records' house songwriter, bass player, producer, and arranger, is perhaps the best example of the latter theme. The song was Waters's biggest hit for Chess Records, reaching Number 3 on the R&B charts in 1954. (Although none of Waters's recordings crossed over to the pop charts, his music was later to play an important role in inspiring rock musicians such as Eric Clapton and the Rolling Stones—who adopted their name from one of his songs.) "Hoochie Coochie Man" typifies Chicago urban blues, with its loud volume and dense sound, its buzzing, growling tone colors, and its insistent beat. The lyric of "Hoochie Coochie Man" is essentially an extended boast, related to the African American tradition of "toasts," fantastic narratives emphasizing the performer's personal power, sexual prowess, and ability to outwit authority.

> *I got a black cat bone, I got a mojo too*
> *I got the John the Conkaroo, I'm gonna mess wit' you*
> *I'm gonna make you girls lead me by my hand*
> *Then the world'll know the hoochie coochie man*

The song draws a direct link between the personal power of the singer (quintessentially expressed through sex) and the southern folk tradition of

Hoodoo, a system of magical charms and medicines, including the black cat bone and John the Conqueror root. This image of supernatural power applied in the service of personal goals was ultimately derived from West African religious tradition, and it tapped a common reservoir of experience among Waters's listeners, many of whom were not many years removed from the folk culture of the rural South. In essence, the lyric of "Hoochie Coochie Man" is an argument for the continuing relevance of deep traditional knowledge in the new urban setting, and it is easy to see why this would have been an attractive message for recent urban migrants. "Hoochie Coochie Man" can also be heard as a direct ancestor of contemporary gangsta rap, which projects a similar outlaw image as a response to the challenging conditions of urban life.

Another important thread in the tapestry of postwar rhythm & blues was *vocal harmony groups*. (Although this tradition is today sometimes called "doo-wop," the earliest performers did not use this term.) Many of these vocal groups were made up of high school kids from the black neighborhoods of cities such as New York, Philadelphia, and Washington, D.C. Few of them initially saw singing as a way to make a living; this perception changed rapidly after the first vocal R&B groups achieved commercial success. These groups specialized in smooth four-voice singing, which sometimes functioned as the background (or "pad") for a lead, high falsetto singer.

One of the most influential vocal harmony groups was the Dominoes, whose 1952 recording of "Have Mercy Baby" pushed vocal group R&B firmly in the direction of a more explicitly emotional sound grounded in the music of the black church. "Have Mercy Baby" was the first record to combine a traditional blues form (see the "Technical Note" on twelve-bar blues later in this chapter, p. 25) and the driving beat of dance-oriented rhythm & blues with the intensely emotional flavor of black gospel singing. The song's commercial success (Number 1 R&B for ten weeks in 1952) was in large part due to the passionate performance of the Dominoes' lead tenor, <u>Clyde McPhatter</u> (1932–72), a former gospel singer from North Carolina. McPhatter, the son of a Baptist preacher and a church organist, was like many other R&B musicians, insofar as the black church played a major role in shaping his musical sensibility. While in formal terms "Have Mercy Baby" is a blues song, it is essentially a gospel performance dressed up in R&B clothing. With a few changes in the lyrics—perhaps substituting the word "Lord" for "baby"—McPhatter's performance would have been perfectly at home in a black Baptist church anywhere in America. The sheer intensity of McPhatter's plea for redemption—you can actually hear him weeping during the fadeout ending—spoke directly to the core audience for R&B, many of whom had grown up within the African American gospel music tradition.

Although it did not appear on the pop music charts, "Have Mercy Baby" attracted an audience among many white teenagers, who were drawn by its rocking beat and emotional directness. In addition, the Dominoes were featured on some of the earliest rock 'n' roll tours, which typically attracted a racially mixed audience. Although McPhatter soon left the Dominoes to form a new group called the Drifters, the impact of his rendition of "Have Mercy Baby" was profound and lasting—the record is a direct predecessor of the soul music movement of the 1960s and of the recordings of Ray Charles, James Brown, and Aretha Franklin.

The artists we have discussed thus far—some of the most successful of the R&B genre—have all been male, and it is worth asking why that should be so. Women (such as Ethel Waters and Bessie Smith) had been the predominant artists in African American popular music from the beginning of the recording industry until well into the 1940s (Wald 2004, pp. 201–202). It is widely accepted that one of the reasons record companies had been willing to support female African American artists in the earlier part of the century is that they were viewed as less "threatening" to potential white listeners than African American men. The emergence of overtly powerful men as major artists in the R&B genre, then, suggests that the genre itself had withdrawn somewhat from attempting to win fans outside of the African American community. Ironically, it may have been this withdrawal—and the sense that the music was not meant to be heard by white listeners—that made it all the more attractive to white teenagers! Whatever the reason for the increasing masculinity of the genre, it is clear that women in R&B in the fifties had to accommodate themselves to it stylistically, in a way that previous generations did not.

Big Mama Thornton (1926–84), born in Montgomery, Alabama, is perhaps the clearest example of this trend. The daughter of a Baptist minister, Thornton began her professional career as a singer, drummer, harmonica player, and comic on the black vaudeville circuit and later settled in Houston, Texas, working as a singer in black nightclubs. Her imposing physique and sometimes malevolent personality helped to ensure her survival in the rough-and-tumble world of con artists and gangsters. One producer and songwriter who worked with Big Mama described her in vivid terms (in the liner notes to the 1992 MCA release *Big Mama Thornton: Hound Dog/The Peacock Recordings*):

> In rehearsal she'd fool around, pick up one of those old microphones with a heavy, steel base with one hand and turn it upside down with the base in the air and sing like that. She was a powerful, powerful woman. She had a few scars, looked like knife scars on her face, and she had a very beautiful smile. But most of the time she looked pretty salty.

In the early 1950s Thornton arrived in Los Angeles and began working with Johnny Otis (Veliotes), a Greek American drummer, promoter, bandleader, and nightclub owner who lived in the black community. Looking for material for Big Mama to record, Otis decided to consult two white college kids who had been pestering him to use some of the songs they had written. After hearing

"Big Mama" Thornton, one of the faces of rhythm & blues in the mid-1950s. Michael Ochs Archives/Getty Images.

Thornton's powerful singing, Jerry Leiber and Mike Stoller ran home and composed a song that they felt suited her style: "Hound Dog." The combination of Leiber and Stoller's humorous country-tinged lyric, Johnny Otis's drumming, and Thornton's powerful, raspy singing produced one of the top-selling R&B records of 1953: Number 1 for seven weeks. (This was the first hit written and produced by the team of Leiber and Stoller, who were to become arguably the most prolific and influential songwriting team in rock 'n' roll history.)

Of course, most people today know "Hound Dog" through Elvis Presley's version of the song, recorded by RCA Victor in 1956. If you are familiar only with Presley's version, then the original recording may come as something of a revelation. From the very first phrase (You . . . ain't . . . *nothin'* . . . but a houn' dog . . .) Thornton lays claim to the song, and to our attention. Her deep, raspy, commanding voice, reprimanding a ne'er-do-well lover, projects a stark image of female power rarely expressed in popular music of the 1950s. The bluntness of the lyric is reinforced by the musical accompaniment, which includes a bluesy electric guitar, a simple drum part played mainly on the tom-toms, and hand clapping on beats 2 and 4 (the "backbeats"). The tempo is relaxed, and the performance is energetic but loose. The final touch, with the all-male band howling and barking in response to Big Mama's commands, reinforces not only the humor of the record but also its feeling of informality, the sense that these are not distant pop stars but people you could get to know and maybe even party with.

COUNTRY AND WESTERN MUSIC

Country and western, the industry's new name for what used to be called hillbilly music, mushroomed in popularity after World War II. Although the South remained a lucrative area for touring performers, the wartime migration of millions of white southerners meant that huge and enthusiastic audiences for country and western music had also been established in the cities and towns of Pennsylvania, Ohio, Michigan, and California. The postwar era saw the rapid spread of country music programming on radio, and by 1949 more than 650 radio stations were making live broadcasts of country performers. The continuing success of WSM's *Grand Ole Opry,* broadcast from Nashville, inspired a new generation of country music shows, including Shreveport's

Louisiana Hayride, Dallas's *Saturday Night Shindig,* Boston's *Hayloft Jamboree,* and *Hometown Jamboree,* broadcast from Los Angeles. As in the R&B field, dozens of independent record labels specializing in country music sprang up after the war, and Nashville, Tennessee, and Southern California began to assert themselves as centers for the production of country music. In 1950—when Capitol Records became the first major company to set up its country music operation in Nashville—it was estimated that country music accounted for fully one-third of all record sales nationwide.

As country music's core audience moved north, west, and upward into the urban middle class, the "mainstreaming" of country music continued apace. Pop artists such as Bing Crosby ("Sioux City Sue," Number 3 Pop in 1946) and Tony Bennett ("Cold, Cold Heart," Number 1 Pop in 1951) had huge chart successes with their adaptations of country material. Since the 1920s, the New York–based music industry had underestimated—and often seemed embarrassed by—the popularity of popular styles based in southern folk music. But by 1950, when Patti Page's pop-style rendition of the nostalgic country song "Tennessee Waltz" became the fastest-selling record in a quarter-century, the record company executives had no choice—country music was off the porch and sitting in the living room. "Tennessee Waltz" held the Number 1 position on the pop charts for thirteen weeks in 1950 and eventually went on to sell more than six million copies. The popular appeal of this record was boosted by two technological innovations: the use of multitrack tape recording, which allowed Page to, in effect, sing a duet with herself, and the fact that this was one of the first songs to be issued as a 45-r.p.m. single record. "Tennessee Waltz" spawned a rash of **cover versions** by other artists, and served notice that a pop-styled approach to country and western music could not only penetrate but actually dominate the mainstream.

A harder-edged style of country music, called "honky-tonk" (after the working-class bars in which it was often played), is represented by <u>Hank Williams</u> (1923–53), the most significant figure to emerge in country music during the immediate post–World War II period. Williams wrote and sang many songs in the course of his brief career that were enormously popular with country audiences at the time; between 1947 and 1953 he amassed an astounding thirty-six Top 10 records on the country charts, including such Number 1 hits as "Lovesick Blues," "Cold, Cold Heart," "Jambalaya (On the Bayou)," and "Your Cheatin' Heart." All of these Number 1 hits—along with many other Williams songs—have remained long-term country favorites and are established "standards" of their genre. In addition, his songs were successfully covered by contemporary mainstream pop artists, thus demonstrating the wide-ranging appeal of the new country material. "Cold, Cold Heart" helped launch the career of Tony Bennett when the young crooner scored a huge success with it in 1951 (Number 1 Pop for six weeks). Again, it is worth noting that Williams was not only a performer but also a songwriter, a combination that would have been extremely unusual in the mainstream pop of the day.

Hank Williams represented for postwar country audiences the enduring myth of the hard-living, hard-loving rambler. Although the details of Williams's life seem in retrospect to have custom-designed him for legendary status, it is important to realize that these were the actual facts of his life: born into crushing poverty in Alabama, this son of a sharecropper learned to make his way at an early age by performing on the street, learning a great deal from a black street singer named Rufe "Tee-Tot" Payne. By the time he was sixteen, Williams, now called "the Singing Kid," had his own local radio show; shortly thereafter he formed a band, the Drifting Cowboys, and began touring throughout Alabama. Enormous success came to Williams by the time he was in his mid-twenties, but it did not come without its problems. By 1952 he was divorced, had been fired from the *Grand Ole Opry* (for numerous failures to appear), and was seriously dependent on alcohol and painkilling drugs. He died on New Year's Day 1953 at age twenty-nine, having suffered a heart attack in the back of his car while en route to a performance.

Along with a few of Williams's other records, the jaunty "Hey, Good Lookin'" was actually something of a minor crossover hit for him (Number 29 Pop, but Number 1 on the Country chart—for eight weeks—in 1951). This should not seem surprising, given its danceable character and its pop-friendly AABA form borrowed from Tin Pan Alley models. With its prominent steel guitar and fiddle parts, not to mention the character of Williams's vocal, there's still no mistaking the record's basis in country music. What is most arresting here, however, is the specific targeting of a youthful audience. The lyrics address cars, dancing, and young romance, and the use of terms like "hot-rod Ford," "soda pop," "go steady," and "date book" create what would—about five years later—have been called a "teen-friendly" piece of material.

Hank Williams performs, while Chet Atkins—soon to be a hugely influential figure in country music himself, as a guitarist and producer—looks on admiringly. Ernie Newton is playing bass. Courtesy of Country Music Hall of Fame and Museum.

In a sense, "Hey, Good Lookin'" came a little too early, and Hank Williams of course died much too young. Had Williams been able to bring this same song, or something like it, to a savvy record producer in late 1955 or early 1956—to a producer aware of the noise being made by the young Elvis Presley or by Carl Perkins (of "Blue Suede Shoes" fame) at the time—that cynical producer might have said something like this: "Hank, you've got something there. Please throw out those fiddles, though—too hillbilly. And replace the steel guitar with a regular electric guitar played R&B-style.

Add some R&B-based drumming, too. I think you'll have a hit rock 'n' roll record." And had Williams been interested, which is questionable, his name might well have been added to the **rockabilly** roster, perhaps even close to the top of it. As it is, Williams's early death leaves us pondering what might have been; but in any case, a song like "Hey, Good Lookin'" attests to the forward-looking character of his creativity.

THREE BIG HITS OF THE PRE–ROCK 'N' ROLL PERIOD

We pause now to consider in detail three representative hit records from the period under discussion. In doing so, we will not only become familiar with characteristic sounds of this decade but will also begin to develop skills in listening critically to popular music, and to become familiar with terminology and concepts that will prove essential in our survey of the history of rock music. The conceptions of *melody*, *rhythm*, *harmony*, and *form* reflected in these examples have their roots in music that substantially predates these particular hits. Yet the influence of these conceptions also extended far into the future, as will soon become evident.

The Weavers (Pete Seeger on banjo, Lee Hays, Fred Hellerman, Ronnie Gilbert). Courtesy Library of Congress.

The three records, representing diverse styles, are "Goodnight, Irene" by the Weavers (1950), "Choo Choo Ch'Boogie" by Louis Jordan's Tympany Five (1946), and "Love and Marriage" by Frank Sinatra (1955). They are considered in this order because, from the standpoint of musical form, "Goodnight, Irene" presents the simplest conception, while the other two present a somewhat more elaborate approach. (This in no way implies that the other two are either "better" records or that they are necessarily more "difficult" to understand or to enjoy!) In this section, the musical aspects of these hits are deliberately isolated, in order to concentrate on the listening experience they provide. Even if you have no formal musical training, you should be able to follow the basic structure of the recordings with a little practice.

"Goodnight, Irene" (Strophic Song Form)

The Weavers' recording of "Goodnight, Irene" was an unexpected but gigantic hit in 1950, one of the biggest records of the entire post–World War II decade (1945–1954). It held the Number 1 spot on the pop charts for thirteen weeks, eventually selling more than two million copies (a remarkable figure for the time). The broad appeal of "Goodnight, Irene" may be attributed to several factors. The Weavers learned the song from the African American musician Huddie Ledbetter (1889–1949), better known as Leadbelly; thus the recording had its source in black folk music. However, "Goodnight, Irene" tells a story— of marital strife, regret, and the need to return to "traditional" values of home and family—that could well have come right out of a contemporary honky-tonk tune. Furthermore, the Weavers' performance of the song avoids any of the rough edges that would have been characteristic of either African American or white country styles; with the considerable assistance of a smooth arrangement provided by Gordon Jenkins (the managing director of Decca Records), they turn "Goodnight, Irene" into an effective pop record designed for a wide, mainstream audience. The success of "Goodnight, Irene," and of several other records by the Weavers over the next few years, helped to define a market niche for folk-based popular music, setting the stage for the later "urban folk" appeal of the Kingston Trio; Peter, Paul, and Mary; and even Bob Dylan. In addition, the Weavers' use of international folk materials, such as the Israeli song "Tzena, Tzena, Tzena" (found on the other side of "Goodnight, Irene," and a substantial hit as well), made them in effect the first "worldbeat" artists—a category of popular music that would not emerge in defined form for another thirty years.

"Goodnight, Irene" is a good illustration of one of the oldest and most enduring of all musical forms: the **strophic** song. (See the "Listening to" discussion, pp. 22–23.) In a strophic song, the same music is heard several times, with changing words. Strophic songs are found in virtually all types and styles of music: in the folk cultures of many countries, in African American blues, in the early "hillbilly" music of the American rural South, and in all the periods of American popular song. It is easy to understand why this is true. Strophic songs, because of the repetitive nature of their music, are easy to learn and to remember. They can also readily be used by performers to encourage listeners to participate by singing along; the Weavers, in fact, made a habit of concluding their public appearances with "Goodnight, Irene," urging their audiences to sing with them.

When an audience member sang along with the lead singer in "Goodnight, Irene," he or she was singing the *melody* of the song. From a technical standpoint, a melody consists of a succession of musical notes, or *pitches*; musicians typically name these pitches with letters (C, D, E-flat, and so forth) that can identify them in terms of written music and in terms of their positions on a keyboard or a guitar. There is more to a melody than just a succession of pitches, however. To make a melody, the notes have to occur in a specific pattern in time. Some notes are longer, some are shorter, and the durations are almost always defined in relation to an ongoing, regular *pulse* or *beat*. This time dimension of music is *rhythm*. When you tap your foot or your finger to a tune, you are feeling its rhythm, its pulse, its beat.

"Choo Choo Ch'Boogie" (Twelve-Bar Blues Form)

"Choo Choo Ch'Boogie" merits our attention as a representative recording by the most popular rhythm & blues act of the post–World War II decade, Louis Jordan and His Tympany Five.

Louis Jordan and His Tympany Five, 1946. Frank Driggs Collection.

LISTENING TO "GOODNIGHT, IRENE"

A closer look at the opening of "Goodnight, Irene" will help introduce some basic examples of melody and rhythm. This opening section (following a brief instrumental introduction) consists of words and music that are repeated regularly together as a unit throughout the song; such a section is called a **chorus**. The chorus may readily be subdivided into four *phrases*, brief building blocks of the melody that are separated from one another by breathing spaces (pauses or *rests*):

> *Irene, goodnight;* [vocal pause]
> *Irene, goodnight;* [vocal pause]
> *Goodnight, Irene, goodnight, Irene,*
>   [brief vocal pause]
> *I'll see . . . dreams.* [vocal pause]

Each phrase has an individual pitch structure, sometimes going higher and sometimes lower, in patterns that mimic the natural inflections of spoken words; phrases that "sing" naturally are generally a hallmark of effective songwriting. As is typical of most speech, the vocal melody tends to fall in pitch at the ends of phrases. Some phrase endings seem musically more conclusive than others; in the chorus of "Goodnight, Irene" this is true of the second and fourth phrases, both of which end on the same pitch. When the melody reaches such a temporary stopping point—what we might call the end of a musical "sentence"—musicians call this a **cadence**.

Now what about the rhythm? In the Weavers' recording of "Goodnight, Irene" the musical instruments start to articulate the beat shortly after the record begins, and this regular beat then persists throughout the rest of the record, right through the fade-out. All beats are not equally intense, however, and a larger, regular rhythmic pattern is created by the significant *accent* given to every third beat:

> **One,** two three; **One,** two three; **One,** two three; and so on

These groups of three beats, defined by the regular accents, are called *measures*, or *bars*. (The three-beat bars—or triple *meter*—of "Goodnight, Irene" evoke the rhythm of the **waltz**, a dance whose popularity dates back to the nineteenth century.) It may also be noticed that

the phrases of the melody in this song all extend over a duration four bars in length. Thus a great consistency characterizes the rhythmic patterns of this song at every level: a regular beat; constant three-beat measures; phrases that are all four measures in length (with cadences occurring regularly at the end of every other phrase); a four-phrase melodic chorus. Such regularity is typical of popular music, since it results in easily remembered, reassuringly predictable patterns that lend themselves readily to singing and dancing. Of course, too much regularity would result in boredom, so most popular songs tread a fine line between what is predictable and what creates novelty and interest.

If we look now at the overall structure of the Weavers' recording, we will be able to appreciate additional aspects of "Goodnight, Irene"; see the Listening Chart that follows. (This is the first example of the charts that are presented regularly throughout this book to facilitate in-depth discussion of some particularly significant recordings. You may want to refer to the chart to reinforce and supplement the discussion that follows, and also to use the chart as a visual aid while listening to the recording.) The recurring chorus sections alternate with **verses**. The melody for all of the verses is the same each time, but this verse melody is recognizably different from that of the chorus. What distinguishes the verses from one another is that new words are sung with each successive verse—while the words to the chorus sections, of course, remain the same each time. Attentive listening will reveal that each of the verses in "Goodnight, Irene" is constructed analogously to the chorus, insofar as each verse also may be divided into four phrases, with each phrase extending over four bars of the ongoing triple meter, and with clear cadences occurring at the ends of the second and fourth phrases.

In "Goodnight, Irene," one verse and one chorus together form a larger structural unit: the **strophe** of this strophic song. (The term *strophe* comes from literature, identifying a section of poetry that contains a certain number of lines, usually with a set pattern of meter and rhyme.) The alternation of verses and choruses creates a continuing source of variety and interest within the strophic form, as each strophe presents one section that

LISTENING CHART "GOODNIGHT, IRENE"
Written by Huddie Ledbetter (Leadbelly) and performed by The Weavers; recorded 1950

FORM		LYRICS
Brief instrumental introduction		
Chorus	0.14	*Irene, goodnight . . .*
Instruments, background voices repeat the chorus tune	0.34	
Strophe 1: Verse	0.54	*Last Saturday night . . .*
Chorus	1.15	*Irene, goodnight . . .*
Strophe 2: Verse	1.35	*Sometimes I live . . .*
Chorus	1.55	*Irene, goodnight . . .*
Strophe 3: Verse	2.15	*Stop ramblin' . . .*
Chorus	2.36	*Irene, goodnight . . .*
Chorus is repeated, fading out	2.56	

remains consistent and completely predictable in terms of both words and music, and another section in which the words change, revealing a new event or twist in the developing story. It seems obvious why this verse-chorus format became a favored approach to strophic form.

In practice, a performance of a strophic song may begin either with a verse or with the chorus. The Weavers' recording begins with the chorus, since this part would be immediately recognizable to anyone even vaguely familiar with the song—a clever selling point!—and the vocal chorus is itself preceded by an instrumental foreshadowing of the chorus melody, which clearly was designed to spur a feeling of anticipation, along with familiarity, in the listener. After the voices first sing the chorus with words, the music for the chorus is repeated without words, by instruments and background voices, reinforcing this essential part of the song before the performance proceeds with the first verse. Performances of strophic songs almost invariably end with the chorus, which brings a sense of comfortable, predictable conclusion, and indeed the Weavers' recording follows this anticipated procedure, even fading out as the chorus repeats, literally bidding the listener "goodnight."

The Weavers' recording of "Goodnight, Irene" was designed to avoid the kind of absolutely predictable structure that would have made for an uninteresting record. An additional factor, which brings interest to the successive vocal choruses, has to do with the aspect of music musicians call *harmony*. In a very basic sense, harmony deals with the interrelationships among different pitches in a musical piece. It may be heard, by the time we reach the chorus following the first verse, that the melody is being enriched here by having different voices sing different pitches at the same time: While the melody remains clearly in the foreground, the other pitches heard simultaneously are creating **chords**, which provide the foundation for harmony in popular music. The employment of three different solo voices to sing the three verses provides yet another source of variety. Notice here how apparent it is that the man who sings verse 3 is not the same man who sings verse 1; it is the specific individual "color," or **timbre,** of the two voices that allows us to differentiate them.

The Weavers' "Goodnight, Irene" exemplifies both the strophic song and the adaptability of this form to various arrangements in performance and recording. In fact, strophic songs can be almost infinitely adaptable, lending themselves to the spontaneous alteration of lyrics and to the creation of additional strophes to fit new occasions, new contexts, new performers, and new audiences—since everybody, presumably, either knows the tune to begin with, or else can learn it in short order.

Released in 1946 by Decca Records, "Choo Choo Ch'Boogie" proved to be the biggest hit of Jordan's entire career, holding the Number 1 spot on the rhythm & blues charts for an astounding eighteen weeks, and crossing over into the Top Ten on the pop charts as well. Although crossing over to mainstream pop success was a relatively unusual achievement for rhythm & blues artists during this period, Jordan managed to do so with some regularity, which indicates the broad appeal of his music and also foreshadows one of the major commercial phenomena—rhythm & blues recordings becoming huge pop hits—that would come to define rock 'n' roll. "Choo Choo Ch'Boogie" will also serve to introduce one of the most important formal patterns in American popular music, the *twelve-bar blues*.

"Choo Choo Ch'Boogie," while obviously very different in musical style from "Goodnight, Irene," is actually quite similar in overall musical structure. It too is a strophic song in which each of the three strophes contains both a verse and a chorus; see the accompanying Listening Chart. (The fact that both of these songs share this basic organization illustrates how useful and flexible the strophic song with verses and choruses can be.)

🎧 LISTENING TO "CHOO CHOO CH'BOOGIE"

One of the most immediately apparent and important differences between "Choo Choo Ch'Boogie" and "Goodnight, Irene" lies in the crucial area of rhythm. The rhythm of the Jordan recording is based on regular *four-beat* bars, as opposed to the regular triple meter of "Irene." That is to say, the rhythmic accents in "Choo Choo Ch'Boogie" create the following steady pattern:

One, two three, four; **One,** two, three, four; **One,** two, three four; and so on.

(By far the most common meters found in all styles and periods of American popular music are quadruple meter, triple meter, and duple—a simple **one**, two—meter.) The four-beat bars of "Choo Choo Ch'Boogie" are arranged into two-bar phrases; each phrase corresponds to one line of the lyrics, as may be seen in the chart. The verses are all twelve bars (six phrases) in length, while the choruses are all eight bars (four phrases) in length, and this in turn creates consistent strophes of twenty bars each.

All this is hopefully straightforward enough to hear and to understand, but it is now important to pause briefly over the *internal* form of those twelve-bar verses. This runs the risk of becoming slightly technical, but these verses all exemplify the musical pattern of *twelve-bar blues*—an arrangement of rhythm and chords that is one of the backbone structures of American popular music. (See "Technical Note," p. 25.) Twelve-bar blues has been so useful and adaptable for musicians, especially in the rock era, that it is worthwhile for any attentive listener to learn to recognize it.

"Choo Choo Ch'Boogie" integrates the twelve-bar blues progression into its overall verse-chorus strophic structure. Verses in twelve-bar blues form alternate with the eight-bar choruses, creating together the twenty-bar strophes. Additional variety is created in the recording by the employment of purely instrumental episodes: an introduction, a concluding "tag," and interludes following the first and second occurrences of the chorus (see the chart).

The instrumental introduction follows the chord pattern of the twelve-bar blues; the horns (a trumpet and

A TECHNICAL NOTE: TWELVE-BAR BLUES

Twelve-bar blues refers to a particular arrangement of four-beat bars. The bars are themselves grouped in phrases of two or four, with characteristic chord changes occurring at certain points. The issue of harmony in the twelve-bar blues is a complex one, especially since the chord progressions in a form as widespread and diverse as the blues will by no means be absolutely systematic or consistent from case to case. Still, the twelve-bar blues does tend to be marked by specific chord changes at particular points, and our present example—"Choo Choo Ch'Boogie"—offers a conveniently straightforward illustration of these changes in each of its verses. (The important thing to remember is that the chord changes in twelve-bar blues need not be limited only to these typical ones.)

If we call our starting chord the "home" chord (musicians would call it the **tonic**), this chart shows the most important, typical points of change in the twelve-bar blues pattern:

BARS: 1   2   3   4
CHORDS: "Home" . . . .
BARS: 5   6   7   8
CHORDS: **Change 1**   "Home"
BARS: 9   10   11   12
CHORDS: **Change 2**   "Home"

Note that the chords at "changes" 1 and 2 are different from one another; thus, there are three essential chords that define the skeleton of this musical structure. (Musicians call the chord at bar 5 the *subdominant*, and the chord at bar 9 the *dominant*.) These are the three chords that define the harmony in the verses of "Choo Choo Ch'Boogie," and they occur at precisely the rhythmic points just shown. To illustrate specifically, here is what happens in the first verse. The numbers of the bars show where the accent (the **one**) of the bar in question falls, and the chord changes always occur on the accented beats; remember to count the four beats in each bar:

BARS: 1   2
LYRICS: *Headin' for the station with a pack on my back*
CHORDS: **Home (tonic)** . . . .
              3   4
I'm tired of transportation in the back of a hack
[home (tonic)] . . . .
              5   6
I love to hear the rhythm of a clickety-clack
Change 1 (subdominant) . . . .
              7
And hear the lonesome whistle, see the
              8
smoke from the stack
Home (tonic) . . . .
              9   10
And pal around with democratic fellows named Mac
Change 2 (dominant) . . . .
              11   12
So take me right back to the track, Jack.
Home (tonic) . . . .

two saxophones) imitate the sound of a train whistle, while the rhythm section (piano, bass, and drums) establishes a characteristic rhythm moving at a medium pace, or medium **tempo**. (This infectious four-beat dance rhythm, common in Louis Jordan's recordings, is also sometimes called a *shuffle*.) After the introduction a verse is sung by Louis Jordan, backed by **riffs** (repeated patterns) in the horn section. Then a chorus, also sung by Jordan, is followed by a twelve-bar blues piano solo. The whole sequence of verse–chorus–instrumental solo is then repeated (with a twenty-bar saxophone solo, representing both verse and chorus, replacing the piano solo). A third strophe is sung, and a slight variation at the end of this chorus leads into the concluding ten-bar tag.

LISTENING CHART "CHOO CHOO CH'BOOGIE"

Music and lyrics by Milt Gabler, Denver Darling, and Vaughan Horton;
as performed by Louis Jordan's Tympany Five; recorded 1946

FORM		LYRICS	DESCRIPTIVE COMMENTS
Instrumental intro			12-bar blues During the first four bars, the horns imitate the sound of a train whistle.
Verse 1	0.17	Headin' for the station with a pack on my back I'm tired of transportation in the back of a hack I love to hear the rhythm of a clickety-clack And hear the lonesome whistle, see the smoke from the stack And pal around with democratic fellows named Mac So take me right back to the track, Jack.	12-bar blues
Chorus	0.34	Choo choo, choo choo, ch'boogie Woo woo, woo woo, ch'boogie Choo choo, choo choo, ch'boogie Take me right back to the track, Jack.	8 bars
Piano solo	0.45		12-bar blues
Verse 2	1.02	You reach your destination, but alas and alack You need some compensation to get back in the black You take a morning paper from the top of the stack And read the situation from the front to the back The only job that's open needs a man with a knack So put it right back in the rack, Jack.	12-bar blues
Chorus [as before]	1.19		8 bars
Saxophone solo	1.30		20 bars (12-bar blues + 8-bar chorus)
Verse 3	1.58	Gonna settle down by the railroad track And live the life of Riley in a beaten-down shack So when I hear a whistle I can peep through the crack And watch the train a-rollin', when it's ballin' the jack Why, I just love the rhythm of the clickety-clack So take me right back to the track, Jack.	12-bar blues
Chorus [as before]	2.14		8 bars
Instrumental tag (with brief vocal interjection)	2.26		10 bars

"Love and Marriage" (AABA Song Form)

The 1955 hit record of "Love and Marriage," a song composed by Sammy Cahn and Jimmy Van Heusen, and sung by Frank Sinatra, serves here to represent several things: the typical Tin Pan Alley song form; the characteristically elaborate and clever arrangements that enhanced recordings of such songs; and the suave and knowing vocal style of one of the greatest singers of this—or any—period. The lasting appeal of this record is reflected in its use as the ironic theme song for the 1990s sitcom "Married, with Children."

"Love and Marriage" introduces us to the four-section **AABA** song, another venerable form in American popular music. Songs constructed along these lines typically have sections of equal length, with the three **A** sections presenting identical (or nearly identical) music accompanied (usually) by different words each time, and the single B section presenting new words *and* new music. The repetitions of the A music assure that the song will quickly become familiar to the listener, while the B section offers some musical variety within the form. The B section in an AABA form is frequently called a **release**—or, even more commonly, a **bridge** (presumably because it links two A sections). The principles behind the AABA formal strategy seem obvious enough: State an effective musical idea to "hook" the listener; restate it (usually with new words) in order to fix it in the listener's mind; then sustain attention with a deviation from the established pattern; and conclude with the gratifying return of the now-familiar basic idea. It is not surprising that many songwriters have turned to AABA organization for the construction of memorable songs. The form itself has endured well past the heyday of Tin Pan Alley, and it continues to influence the structure of some popular music to this day.

Frank Sinatra: The "Sultan of Swoon" in the 1940s, the ultimate cool "saloon singer" in the 1950s. © Corbis; Frank Driggs Collection.

CONCLUSION

The mainstream music industry had been designed to capitalize on the value of *songs* rather than *performances*. In order to maximize their profit, songwriters and publishers had taken a number of understandable steps: They created standardized song forms that allowed them to compose music quickly and efficiently. They created ASCAP to protect their intellectual property rights, and used it to forge a relationship with the radio industry that was so strong that it bordered on monopoly. They built strong ties with the record companies

LISTENING TO "LOVE AND MARRIAGE"

It is a simple matter to hear the AABA organization in "Love and Marriage," especially since each of the A sections begins with identical words: the words of the title, which thus serve as a recurring verbal and musical reference point for the listener. After a brief instrumental introduction, the song proceeds as follows:

A *Love and marriage, love and marriage, go together . . .*
A *Love and marriage, love and marriage, it's an institute . . .*
B *Try, try . . .*
A *Love and marriage, love and marriage, go together . . .*

Following the completion of the form, an instrumental interlude presents the A music again, after which Frank Sinatra reenters and sings the last two sections, B and A, once more. A brief instrumental passage ends the recording.

"Love and Marriage" is typical of AABA songs of this period insofar as it is organized rhythmically in regular four-beat bars that are grouped into sections of eight-bar length. We may also call attention to a few formal subtleties that lend interest and distinction to this particular example of AABA song form. It will be noticed that the music of the second A section is indeed identical to that of the first A—with one small but important exception: it ends on a different pitch from the first. This is significant because, as a result of this alteration in the vocal melody (and in the accompanying chord), there is a cadence at the end of the second A whereas there was no cadence concluding the first A. In a sense, then, the first A section sets up the second A, which in turn musically rounds off the first. The beginning of the B section is marked by a particularly striking new chord, which helps to set the music of this section strongly apart. The final A of "Love and Marriage" restates not only the music but also many of the words of the opening section. Monotony is decisively avoided in this case, however, for two reasons. First of all, this concluding section is extended beyond the expected eight bars to reach a length of eleven bars. Secondly, unlike the first A, this section does reach a cadence (although we are, effectively, forced to wait for it), so it provides a definitive feeling both of rounding and of conclusion to the overall form. Because of the differences among the three A sections in "Love and Marriage," the form is perhaps best represented as A-A^{1}B-A^2.

---

that sold their music to the public. In short, they streamlined every aspect of the business, from songwriting to recording to promotion, in order to make it work as efficiently as possible. As the business model became more efficient, it naturally became more narrowly focused. Musicians and songwriters whose musical style or business model did not fit the norm were often excluded from participation. From its own point of view, this approach makes perfect sense: Tin Pan Alley publishers had created an extremely profitable industry, and they had little to gain by sharing it with other composers and musicians, especially those whose music and culture seemed strange and even threatening.

From the outsiders' perspective, however, the picture looked very different: The mainstream music industry was preventing entire communities from having their music heard, and—not incidentally—reaping the profits that that could bring. At the same time, the fact that these artists were excluded from radio and mainstream performance venues meant they did not have to be concerned with the strict—and often overtly repressive—standards of propriety that these venues demanded. The result was that non-mainstream musical forms—especially country and western and rhythm & blues—were able to be more daring, more openly sexual, and more rebellious than mainstream musical forms. It is not difficult to see how this would be appealing to teenagers. And, as teenagers became an increasingly dominant consumer demographic, they would bring this music with them into the mainstream, as rock 'n' roll.

2

THE RISE OF
ROCK 'N' ROLL, 1954–1959

Like many cultural developments, the birth of rock 'n' roll occurred in two stages: the organic emergence of a new phenomenon, followed by the recognition, definition, and (often) exploitation of that phenomenon. In this case, the first stage occurred when disc jockeys and independent record companies noticed white teenagers' attraction to rhythm & blues music, a genre originally produced by and for African American adults. The second stage developed when artists responded to that attraction by developing a new form of rhythm & blues that was specifically tailored to a white teen audience. It may seem strange to define musical appeal in such specifically racial terms, but the racial implications of rock 'n' roll—and arguments over those implications—were absolutely central to the way the genre was defined at the time.

Since the musical genres that would become rock 'n' roll (and the cultural groups that created them) had been largely excluded from participation in the mainstream music industry up to that point, their sudden embrace by the teen audience caught many people off guard. In many cases, it didn't take much to turn that surprise into fear. As it turned out, rock 'n' roll was uniquely situated to evoke a wide range of concerns, most of which had little relationship to each other—or, in many cases, to reality. These concerns included worries about the continued viability of the Tin Pan Alley business model, a sense that rock's musical characteristics indicated a general decline in American taste, suspicions of communist influence on American society, and anxieties about interracial interaction. Somewhat ironically, the fact that rock 'n' roll inspired such fears was an important part of its appeal to its core audience, teenagers.

The term "rock 'n' roll" was probably first used for commercial and generational purposes by disc jockey Alan Freed (1922–65). In the early 1950s Freed discovered that increasing numbers of young white kids were listening to and requesting the rhythm & blues records he played on his *Moondog Show* nighttime program in Cleveland—records he then began to call "rock 'n' roll" records. Freed also promoted concert tours featuring black artists, playing to a young, racially mixed audience, and promoted them as "rock 'n' roll revues." The term "rock 'n' roll" itself was derived from the many references to "rockin'"

Disc jockey **Alan Freed** in Cleveland. Courtesy of Library of Congress.

and "rollin'" (sometimes separately, sometimes together) that may be found in rhythm & blues songs, and on race records dating back at least to the late 1920s. Among the relevant recordings that would have been known to Freed and his audience were the late-1940s rhythm & blues hit "Good Rockin' Tonight" (recorded by a number of different artists after first becoming a hit for its composer, Roy Brown) and the huge 1951 hit by the Dominoes, "Sixty Minute Man" (which featured the lyric "I rock 'em, roll 'em, all night long, I'm a sixty-minute man"). "Rock" and "roll" are clearly associated in these and other songs with sexual implications, but these implications faded as "rock 'n' roll" increasingly came to refer simply to a type of music.

Why did Freed feel he needed a new term for this music in the first place? There were two major reasons. On an immediate level, he probably wanted to corner the market on the new genre for himself. If he used the term rock 'n' roll to refer to the specific mix of rhythm & blues records played on his show, then—by definition—he would be the *only* rock 'n' roll deejay. As we will see, Freed very calculatingly leveraged his position as a cultural gatekeeper into better jobs for himself as a deejay, concert promoter, and songwriter.

On a more general level, the term was clearly intended to sidestep the racial prejudices of the era. In the wake of the 1954 Supreme Court decision in *Brown v. Board of Education*, which declared school segregation unconstitutional, Americans were facing a new era of racial integration, particularly among school-aged young people. In the wake of this change—and the Civil Rights movement it inspired—the idea of young white people falling in love with the music of African Americans was viewed by many of their parents as an inherently negative development. The term "rock 'n' roll"—by sounding almost-but-not-quite-exactly like "rhythm & blues"—could thus send two very different messages to teenagers and their parents. To potentially racist parents, it sent a misleading message of reassurance, presenting rock 'n' roll as something significantly different from the popular African American music of the time. To teenagers, by contrast, the term referred to a specific repertoire of rhythm & blues songs that Alan Freed had chosen to appeal to his young audience. In other words, the message that "rock 'n' roll" sent to teens was that Freed took them seriously as consumers.

In short, Alan Freed—and other early promoters of rock 'n' roll—were trying to have it both ways, particularly when it came to the controversial issue of race. When it suited their purposes, they made every effort to exploit the music's connections to African American culture. But in situations where they felt it worked against them, they tried to disassociate the genre from African American culture as much as possible. In addition to being an obvious contradiction, this was also a position that was very difficult to maintain from a practical standpoint, and they were not always successful in doing so. As a result, the ground-level decisions that were being made in this era paint a complex and sometimes confusing picture of rock 'n' roll's relationship to African American culture. In the end, that itself may be the most significant generalization to be made; the contradictions and ambiguities of rock 'n' roll's social position in the fifties reflected similar issues in American society generally.

Alan Freed's new audience was dominated by those born into the so-called baby boom generation at the end of, and immediately following, World War II. It was a much younger audience than had ever before constituted a target market for music, and it was a large audience that shared some specific and important characteristics of group cultural identity. These were kids growing up in the 1950s, a period of relative economic stability and prosperity, but also a period marked by a self-conscious return to "normalcy" defined in socially and politically conservative ways, following the enormous destabilizing traumas of world war. In terms of the entertainment industry, this was the first generation to grow up with television as a readily available part of its culture; this powerful new mass medium proved a force of incalculable influence and offered another outlet for the instantaneous nationwide distribution of music.

Yet the 1950s was a period characterized by its own political and cultural traumas. In addition to the end of segregation, Cold War tension between the United States and the Soviet Union fed an intense anticommunism in America that

Reverend Bob Gray preaching against Elvis Presley's "spiritual degeneracy" (Jacksonville, Florida, 1956). Photo by Robert W. Kelley/Time Life Pictures/Getty Images.

resulted in such controversial phenomena as congressional hearings concerning "un-American activities" and the blacklisting of many writers, musicians, and entertainment personalities who had been involved in suspect left-wing groups and actions in the 1930s, 1940s, and 1950s. A major pillar of the anticommunist movement was the belief that Soviet agents were trying to destabilize America politically by destroying its culture from within. This belief often served to reinforce other concerns about rock 'n' roll; it would be bad enough if rock 'n' roll were harming the music industry and encouraging bad taste among the youth, but what if all of that was only part of a larger plot to bring down America itself?

Perhaps the most important factor of all for adolescents during the 1950s was simply their identification by the larger culture itself as a unique generational group, even as they were growing up. Thus they quickly developed a sense of self-identification as teenagers (this category was not necessarily limited to young people between the ages of thirteen and nineteen; many ten-, eleven-, and twelve-year-olds participated fully in "teen" culture). Naturally such a group, from a young age, had to have its own distinctive emblems of identity, including dance steps, fashions, ways of speaking, and music. The prosperity of the 1950s gave these young people an unprecedented collective purchasing power, as the allowances of millions of kids went toward leisure and entertainment products geared especially to this generation's tastes and sense of identity. What resulted was an increasingly volatile give-and-take between, on the one hand, products and trends that were prefabricated for teens by the adult commercial culture, and on the other hand, products and trends chosen and developed unpredictably by the members of the new generation themselves. Rock 'n' roll music was at the center of this give-and-take. It emerged as an unexpected musical choice by increasing numbers of young people in the early to mid-1950s; it then became a mass-market phenomenon exploited by the mainstream music industry in the later 1950s; and eventually it was to some extent reclaimed by these teenagers themselves in the 1960s as they grew old enough to make their own music and, increasingly, to assume some control of the production and marketing of it.

In 1954, Alan Freed moved to station WINS in the larger New York radio market, taking the phrase "rock 'n' roll" with him to identify both the music he played and his target audience. Freed continued to promote African American musicians, in the face of considerable resistance in the society as a whole to the idea of racial integration. In 1957, a TV show sponsored by Freed was canceled after the black teenage singer Frankie Lymon was shown dancing with a white girl. In 1958 Freed himself was arrested for anarchy and incitement to riot after a fight broke out at one of his rock 'n' roll concerts in Boston. But it would be payola—the illegal practice, common throughout the music industry, of paying bribes to radio disc jockeys in order to get certain artists' records played more frequently—that would ultimately destroy Alan Freed.

As discussed in the previous chapter, the small independent record companies that produced rhythm & blues music often had little contact—

commercially or socially—with the mainstream music industry. Many of them were located outside of New York, were run according to a different business model, and were staffed by people who would not have fit into the Tin Pan Alley social world even if they had the opportunity to try. As a result, many of the independent labels, lacking other options, resorted to payola to get their records played on the radio. Unfortunately for them, this strategy backfired. The illegality of the practice led many of those involved to be prosecuted, which not only removed them from their jobs in the music industry but also associated rock 'n' roll itself with criminality. At the same time, it also reinforced the message that rock 'n' roll was an inferior musical product— after all, if the music was good, you wouldn't have to bribe someone to play it on the radio, would you? In the early 1960s, Alan Freed was prosecuted for accepting payola, while promoters like Dick Clark (who handled mainly white rock 'n' roll artists and had deeper connections to the old music industry) escaped relatively unscathed. Freed was blackballed within the music business, and he died a few years later, a broken man.

Whatever his indiscretions, Alan Freed was clearly in the vanguard of an increasing number of disc jockeys, all over the country, who wished to capture the new, large audience of young radio listeners and potential record buyers, and who consequently embraced the term "rock 'n' roll" to refer to virtually any kind of music pitched to that audience. This included records that would previously have been marketed purely as rhythm & blues or to a lesser degree as country and western, along with an expanding group of hybrid records that drew freely on multiple stylistic influences, including those associated with mainstream Tin Pan Alley–type music. Strange as it now seems, in the early heyday of rock 'n' roll Chuck Berry, Pat Boone, Fats Domino, Ricky Nelson, the Everly Brothers, and Elvis Presley were all lumped together as "rock 'n' roll singers"—meaning simply that they all had records being listened to and purchased by large numbers of teenagers. This was a period of remarkable heterogeneity on radio and on the record charts, as all of the preceding singers, along with the likes of Frank Sinatra and Patti Page, could be heard jostling each other on Top 40 radio stations and seen nudging each other on the pop charts. In the marketing confusion that resulted, rock 'n' roll records appeared on different, previously exclusive, charts simultaneously; early in 1956 Carl Perkins's "Blue Suede Shoes" and Elvis Presley's "Heartbreak Hotel" both made chart history by climbing to the upper reaches of the country and western, rhythm & blues, and pop charts all at the same time.

The purchase of rock 'n' roll records by kids in the 1950s proved a relatively safe and affordable way for those kids to assert generational identity through rebellion against previous adult standards and restrictions of musical style and taste. Thus the experience of growing up with rock 'n' roll music became an early and defining characteristic of the baby boom generation. Rock 'n' roll records accompanied the boomers in their progress from preadolescence through their teenage years. It is consequently not surprising that this music increasingly and specifically catered to this age group, which by the late 1950s had its own distinctive culture (made possible by abundant leisure time and economic prosperity) and its associated rituals: school and vacation (represented in rock 'n' roll songs such as "School Day" and "Summertime Blues"), fashions ("Black Denim Trousers and Motorcycle Boots" and "Itsy Bitsy Teenie Weenie Yellow Polkadot Bikini"), social dancing ("At the Hop" and "Save the Last Dance for Me"), and courtship ("Teen-Age Crush," "Puppy Love," "A Teenager in Love," and "Poor Little Fool"). Some rock 'n' roll songs—for example, "Roll over Beethoven" and "Rock and Roll Is Here to Stay"—self-consciously announced themselves as emblems of a new aesthetic and cultural order, dominated by the tastes and aspirations of youth. In fact, the demographic strength of the baby boom generation has made them an attractive market even to the present day. In many ways, the development of rock itself for at least its first three decades runs parallel to the general chronology of baby boomers' lives: aimed at teens in the fifties, rebellious college students in sixties, and maturing young adults in the seventies.

It would not be an exaggeration to say that the 1950s essentially invented the teenager as a commercial and cultural entity, and that rock 'n' roll music, along with television and, to some extent, movies, played an essential role in this invention. Although popular music of all eras has reached out to young audiences with plentiful songs about love and courtship, the virtually exclusive emphasis on appeal to one particular, extremely young, generation is what most distinguishes the phenomenon of rock 'n' roll. It is thus not surprising that teenagers themselves were recruited, with increasing frequency, as performers to market this music, beginning with the popular group Frankie Lymon and the Teenagers (who scored their first and biggest hit "Why Do Fools Fall in Love?" early in 1956, when lead singer Lymon himself was only thirteen years old), and continuing in the following years with such teenage performers as Paul Anka and Ricky Nelson. (The popularity of Nelson was closely linked to television; he was already well known to audiences as the younger son on *The Adventures of Ozzie and Harriet* show before he started making records.) The association of rock 'n' roll with adolescence and adolescents was so complete that, in the 1960s, practitioners of the music who had grown out of their adolescent years, and who wanted to appeal to a maturing audience of their peers, rechristened their music simply *rock*.

For all this appropriate emphasis on the generational culture of rock 'n' roll, we should not ignore the fact that the shift in musical marketing away from primarily racial and regional considerations (and their associated class-related aspects) toward primarily generational considerations had some unforeseen and extremely significant consequences, profoundly affecting the American cultural landscape. There was a period in the later 1950s when much of the same popular music—rock 'n' roll records—would be played for dances at inner-city, primarily black, public schools; for parties at exclusive white suburban private schools; and for socials in rural settings catering to young people. This was a new kind of situation, especially in the society of the 1950s, which was in most respects polarized in terms of race, class, and region. While musicians and styles have often crossed between cultures throughout the history of American music, rock 'n' roll seemed to offer a bridge connecting supposedly exclusive *audiences*. If you were young in the 1950s, no matter where you lived, no matter what your race or class, rock 'n' roll was *your* music. An important, if ultimately fragile, potential of popular music to create new connections and relationships among audiences in a highly fragmented society was first glimpsed on a large scale in the period of rock 'n' roll. For those that loved rock 'n' roll, this was part of its appeal. For those that didn't, this was part of what made it seem so threatening.

COVER VERSIONS AND EARLY ROCK 'N' ROLL

One of the most important precedents for the rise of rock 'n' roll was a commercial and musical phenomenon known as the *cover version*. In the broadest sense, this term simply refers to the practice of recording a song that has previously been recorded by another artist or group. However, practitioners, merchants, and scholars of popular music have usually used the term in a more restricted sense, to refer to a version—sometimes an almost exact copy—of a previously recorded performance, often involving an adaptation of the original's style and sensibility, and usually aimed at cashing in on its success. Of course, the process of musical borrowing is no doubt as old as music itself. But this process takes on new significance when the element of financial profit is introduced, and when issues of social inequality are involved. In such contexts, the influence of one tradition, style, or performer on another can also be seen as a kind of musical appropriation, and borrowing becomes something more akin to stealing.

While cover versions of various kinds had existed before in other forms of popular music, those most important for understanding the rise of rock 'n' roll in the mid-1950s involved white performers covering the work of African American recording artists. In many cases, despite sounding very similar, the recording by the white artist was considered part of the rock 'n' roll genre while the recording by the black artist was classified as rhythm & blues. This supports the idea discussed previously: that the term rock 'n' roll itself was viewed as a way to separate the new genre from its African American roots.

At the same time, this was a relationship not simply between individual musicians but also between competing institutions, since the underlying motivation for covering a recording typically involved the major record companies' attempt to capitalize on the musical discoveries of small independent record labels. It is not difficult to see how these two goals (obscuring the music's associations with African American culture and moving its ownership to mainstream record labels) could work together.

To better our understanding of this phenomenon, let's look at specific examples of cover versions. In 1947 a black singer and pianist named Paula

Watson recorded a song called "A Little Bird Told Me" for the independent label Supreme. Watson's version of the song, released in 1948, reached Number 2 on the R&B charts and made an impact on the pop charts, peaking at Number 14. This early crossover hit attracted the attention of Decca Records, which immediately issued a cover version of the song performed by a white singer named Evelyn Knight. Knight's version of the song reached Number 1 on the pop charts, in large part owing to the promotional power of Decca Records and the fact that white performers enjoyed privileged access to radio and television play.

The tiny Supreme label sued Decca Records, claiming that its copyright to the original had been infringed. In this case the crux of the matter was not the song per se—its author, Harvey Brooks, collected composer's royalties from both record companies. Rather, Supreme claimed that Decca had stolen aspects of the original recording, including its arrangement, basic sound, and vocal style. Although Evelyn Knight had indeed copied Paula Watson's singing precisely—to the degree that it fooled musical experts brought in as witnesses—the judge ultimately decided in favor of the larger company, ruling that musical arrangements were not copyrighted property and therefore not under legal protection.

This decision affirmed the legal principle that the song (published in the form of sheet music) was a copyrightable form of intellectual property, but that individual interpretations or arrangements of a given song could not be protected under the law. This meant the continuation of an older conception of music's legal status—focused on the written document—in an era when recordings, rather than sheet music, had become the dominant means of transmission. The decision confirmed the idea that, from a legal and thus monetary standpoint, the contributions of the songwriter would remain more important than those of the song's performer, no matter what those contributions may be. This discrepancy became even more pronounced in later years as changes in recording and production technology began to blur the distinction between songwriting and performance.

The "Little Bird Told Me" decision opened the floodgates for cover versions during the 1950s, for better or worse. Now let's take a closer look at three more examples of cover versions, each of which gives us a different perspective on the complex musical, economic, and social forces that converged to create rock 'n' roll in the mid-1950s.

THE ROCK 'N' ROLL BUSINESS

To comprehend the emergence of rock 'n' roll as both a musical genre and a commercial category, it is important that we summarize the economics of the music business in the mid-1950s. The overall vitality of the American economy after World War II helped push the entertainment industry's profits to new levels. Sales of record players and radios expanded significantly after the war. Total annual record sales in the United States rose from $191 million in 1951 to $514 million in 1959. This expansion was accompanied by a gradual diversification of mainstream popular taste and by the reemergence of independent ("indie") record companies, whose predecessors had been wiped out twenty years before by the Great Depression. Most of these smaller companies—established by entrepreneurs in New York and Los Angeles, and in secondary centers such as Chicago, Cincinnati, Nashville, Memphis, and New Orleans—specialized in rhythm & blues and country and western recordings, which had begun to attract a national mass audience. This process was viewed with a mixture of interest and alarm by the directors of the "majors" (large record companies such as RCA Victor, Capitol, Mercury, Columbia, MGM, and Decca), which still specialized mainly in the music of Tin Pan Alley, performed by crooners. A few of the majors—for example, Decca, which had already made millions from the sale of R&B and country records—did manage to produce some early rock 'n' roll hits. Other large record companies took a couple of years to react to the emergence of rock 'n' roll. RCA Victor, for example, scored a Number 1 hit in 1956 with Kay Starr's rendition of "Rock and Roll Waltz" (a song that described a teenager watching her parents try to dance to the new music, accompanied by music more akin to a ballroom waltz than to rock 'n' roll). But RCA also signed the rockabilly singer Elvis Presley and set to work transforming him into a Hollywood matinee idol and rock 'n' roll's first bona fide superstar.

The sales charts published in industry periodicals like *Billboard* and *Cashbox* during the 1950s chronicle changes in popular taste, the role of the indies in channeling previously marginal types of music into the pop mainstream, and the emergence of a new teenage market. The charts also reveal a complex pattern of competition among musical styles. As an example, let's have a look at the *Billboard* charts for July 9, 1955, when Bill Haley and the Comets' "Rock Around the Clock" became the first rock 'n' roll hit to reach the Number 1 position on the "Best Sellers in Stores" chart. This event is cited by rock historians as a revolutionary event, the beginning of a new era in American popular culture. However, two very different recordings, reminiscent of earlier styles of popular music, held the Number 1 positions on the jukebox and radio airplay charts on the same date (July 9)—the Latin American ballroom dance hit "Cherry Pink and Apple Blossom White," by Perez Prado and His Orchestra, and "Learning the Blues," performed by the former big-band crooner Frank Sinatra with the accompaniment of Nelson Riddle and His Orchestra. And lest we assume that this contrast in styles represented a titanic struggle between small and large record companies, it should be noted that all three of these Number 1 records were released by majors (Decca, RCA Victor, and Capitol, respectively).

🎧 LISTENING TO THREE R&B RECORDS AND THEIR "COVERS"

"Shake, Rattle, and Roll," original version performed by Big Joe Turner (Number 1 R&B, Number 22 Pop, 1954); cover version performed by Bill Haley and the Comets (Number 7 Pop, 1954); "Sh-Boom," original version composed and performed by the Chords (Number 2 R&B, Number 5 Pop, 1954); cover version performed by the Crew Cuts (Number 1 Pop for nine weeks, 1954); "Mystery Train," original version composed and performed by Junior Parker (no chart appearance, 1953); cover version performed by Elvis Presley (Number 11 Country and Western, 1955)

Perhaps the most famous example of a mid-1950s cover version is the song "Shake, Rattle and Roll," composed in 1954 by Jesse Stone, a black producer and talent scout for Atlantic Records. (The song was actually published under the pseudonym Charles Calhoun.) "Shake, Rattle and Roll" is a twelve-bar blues; a recurring section with identical lyrics functions like a chorus (*Shake, rattle and roll . . .*). The original recording of the song, released by Atlantic in 1954, is in the jump blues R&B style. It features Big Joe Turner (1911–85), a forty-three-year-old vocalist who had begun his career as a singing bartender in the Depression-era nightclubs of Kansas City and had sung with various big bands during the swing era. Turner was one of Atlantic's early stars, and his recording of "Shake, Rattle and Roll" not only held the Number 1 position on the R&B charts but also crossed over to the pop charts, where it reached Number 22.

This crossover hit soon caught the attention of executives at Decca Records and of a former country and western bandleader named Bill Haley (see Box at the end of this chapter). Later in 1954, Bill Haley and the Comets recorded a rendition of "Shake, Rattle and Roll" that was clearly indebted to Turner's original but also departed from it in significant ways. While the Atlantic recording features a band made up of veteran jazz musicians, playing a medium-tempo shuffle rhythm, the Haley recording emphasizes guitars rather than saxophones, and his group plays with a rhythmic feeling more like that of a western swing band than that of a jump blues R&B band. One of the most obvious differences between the two versions lies in the song's text. The original lyric, as written by Jesse Stone and embellished by Big Joe Turner, is full of fairly obvious sexual references. Presumably because these lyrics would have proved too wild for AM radio and would have offended many in the predominantly white pop music audience, Haley sang a bowdlerized (censored) version of the song.

The other major difference between Turner's and Haley's versions of "Shake, Rattle and Roll" is the level of profit generated by the two recordings. In fact, this is not the most egregious example of a white band and major record company reaping profits from a song originally recorded by black musicians for an independent label, since both versions appeared on the pop charts, and each sold over a million copies. There are crucial differences between the two, however. While Big Joe Turner's version crossed over to the pop chart (and the expanding white teenage audience for black popular music), the majority of Atlantic's sales was nonetheless focused in the black community. Haley's version reached Number 7 on the pop chart but did not appear on the R&B charts at all, indicating that black audiences preferred Turner's jump band–style approach to the country-tinged style of the Comets. While Haley built on his early hit success, going on to become the first "king" of rock 'n' roll music, Turner was never again able to score a Top 40 pop hit or a Number 1 R&B hit. Atlantic sought to promote the middle-aged blues shouter to the teen audience for rock 'n' roll, but his time had passed. Turner himself claimed that "rock 'n' roll" was just another name for the same music he had always sung, but that he got "knocked down" in the traffic of a newly crowded scene.

The two versions of "Shake, Rattle and Roll" represent a pivot point between early 1950s R&B and later 1950s rock 'n' roll. And they are also a junction at which two popular musicians crossed paths—Big Joe Turner on his way down, and Bill Haley on his way up.

"**Sh-Boom**" is one of the most famous cover versions of the early rock 'n' roll era. In fact, its original recording by the Chords is often cited as one of the very first rock 'n' roll records. Certainly the Chords' "Sh-Boom" is a prime example of the rhythm & blues black vocal group style and, as a Top 10 pop hit, was also one of the first records to demonstrate the huge appeal that style could have to a mass audience. It is particularly significant that the Chords managed to place their record near the top of the pop charts in spite of a massively successful cover version of the tune by the white group the Crew Cuts. The Crew Cuts' "Sh-Boom" was one of the two biggest pop hits of 1954 and thus offers a particularly instructive example of the "cover record" phenomenon. A splendid irony underlying all this is the fact that the Chords' original "Sh-Boom" was in fact on the "flip" side of their own cover version (for the R&B market) of white pop singer Patti Page's hit "Cross over the Bridge"! If some discerning listeners and some enterprising disc jockeys hadn't turned the Chords' record over and enthused over the apparent throwaway number on the B-side, you wouldn't be reading this right now.

The Chords' "Sh-Boom" also illustrates how the presence of unexpected elements in the arrangement and performance of a rather ordinary tune can help create an extraordinary and original pop record. Essentially, the song is a standard AABA love ballad whose sentimental lyrics and stereotypical chord changes would suggest, on paper, either a slow rhythm & blues ballad or some grist for a latter-day pop crooner's mill. However, the Chords made the striking decision to treat the song as an up-tempo number and to add some novel touches that were appropriate to an up-tempo record but that also made this one really stand out. Among these novel touches on the Chords' recording (see the outline that follows) are: an **a cappella** (unaccompanied) vocal introduction; the incorporation of brief passages of **scat singing** (nonsense syllables), borrowed from jazz, at strategic points in the performance; a long and sizzling instrumental break, in the form of a saxophone solo—accompanied by the vocal group's rhythmic "doo-wop" nonsense syllables in the background—right in the middle of the record; and an unexpected ending on the term "sh-boom" itself, intoned by the group on an especially rich chord. This record anticipates the kind of unexpected syntheses from different musical styles that would come to characterize the most inventive rock 'n' roll records. For example, the sax solo would have been typical of an up-tempo jump blues or dance-oriented R&B recording, but would probably not have been expected in a record with love ballad lyrics, while "doo-wop" vocal sounds—expected in R&B love ballads—were not typically paired with hot instrumental solos. The association made in the record between jazz-related scat vocal solos and the nonsense syllables of vocal group doo-wop, while logical, was also quite original.

There are novel touches in the Crew Cuts' recording as well, which help account for its great popular success. As shown in the outline that follows, this version begins with scat singing. In the middle of the record, instead of a saxophone solo, there are two brief sections of group nonsense-syllable singing—each of which is punctuated by an isolated, loud, and humorous kettledrum stroke. Toward the end of the recording there are not one but *two* "false" endings (see outline). Arguably, all these effects tend to push this version into the category of a full-fledged novelty record (whereas the Chords' version comes across as an up-tempo R&B record with some novel aspects).

In terms of singing style, the Crew Cuts are crooners. The alternation between phrases where a solo voice takes the lead and phrases that are sung by the full group produces some agreeable variety in their arrangement, but there is really no difference in vocal coloration between the solo and the group; that is to say, the group passages are, in effect, "crooning times four." In contrast, the Chords' vocal arrangement is typical of a rhythm & blues approach insofar as it exploits differences in vocal timbre among the group's members, as well as the opposition between solo and group singing. This is heard most clearly in the B section (bridge) of the Chords' version, where the lead is taken by a solo bass voice that presents a strong contrast to the sound of the lead tenor heard in the first two A sections. Of course, the Chords' general approach throughout is rougher in sound than that of the Crew Cuts, underlining the much more aggressive rhythmic feeling of their recording as a whole. And the overriding difference between the Chords' and the Crew Cuts' recordings of "Sh-Boom" has to do precisely with that rhythmic feeling: Simply put, the former swings hard and the latter does not.

LISTENING CHART OUTLINE: THE CHORDS' "SH-BOOM"		
FORM		**LYRICS**
INTRODUCTION (full group a cappella, then band enters)		
A	0.07	("Life could . . . "; tenor lead)
	0.22	(scat singing interlude)
A	0.29	("Life could . . . "; tenor lead)
B	0.43	("Every time . . . "; bass lead)
A	0.57	("Life could . . . "; full group)
	1.11	(scat singing interlude)
Sax solo	1.22	(with group "doo-wop" sounds in background; this is the length of two A sections)
A	1.53	(full group; same words as first A section)
	2.07	(scat singing interlude, leading to sudden ending with the full group)

LISTENING CHART OUTLINE: THE CREW CUTS' "SH-BOOM"		
FORM		**LYRICS**
INTRODUCTION (scat singing)		
A	0.08	(tenor lead)
A	0.23	(tenor lead)
B	0.37	(tenor lead, then full group)
A	0.52	(tenor lead)
	1.07	Group "nonsense" singing (two sections, each the length of an A section, punctuated by kettledrum strokes)
B	1.37	(full group)
A	1.51	(full group, then tenor lead; same words as first A section)
	2.06	(scat singing interlude, leading to first "false" ending, then to:)
A	2.18	(full group, then tenor lead; same words as the second A section) ("False" fade-out leads to sudden loud conclusion with the full group)

The biggest star of the rock 'n' roll era—and arguably of the entire history of American popular music—was Elvis Presley (1935–77). Presley was born in Tupelo, Mississippi, the only child of a poor family, and his musical taste was shaped at a young age by the white gospel music he heard at church, by radio broadcasts of country music and rhythm & blues, and by the popular crooners of the postwar era, especially Dean Martin. (At the age of eight Presley won a talent contest at a Mississippi county fair, singing an old country song called "Old Shep.") As a teenager he moved to Memphis, took a job as a truck driver, and nurtured his ambition to become a singing film star.

In 1954 Presley came to the attention of Sam Phillips, the owner of Sun Records, a small independent label in Memphis, Tennessee, that specialized in country and rhythm & blues recordings and had scored a few regional hits. Phillips teamed Presley with two musicians from a local country band called the Starlite Wranglers, Scotty Moore (b. 1931) on electric guitar and Bill Black (1926–65) on string bass. Presley made a series of recordings with an R&B cover version on one side and a country song on the other. In essence, Sam Phillips was fishing with Elvis as bait, trying to see if he could develop a single artist who could sell to both white and black audiences. In his early live appearances, Elvis was billed as "the King of Country Bop," an attempt to indicate his idiosyncratic combination of black and white influences. The last record that Elvis made with Sam Phillips—just before he signed with RCA Victor and went on to become a national celebrity—was a cover version of an R&B song called **Mystery Train**," and it is this recording that we now examine in some detail.

In 1953 Herman ("Little Junior") Parker (1927–71), a singer, songwriter, and harmonica player who was achieving some success with his rhythm & blues band Little Junior's Blue Flames, had recorded a tune called

The young **Elvis Presley** in action. CBS/Landov.

"Mystery Train" for Sam Phillips's Sun label. The song received little attention at the time of its release, but at some point the young Elvis Presley must have noticed it, for he recorded "Mystery Train" early in 1955—also for Sun Record Company. Examining these two versions of "Mystery Train" will assist us in understanding the developing synergy between rhythm & blues and country music that played a strong role in the phenomenon called rock 'n' roll. It will also serve to underline the essential role of small independent record labels in disseminating "marginal" music and thus in contributing to this synergy. And it will help trace the origins of Elvis Presley's unique style, illuminating what Sam Phillips (who worked extensively with both black and white artists during the heyday of Sun Record Company) had in mind when he made his oft-quoted, oft-paraphrased observation that if he could find a white man with "the Negro sound and the Negro feel," then he could become a millionaire.

"Mystery Train" as a composition is credited to Parker and Phillips, and it is a strophic twelve-bar blues structure, at least in its original version (with one harmonic irregularity: some strophes begin on the subdominant chord rather than on the **tonic**, so that the first two four-bar phrases of these particular strophes are harmonically identical). Both Parker's original performance and Presley's cover version are individually fine recordings. What is most remarkable,

however, is how *different* they are from one another. Although Presley obviously learned a great deal from listening to Parker, and to dozens of other fine rhythm & blues artists, Presley's "Mystery Train" is arguably less a traditional cover than a reconceptualization of the song—a reconceptualization that reflects both Presley's distinctive self-awareness as a performer and his emerging (if probably implicit) ideas regarding his listening audience and how to engage it.

Junior Parker's original "Mystery Train" is a darkly evocative record with obvious roots both in rural blues and in rhythm & blues traditions. The train was a favorite subject and image for rural blues singers, and the spare, nonlinear lyrics in Parker's song are clearly aligned with rural blues traditions; this train is certainly "mysterious." In the first strophe, the "long black train," with its "sixteen coaches" taking the singer's "baby" away, paints a funereal picture. By the time we reach the third and final strophe, the train is bringing "baby" back to the singer, and the mood has brightened. But that brightening is darkened by the certainty already communicated in the second strophe: the train that took her away will "do it again." Parker's "Mystery Train" articulates a pessimistic worldview characteristic of the blues by asserting that the singer may triumph over adversity, but only temporarily—that is to say, life is a cycle of misfortunes offering, at best, periodic relief, but no permanent reprieve. (Two out of the three strophes portray "baby's" departure, while only one depicts her anticipated return.)

Parker's band constitutes a fairly typical rhythm & blues lineup for its time: electric guitar, acoustic bass, piano, drums, and saxophone. The "chugging" rhythm conveys a perfect sense of the train's steady, inexorable momentum. The saxophone is confined basically to long, low notes that evoke the train's whistle, while an additional atmospheric touch is added at the end of the recording, with a vocal imitation of the sound of the train's brakes as it finally comes to a stop (an event marked by the concluding guitar chord and the cessation of the "chugging" rhythm).

Elvis Presley's "Mystery Train," recorded when the "hillbilly cat" was barely twenty years old, conveys a breathless sense of intensity, excitement, and even enthusiasm (listen to Presley's spontaneous-sounding, triumphant "whoop" at the end of the recording!) that makes for a totally different experience from that offered by Parker's rendition. The much faster tempo of the Presley record is of course a decisive factor, but it is only the most obvious of many reasons that may be cited for the essential transformation "Mystery Train" undergoes here. There is little, if any, attempt at naturalistic evocation of the train by Presley's band, which consists simply of electric guitar, acoustic guitar, acoustic bass, and drums. One might hear a trainlike rhythm in the music, but the speed of the recording encourages one to imagine a roller coaster rather than a train (especially by 1955 standards). In fact, unlike Parker's record, Presley's version focuses on the singer rather than the train. Parker's protagonist seems ultimately at the mercy of the train, which has taken away his "baby" and will do so again, even if it occasionally brings her back. But Presley's vocal portrays a confident protagonist who projects control over his own future.

Presley's version presents significant alterations of Parker's original in the internal structuring of both the words and the music. In the lyrics to the second strophe, Presley makes a crucial substitution, asserting that while the train took his "baby," "*it never will again*"! As if to emphasize this essential change, Presley repeats this second strophe, with its altered lyrics, at the end of his record, so that now there are a total of four strophes, three of which look toward the return of his "baby," while only one (the first one) emphasizes her departure. That departure now becomes a one-time occurrence, as the song assumes a linear narrative shape that it did not have in Parker's original version. Even more importantly, this revision of the lyrics expresses and underlines the singer's feeling of control over the situation—definitely not an attitude traditionally associated with the blues. (It would be hard to imagine Parker asserting that the train will never take his lover away again.) In Parker's "Mystery Train," the instrumental break occurs between the second and third strophes, emphasizing, and allowing the listener to ponder, the singer's assertion that the train is going to take his "baby" again; arguably, this structural arrangement colors significantly our entire perception of the song. In Presley's version, by contrast, the instrumental break occurs after the third strophe, leaving the singer's words "she's mine, all mine" resonating in the listener's ears.

While Parker's "Mystery Train" follows the standard format of twelve-bar blues in the rhythmic arrangement of all its phrases and strophes, Presley's version is highly irregular by comparison. Many of the phrases in Presley's "Mystery Train" are longer than they "should" be; if we attempted to notate his performance in terms of a twelve-bar blues paradigm, we would find ourselves constantly having to add "half-bar" extensions (two extra beats) to many phrases. While there seems to be a general pattern formed by these extensions throughout the first three strophes, Presley breaks free of even this suggested pattern in his final strophe, extending one of the phrases yet further than before, while constricting another. (One of the truly remarkable things about this "Mystery Train" is that Presley's band was able to follow the apparent spontaneity, and consequent unpredictability, of his phrasing—especially given the breakneck speed of the performance.) Clearly, this singer is constrained by nothing; the rhythmic freedom of the music itself is reflective of his apparently limitless confidence.

With all these differences, we still should not ignore Presley's obvious debts to the blues and rhythm & blues traditions represented by Parker's original composition and recording. It is not difficult to hear strong aspects of what Sam Phillips called "the Negro sound and the Negro feel" in Presley's performance: in particular, the strong regional accent and the frequency of **blue notes** (see Glossary) and of sliding between pitches. These characteristics are, of course, points of intersection between black blues and white country traditions. What is important is to understand how Presley emphasized these common elements to form a style that sounded significantly "blacker" (particularly to white audiences) than that of virtually any other white singer who had emerged in the post–World War II era. (Presley also incorporated some vocal effects more specifically associated with white traditions—especially the kind of rapid stuttering, "hiccuping" effect heard in lines like "comin' dow-*hown* the li-*hine*" or "she's mine, a-*hall* mine.") Even the kind of rhythmic freedom that we have observed in Presley's "Mystery Train" reflects practices common in African American music, although one would have to go back to rural blues recordings to find anything comparably irregular, as most rhythm & blues records were tied to the kind of regularity in phrasing that was usually expected in music designed to be suitable for dancing.

This observation brings us to our final point. In sum, Elvis Presley's "Mystery Train" is unique in our experience of cover records thus far because it is more aggressive and "raw" than the original on which it was modeled. But the freedom and rawness of Presley's version is not primarily in the service of a vision that seeks to return us to the original flavor and context of rural blues—far from it. Rather, Presley's "Mystery Train" is the expression of a young white singer who is looking with optimism toward an essentially unbounded future, flush with new possibilities for stylistic synthesis that would help assure both intensely satisfying personal expression and an unprecedented degree of popular success. Unlike Parker's "Mystery Train," which is the expression of a man working knowledgeably within a tradition that both defines and confines the outlines of his music, and of his worldview, Presley's "Mystery Train" offers a totally new kind of ride, a ride without preconceived limits or conditions. No wonder so many other young singers, and a remarkably large young audience, wanted to climb aboard!

The record that pushed "Rock Around the Clock" out of the Number 1 position two months later was "The Yellow Rose of Texas" (a nineteenth-century minstrel song), performed in a deliberately old-fashioned sing-along style by the Mitch Miller Singers. Miller was the powerful director of the A&R (artists and repertoire) department at Columbia Records, and in that role had helped to establish the careers of pop crooners such as Doris Day, Tony Bennett, and Frankie Laine. He was also an archenemy of rock 'n' roll music and of its increasing influence on AM radio programming, which he derided as being geared to "the eight- to fourteen-year-olds, to the pre-shave crowd that make up twelve percent of the country's population and zero percent of its buying power" (Clarke 1995, p. 410). It is not hard to understand Miller's anger over the domination of radio by Top 40 playlists—predetermined lists of records by a limited number of artists, often backed up by bribes from record company officials to radio station personnel. One could see the free-form FM radio broadcasts of the late 1960s and the rise of alternative stations in the 1980s and 1990s as similar reactions against the playlist concept. But his refusal to recognize the teenage market was nothing if not short-sighted. A 1958 survey of the purchasing patterns of the nineteen million teenagers in the United States showed that they spent a total of nine billion dollars a year and strongly influenced their parents' choices of everything from toothpaste and canned food to automobiles and phonographs. And, of course, they bought millions and millions of records.

CONCLUSION

In many ways, the birth of rock 'n' roll was even more of a cultural and economic shift than a musical one. The move toward racial integration, the postwar economic boom, resistance to the perceived restrictiveness of the Tin Pan Alley

BILL HALEY AND "ROCK AROUND THE CLOCK" (1955)

<u>Bill Haley</u> (1925–81) would seem an unlikely candidate for the first big rock 'n' roll star, but in the early 1950s this leader of various obscure western swing groups was seeking a style that would capture the enthusiasm of the growing audience of young listeners and dancers, and he accurately sensed which way the wind was blowing. He dropped his cowboy image, changed the name of his accompanying group from the Saddlemen to the Comets, and in 1953 wrote and recorded a song, "Crazy, Man, Crazy," that offered a reasonable emulation of dance-oriented black rhythm & blues music. The record, released by a small indie label, rose as high as Number 12 on the pop charts. In 1954 the Comets were signed by Decca Records, where they worked in the studio with Decca's man in charge of artists and repertoire (**A&R**), Milt Gabler. Gabler, who had produced a series of hit records with Louis Jordan and His Tympany Five (see Chapter 1), helped to push Haley's style further in the direction of jump band rhythm & blues—"I'd sing Jordan riffs to the group that would be picked up by the electric guitars and tenor sax," he later said.

As we have already noted, Bill Haley and the Comets recorded commercially successful cover versions of rhythm & blues hits in the mid-1950s, notably "Shake, Rattle and Roll" (Number 7, 1954) and "See You Later, Alligator" (Number 6, 1956). But they attained their unique status in pop music history when their record of "Rock Around the Clock" became, in 1955, the first rock 'n' roll record to be a Number 1 pop hit. It stayed in the top spot for eight consecutive weeks during the summer of 1955 and eventually sold over twenty-two million copies worldwide.

"Rock Around the Clock," written by Max C. Freedman and Jimmy DeKnight, was actually recorded in 1954 and was not a big hit when first released. But then the record was prominently featured in the opening credits of the 1955 movie *Blackboard Jungle*, which dealt with inner-city teenagers and juvenile delinquency, and "Rock around the Clock" quickly achieved massive popularity—and

forged an enduring link that has connected teenagers, rock 'n' roll, and movies ever since. Bill Haley's claim to have "invented" rock 'n' roll deserves little credibility. But Haley proved to be an important popularizer of previously marginalized musical sounds and ideas, and he paved the way for the widespread acceptance of many more creative artists working with rock 'n' roll.

"Rock Around the Clock" demonstrated the unprecedented success that a white group with a country background could achieve playing a twelve-bar blues song driven by the sounds of electric guitar, bass, and drums. It proved a portent of the enormous changes that were about to overtake American popular music and opened the floodgates for artists like Elvis Presley, Carl Perkins, and Buddy Holly. "Rock Around the Clock" also helped prepare a receptive mass audience for the sounds of rhythm & blues, and for black artists building on rhythm & blues traditions. While the song was still at the top of the pop chart in 1955, Chuck Berry's trailblazing "Maybellene" (see Chapter 3) made its appearance on the same chart, and before long was itself in the Top 10.

Bill Haley and the Comets shake up a crowd at the Sports Arena in Hershey, Pennsylvania, 1956. Courtesy of Library of Congress.

system, the growth of independent record labels, and the rise of the teenager as a demographic force all combined to set the stage for a new genre that would bring the music, style, and business model of previously marginalized groups into the mainstream.

3
EARLY ROCK 'N' ROLL
MUSICIANS

THE FIRST GENERATIONS

Though it may seem strange, the first generation of rock 'n' roll stars did not necessarily see themselves primarily as rock 'n' roll musicians, at least initially. Emerging from the African American tradition of rhythm and blues, they eyed their young white audience with a mixture of enthusiasm and skepticism. As noted previously, "rock 'n' roll" was initially seen as a marketing term used to sell rhythm & blues records to young white audiences. For that reason, many musicians who fell into this category continued to view their older, African American listeners as their core audience, only slowly coming to recognize the potential of their new listeners. The extent to which the first generation of rock musicians consciously pursued this new audience at various points in their careers is closely tied to the extent to which they considered themselves to be part of rock 'n' roll.

The three most prominent musicians to fall into this category are Chuck Berry, Little Richard, and Fats Domino, all of whom began their careers as rhythm & blues musicians. Of the three, Chuck Berry was the songwriter/performer who most obviously addressed his songs to teenage America (white and black) in the 1950s; Little Richard was the cultivator of a deliberately outrageous performance style that appealed on the basis of its strangeness, novelty, and sexual ambiguity; and Fats Domino's work most directly embodied the continuity of rhythm & blues with rock 'n' roll. As might be expected from this description, Domino was the earliest of the three to become an established performer (although he was slightly younger than Berry)—he cut his first rhythm & blues hit, "The Fat Man," in 1949 at the age of twenty-one. But all three crossed over to the pop charts and mainstream success within the first few months following the massive success of Bill Haley's "Rock around the Clock."

Chuck Berry

Charles Edward Anderson ("Chuck") Berry (b. 1926) burst precipitously onto the pop music scene with his first record, "Maybellene." It was a novel synthesis that did not sound precisely like anything before it, and it introduced listeners to an already fully formed style of songwriting, singing, and guitar playing that would exercise a primal influence on virtually all of the rock 'n' roll to follow.

Berry was born in St. Louis, Missouri, where he absorbed blues and rhythm & blues styles. He was one of the first black musicians to consciously forge his own version of these styles for appeal to the mass market—and he was certainly the most successful of his generation in this effort. Like many other black musicians, Berry also knew country music, and he found that his performances of country songs in clubs appealed strongly to the white members of his audience. He put this knowledge and experience to good use: "Maybellene" was distantly modeled on a country number called "Ida Red." Nevertheless, the primary elements of "Maybellene" trace their roots clearly to rhythm & blues: the thick, buzzing timbre of Berry's electric guitar; the blue notes and slides in both voice and guitar; the socking backbeat of the drum; and the form, derived from twelve-bar blues structures.

After the success of "Maybellene," Chuck Berry went on to write and record other excellent rock 'n' roll songs that became more and more explicit celebrations of American teenage culture and its

Chuck Berry in 1959. Courtesy of Library of Congress.

music. "Roll Over Beethoven" (1956) praises rhythm & blues at the expense of classical music. "School Day" (Number 3 Pop, Number 1 R&B in 1957) describes drudgery relieved by an after-school trip to the "juke joint," at which point the record becomes literally an advertisement for itself and an anthem

🎧 LISTENING TO "MAYBELLENE"

What, then, made "Maybellene" sound so startlingly new? The explosive tempo, for one thing; while swing bands occasionally may have played for dancing at a tempo like this, no vocal-based rhythm & blues had ever gone at this pace, because it is exceptionally hard to articulate words, and have time to breathe, when trying to sing at this tempo. But Berry pulled it off, articulating the words with clarity and remarkable force. This brings up another essential aspect of the record's novelty and appeal, which is the lyrics themselves. The lyrics to "Maybellene" provide an original and clever description of a lovers' quarrel in the form of a car chase, complete with a punning invented verb form (*motorvatin'*), humorous details ("Rain water blowin'" under the automobile hood, which is "doin' my motor good"), and a breathless ending in which the singer catches Maybellene in her Cadillac at the top of a hill—an ending that still leaves listeners room to imagine a wide range of sequels. And what could reach out to a young audience more effectively than a story featuring both cars and sex appeal?

In addition, we should not miss the implied class distinction the lyrics make between Maybellene, in her top-of-the-line Cadillac Coupe de Ville, and the narrator, in his more humble, middle-class, but eminently functional "V-8 Ford." As he chases and finally catches the Cadillac (and Maybellene), there is a sense of the underdog's triumphing in the race, and the boastful claim of the first verse, that nothing could outrun his V-8 Ford, is vindicated. (Cars have long been an important status symbol in American culture, and African American culture is certainly no exception to this. A song recorded by Bessie Smith in 1928, a generation before "Maybellene," called "Put It Right Here (Or Keep It Out There)," described the singer's deadbeat lover as follows: "Once he was like a Cadillac, now he's like an old worn-out Ford." The concern with cars persists into rap music; an early example of this is "Sucker M.C.' s," a 1983 hit by Run-D.M.C.).

All the basic ingredients that would inform a string of successive, successful Chuck Berry records are present in "Maybellene." These elements became his trademarks: an arresting instrumental introduction for unaccompanied electric guitar; relentless intensity produced by a very fast tempo and a very loud volume level; formal and stylistic elements strongly related to earlier rhythm & blues music; and witty lyrics, clearly enunciated and designed to appeal to the lifestyle and aspirations of his young audience.

Form

The form of "Maybellene" is clearly based on the twelve-bar blues. The chorus ("Maybellene, why can't you be true?") adheres to the traditional twelve-bar structure in every respect: three four-bar phrases with a standard chord pattern. The three-line poetic structure of the chorus lyrics, in which the second line is a repetition of the first, presents a pattern that dates back to some of the oldest known blues songs. The verses, however, while twelve bars long, completely suppress chord changes, remaining on the "home" (or tonic) chord throughout while the voice delivers rapid-fire lyrics using brief, repetitive patterns of notes (see Listening Chart). Ironically, by eliminating chord changes and restricting melodic interest in the verses, Berry turns what could have been a static, repetitive form into something more dynamic. Instead of a string of standard twelve-bar blues stanzas, we hear an alternating verse–chorus structure that allows Berry to tell his story, and to build his record, in a more exciting way.

The stripped-down music of the verses focuses all attention on their lyrics—which is appropriate, as it is the verses that relate the ongoing progress of the car chase. Their repetitive melodic formulas allow Berry to concentrate on articulating the densely packed words; the continuous verbal activity more than compensates for the lack of musical variety. Actually, the verses build enormous tension, so that when the choruses at last bring some chord changes—basic as they are—there is a feeling of release and expansion. The pace of the lyrics also slows down momentarily for the choruses, which reinforces this effect of expansion and allows Berry to lean expressively on the crucial name, "Maybel*lene*." Yet, while the choruses provide variety and release, they create tension of another sort, as they postpone the continuation of the story being told in the verses. This same effect is created on a larger scale by the instrumental break before the final verse: variety and release on the one hand (and an opportunity for Berry to showcase his considerable guitar chops), along with a real sense of racing along down the highway, but tension and postponement of the story's climax on the other.

The manipulation of a limited set of musical materials to achieve maximal results of variety, novelty, and excitement is the essence of effective rock 'n' roll. "Maybellene" is an outstanding case in point. The formal issues discussed previously may seem either obvious or all but lost in the pure visceral intensity of the record, but the seamlessness of Chuck Berry's artistry should not blind us to the man's brilliance. Above all, "Maybellene" is a beautifully formed record, building inexorably from start to finish, where everything is made to count, without a single word or note wasted.

The Song/The Recording

In Chuck Berry's "Maybellene," the song *is* the recording. When people think of or cite "Maybellene," they are referring to Berry's original recording of it—the ultimate, and really the only important, source material. The culture of rock 'n' roll centered to an unprecedented extent on records: records played on the radio, records played at dances, records purchased for home listening. Studio recordings thus increasingly came to represent the original, primary documents of the music, often preceding and generally taking precedence over any live performances of the material, and certainly over any published sheet music. Baby boomers went to hear rock 'n' roll stars perform the hits they already knew from the records they heard and bought; on the nationally broadcast television program *American Bandstand*, singers came without accompanying bands and lip-synched their songs while the records played in the background. The issuing of sheet music was becoming an afterthought, an ancillary to the recording. In many future discussions, consequently, we will be discussing the song and the recording as one, rather than as separate entities.

This change also suggests another reason why rock 'n' roll was so threatening to the Tin Pan Alley business model. It is difficult to imagine anyone viewing the experience of playing "Maybellene" at home on a piano as being in any way comparable to the experience of hearing Chuck Berry's recording of it. This was a problem,

because from the Tin Pan Alley point of view, the product was supposed to be the *song*, not the *performance*, and to change that formula was to change the whole foundation of the system. In other words, by being a songwriter and performer simultaneously, Chuck Berry was effectively neither. He was not writing songs for others to perform, since, even if they tried, their performances would pale in comparison to his own. He was also not a performer who needed professional songwriters to provide him with material, since he wrote his own songs. If this approach became standard practice for the whole industry, it would make the jobs of both Tin Pan Alley songwriters *and* Tin Pan Alley performers obsolete. In many ways, that is exactly what happened.

At the same time, the legal principles that underlie the music business are still based on the Tin Pan Alley model, even to the present day. This, in turn, has created a discrepancy between the *culture* of rock, which emphasizes the performer, and the *business* of rock, which emphasizes the songwriter. Perhaps the most obvious way this discrepancy has affected rock musicians is the all-too-common story of the naïve young artist who signs away songwriting royalties in exchange for a greater share of performance royalties, a deal which seems reasonable on the surface, but which is in fact greatly to the artist's disadvantage. This discrepancy was manifested in the case of "Maybellene" by the fact that the deejay Alan Freed was listed as a coauthor of this song. Freed was given the composer credit by Berry's record label Chess Records, essentially as a bribe to publicize the song (Cohen 2004: 163). At the time, this move probably seemed like a minor expenditure, but it almost certainly wound up costing Chuck Berry millions of dollars over time.

"Maybellene" opens arrestingly with the sound of Berry's hollow-body electric guitar playing a bluesy lick that sizzles with sonic energy. The impact of "Maybellene" is in no small part due to the infectious rhythmic **groove** and sound established by Berry and a gifted group of sidemen, including the great blues composer and bassist Willie Dixon, an integral part of Muddy Waters's recordings for Chess Records (see Chapter 1); Jerome Green, on maracas; and pianist Johnny Johnson, who may well have played a role in the creation of Berry's songs. Some credit for the overall sound of the recording must

LISTENING CHART "MAYBELLENE"

Music and lyrics by Chuck Berry (also credited to disc jockeys Russel Fratto and Alan Freed);[1] as performed by Chuck Berry and his combo; recorded 1955

FORM		LYRICS	DESCRIPTIVE COMMENTS
Instrumental intro			Solo electric guitar "hook" establishes characteristic sound (suggesting auto horns) and tempo.
Chorus	0.04	*Maybellene . . .*	Twelve-bar blues.
Verse 1	0.17	*As I was . . .*	Twelve bars, without any chord changes; very fast pacing of lyrics.
Chorus	0.29	*Maybellene . . .*	As before.
Verse 2	0.41	*The Cadillac . . .*	As in verse 1.
Chorus	0.53	*Maybellene . . .*	As before.
Instrumental break	1.05		Two successive twelve-bar sections.
Chorus	1.30	*Maybellene . . .*	As before.
Verse 3	1.42	*The motor . . .*	As in verse 1.
Chorus	1.55	*Maybellene . . .*	As before.
Instrumental coda	2.07		Fades out.

1. In the early years of rock 'n' roll, the record market was fluid and unpredictable, and agents, promoters, distributors, and disc jockeys were often given (or would take) songwriting credits in exchange for the "favor" of pushing particular artists or records. There was nothing new in this practice; it just became much more widespread. In any case, it is doubtful that Fratto and Freed had anything substantial to do with the creation of "Maybellene," although they certainly helped it to be heard and to become popular.

also go to Phil and Leonard Chess, who in their years of recording Chicago blues musicians such as Muddy Waters and Howlin' Wolf had learned how to stay out of the way of a good recording. They sometimes offered advice but never tried to radically alter a musician's style for commercial effect.

Amid the numerous elements borrowed from rhythm & blues and urban blues, we may also hear in "Maybellene" a prominent, and very regular, bass line, alternating between two notes on beats 1 and 3 of each bar. The rhythmic feel of this bass line is stylistically much more suggestive of country music than of anything found typically in rhythm & blues, and its presence here points to Berry's knowledge of country music and to what Berry himself has identified as the country origins of "Maybellene." As we shall see repeatedly, rock 'n' roll music is often based on a synthesis of widely diverse stylistic elements.

for the music it represents: "*Hail! Hail! Rock 'n' roll! Deliver me from the days of old!*" "Rock and Roll Music" (Number 8 Pop, Number 6 R&B, also in 1957) articulates the virtues of its subject, as opposed to the limitations of "modern jazz" or a "symphony." "Sweet Little Sixteen" (Number 2 Pop, Number 1 R&B in 1958) wittily describes the young collector of "famed autographs," coping with growing up ("tight dresses and lipstick"), for whom a rock 'n' roll show becomes—in her mind, at least—a national party where all the "cats" want to dance with her.

Berry's consummate statement on rock 'n' roll mythology is doubtless "Johnny B. Goode" (Number 8 Pop, Number 2 R&B in 1958). Here he relates the story of a "country boy" who "never learned to read or write so well" but who "could play a guitar just like a-ringin' a bell." (Berry's autobiography states that the "country boy" was originally a "colored boy," but Berry opted to make his tale color-blind, recognizing the diversity of his audience and the potential universality of his myth.) The boy's mother predicts his coming success as a bandleader with his "name in lights, saying 'Johnny B. Goode tonight'"—as one of pop music's greatest verbal puns embodies the dream of every teenager with a guitar and a wish to succeed as a rock 'n' roller (with parental approval and appreciation, no less)!

It cannot be known how many careers in music were inspired or encouraged by "Johnny B. Goode," but a list of pop musicians who have been obviously and singularly influenced by Chuck Berry would read like a who's who of rock stars from the 1960s and beyond. He is probably the only musician of his generation to be inescapably influential on three different, and essential, fronts: as a brilliantly clever and articulate **lyricist** and songwriter; as a fine rock 'n' roll vocal stylist; and as a pioneering electric guitarist. The mass adulation belonged to Elvis Presley, but the greatest influence on musicians unquestionably was made by Berry.

The Electric Guitar and Rock 'n' Roll

It is almost impossible to conjure up a mental image of Chuck Berry—or Buddy Holly or Jimi Hendrix—without an electric guitar in his hands. Certainly, one of rock 'n' roll's most significant effects on popular music was its elevation of the electric guitar to the position of centrality that the instrument still enjoys in most genres of popular music today. The development of the electric guitar is a good example of the complex relationship between technological developments and changing musical styles. Up through the end of World War II, the guitar was found mainly in popular music that originated in the South (blues and hillbilly music), and in various "exotic" genres (Hawai'ian and Latin American guitar records were quite popular in the 1920s and 1930s). Because of its low volume, the acoustic guitar was difficult to use in large dance bands and equally difficult to record. Engineers began to experiment with electronically amplified guitars in the 1920s, and in 1931 the Electro String Instrument Company (better known as Rickenbacker) introduced the first commercially produced electric guitars. Laid across the player's knees like the steel or Hawai'ian guitars used in country music and blues, these instruments were called "frying pans" because of their distinctive round bodies and long necks. By the mid-1930s the Gibson Company had introduced a hollow-body guitar with a new type of pickup—a magnetic plate or coil attached to the body of the guitar, which converts the physical vibrations of its strings into patterns of electric energy. This pickup later became known as the *Charlie Christian* pickup, after the young African American guitarist from Texas (1916–42) who introduced the guitar into Benny Goodman's band and helped to pioneer the modern jazz style called *bebop*. Despite Christian's innovations with the Goodman band, few of the big swing bands introduced the instrument, and none allowed it to play a prominent role.

The *solid-body electric guitar* was developed after World War II and was first used in rhythm & blues, blues, and country bands—the country musician Merle Travis (1917–83) had one designed for him as early as 1946, and blues musicians such as T-Bone Walker (1910–75) and Muddy Waters were also recording with electric guitars by the late 1940s. For the most part, guitars were used as a rhythm instrument at this time. In other words, they were viewed as being similar to a piano—their job was mainly to play chords behind a solo instrument. Only in rare cases would the guitar itself be used to perform a solo. In fact, one of the developments that began to significantly distinguish rock 'n' roll from rhythm & blues in the late 1950s was the replacement of the saxophone by the guitar as a solo instrument. This change was emphasized by Buddy Holly's decision to have two guitarists in his band: a "rhythm" guitarist to play chords and a "lead" guitarist to play solos. Previous to this, a single guitar player would have fulfilled both duties.

The first commercially produced solid-body electric guitar was the Fender Broadcaster (soon renamed the Telecaster), brainchild of Leo Fender and George Fullerton. This model, released in 1948, featured two electronic pickups, knobs to control volume and timbre, and a switch that allowed the two pickups to be used alone or together, allowing the player to create a palette of different sounds. In 1954 Fender released the Stratocaster, the first guitar with three pickups, and the first with a "whammy bar" or "**vibrato** bar," a metal rod attached to the guitar's bridge that allowed the player to bend pitches with his right as well as his left hand. Fender's most successful competitor, the Gibson Company, released a solid-body guitar in 1952, christening it the Les Paul in honor of the celebrated guitarist who helped to popularize both the new instrument and the use of multiple-track tape recording. The first widely popular electric bass guitar, the Fender Precision Bass, was introduced in 1951.

What is it about electric guitars that makes them such objects of fascination—sometimes bordering on fetishism—for musicians and fans alike? As with any kind of influential technology—say, the automobile or the phonograph—the meaning of the guitar is a complex matter. To begin with, the instrument came into the popular mainstream with a somewhat dubious reputation, perhaps a carryover from the medieval European association of stringed instruments with the Devil, and was associated with the music of marginalized regions (the South, Latin America) and people (sailors and railway men, sharecroppers and hobos,

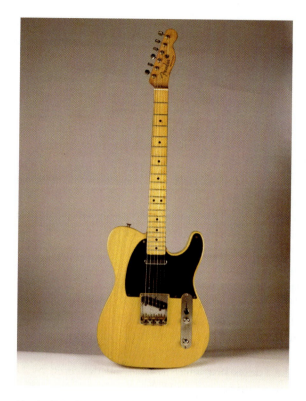

Fender Broadcaster, the first commercially produced solid-body electric guitar (photo by Steve Catlin/Redferns); 1952 Gibson Les Paul Gold Top (photo by Nigel Osbourne/Redferns).

blacks, Latinos, and poor southern whites). A lot of the put-downs aimed at young rock 'n' rollers by the mainstream music press of the 1950s ridiculed the guitar, suggesting that it was an instrument that anyone could play. (If you believe *that,* we suggest that you take a few guitar lessons!) The electric guitar became a symbol of the energetic diversity that was elbowing its way into the mainstream of American popular music during this period. The feeling of excess and invasion was reinforced by the development of portable tube amplifiers, which, if pushed hard enough, could provide a dense, sizzling, and very loud sound, eventually augmented by special-effects devices such as wah-wah pedals and "fuzz boxes" that were perfectly designed to drive parents and other authority figures nuts. In addition, the suitability of the guitar for use as a phallic symbol—a formerly male practice more recently appropriated by female rockers—added to the instrument's aura of danger and excitement.

Little Richard

The centrality of records to the culture of rock 'n' roll didn't negate the significance of live performances. Indeed, live performances disseminated via the new mass medium of television, or on the movie screen, assumed a new importance for performers of rock 'n' roll music, and individual artists and vocal groups sought to cultivate visual characteristics or mannerisms that would set them apart from others and encourage listeners to remember them—and to go out and buy their records. Chuck Berry had his famous "duck walk" as a stage device. But no performer in the early years of rock 'n' roll was as visually flamboyant as Little Richard.

<u>Richard Wayne Penniman ("Little Richard")</u> (b. 1932) spent several lackluster years as a journeyman rhythm & blues performer before hitting the pop charts early in 1956 with his wild performance of the nonsensical song "Tutti-Frutti." Based on the twelve-bar blues, "Tutti-Frutti" alternated nonsense choruses ("Tutti-frutti, au rutti, a-wop-bop-a-loom-op a-lop-bam-boom!"—and variants thereof) with nonspecific but obviously leering verses ("I got a gal named Sue, she knows just what to do"), all delivered by Little Richard in an uninhibited shouting style complete with falsetto whoops and

accompanied by a pounding band led by Little Richard's equally uninhibited piano. In retrospect, it seems surprising that records like "Tutti-Frutti" and its even more successful—and more obviously salacious—follow-up, "Long Tall Sally," got played on mainstream radio at all. It must have been assumed by programmers that Little Richard was a novelty act and that therefore nobody would pay attention to, or understand, the words of his songs. But teenage listeners in the 1950s certainly understood that Little Richard embodied the new spirit of rock 'n' roll music in the most extroverted, outrageous, and original way.

Any doubts on the matter would surely have been resolved by seeing Little Richard's performances in any of the three rock 'n' roll movies in which he appeared during the two years of his greatest popular success, 1956–57: *Don't Knock the Rock, The Girl Can't Help It,* and *Mister Rock 'n' Roll.* Heavily made up, with his hair in an enormous pompadour, rolling his eyes, playing

Little Richard in 1957. Frank Driggs Collection.

🎧 LISTENING TO "LONG TALL SALLY"

Like most of Little Richard's songs, "Long Tall Sally" is built on the twelve-bar blues. Like Chuck Berry and other artists who came out of rhythm & blues to seek pop stardom, Little Richard adapted the twelve-bar blues structure so as to reflect the more traditionally pop-friendly format of verse-chorus. Here, the first four bars of each blues stanza are set to changing words—verses—while the remaining eight bars, with unchanging words, function as a repeated chorus. This simple but surprisingly effective formal arrangement is reflected in both identical and varied ways in many rock 'n' roll songs of the period; for examples of variations on this structure, see the listening charts for Elvis Presley's "Don't Be Cruel" and for the Coasters' "Charlie Brown."

LISTENING CHART "LONG TALL SALLY"
Music and lyrics credited to Enotris Johnson, Richard Penniman, and Robert Blackwell;
as performed by Little Richard and unidentified band; recorded 1956

FORM		LYRICS	DESCRIPTIVE COMMENTS
Verse 1		*Gonna tell Aunt Mary . . .*	Underlying rhythmic and chord structure is that of the twelve-bar blues, with the first four bars constituting the verse and the final eight bars the chorus; loud, flamboyant vocal style throughout.
Chorus	0.05	*Oh, baby . . .*	
Verse 2	0.16	*Well, Long Tall Sally . . .*	Twelve-bar blues pattern persists throughout the song.
Chorus	0.21	*Oh, baby . . .*	
Verse 3	0.32	*Well, I saw Uncle John . . .*	
Chorus	0.37	*Oh, baby . . .*	
Instrumental break	0.47		Two twelve-bar blues sections; intense saxophone solo reflects the mood of the vocal.
Repetition of verse 2 + chorus, then verse 3 + chorus	[begins 1.18]		
Conclusion	1.49	*We're gonna have some fun tonight . . .*	Extended choruslike section; twelve-bar blues structure.

the piano while standing and gyrating wildly, Little Richard epitomized the abandon celebrated in rock 'n' roll lyrics and music. Both the sound of his recordings and the visual characteristics of his performances made Little Richard an exceptionally strong influence on later performers; the white rockabilly singer-pianist Jerry Lee Lewis was inestimably in his debt, and in the 1960s the English Beatles and the American Creedence Clearwater Revival—along with many other bands—played music whose roots could readily be traced back to Little Richard. Moreover, the lingering (and carefully crafted) ambiguity of Little Richard's sexual identity—available evidence suggests that he might best have been classified in the early days as an omnivore—paved the way for the image of performers such as David Bowie, Elton John, and Prince.

Boogie-Woogie Piano Music

One important influence on the rhythmic conception of early rock 'n' roll musicians was the *boogie-woogie* blues piano tradition, which sprang up during the early twentieth century in east Texas, and soon spread to the neighboring states of Louisiana, Arkansas, Missouri, and Oklahoma and eventually to Chicago via the railroad. The style developed in the environment of the barrelhouses, rowdy nightspots patronized by the men who worked in the lumber and turpentine camps of the area. Solo pianists, a cheap and readily available form of entertainment, responded to the rowdy environment of the barrelhouses by developing a powerful style that could be heard over the crowd noise. In boogie-woogie performances the pianist typically plays a repeated bass pattern with his left hand, down in the low range of the piano, while improvising **polyrhythmic** patterns in his right hand. The greatest boogie-woogie piano players—men like Pete Johnson, Albert Ammons, Meade Lux Lewis, and Pine Top Smith—were said to have "a left hand like God," an admiring reference to the volume, steadiness, and authority of their bass patterns. During the Second World War boogie-woogie became a national fad, spawning a series of hit records, including "Boogie Woogie," "Boogie Woogie Bugle Boy," and even "The Booglie Wooglie Piggy." After the war the strong bass rhythms of boogie-woogie were an important influence on jump-band R&B artists such as Louis Jordan (including his hit record "Choo Choo Ch'Boogie," which we discussed in Chapter 1), and on early rock 'n' roll, particularly the work of southern-born pianists such as Little Richard, Fats Domino, and Jerry Lee Lewis.

Fats Domino

Antoine "Fats" Domino (b. 1928), a singer, pianist, and songwriter, had been an established presence on the rhythm & blues charts for several years by the time he scored his first large-scale pop breakthrough with "Ain't It a Shame" in 1955 (Number 10 Pop, Number 1 R&B). In this case, mainstream success was simply the result of the market's catching up with Domino; there is no significant stylistic difference between his earlier rhythm & blues hits and his rock 'n' roll bestsellers like "I'm in Love Again" and "I'm Walkin'." Domino himself remarked that he was always playing the same music, that they called it "rhythm & blues" first and "rock 'n' roll" later, and that it made no difference to him—although it surely did make a difference to him when the rock 'n' roll market catapulted his record sales into the millions and eventually made him the second-biggest-selling recording artist of the 1950s, right behind Elvis Presley.

Domino was born in New Orleans and grew up bathed in the rich and diverse musical traditions of that city. His distinctive regional style best exemplifies the strong connections between rock 'n' roll and earlier music. Jazz, especially boogie-woogie, was a strong early influence on him, along with the rhythm & blues piano style of <u>Professor Longhair</u> (1918–80; real name Henry Roeland Byrd) and the jump band style of trumpeter Dave Bartholomew's ensemble. Bartholomew became Domino's arranger, producer, and songwriting partner, and their collaboration produced a remarkable string of consistently fine and successful records. Their "New Orleans" sound was also widely admired and imitated among musicians; Domino played piano on hit records by other artists, and Little Richard recorded in New Orleans to use the city's distinctive sidemen and thus try to capture some of the city's rock 'n' roll magic. (Little Richard's "Long Tall Sally" is modeled directly on Domino's "Ain't It a Shame," both in formal layout and musical arrangement.)

Antoine "Fats" Domino in 1958. Michael Ochs Archives/ Getty Images.

Given his strong links to tradition, it is not surprising that Fats Domino recorded a number of Tin Pan Alley standards—in contradistinction to artists like Chuck Berry and Little Richard, who concentrated on novel songs and styles to appeal to their new audience. In fact, Domino's 1956 remake of "Blueberry Hill" proved to be his most popular record, reaching the Number Two position on the pop charts and topping the R&B charts. "Blueberry Hill" was a Tin Pan Alley tune that had originally been a big hit in 1940 for the Glenn Miller Orchestra (with vocal by Ray Eberle). Domino preserved his own rhythm & blues–based style when performing "Blueberry Hill" and other standards, however, thus bringing a new kind of musical hybrid to mass-market attention, and with this phenomenon a new and important musical bridge was crossed. We might say that, rather than crossing over himself, Domino made the music cross over to him. Smooth Tin Pan Alley–style crooning and uninflected urban diction were replaced by Domino's rhythmically accented, full-throated singing in his characteristic New Orleans accent, and it certainly wasn't the sound of a sweet band backing him or shaping his own piano accompaniment.

Fats Domino, Little Richard, and Chuck Berry all achieved their successes recording on independent labels, thus demonstrating the great importance of the indies to the popularization of rock 'n' roll. Domino recorded for Imperial, a Los Angeles–based concern headed by Lew Chudd, which also issued records by the important rhythm & blues electric guitar stylist Aaron "T-Bone" Walker. Little Richard was an artist for Specialty Records, Art Rupe's Hollywood label, which had on its roster such rhythm & blues stars as Percy Mayfield, Lloyd Price, and Guitar Slim, along with important African American gospel groups and soloists. Berry's records were issued on Chess, the Chicago label of the Chess brothers Leonard and Phil, which also served as home for an impressive list of blues-based artists like Muddy Waters, Howlin' Wolf, and Willie Dixon, along with other rock 'n' rollers like Bo Diddley and the vocal group the Moonglows.

THE NEXT GENERATION

As rock 'n' roll became established as a genre unto itself, it soon gave rise to a new generation of musicians. While they may have had a background in rhythm and blues or country (or both), these artists saw themselves as *primarily* rock 'n' roll musicians, as opposed to musicians from other genres who *happened to be playing* music that was promoted as rock 'n' roll.

Elvis Presley

The biggest rock 'n' roll star to fit this profile was, of course, Elvis Presley. Presley's early career with the independent label Sun Records was briefly considered in the previous discussion of "Mystery Train" (see Chapter 2). When RCA Victor bought out Presley's contract from Sun in late 1955, at the then-extravagant price of thirty-five thousand dollars, this mainstream major label set about consciously trying to turn the "hillbilly cat" into a mainstream performer without compromising the strength of his appeal to teenagers. In this they were assisted by two major players. First, there was Presley's manager, Colonel Thomas Parker, who saw to it that Presley was seen repeatedly on television variety shows and in a series of romantic Hollywood films. Second was RCA's Nashville producer Chet Atkins, who saw to it that Presley's records for the label were made pop-friendly, according to Atkins's standards. (In the 1960s Atkins became the producer most credited with developing the "Nashville Sound" of pop-oriented country music.) They succeeded beyond anyone's expectations. Although Presley's television performances were denounced by authorities as vulgar because of the singer's hip-shaking gyrations, the shows were attended by hordes of screaming young fans and were admired on the screen by millions of young viewers. And Presley's records racked up astronomical sales as he dominated the top of the pop charts steadily from 1956 on into the early 1960s, quickly establishing himself as the biggest-selling solo artist of rock 'n' roll, and then as the biggest-selling solo recording artist of *any* period and style—a title he still held at the beginning of the twenty-first century.

Presley's biggest hit, "Don't Be Cruel," topped the charts for eleven weeks in the late summer and fall of 1956, eventually yielding pride of place to another Presley record, "Love Me Tender."

Elvis Presley on stage in 1956. Michael Ochs Archives/Getty Images.

On the other side of "Don't Be Cruel" was Presley's version of "Hound Dog," a song that had been a major rhythm & blues hit in 1953 for Big Mama Thornton. Comparing Presley's cover of "Hound Dog" for RCA with the earlier cover he did for Sun of the rhythm & blues tune "Mystery Train" sheds further light on the shaping of Elvis's image for mainstream consumption. Whereas his rockabilly "Mystery Train" is noticeably faster, looser, and wilder than Junior Parker's original, his "Hound Dog" has lost some of its teeth—so to speak—as a result of the bowdlerization of the original words. Big Mama Thornton's version is full of sexual innuendo, making it clear that the term "hound dog" is being used metaphorically, not literally ("daddy, I know you ain't no real cool cat"; "you can wag your tail, but I ain't gonna feed you no more"; see the discussion

🎧 LISTENING TO "DON'T BE CRUEL"

"**D**on't Be Cruel" is based on the twelve-bar blues. Presley's vocal is heavy with blues-derived and country inflections; we hear a striking regional accent, and the occasional "hiccuping" effect ("baby, it's just you I'm a-thinkin' of") is one associated particularly with rockabilly singers like Presley, Gene Vincent, and Buddy Holly. The strong backbeat throughout evokes rhythm & blues, while the repeated electric guitar figure at the opening is reminiscent of rhythmic ideas favored by western swing bands (and ultimately derived from boogie-woogie). Imposed on all these diverse and intense stylistic elements is a wash of electronic **reverb**—an attempt by the engineers at RCA's Nashville studios to emulate the distinctive (and decidedly low-tech) "**slap-back**" echo sound of Presley's previous recordings on Sun Records. There is also the sweetening sound of the backing vocal group, the Jordanaires, whose precise "bop, bop"s and crooning "aah"s and "ooo"s are doubly rooted in white gospel music and in the most genteel, established, mainstream pop style. Whether this odd amalgam is

LISTENING CHART "DON'T BE CRUEL"

Music and lyrics by Otis Blackwell and Elvis Presley;[1] as performed by Elvis Presley, vocal and guitar, with the Jordanaires and backing instrumentalists; recorded 1956

FORM		LYRICS	DESCRIPTIVE COMMENTS
Instrumental intro			Repetitive guitar hook, strong backbeat (four bars long).
Verse 1	0.05	*If you know . . .*	Twelve-bar blues structure, arranged to suggest a verse-chorus pattern, with the first eight bars constituting the verse and the final four bars the chorus.
Chorus	0.16	*Don't be cruel . . .*	
Verse 2	0.23	*Baby, if I made you mad . . .*	Twelve-bar blues structure, with an extension added (six bars in length) to the chorus.
Chorus + extension	0.33 (0.40)	*Don't be cruel . . . I don't want . . .*	
Verse 3	0.48	*Don't stop a-thinkin' of me . . .*	Twelve-bar blues, plus extension (as before).
Chorus + extension	0.59 (1.05)	*Don't be cruel . . . Why should we . . .*	
Verse 4	1.13	*Let's walk up . . .*	Twelve-bar blues, plus extension (as before).
Chorus + extension	1.24 (1.30)	*Don't be cruel . . . I don't want . . .*	
Concluding chorus + additional extension	1.39 (1.50)	*Don't be cruel . . . Don't be cruel . . . I don't want . . .*	

1. Presley, though not generally known as a songwriter, was credited as coauthor of a handful of his early hits for RCA.

deemed to work as a source of stylistic enrichment, or whether listening to Presley and the Jordanaires together on this record seems like listening to the Chords and the Crew Cuts *simultaneously* performing "Sh-Boom" (see the discussion of cover versions on pp. 41–42) will obviously be a matter of personal taste. It can never be known how much the Jordanaires added, or if they added at all, to the appeal of this and many other records Presley made with them for RCA. But the commercial success of these records was unprecedented, and their mixture of styles was yet another indication of the extent to which the traditional barriers in pop music were falling down. (Major labels often tended to sweeten recordings by rock 'n' roll singers for the mass market, while the indies went for a rawer, more basic sound. For example, many of Jackie Wilson's rhythm & blues–based recordings for the Brunswick label—a subsidiary of the major Decca—featured elaborately arranged backing choruses and orchestral arrangements.)

in Chapter 1). Such sexual implications are gone in Presley's rendition, which seems to be literally about a pathetic mutt who is "cryin' all the time" and "ain't never caught a rabbit." With the lyrics cleaned up in this way for mass consumption, the undeniable passion of Presley's performance seems a bit over the top for the subject matter, turning the record into a kind of novelty song. But this certainly didn't bother the singer's audience, most of whom could not have been familiar with Thornton's original anyway; "Hound Dog" proved just about as popular as "Don't Be Cruel" itself.

Presley's extraordinary popularity established rock 'n' roll as an unprecedented mass-market phenomenon. His reputation as a performer and recording artist endured up to his death in 1977 at the age of forty-two—and continues beyond the grave; Graceland, his home in Memphis, Tennessee, is now a public museum dedicated to his memory and is visited by upwards of 600,000 people annually. Presley gave strong performances and made fine records at many points throughout his career, and he starred in many movies. But it cannot be denied that Elvis Presley's principal importance as a musical influence and innovator—like that of Chuck Berry, Little Richard, and Fats Domino—rests upon his achievements during the early years of rock 'n' roll. In 1956 Presley cut a handful of records that literally changed the world for himself and for those around him, and the unbridled exuberance of his live performances at that time became the model for every white kid who wanted to move mountains by strumming a guitar, shaking his hips, and lifting his voice.

Jerry Lee Lewis

Jerry Lee Lewis (b. 1935) is a piano player in the same boogie-woogie blues-influenced tradition as Little Richard and Fats Domino. Also like Little Richard, Lewis was known for his personality and performance style as much as for his music. On stage, he was known to pound the piano keys, flip his long hair around, and jump up on the piano (and in one instance when he was opening for Chuck Berry, even light it on fire). With titles like "Whole Lotta Shakin' Goin' On" and "Great Balls of Fire" (both 1957), his songs reinforced his image as a wild man, as did his nickname: The Killer.

Growing up in Louisiana, Lewis had been exposed not only to the country and R&B traditions, but also to Christian gospel music in the Pentecostal Assemblies of God denomination, which was home to his cousin, the well-known televangelist Jimmy Swaggart. Many of his apparently wild performance gestures and stylistic flourishes were, in fact, drawn from the religious tradition in which he was raised. At the same time, much of Lewis's music was driven by his own spiritual discomfort over having rejected the church in favor of rock 'n' roll, a discomfort that he openly discussed on many occasions.

Jerry Lee Lewis ("The Killer") in action, 1957. Michael Ochs Archives/Getty Images.

In 1958, while on tour in England, the news broke that Lewis had not only married his 14-year-old second cousin, but had done so without divorcing his previous wife, causing a scandal that effectively drove him out of the music business for several years. Though his career began to recover in the 1960s, and he continued performing into the twenty-first century, he was never again to regain his initial popularity.

Jerry Lee Lewis's significance to rock 'n' roll can be seen in several areas. Like other rock 'n' roll artists of his era, Lewis represented the wild and untamed—even frightening—image that would come to characterize rock as a whole. At the same time, it is worth thinking about the extent to which the "wildness" of early rock 'n' roll reflected these artists' actual attitudes, how much of it was a result of stereotypes based on their class or racial background, and how much was a result of the artists (or their handlers) intentionally playing up to the stereotypes. In Lewis's case, all of these factors probably came into play.

A related aspect of Lewis's significance to rock culture was the fact that he viewed rock 'n' roll—and especially his own music—as being sinful in the most profound sense of the word. Most of the first generation of rock 'n' roll artists—black and white—were raised in a very strong evangelical Christian culture, a culture that took an especially dim view of rock 'n' roll. Many of these artists—especially Lewis and Little Richard—were deeply conflicted about their work as rock musicians. Lewis, in particular, has stated on numerous occasions that he believes himself to be literally damned for playing rock 'n' roll. Ironically, Lewis's espousal of the idea that rock is a powerful force of sin and temptation may well have been part of what made him attractive to his fans. The romanticized spiritual dissolution defined by these early rockers has continued to be a central theme of rock music to the present day.

Finally, Jerry Lee Lewis's music fits clearly into a Louisiana tradition of piano-based rhythm & blues, despite the fact that he is not African American. Like many of the white rock musicians of his era, Lewis was not simply imitating African American musical culture—this was the music that he had been raised on and with which he identified. That such a state of affairs could, and did, exist in the Deep South at the height of segregation again shows the complexity of the racial politics that gave birth to rock 'n' roll.

Buddy Holly

<u>Buddy Holly (Charles Hardin Holley)</u> (1936–59) offered an image virtually the opposite of Lewis's and Presley's intense, aggressive, suggestively sexual stage personae. Here was a clean-cut, lanky, bespectacled young man—obviously nobody's idea of a matinee idol, but one who certainly knew his way around a guitar and a recording studio. The Texas-born Holly began his career with country music but soon fell under the influence of Presley's musical style and success and formed a rock 'n' roll band, the Crickets.

Buddy Holly performing with the Crickets in 1957. CBS/Landov.

Holly's first record in his new style, "That'll Be the Day," rose to Number One on the pop charts in late 1957 and established his characteristic and highly influential sound. "That'll Be the Day" combined elements of country, rhythm & blues, and mainstream pop in the kind of synthesis that typified rock 'n' roll in a general sense, but which nevertheless projected a distinctive approach and sensibility. Holly's vocal style, full of country twang and hiccups, along with expressive blue notes, projected that mixture of toughness and vulnerability that forms the essence of both fine country singing and fine blues singing. The Crickets' instrumental lineup of two electric guitars (lead and rhythm), bass, and drums provided an intense support for Holly's voice, and during instrumental breaks, Holly's lead guitar playing was active, riff-based, and hard-edged in a way that reflected the influence of Chuck Berry. Both of these characteristics would become major influences on rock to the present day. "That'll Be the Day" is structured like a typical pop song, alternating verses and choruses of eight bars each; but when it comes time to provide an instrumental break, the Crickets play a twelve-bar blues pattern. This works, because important aspects of both vocal and instrumental style throughout the record are based on blues- and rhythm & blues–derived elements. On some later records, like "Oh, Boy!" and "Peggy Sue," Holly used a twelve-bar blues structure for the song itself.

Buddy Holly's career was tragically cut short when he was twenty-two by a plane crash that also claimed the lives of two other prominent rock 'n' roll personalities: the promising seventeen-year-old Chicano singer and songwriter Ritchie Valens, whose music proved to be an important stimulus for later Mexican American musicians like Carlos Santana and the members of the group Los Lobos (see Listening to: "La Bamba"); and the Big Bopper (J. P. Richardson), who had achieved success with novelty records. A measure of Holly's importance for later pop music may be seen in the fact that the Beatles modeled their insect-based name, their four-piece instrumental lineup, and aspects of their vocal style on the Crickets—and through the Beatles, of course, the influence passed on to innumerable bands. Holly was also, like Chuck Berry, an important rock 'n' roll songwriter; in addition to the songs already mentioned, he wrote and recorded "Everyday," "Not Fade Away," "Rave On," and others, which became increasingly popular in the years after his death and were covered by rock bands. Furthermore, Holly's work with arrangements and studio effects looked forward to some of the recording techniques of the 1960s. He frequently used *double-tracking* on his recordings—a technique in which two nearly identical versions of the same vocal or instrumental part are recorded on top of one another, foregrounding that part so that it seems to come right out of the speaker at the listener.

Latin American Influences

Latin American music was an important source of influence on the popular genres that contributed to the rise of rock 'n' roll in the mid-1950s. The Latin tinge in rhythm & blues reflected the long-standing appreciation of Latin music in America's black communities. Afro-Cuban music and its derivatives in the United States—including the rumba, the bolero, and the mambo—exerted a pervasive, if underrecognized, influence on R&B, an influence particularly evident in the work of musicians who grew up, played regularly, or recorded in New Orleans. As the writer and musician Ned Sublette has noted, there were also Latin influences—such as the widespread use of maracas or the *cha-cha-chá* rhythm—that are overlooked simply because they have subsequently become so commonplace that they are no longer viewed as being distinctively Latin. The strongest Latin influences on country and western music came from Mexico and from Mexican American communities in the American Southwest. Western swing musicians such as Bob Wills and the Texas Playboys made the incorporation of elements from Mexican music quite explicit.

The Latin influence on rock 'n' roll is perhaps best exemplified by recordings made during the late 1950s in Los Angeles. The most popular of the musicians to emerge from the Los Angeles scene was Richard Valenzuela, a.k.a. Ritchie Valens (1941–59), born in Pacoima, California, to working-class Mexican-American parents. Although Valens's recording career lasted only eight months—cut short by the plane crash that also killed Buddy Holly and the Big Bopper—his recordings, released on the independent label Del-Fi Records, helped to create a distinctive Los Angeles rock 'n' roll sound. (Other such recordings included the Champs' Number 1 Pop and R&B single, "Tequila" (1958), an instrumental number written by Mexican American drummer Danny Flores.)

Valens grew up surrounded by Mexican and country and western music, but also listened keenly to rhythm & blues groups like the Drifters and to rock 'n' rollers Buddy Holly, Bo Diddley, and Little Richard. His parents bought him a guitar and he joined a local dance band, the Silhouettes, at sixteen. In 1958 Valens auditioned for Del-Fi owner Bob Keane and recorded his debut single, "Come On, Let's Go" (Number 42 Pop, Number 27 R&B), at Gold Star Studios in Los Angeles. (This song was later covered by the Ramones, a punk rock band.) Valens's second recording date produced "Donna" and "La Bamba," hurriedly released on two sides of a 45 r.p.m. single after a deejay played a test-pressing of

Ritchie Valens. Michael Ochs Archives/Getty Images.

the former song on a popular Los Angeles radio station. "Donna," which reached Number 2 on both the pop and R&B charts, was a classic teen love song written for a girl Valens knew in high school. Valens made a trip to New York in late 1958 to promote the record, appearing on Dick Clark's *American Bandstand* and Alan Freed's Christmas Show, alongside his idols Chuck Berry and Bo Diddley. Tragically, "Donna"/"La Bamba" was the last of Valens's records to be released during his lifetime. (See the listening discussion, pp. 70–71.)

WILD, WILD YOUNG WOMEN: THE LADY VANISHES

While reading this completely male-dominated account of the early history of rock 'n' roll, it is only natural to ask: Where were the women? There was a significant, occasionally empowered, female presence both in rhythm & blues and in country music by the early 1950s (recall Big Mama Thornton's "Hound

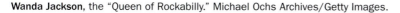

Dog," to offer just one example); didn't some of this carry over into rock 'n' roll? Even the conservative mainstream pop music of the early- to mid-1950s featured among its "big singers" strong female vocalists such as Patti Page, Jo Stafford, and Doris Day.

The truth of the matter is paradoxical. It is both correct and incorrect to claim that there were no female rock 'n' rollers comparable to the men we have been discussing. It is correct simply because, during the formative years of rock 'n' roll as a commercial phenomenon, women who aggressively embraced the new stylistic trends were a negligible presence on the charts. But it is incorrect because this lack of hit records doesn't mean that such women didn't exist—far from it!

The example of Wanda Jackson, probably the most remarkable of the pioneering rock 'n' roll women, illustrates the situation perfectly. Jackson (born 1937 in Oklahoma), a multitalented singer, instrumentalist, and songwriter,

Wanda Jackson, the "Queen of Rockabilly." Michael Ochs Archives/Getty Images.

🎧 LISTENING TO "LA BAMBA"

Traditional Mexican folk song, adaptation by Ritchie Valens; performed by Ritchie Valens; recorded 1958 in Los Angeles

While his other recordings were excellent but conventional rock 'n' roll, Valens's most original contribution was the song "La Bamba" (Number 22 Pop), an adaptation of a folk song from the Mexican region of Veracruz. To understand the creativity of his reworking of the song, we need to know a bit about the genre from which it sprang, a three-hundred-year-old tradition called *son jarocho*.

Situated on Mexico's Caribbean coast, Veracruz is one of the historical centers of Afro-Mexican culture, and the region's music reflects a blend of Spanish, African, and Native American elements. *Son jarocho* is a fiery, up-tempo song genre that alternates vocal refrains (*estribillos*) with rapid improvisational passages, accompanied by an ensemble of stringed instruments. The typical *jarocho* group consists of *arpa* (a wooden harp) and two smaller relatives of the guitar, the *jarana*, and the *requinto*. The harpist usually plays a bass line with one hand and rapid melodic figures on the higher strings with the other hand, while the *requinto* adds improvisational lines complementing the harp, and the *jarana* provides a vigorously strummed chordal accompaniment. Although jarocho groups play in a variety of social contexts—including tourist hotels—the genre is particularly associated with wedding ceremonies, at which the bride and groom together perform a subtle dance that symbolizes their unity.

Although the *son jarocho* was not as well known to American audiences as northern Mexican genres like mariachi, a number of musicians from Veracruz moved to Mexico City in the 1940s and made recordings and appeared in films which gained the tradition wider exposure. This is very likely how the song "La Bamba" came to the attention of the young Ritchie Valens, living in a ranch house in the San Fernando Valley. While the text of "La Bamba" varies from performance to performance in the traditional setting, there are a few stable verses that identify the song, and these are the elements that

Ritchie Valens held on to as he adapted the song to the aesthetics of American rock 'n' roll:

> *Para bailar la bamba, para bailar la bamba*
> *Se necesita una poca de gracia*
> *Una poca de gracia pa' mi pa' ti*
> [In order to dance the Bamba, in order to dance the Bamba
> A little grace is needed
> A little grace for me and for you]
> *Ay arriba y arriba, ay arriba y arriba*
> *Por ti seré, por ti seré*
> [Faster and faster, faster and faster
> I'll be for you, I'll be for you]
> *Yo no soy marinero, yo no soy marinero*
> *Soy capitán, soy capitán, soy capitán*
> [I'm not a sailor, I'm not a sailor
> I'm a captain, I'm a captain, I'm a captain]
> *Bamba, bamba. . . .*

The *arriba* (literally "up") reference in the text suggests the nature of the jarocho dance, in which the footwork, or *zapateado*, is done faster and faster as the tempo of the music increases. The stanza *Yo no soy marinero, soy capitan* ("I am not a sailor, I am a captain") refers to Veracruz's role as a seaport and to the husband's promise that he will behave with dignity (like a captain, not a sailor) and remain faithful to his wife.

In comparison to a more traditional rendition of "La Bamba," with its improvisation and dense interweaving of melodic-rhythmic patterns, Valens's version will likely seem much simpler and spare. The recording opens abruptly with a brief ascending line on the electric bass, followed by the rhythm guitar playing the basic chord pattern, which is soon doubled by the bass. The "La Bamba" pattern consists of a three-chord sequence heard later in thousands of other rock 'n' roll songs (e.g., "Twist and Shout"), and it became one of the most enduring riffs in popular music history, part of the repertoire of every aspiring rock 'n' roll guitarist or bassist.

After a quick pause, Valens sings the traditional verses without any improvisation (more like a pop tune than a traditional *son jarocho* performance). The dance pulse, played by the great session drummer Earl Palmer, is reinforced by his use of a woodblock—reminiscent of the Cuban claves used in Latin dance music—to play a rhythm derived from the then-popular *cha-cha-chá*, a rhythmic feel suitable for the driving rock 'n' roll groove. The two-minute, five-second recording—quite short for a 45 r.p.m. single—features an energetic guitar solo by Valens in the middle.

"La Bamba" is unique among early rock 'n' roll records not only because of the source of the inspiration—a Mexican folk song—and because the lyric is exclusively in Spanish, but also because of the sound of the recording, shaped by the unique timbres of the instruments used. The iconic opening rhythm guitar part is played by the renowned studio musician Carol Kaye on a large, hollow-bodied electric guitar. The Gibson Super 400 has what guitarists sometimes call a "woody" sound, here given a slightly "fuzzy" timbre by the distortion of the tube amplifier through which it is played. Valens plays his guitar solo on another hollow-bodied electric guitar, a Harmony H44 Stratotone. The bass part is played on a Danelectro bass guitar, which had previously been used mainly on country and western recording sessions, often in combination with an acoustic string bass. (This combination was also used to great effect on Nancy Sinatra's 1966 Number 1 single "These Boots Are Made for Walkin'") When played with a guitar pick, the Danelectro produces a slight percussive "click" on each note, and its thick, heavy sound gives the bass guitar in "La Bamba" a more immediate presence than is typical of early rock 'n' roll records.

It is hard to know what impact Ritchie Valens might have exerted on the emergence of a Latin-influenced variant of rock 'n' roll had he not died so young. But his influence lives on, not least in the cover version of "La Bamba" performed by Los Lobos, a Chicano rock group formed in East Los Angeles in 1973. Their version of "La Bamba," featured in a semifictionalized film account of Valens's life (La Bamba, 1987), was a Number 1 pop single for three weeks in 1987.

had already achieved success in the country music field singing and touring with Hank Thompson (of "The Wild Side of Life" fame) when—still a teenager—she encountered Elvis Presley as the career of the "hillbilly cat" was just beginning to take off. Presley astutely sensed that Jackson would have a gift for performing rockabilly music, and he encouraged her to record in the style. Jackson's own rockabilly career began with "I Gotta Know" in 1956, a kind of transitional song for her that presented the unique pairing of breakneck, rocking verses with a moderately paced, country-waltz chorus. Following this, between late 1956 and early 1958, Jackson recorded fierce performances of unapologetic rockers like "Hot Dog! That Made Him Mad," "Fujiyama Mama," "Let's Have a Party," and her own "Mean Mean Man," performances that established her as one of the most powerful and convincing rockabilly musicians of her time. In terms of pure energy, vocal charisma, aggressive sexuality, and her stylistic mastery of both rhythm & blues and country elements, Jackson stands revealed on these records as a performer who could readily go toe-to-toe (or pelvis to pelvis!) with Elvis Presley or with any of the other major male rock 'n' rollers of this period.

In the first flush of rock 'n' roll, one would have thought that Wanda Jackson had everything possible going for her: She was an exceptional recording artist, a young and extremely photogenic woman, and an enthusiastic live performer who had the support of a major label (Capitol). Her records are rockabilly "classics" in every respect—except for one: none of them was a hit! Following the modest showing of "I Gotta Know" on the country "disk jockey" chart (Number 15 in 1956, indicating that the record was getting some airplay on country music stations), Jackson vanished from all the charts for nearly four years. Capitol Records finally released "Let's Have a Party," originally an album track, as a single in 1960, two years after it was recorded, and Jackson scored her first entry on the mainstream pop chart with it (but it peaked at Number 37). By this time, however, Jackson's hopes for becoming a major rock 'n' roll star had understandably soured, and she was well on her way back to concentrating on more traditional-sounding country music—a style that enabled her to maintain some chart presence into the early 1970s.

If Wanda Jackson's story were unique, her lack of mainstream success could be attributed simply to the kind of "accidental" bad luck that all too frequently befalls very gifted people. And it must be granted that, in some respects, Jackson courted controversy. She embraced the implicit interracial character of rock 'n' roll to the explicit extent of touring with an integrated band—a daring move for the time—and she refused to perform in any venues where her African American pianist, Big Al Downing, would face prejudicial treatment. (She also threatened, in the lyrics of "Fujiyama Mama," to "blow your head off" with nitroglycerine if you spoke ill of her!) Nevertheless, there were other talented candidates for a "female Elvis Presley" among young white southern women in the 1950s, and each of them met an analogous fate.

Janis Martin (born 1940 in Virginia; died 2007) was barely sixteen years old when RCA Victor (Presley's own label) began promoting her as literally "the female Elvis" in 1956. Her teen-friendly records, like "My Boy Elvis" and her own composition "Drugstore Rock 'n' Roll," are energetic, thoroughly professional rockabilly, and compare favorably with many a big hit from the period. Yet Martin proved unable to make the hoped-for big impact, and by 1958—when what had been her secret marriage unavoidably became public knowledge as a result of her pregnancy—she had been dropped by RCA and quickly consigned to obscurity. Jo-Ann Campbell (born 1938 in Florida) was showcased by disc jockey Alan Freed as "the blonde bombshell" on radio, in his "rock 'n' roll revues," and in his movie *Go, Johnny Go!* (1959); in spite of this public exposure, such fine Campbell recordings as "Wait A Minute" and "You're Driving Me Mad," both of which exhibit the strong influence of rhythm & blues in their driving band arrangements, failed to achieve commercial success. Lorrie (Lawrencine) Collins (born 1942 in Oklahoma) performed with her even younger brother Larry as the "Collins Kids" duo; their act became well known through television in the mid-1950s, and they also cut some scintillating rockabilly records for Columbia between 1956 and 1958. In particular, "Heartbeat" and "Mercy," both written by the Collins Kids themselves, feature the intense sound of Lorrie Collins's solo voice, but neither these nor any of their other recordings made the charts. Martin, Campbell, and Collins—like Wanda Jackson—all were gifted rock 'n' roll performers at a young (even very young) age, whose talents extended to the occasional writing of their own material, and who did not lack for publicity. Yet these three are so obscure today that neither the eleven-hundred-page *Rolling Stone Encyclopedia of Rock & Roll* nor even the wide-ranging *Trouble Girls: The Rolling Stone Book of Women in Rock* so much as mentions any of them. In effect, these women—and who knows how many others like them?—have been written out of history. The phenomenon cries out for some larger explanation than multiple individual instances of bad luck.

Clearly the essential conservatism of the 1950s, politically and culturally, made it a particularly inauspicious time to be seen as a rebellious and empowered young woman. The rebellious, empowered young men of early rock 'n' roll proved controversial enough, and most teenagers of the period—male and female—were happy admiring these men from a safe distance, and without wishing the rock 'n' roll attitude to cross the gender divide. The post–World War II ideal of domestic femininity proved to be extremely powerful and provoked no widespread and enduring challenges until the 1960s.

Given the tenor of the times, an empowered *black* female rock 'n' roll "idol" would have been even more unlikely—which is why African American women have played no part in this discussion. Only a few female black artists, such as LaVern Baker and Sarah Vaughan, achieved even modest success on the pop charts during the early years of rock 'n' roll. (In 1957 the Bobbettes, a group of five African American schoolgirls from New York's Harlem, seemed to come out of nowhere with an irresistible rock 'n' roll hit about their fifth-grade teacher, "Mr. Lee" [Number 6 Pop, Number 1 R&B], after which the girls just as abruptly disappeared into oblivion.)

The first woman who could be called a real recording "star" of the rock 'n' roll era is Italian American <u>Connie Francis</u> (born Concetta Rosa Maria Franconero, 1938, in New Jersey), whose string of hit records only began in 1958 with her revival of a Tin Pan Alley tune from 1923, "Who's Sorry Now." Although Francis did occasionally perform bona fide rockers (such as "Stupid Cupid," Number 14 Pop in 1958, and "Lipstick on Your Collar," Number 5 Pop in 1959), her output overall is highly eclectic and is best understood as that of

Connie Francis on the set of *American Bandstand* in 1958. Photo by Paul Schutzer/Time Life Pictures/Getty Images.

a mainstream pop singer who appreciated the importance of appealing to the new young audience. Compared with someone like Wanda Jackson, Connie Francis—both on records and in her public image—seemed, if not demure, at least utterly unthreatening. By 1960 America was at last ready to embrace a young female recording artist with at least a somewhat feisty public image, and the teenage <u>Brenda Lee</u> (born Brenda Mae Tarpley, 1944, in Georgia), who became known as "Little Miss Dynamite," was there to fill the bill with engaging rock 'n' roll songs like "Sweet Nothin's" (Number 4 Pop, 1960) and "Rockin' around the Christmas Tree" (Number 14 Pop, 1960). Lee also recorded a large proportion of slow, sentimental love songs, but the real measure of just how far she was from being a true "female Elvis" may be taken by comparing any of her rock 'n' roll records to Jackson's "Fujiyama Mama," or even to Lorrie Collins's "Mercy."

But the fact that such distinctions can even be made in the first place suggests a deeper story: rock 'n' roll in this era was largely viewed as a masculine endeavor, forcing women who wanted to become involved as artists to face divided loyalties. Should they "rock 'n' roll" or should they be "feminine"? Almost by definition, they could not be both. As rock 'n' roll moved into the sixties, this issue would manifest itself in a number of different ways, most notably in a general feeling that to make rock 'n' roll more open to women's perspectives was to restrict or even "emasculate" it. The way that both men and women have negotiated this issue continues to have a profound effect on rock even to the present day.

SONGWRITERS AND PRODUCERS OF EARLY ROCK 'N' ROLL

The relatively clear lines of division between songwriters and performers that characterized the world of mainstream pop music up to around 1955 no longer held up in the early years of rock 'n' roll's mainstream success. And it has been established that this is because the roots of rock 'n' roll lie with rhythm & blues and country music, areas of activity where, as we have seen, performers often wrote their own songs and, conversely, songwriters frequently performed and recorded their own works. This diminishing importance of the independent songwriter represented another major shift brought about by the rock 'n' roll revolution. In time, it came to be expected that performers would be the composers of their own songs, and this led to a correspondingly stronger identification of artists with specific material. Here lie the origins of the mystique of the pop music personality as a creative artist, rather than as merely an interpreter—a mystique that came into its own in the later 1960s.

None of this meant that important nonperforming songwriters ceased to exist, of course. As we shall see in the next chapter, the early 1960s actually brought, if temporarily, a renewed emphasis on songwriting as an independent craft, prior to the heyday of songwriting bands like the Beatles and songwriter-performers like Bob Dylan. And with the increasing importance of the recording itself as the basic document of rock 'n' roll music, another behind-the-scenes job grew steadily in importance in the later 1950s and the early 1960s: that of the record producer. Producers could be responsible for many things, from booking time in the recording studio, to hiring backup singers and instrumentalists, to assisting with the engineering process. Essentially, though, the producer was responsible for the characteristic *sound* of the finished record, and the best producers left as strong a sense of individual personality on their products as did the recording artists themselves. When the producer and the songwriter were the same person (or persons), his or her importance and influence could be powerful indeed.

This was the case with the most innovative songwriting/producing team of the early rock 'n' roll years, Jerry Leiber and Mike Stoller (both born 1933). Leiber and Stoller were not recording artists, but they were already writing rhythm & blues songs when they were teenagers. Eventually they wrote and produced many hits for Elvis Presley, and they did the same for one of the most popular vocal groups of this period, the Coasters. (They also produced and did occasional writing for the Drifters, and the elaborately produced orchestral sound of these records in the early 1960s was possibly even more influential than Leiber and Stoller's previous records had been in the later 1950s.) The team constructed what they called "playlets" for the Coasters, scenes from teenage life of the 1950s distilled into brilliantly funny rock 'n' roll records. Like many by Chuck Berry, the Coasters' hits were specifically about, and for, their intended audience. An examination of "Charlie Brown" (see next page) will enable us to appreciate in detail this targeting of the teenage audience, along with the vocal artistry of the Coasters and the behind-the-scenes writing and production artistry of Leiber and Stoller.

CONCLUSION

The rise of rock 'n' roll in the mid-1950s transformed the landscape of American popular music, further cementing the popularity of southern-derived styles ultimately derived from the blues and country music, and transforming the teenager into both a marketing concept and a cultural icon. Then, in a series of developments that seems so tragically poetic as to be almost predestined, virtually every major rock 'n' roll artist of the era either withdrew from the music scene or died at the end of the fifties. In 1957, after a brush with death, Little Richard rejected rock 'n' roll and became a preacher. In 1958, Elvis was drafted into the U.S. Army, putting his recording career on hold. That same year, Jerry Lee Lewis's scandals essentially forced him out of the music business. In February of 1959, Buddy Holly and Richie Valens were killed in a plane crash while on tour together. In March of 1960, Chuck Berry was sentenced to five years in prison due to a violation of the Mann Act.

Youth culture—and the music industry's sometimes clumsy attempts to interpret and shape it—was to become even more predominant during the

🎧 LISTENING TO "CHARLIE BROWN"

Music and lyrics by Jerry Leiber and Mike Stoller; as performed by the Coasters with accompanying band (King Curtis, sax solo); recorded 1958

"Charlie Brown" presents an indelible portrait of a ubiquitous figure, the class clown. Although such a song topic would probably not have occurred to anyone prior to the 1950s, it certainly made an effective choice at a point when, for the first time ever, the biggest market of potential record buyers consisted of schoolkids: the junior high schoolers and high schoolers, even elementary schoolers, each of whom probably knew a "Charlie Brown" in at least one of his or her classes. The specific time period and culture of the 1950s is evoked through a sparing but telling use of then-current slang terms like "cool" and "daddy-o."

From the first arresting vocal **hook**, "Fee fee, fie fie, fo fo, fum," the record brims with unrelenting high energy.

Like Chuck Berry, the Coasters were adept at delivering a dense, cleverly worded text very clearly at a fast tempo. The intensity of the Coasters' vocal style owes much to rhythm & blues, although certain comic effects—like the low bass voice repeatedly asking, "Why's everybody always pickin' on me?" and asking, "Who, me?" in the bridge—suggest roots going back to early twentieth-century stage routines. (The low bass voice was also a staple element of rhythm & blues group singing style; see the discussion of the Chords' "Sh-Boom" in Chapter 2.) Highly effective are the contrasts between passages that are essentially vocal solos, with occasional, minimal contributions by the rhythm instruments (at the start of each A section—see the Listening Chart), and the

LISTENING CHART "CHARLIE BROWN"
Music and lyrics by Jerry Leiber and Mike Stoller; as performed by the Coasters with accompanying band (King Curtis, sax solo); recorded 1958

FORM		LYRICS	DESCRIPTIVE COMMENTS
A (verse) (chorus)	0.08	*Fee, fee, fie, fie . . .* *I smell smoke . . .* *Charlie Brown,* *Charlie Brown . . .*	Twelve-bar blues stanza, divided into a four-bar verse (vocal solo) and an eight-bar chorus with full accompaniment and call and response between the voices and the saxophone.
A (verse)	0.23	*That's him . . .*	As before.
(chorus)	0.31	*Charlie Brown . . .*	
B	0.46	*Who's always . . .*	Bridge section.
A (verse)	1.01	*Who walks . . .*	As before.
(chorus)	1.08	*Charlie Brown . . .*	
Instrumental break	1.24		Twelve-bar blues stanza, constructed exactly like the A sections, but with the voices absent and the saxophone freely improvising over the rhythmic and chordal structure; blue notes are noticeable in the sax solo.
Repetition of final A section	1.46		
Instrumental fade-out	2.09		

following passages where the full band offers a steady accompaniment and the saxophone engages in **call-and-response** with the vocal group.

Form

"Charlie Brown" combines aspects of two different formal designs we have seen in previous musical examples. The song reveals its mainstream pop roots in its overall AABA structure. But the A sections are twelve-bar blues stanzas, which would not of course be typical of a Tin Pan Alley tune; furthermore, each A section divides the twelve bars into a little verse-chorus structure of the type we have seen in "Long Tall Sally" and "Don't Be Cruel." The most direct kinship is with "Long Tall Sally": four bars of verse, followed by eight bars of chorus. The kinship is that much more marked because of an additional similarity between the two; in both "Charlie Brown" and "Long Tall Sally" the twelve-bar blues stanzas start off with vocal solos, and a continuous full accompaniment does not join in until the chorus portions at the fifth bar of the structure. The B section, in contrast, is eight bars in length, providing a harmonic and rhythmic release from the succession of blues structures.

The Song/The Recording

As songwriters, Leiber and Stoller always had an interest in mixing—even scrambling—elements derived from rhythm & blues music, which they knew well and loved, with elements derived from mainstream pop. This interest is evident in the form of "Charlie Brown" itself, as we have discussed, but it may also be seen in certain details. For example, the twelve-bar blues stanzas in the song are noticeably *lacking* in blue notes; Leiber and Stoller wrote a simple pop-oriented melody and just directed the bass singer to speak his solo line. But as producers, Leiber and Stoller brought in King Curtis, a Texas-born rhythm & blues saxophonist, to play on the record. In his twelve-bar instrumental break Curtis emphasized blue notes, jumping in front of and behind the beat in a **syncopated** manner evocative of stuttering. (This style, as much indebted to country hoedown music as to R&B, was also used successfully by the country and western saxophonist Boots Randolph.) Curtis's "yackety sax" sound links the Coasters' record to both rhythm & blues and country music, and creates a humorous, goofy effect perfectly suited to the comic tale of Charlie Brown.

Apart from the sparkling clarity of the recording, there is only one prominent production effect in "Charlie Brown": the artificially high voices in the bridge on "Yeah, you!" This effect was produced by playing a tape of normal voices at double speed, a device that was popular on novelty records at this time. Here we see the modest beginnings of the kind of artificial studio effects that would be found on more and more records as producers took increasing advantage of increasingly sophisticated recording studios and techniques.

following decade, as rock 'n' roll gave way to rock. In the next two chapters we follow this story in some detail, from the emergence of a new generation of American teen pop stars and the onset of the so-called British Invasion through the rise of soul music and the musical experimentalism of the late 1960s counterculture.

4

POP MUSIC IN THE EARLY
1960s

As rock 'n' roll artists came to participate more fully in the music business, their concerns began to fall in line with those of an earlier generation of mainstream popular musicians. For many, it seemed almost self-evident that if rock 'n' roll was going to be pop music, it should adjust itself to the mainstream music industry's business model and cultural expectations. But exactly how this could be done without losing the essence of rock 'n' roll itself was an open question, and the early sixties was a time when many artists and businesspeople were experimenting with different answers. At the same time, some musicians and fans resisted that trend altogether, continuing to embrace and develop the genre's outsider status. Like the more commercial side of the spectrum, this side also featured many different approaches and perspectives. For those who wished to focus on the commercial possibilities, the most obvious answer for many was simply to create a new version of the traditional approach that was essentially a hybrid: a Tin Pan Alley business model married to a rock 'n' roll sound.

Because of this, the early 1960s are often described as a lackluster period in the development of American popular music: a time of relative stasis between the excitement of the early rock 'n' roll years and the coming of the Beatles to

America in 1964. Many have gone even further, viewing the commercialization of rock 'n' roll as an intentional "taming" of its rebellious spirit in order to make it more commercially appealing. And in some senses, it was. At the same time, there is often an unspoken gender dynamic at work in such criticisms. Specifically, this era saw a notable increase in the prominence of female songwriters and performers, as well as a pronounced effort to reach out to female consumers. What some may see as a curtailing of rock's masculine essence in order to attract a larger fan base, others may see as an increased responsiveness to women's and girls' points of view. Was it possible for rock to make this transition without losing something essential in its character? If so, how? If not, what does that say about rock itself? These were questions that rock 'n' roll was struggling with in this era.

In order to understand the evolution of rock 'n' roll in the early 1960s we need to take into account several important trends. Black artists such as Ray Charles and Sam Cooke, whose careers started in the 1950s, created styles that were deeply grounded in African American musical traditions, dominating the rhythm & blues charts and expanding the appeal of a more gospel-influenced style of performance. A new kind of social dancing, also inspired by African American styles, gave rock 'n' roll music for the first time a new and distinctive set of movements and social customs to accompany it, quintessentially represented by Chubby Checker's enormously popular recording, "The Twist." Simultaneously, changes were beginning to take place in the music business, as members of the first generation to grow up with rock 'n' roll began to assume positions of power in the industry as writers and producers, and the Tin Pan Alley system was reinvented for the new music and its new audiences at the Brill Building in New York, at Gold Star Studios in Los Angeles, and at the Motown headquarters in Detroit. Finally, new stylistic possibilities (and cultural contexts) for rock 'n' roll began to emerge out of California, spearheaded by the Beach Boys, whose leader, Brian Wilson, established a model for many to follow by being an innovative performer, writer, and producer all rolled into one.

In the mid-fifties, Alan Freed and others had chosen rhythm & blues songs that they felt would appeal to suburban teenagers, and called this subgenre rock 'n' roll. In the late fifties, young musicians who had not emerged from the African American tradition started creating their own versions of rock 'n' roll. The most obvious implication of this fact—both at the time and in retrospect—was that non–African American audiences were embracing African American music. In the early sixties, however, this trend began to reverse. Rock 'n' roll was combined with a Tin Pan Alley business approach, in an overt attempt to bring it back into the orbit of the mainstream music industry. As we shall soon see, many of the first generation of rock fans were also beginning to become interested in so-called folk music, a genre associated with rural traditions, particularly those of the British Isles and the American South. Meanwhile, as part of the civil rights era, African American musicians began to draw more explicitly on African American cultural themes and musical characteristics. Ultimately, these trends resulted in a kind of re-segregation of American popular music, with the term "soul" coming to represent the African American side of the equation and the term "rock" generally coming to represent the European American side. But there were many exceptions to this trend, and we must be careful not to assume that musicians and their audiences saw it this way at the time. Many musicians who are now considered to fall primarily into the soul genre, for example, were also considered at the time to be rock artists. As always, the relationship between musical style and social identity is more complex in reality than in theory.

THE RISE OF SOUL MUSIC: RAY CHARLES AND SAM COOKE

Among many significant African American artists of the early 1960s who developed styles that would eventually be marketed as "soul music," Ray Charles (the "Genius of Soul") and Sam Cooke ("The King of Soul") had the greatest success at "crossing over" from the rhythm & blues to the pop charts. The two men were born only four months apart, both in the deep South, but in some respects their lives and musical styles were very different. Charles was born into extreme poverty, completely lost his sight at the age of seven, was orphaned in his early teens, and left the South at age sixteen to establish his professional career as a jazz and rhythm & blues musician in far-away Seattle. Cooke was the son of a successful Baptist preacher who relocated from Mississippi to Chicago, where young Sam joined the Soul Stirrers, a leading gospel vocal group. Charles's gritty, directly emotional vocal sound, which incorporated dramatic effects from the African American preaching tradition, can immediately be distinguished from Cooke's cooler, smoother approach, shaped by the vocal quartet tradition and by crooners like Nat "King" Cole. Charles's storied career spanned more than half a century, while Cooke died tragically at the age of thirty-three, leaving his fans to wonder what he might have accomplished had he lived longer.

Despite these differences, it is not difficult to find meaningful parallels between the two men's musical careers. As we have suggested, both Charles and Cooke were strongly influenced by African American sacred music. In bringing aspects of gospel singing to bear upon their performances of secular material, each faced protests from church leaders who wanted to keep Saturday night and Sunday morning as far apart as possible. Ray Charles and Sam Cooke each succeeded at appealing to, and selling records to, a racially diverse audience—including black and white teenagers and, increasingly, their parents. Both Charles, who maintained notoriously tight managerial control over his career, and Cooke, who started his own publishing firm and record label, were among the first black performers of their generation to achieve success as businessmen. Finally, the personal struggles that both men experienced—Charles's blindness and addiction to drugs and alcohol, the tragic death of Cooke's infant son and his own early, violent demise—allowed them to stand as powerful symbols for the struggle of the black community to achieve equality in an age of racial segregation and civil rights activism.

Ray Charles and Soul Music

Ray Charles (born Ray Charles Robinson, 1930–2004) was a constant presence on the rhythm & blues charts during the 1950s, but major crossover success eluded him until 1959, which is why we have not grouped him with early African American rock 'n' roll stars like Chuck Berry, Little Richard, and Fats Domino. In any case, Charles was never interested in being typecast as a rock 'n' roller, and he never consciously addressed his recordings to the teen market—or to any obviously delimited market, for that matter. Characteristically, as soon as he established himself as a mass-market artist with the stunning blues-based and gospel-drenched "What'd I Say" (Number 6 Pop, Number 1 R&B, 1959), he immediately sought new worlds to conquer;

"The Genius," **Ray Charles**, performing in 1960. David Redfern/Redferns/Retna, Ltd.

his next record was a highly individual cover of Hank Snow's 1950 hit "I'm Movin' On," one of the biggest country records of all time. Within a year, Charles had achieved his first Number 1 pop hit with his version of the old Tin Pan Alley standard "Georgia on My Mind" (by Stuart Gorrell and Hoagy Carmichael), which also made it to Number 3 on the rhythm & blues chart. But Charles's most astounding success was with his version of country artist Don Gibson's "I Can't Stop Loving You," which brought Charles's unique take on country music to the top spot on *both* the pop and rhythm & blues charts (five weeks Number 1 Pop, ten weeks Number 1 R&B) in 1962 and gave him the biggest hit record of that entire year.

Ray Charles was certainly not the first artist to assay many different genres of American popular music, and he was, of course, only one of many to achieve remarkable crossover success. What is it, then, that made his career so distinctive, that made him such a universally admired pop musician—by audiences, critics, and other musicians—that the appellation "genius" has clung to his name for decades, as if he had been born to the title?

Part of it is the astounding range of talents Charles cultivated. He was a fine songwriter, having written many of his early rhythm & blues hits, including classics of the genre like "I've Got a Woman" and "Hallelujah I Love Her So." He was a highly skilled arranger, as well as an exceptionally fine keyboard player who was fluent in jazz as well as mainstream pop idioms. And, above all, he was an outstanding vocalist, with a timbre so distinctive as to be instantly recognizable and an expressive intensity that, once heard, is difficult to forget. But this still is not the whole story. Charles's most characteristic recordings are not only distinguished, individual statements but also unique and encompassing statements about American popular music *style*.

After an apprenticeship period, during which he emulated the pop-friendly vocal and instrumental approach of Nat "King" Cole and the King Cole Trio, Ray Charles established a style that immediately expressed his interest in synthesis. Charles's first Number 1 rhythm & blues recording, "I've Got a Woman" (recorded in 1954), is an obviously secular song based on gospel models, performed by Charles in a manner clearly related to gospel vocal stylings. Although black gospel music had been a long-term influence on aspects of secular "race" records and rhythm & blues, arguably nobody before Charles had brought the sacred and secular idioms into such a direct and intimate relationship; by the time of "Hallelujah I Love Her So" (Number 5 R&B, 1956) he was expressing the connection in the song's very title! Needless to say, some people were scandalized by this. The final portion of "What'd I Say," in which Charles shouts and groans in call and response with a female chorus to produce music that simultaneously evokes a wild Southern Baptist service and the sounds of a very earthly sexual ecstasy, was banned on many radio stations in spite of the record's status as a national hit.

Although the term "soul music" would not enter the common vocabulary until the later 1960s, it is clearly soul music that Ray Charles was pioneering in his gospel-blues synthesis of the 1950s. He is now widely acknowledged as the first important soul artist, and his work proved an incalculable influence on James Brown, Aretha Franklin, Curtis Mayfield, Otis Redding, Sly Stone, and innumerable others. When Charles went on to record Tin Pan Alley and country material in the 1960s, far from leaving his soul stylings behind, he brought them along to help him forge new, wider-ranging, and arguably even braver combinations of styles.

When Charles recorded "Georgia on My Mind," he did not attempt to turn the Tin Pan Alley standard into a rhythm & blues song (the way Fats Domino had done earlier with "My Blue Heaven," for example). Neither did he remake himself into a crooner (the way Elvis Presley often did when performing mainstream pop-oriented material). Rather than using the jump band group that had backed him on most of his earlier records—and then perhaps adding some superficial sweetening with strings and crooning background chorus—Charles wholeheartedly embraced the Tin Pan Alley heritage of the song and presided over a sumptuous arrangement of it, with orchestral strings and accompanying chorus, that virtually outdid Tin Pan Alley itself in its elaborateness and unrestrained sentiment. But against this smooth and beautifully performed backdrop (Charles always insisted on the highest musical standards from all personnel involved in his performances), Charles sang "Georgia on My Mind" as if he were performing a deeply personal blues. While the original words, melody, and phrasing of the song were clearly conveyed, Charles employed an intense and sometimes rough-edged vocal timbre, used constant syncopation, and selectively added shakes, moans, and other improvised touches ("*I said-a, Georgia*") to reflect what was at this point his natural, individual vocal approach, rooted in gospel and blues. And he occasionally provided jazz-based fills in his piano part between vocal phrases, to evoke call and response within his own performance, while the backing chorus echoed his words at strategic intervals, producing call and response between them and Charles himself.

The result of all this was an extraordinary and unprecedented juxtaposition and dialogue of styles within a single recording. And, as the preceding description indicates, this was no haphazard jumble of different elements; it came across as expressive and utterly purposeful. In effect, Ray Charles did more than reinterpret "Georgia on My Mind"; he virtually reinvented the song for a new generation of listeners and left his mark on the song permanently. It seems only appropriate that in 1979 his recording was named the official song of the state of Georgia.

In 1962 Charles cast his stylistic net still wider, producing a concept album, *Modern Sounds in Country and Western Music,* which stands as a milestone in the history of American popular music. When Charles first announced to his record company that he wanted to do an album of country songs, the project was derisively labeled "Ray's folly"; it was thought that he would lose his audience. Charles was not a man to be crossed, however, and he persevered, with the result, of course, that he enlarged his audience even further—and beyond anyone's expectations. By this point, Charles was aggressively and creatively playing with stylistic mixtures, and the album essentially redrew the map of American popular music, both appealing to and challenging fans of radically different genres.

Every song on *Modern Sounds in Country and Western Music* was transformed from its origins into something rich and strange. The Everly Brothers' "Bye, Bye, Love" and Hank Williams's "Hey, Good Lookin'" became big-band shouts to bookend the album, while other songs received orchestral treatments worthy of the best Tin Pan Alley arrangements—or of Charles's own "Georgia on My Mind." It's hard to think of any major aspect of American pop that isn't represented, or at least implied, somewhere on this amazingly generous record, which weaves a tapestry of stylistic and historical associations, reaching across space, time, and race to build radically new bridges. The enormously popular "I Can't Stop Loving You" merges aspects of country, Tin Pan Alley, gospel, and blues, and even (as in "Georgia") a hint of jazz piano. Here Charles engages in stylistic call and response with the large background chorus, personalizing the lyrics that they sing in smooth massed harmony. The deliberateness of this dialogue is clearly revealed toward the end of the record by Charles's seemingly offhand, but illuminating, aside to the chorus: "Sing the song, children" (a remark that also confirms, as if there could be any doubt, exactly who's in charge here).

Although Ray Charles's many country-oriented records of the 1960s did extremely well on both the pop and rhythm & blues charts, they did not register on the country charts of the time. Perhaps Charles's genre-bending approach was a bit too exotic for the typical country music fan. Still, these records were heard and deeply appreciated by many country musicians. We can take the word of no less an authority than Willie Nelson, who is quoted in the booklet accompanying the Ray Charles box set *Genius & Soul*: "With his recording of 'I Can't Stop Loving You,' Ray Charles did more for country music than any other artist." Charles finally did crack the country charts in the 1980s with some of his later efforts in the genre.

Ray Charles remained active almost until his death, performing and recording in all the many genres (and mixed styles) of which he was a seasoned master. In summarizing an astounding career that steadfastly resists summarizing, we might paraphrase what Jerome Kern reportedly said about Irving Berlin: This man has no "place" in American music; he is American music! Or perhaps we can leave the last word to Charles himself (as quoted by Quincy Jones in the booklet accompanying *Genius & Soul*): "It's all music, man. We can play it all."

Sam Cooke

<u>Sam Cooke</u> (1931–1964) was an important soul artist who both influenced and was influenced by rock music. After a successful career as a gospel singer with his group the Soul Stirrers, Cooke began to explore secular music in 1956. He initially recorded under the pseudonym "Dale Cooke," so as not to arouse the suspicions of his gospel audience; he feared they would question the sincerity of his Christian beliefs if they discovered he was also singing nonreligious music. His fear proved to be well founded, and he was ultimately forced to choose between the two worlds. He chose secular music, and the gospel community never completely accepted him again.

Cooke thus moved from a self-selected community that prided itself on its high moral standards to the wider, grittier world of popular music, and he ultimately combined the two influences into a whole that directed the power of

Sam Cooke in 1960. Photo by RB/Redferns.

older traditions into new forms. Viewed from the gospel point of view, Cooke was debasing sacred music by using its style to sing songs about romance, partying and, ultimately, secular politics. But from the pop point of view, Cooke was bringing a spiritual perspective *to* soul and rock 'n' roll music. In many ways, Cooke's struggle was very similar to that which Bob Dylan was just beginning to face in the folk world (see Chapter 5), and in fact he often covered Dylan's song "Blowin' in the Wind" in concert. Eventually, this inspired Cooke to write his most political song, "A Change Is Gonna Come," which he openly described as a response to "Blowin' in the Wind."

Though not primarily viewed as a "political" artist today, Sam Cooke's career set the stage for later expressions of politics in both soul and rock music. Beyond "A Change Is Gonna Come," Cooke's politics resided more in his life than in his songs. His devotion to the African American community was manifest in his admiration for Malcolm X and his friendship with Muhammad Ali (both highly controversial figures in the early sixties). His commitment to black self-determination was also apparent in the way he conducted his business. Rather than trust music industry insiders, Cooke took great pains to control every aspect of his career himself, an approach that was highly unusual for an African American artist in the late fifties and early sixties. (One of the few others to accomplish this was Ray Charles.)

Cooke was shot and killed on December 11, 1964, by Bertha Franklin, the manager of the Hacienda Motel in Los Angeles, after he burst into her office in pursuit of another woman who had just fled from his room. The precise details of the incident remain in dispute to the present day.

In addition to his status as a soul icon, Sam Cooke was also a major influence on rock, in several ways. First, many of the songs that he wrote—including "Wonderful World," "You Send Me," and "Let the Good Times Roll," are considered to fall into *both* the soul and rock 'n' roll categories, and are still covered by rock musicians to the present day. Second, his vocal style—more measured than that of early rhythm & blues singers, but still powerful—is cited as an influence by many rock singers, including Van Morrison, Steve Perry of Journey, and Rod Stewart. Finally, Sam Cooke was a musician who was becoming overtly political in an era when that was still very unusual for a popular musician. Within a few years of his death, it would become much less unusual.

To get a sense of the range and evolution of Sam Cooke's musical career, we can examine three of his recordings: the love song "You Send Me," his very first pop hit, and the A- and B-sides of the first single released after his untimely death, "Shake" and "A Change Is Gonna Come."

"You Send Me" was recorded in Los Angeles and released in 1957 on the independent label Keen Records. At the time, Sam and the other members of the Soul Stirrers were under contract with another Los Angeles–based independent label, Specialty Records. In 1956 Sam Cooke had written to Specialty's owner, Art Rupe, asking his permission to record "some popular ballads for one of the major recording companies" (Guralnick 2005: 131). Rupe agreed but insisted that the recording—"Loveable," a thinly disguised secular cover version of one of the Soul Stirrers' biggest gospel hits—instead be released by Specialty. As we have already noted, the release of this record caused consternation in the gospel music community, and it was a major influence on Sam's decision, only four months later, to jump into the pop field with both feet.

"You Send Me" was produced by Robert "Bumps" Blackwell, who had achieved success for Specialty Records a few years before as the producer and cowriter of Little Richard's hits "Good Golly Miss Molly" and "Long Tall Sally." According to eyewitnesses, Art Rupe stormed into the recording session, objecting to Blackwell's decision to use a white vocal group as backing for Sam Cooke's singing and pushing for a less pop-oriented sound more firmly grounded in rhythm & blues. Blackwell held his ground, resigned from Specialty Records, and decamped for a new label called Keen Records, taking Sam Cooke with him. To Art Rupe's great consternation, "You Send Me" shot straight to the top of both the pop and R&B charts, selling almost two million copies for Keen Records and establishing Sam Cooke as a major pop star. Although "You Send Me" was written by Sam Cooke, the copyright to the song was registered in the name of his brother, L. C. Cook, so that Rupe could not claim publishing royalties. (The fact that Rupe, a white label owner, took the position of arguing for a sound more closely related to rhythm & blues, while Blackwell, an African American producer and songwriter, opted for a "whiter," more commercial sound, illustrates how important it is not to assume a straightforward link between social identity and musical style, particularly when business interests are at stake.)

Listening to the eloquence of "A Change Is Gonna Come," its emotional force redoubled by Cooke's impassioned performance, it is easy understand how this song was adopted as an anthem of the 1960s Civil Rights Movement in the years following his death. In 1964 Cooke donated the use of the recording for an album benefiting Martin Luther King's Southern Christian Leadership Conference, and director Spike Lee used the song at a critical point in the 1992 biographical film *Malcolm X*. In this context, and given Cooke's close association with the struggle against racial inequality, it is relevant to consider the impact of race and racial attitudes on his career. The stylistic differences between Cooke's performances before white and black audiences are best represented in the live albums *Live at the Harlem Club, 1963* (released in 1985) and *Sam Cooke at the Copa* (1964, released in 1965). The former album, recorded before a predominantly African American audience in Miami, Florida, is a spellbinding performance, energized by Cooke's close interaction with the audience, which combines the tenderness of his songs with a gritty sensibility firmly grounded in gospel and rhythm & blues music. On the latter album, recorded a year later at New York's swanky Copacabana Club (which until the late 1950s had a strict "no blacks" policy) Cooke's performance is much tamer, less assertive,

🎧 LISTENING TO "YOU SEND ME," "SHAKE," AND "A CHANGE IS GONNA COME"

"You Send Me," written and performed by Sam Cooke, recorded 1957; "Shake," written and performed by Sam Cooke, recorded 1964; "A Change Is Gonna Come," written and performed by Sam Cooke, recorded 1964

In its style and form, "You Send Me" is quite clearly designed to appeal to a broad audience. The recording opens with Cooke gently singing the single word "Darling," followed, a breath later, by the entrance of a small and subdued rhythm section (acoustic string bass, electric guitar, and drums—played in a quiet, subtle manner with wire brushes rather than wooden sticks), and a lush vocal background. "You Send Me" fits firmly within the framework of popular romantic songs of the time and is a good example of the classic AABA Tin Pan Alley form that we discussed in Chapter 1:

> A *You send me . . .*
> A *You thrill me . . .*
> B *At first . . .*
> A *You send me . . .*

So, what separates this record from literally hundreds of others like it being released at the time? The answer is self-evident: Cooke's voice and, by extension, his personality. Simultaneously self-deprecating and confident, his gentle yet emotionally intense performance fits squarely within the framework of romantic crooning, while selectively drawing upon aspects of his gospel experience, particularly in his use of **melisma** (a technique in which a single word or syllable of the text is stretched out over multiple pitches). It is Cooke's supple, agile voice—not the song, not the band, nor the "angelic" vocal chorus—that helped this recording "send" millions of listeners to their local record stores and inspired Coral Records (a subsidiary of the major record company Decca) to record a Top 10 cover version of the song by the white pop singer Teresa Brewer within months of its initial release.

The song "Shake" was recorded in Los Angeles in November 1964, just a month before Cooke's death. "Shake" is a hard-driving dance number and was in some ways a departure for Cooke, whose prior hit records had, by and large, taken a smoother, less aggressive musical approach. Interviews conducted just before his death indicate that he was thinking of moving in a harder-edged direction, in line with the emergence of what was then just beginning to be marketed as soul music. Like "You Send Me," "Shake" begins abruptly with a single word, but the sound and sensibility of the two records could scarcely be more different. The band includes two electric guitars—one playing a percussive rhythmic pattern on a single string and the other playing mildly distorted Chuck Berry–style chords—and a six-piece horn section, a sound more akin to a fusion between jump band rhythm & blues and rock 'n' roll than to the more slick, pop-oriented style of many of Cooke's previous hits. The song itself combines elements of blues form and Tin Pan Alley form, and it is interesting to speculate in what direction Cooke might have extended this impulse had he lived through the late 1960s, when the soul music recordings of James Brown and Aretha Franklin dominated the charts. (A variety of artists covered "Shake" in later years, including Eric Burdon and the Animals, the Supremes, the Small Faces, and Otis Redding, who performed the song at the first Monterey Pop Festival in 1967.)

"A Change Is Gonna Come," the B-side of "Shake," is generally regarded as Sam Cooke's greatest song, and although it did not rise as high on the Pop and R&B charts as many of his earlier singles, the song has gained in popularity and stature in the decades since its release. ("A Change Is Gonna Come" is ranked Number 12 on Rolling Stone's list of the *500 Greatest Songs of All Time* and Number 3 in the webzine Pitchfork Media's *Greatest Songs of the 60s.*) Although it was first recorded in December 1963, the single version was not released until a year later, just a few weeks after Cooke's death.

According to Cooke's biographer, Peter Guralnick, the song was inspired not only by Bob Dylan's song "Blowin' in the Wind," but also by Cooke's experiences while on tour, including a conversation with sit-in demonstrators in Durham, North Carolina, and his arrest in Shreveport, Louisiana, for attempting to check in to a racially segregated motel. The centrality of Cooke's personal experiences to the lyric of "A Change Is Gonna Come" is indicated by his decision to write it in the first person, creating a testimony of the sort common in the gospel music tradition.

The recording opens with a majestic orchestral introduction, complete with eleven strings, five brass, and tympany—an arranging strategy that, through its association with classical music, announces the seriousness of what is to follow—and then Sam Cooke begins to sing his story:

I was born . . .

In keeping with the lyric, the song's chorus seems to flow seamlessly from the verse:

It's been a long . . .
but I know . . .

According to his close friend and business partner, J. W. Alexander, Cooke reported that the song came to him whole-cloth, as if he had dreamed it: "He was very excited, and when he finished it, he explained it to me—his reason behind the lyrics. Like, 'I don't know what's up there beyond the sky'—it's like somebody's talking about I want to go to heaven, really, but then who knows what's really up there? In other words, that's why you want justice on earth" (Guralnick 2003: 18). Other verses of the song resonate with Cooke's firsthand experience of racial discrimination ("*I go to the movie and I go downtown, somebody keep tellin' me, don't hang around*") and with the drowning death of his 18-month old son just a few months prior ("*There have been times that I thought I couldn't last for long, but now I think I'm able to carry on*").

and crafted to appeal to the musical aesthetic of a largely white, middle-class, middle-aged audience. This sort of stylistic code-switching has been used by many African American artists striving to "cross over" in the recording studio and in live performances. American racial attitudes and customs—which dictated that the diverse people who might buy a hit record often did not want, or were not allowed, to sit in the same room together when the same song was performed live—presented Sam Cooke with a challenge to which he not merely adapted, but *responded*, proactively and creatively, over the course of his all-too-brief career.

"THE TWIST"

"The Twist" began its popular career inauspiciously, as the B-side of a 1959 single by the veteran rhythm & blues group Hank Ballard and the Midnighters. Ballard was convinced that he had written a smash hit with "The Twist," a teen-oriented rock 'n' roll song using a twelve-bar blues structure; it celebrated a simple, hip-swiveling dance step that was gaining some popularity among young African Americans. But the decision makers at Ballard's indie label, King, didn't agree, so they promoted the other side of the record, a perfectly fine but more old-fashioned rhythm & blues ballad called "Teardrops on Your Letter." This tune peaked at Number 89 on Billboard's Hot 100 chart (although both sides of the record enjoyed popularity among rhythm & blues fans) and promptly disappeared from view—along with, one would have assumed, "The Twist." However, the dance named in Ballard's song continued its still somewhat obscure existence.

Meanwhile, somebody must have paid serious attention to that flip side of "Teardrops on Your Letter," somebody with connections at another indie label, Parkway. Since Parkway was based in Philadelphia, its artists had particularly easy access to *American Bandstand*, the teen-oriented, nationally broadcast television show that originated in the same city. American Bandstand was all about dancing: Rock 'n' roll records were played, and the camera showed the teenagers in the studio dancing to them. It was the perfect venue for promoting a new dance record, and a new dance, to the broad rock 'n' roll audience.

Parkway recording artist Chubby Checker was himself all of eighteen when he cut a cover of Hank Ballard's "The Twist" in 1960. (His real name was Ernest Evans; his stage name had in fact been suggested by the wife of *American Bandstand* host Dick Clark, based on Evans's resemblance to a young Fats Domino.) This record was heavily promoted, and this time around Ballard's conviction about the song proved justified: It reached the Number 1 position on the charts. Checker's version adhered so closely to the vocal inflections and the arrangement of the original that Ballard (when interviewed for the 1993

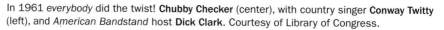

In 1961 *everybody* did the twist! **Chubby Checker** (center), with country singer **Conway Twitty** (left), and *American Bandstand* host **Dick Clark**. Courtesy of Library of Congress.

documentary movie *Twist*) claimed he mistook it for his own record the first time he heard it on the radio!

Even more than the song, the dance itself caught the imagination of young people nationwide as they had the opportunity to observe it on *American Bandstand*. (In fact, Ballard's original recording also entered the pop charts at this time, swept there by the wave of enthusiasm engendered by the dance.) The twist was essentially an individual, noncontact dance without any real steps. Although it was generally done by a boy-and-girl couple facing one another, there was no inherent reason why it had to be restricted to this format; it could at least hypothetically be performed by any number of people, including one, in any dance floor pattern, in any gender combination. This had two related benefits: Being able to dance with a group of friends meant that boys no longer had to ask girls to dance, thus equalizing the gender dynamic and reducing the threat of rejection on both sides. This, in turn, allowed shy and self-conscious teens to participate in dance culture, which increased the potential audience for dance records. At the same time, the lack of physical contact between dancers reduced the inherent sexuality of partner dancing, thus making the whole enterprise appear more wholesome to protective parents (needless to say, teenagers usually managed to find a way around that restriction). The twist was not the first noncontact, free-form dance to emerge in the history of American social dancing, but its enormous popularity signaled a sea change in the entire culture of popular dance. Against all apparent odds, it turned out to be much more than a passing novelty.

Soon adults of all ages and classes and races were doing the twist, along with the teenagers. In turn, the popularity and wide social acceptance of this free-form dancing brought rock 'n' roll music to a significantly broader audience than ever before: It was no longer just music for teenagers but an accepted fact of American social life. Clubs called discotheques, dedicated to the twist and other free-form dances that followed in its wake—the pony, the mashed potatoes, the monkey, and countless others—sprang up all over; one of the most famous, New York's Peppermint Lounge, gave its name to one of the biggest hits of early 1962, "Peppermint Twist," recorded by the club's house band, Joey Dee and the Starliters. Less than a year after it completed its first chart run, Chubby Checker's "The Twist" was back on the Hot 100 for another go-round and reached Number 1 a second time. (This feat has been accomplished by only two records in the history of the pop charts; that the other one is Bing Crosby's "White Christmas" gives some indication of the extraordinary level of popularity of both the twist as a dance and "The Twist" as a record.) Live rock 'n' roll shows began to include female "go-go" dancers along with the singing acts; in the later 1960s these dancers also began to be featured, with or without their clothes, in clubs where recorded rock music was played.

The free-form dances that have accompanied, and in some cases inspired, so much of American popular music from the 1960s to the present thus all find their point of origin in the twist. The discotheques of the 1960s were the ancestors of the discos of the 1970s, and the spirit of bodily freedom represented by those institutions persisted in the mosh pits and related venues of the 1990s and beyond. Rock 'n' roll had found a social body language that matched the novelty of the music and the feeling of liberation that it celebrated.

It should come as no surprise that, in the wake of "The Twist," many other popular songs of the early 1960s were dance-oriented. To cite only a few representative examples: Chubby Checker recorded "Let's Twist Again" in 1961; teenager Dee Dee Sharp cut a duet with Chubby Checker, "Slow Twistin'," as well as "Mashed Potato Time" (both 1962) and "Do the Bird" (1963); songwriter Carole King tapped her babysitter, sixteen-year-old Little Eva (Eva Narcissus Boyd), to record her song "The Loco-Motion" in 1962; and the Motown group the Miracles sang about "Mickey's Monkey" (1963). (As we will see, the later disco craze of the 1970s inspired an analogous flood of dance-oriented songs. Popular music designed specifically for dancing remained popular through the 1980s and beyond.) For the most part, the dance songs of the 1960s, like their later counterparts, were catchy and functional and tended to break no new ground musically or lyrically—which may account, at least somewhat, for the poor reputation of this period in many histories of American pop. Simple verse-chorus formats predominated. But if the songs were not in themselves novel or important, the new dance culture to which they contributed certainly was. And a few of these songs retained the affection of a large public for a surprisingly long time: Chubby Checker joined with the rap group Fat Boys in a successful revival of "The Twist" (subtitled "Yo, Twist!") in 1988, and "The Loco-Motion" was a Number 1 song for the hard-rock group Grand Funk Railroad in 1974 and for the Australian singer Kylie Minogue in 1988.

From a business standpoint, these records could also be seen as the mainstream music industry's attempt to create a new approach that combined the youthful appeal of rock with the commercial foundation of the old Tin Pan Alley model. The songs and the dances were often designed together by professional songwriters as part of a complete package, with each meant to promote the other. The dance's name would be the title of the song, and the lyrics often contained instructions on how to perform the dance. The dance moves were designed to be relatively easy to master for even the most uncoordinated teen, who in any case could gather additional instruction from teen-oriented televised dance programs like *American Bandstand*. And as teens watched, learned, and danced to the song, they also would want to *buy* it, if only so they could practice at home to prepare for the next time they had to dance in public. After all, who would want to be the only teen that couldn't do the latest dance? And, best of all, it only took a few months (at most) for each dance to go out of style, at which point the whole process would begin again. A nation of insecure teens desperate to buy a whole new collection of carefully manufactured dance records every few months was a concept that even the most old-fashioned Tin Pan Alley songwriter could easily understand.

"TEENAGE SYMPHONIES": PHIL SPECTOR

Another major figure in the quest to create a rock 'n' roll version of Tin Pan Alley was Phil Spector. As we have seen, many teenagers achieved success as recording artists in the early years of rock 'n' roll. At the age of seventeen, Phil Spector (b. 1940) had a Number One record as a member of a vocal group, the Teddy Bears, whose hit song "To Know Him Is to Love Him" was also composed and produced by Spector. (The multitalented young man also played guitar and piano on the record, which was the first one he ever made!) It may initially seem surprising, then, that Spector elected not to follow the path of songwriting performers like Chuck Berry and Buddy Holly. Instead he emulated Jerry Leiber and Mike Stoller (see previous chapter), with whom he apprenticed, and by the early 1960s Spector had established himself as a songwriter-producer, working behind the scenes of rock 'n' roll rather than in its spotlights. But Spector must have sensed where the real emerging power was in this young music business: with the people who actually shaped the sounds of the records. The wisdom of his decision is reflected in the fact that his name today is probably better known, and certainly more widely revered among pop musicians, than that of Chubby Checker, Little Eva, and any number of young performers active in the early 1960s.

By the time he was twenty-one years old, Spector was in charge of his own independent label, Philles Records (derived from the simple combination of his name with that of his partner Lester Sill—one area in which rock remained less-than-innovative was in the naming of record labels!), and he brought a new depth of meaning to the phrase "in charge." Working with personally selected songwriters (and often serving as a collaborator in their writing) and with hand-picked vocalists, instrumentalists, arrangers, and engineers, he supervised every aspect of a record's sound. Spector's level of involvement, and his obsession with detail, became legendary; as a result, a Philles record has a distinctive kind of sonority, tied more closely to Spector's personal talents and vision than to the contributions of any other songwriters, or of the technicians, or even of the actual performers. That is to say, more than records by the Crystals or the Ronettes, these are "Phil Spector records."

The characteristic Philles sound was at once remarkably dense and remarkably clear, and it became known as the "wall of sound." Spector achieved this effect by having multiple instruments—pianos, guitars, and so forth—doubling each individual part in the arrangement, and by using a huge amount of echo, while carefully controlling the overall balance of the record so that the vocals were pushed clearly to the front. The thick texture and the presence of strings on these records led them to be called "teenage symphonies." A perfect example is "Be My Baby," to be discussed in detail shortly. However, Spector explored many different types of sound textures on his recordings, and a record like "Uptown," also discussed herein, has a decidedly different and more intimate—while no less impressive—impact.

Philles Records helped establish a new and important model for the production and marketing of pop records. Many indie companies, mimicking the practice of major labels with earlier styles of pop music, rushed as many records as they could into the rock 'n' roll market, often without much thought for quality control, hoping for the occasional hit. In contrast, as would be expected from the description provided previously, Phil Spector turned out an exceptionally small number of records, about twenty in a two-year period, an astoundingly large percentage of which were hits. Of course, the increasingly high profile of record producers through the later 1960s and up to the present (one need only recall the importance of George Martin's work with the Beatles) is a direct outgrowth of Spector's contribution and notoriety; a 1965 essay by the noted writer Tom Wolfe dubbed the then-twenty-four-year-old millionaire "the first tycoon of teen." And when today's bands labor painstakingly for a year or more over the studio production of a disc, they are demonstrating, knowingly or not, Spector's legacy at work.

It is also significant that Spector's own preferred recording venue was Gold Star Studios in Los Angeles; this was an early indication of the coming shift away from New York as the dominant power center of the pop music industry. The studio musicians with whom Spector worked regularly at Gold Star Studios came to be known as the "Wrecking Crew"; individually and collectively they made essential contributions to a remarkable number of hit records from the 1960s on. Among the best known of these musicians are Jack Nitzsche, arranger and percussionist; Hal Blaine, drummer; and Carol Kaye, bassist.

It is worth lingering for a moment on Carol Kaye—not to be confused with Carole King—who, although not well known to the general public, is possibly the single most influential bassist in rock history. Kaye (born in Everett, Washington, in 1935) is said to have played in more than ten thousand recording sessions since 1949, including many of the most popular rock songs recorded in Los Angeles during that time. As one of the few women studio musicians working during the 1950s, '60s, and '70s, she would be significant for that fact alone. As the musician, arranger, and producer Quincy Jones once put it, "the Fender bass player Carol Kaye . . . could do anything and leave the men in the dust" (Jones 2002: 126). However, the significance of Kaye's contribution to rock music goes beyond her gender. In contrast to the majority of professional electric bassists of her era, Kaye began her career as a guitarist, rather than as an acoustic bass player. This meant that her technical vocabulary and general approach to the instrument contrasted in many ways with the traditional approach to bass used by other players. In particular, Kaye plucked the strings with a guitar pick rather than with her fingers, which gave her playing a hard-hitting, percussive quality that was well suited to rock music. Transmitted through her work on recordings by the Beach Boys, Ray Charles, Ike and Tina Turner, Simon and Garfunkel, the Doors, Frank Zappa, and other artists, this sound exerted a profound and lasting influence on rock bassists.

Phil Spector preferred to work with vocal groups over individual artists (although he did do some work with soloists), and his output as producer helped assure, as a result both of its own quality and of its influence, that the early 1960s were a golden age for rock 'n' roll vocal groups. Spector's predilection for vocal groups—shared by many songwriters and producers at the time—was probably due to several factors. The groups offered great potential for intricate and varied vocal textures, of course. But the focus on vocal groups also allowed Spector to use essentially the same backing musicians on every recording, a practice that was fundamental to maintaining the aforementioned "Phil Spector sound." In a very real sense, all Phil Spector productions were by the same "group"—Phil Spector and the Wrecking Crew—regardless of whose name happened to appear on the label. With a few exceptions, the individual vocalists were essentially anonymous as far as the listening public was concerned, so their personnel could be reduced, augmented, or otherwise altered at the will of the producer. The Crystals, for example, are now known to have been at least two completely different groups, possibly more.

The increased power of the producer in this situation was most likely the critical issue here. Cultural historians would also attach significance to the fact that the producers of vocal group rock 'n' roll in this period tended to be, like Phil Spector, male and white, while a large proportion of the most popular vocal groups were female (the so-called girl groups), and of these, a significant number were composed exclusively of African Americans. In effect, the increased specialization and resulting hierarchical arrangement of power and influence that occurred in an operation like Philles Records restored a Tin Pan Alley–like model to the creation and marketing of some of the most successful rock 'n' roll.

An important part of that model was, of course, that the groups should not write their own songs. To list the songwriters with whom Spector worked is to list some of the most prodigious talents of the early 1960s, including the teams of Carole King (not to be confused with Carol Kaye!) and Gerry Goffin, Barry Mann and Cynthia Weil, and Jeff Barry and Ellie Greenwich. For these and many other aspiring songwriters of the time, New York's Brill Building (at 1619 Broadway) and other nearby office buildings served as a base of operations, where they worked in little cubicles with pianos, all packed tightly together, turning out songs for large numbers of artists and (mostly indie) labels. Producers and label executives were constantly in attendance or close at hand, and these office buildings became quite literally rock 'n' roll's vertical Tin Pan Alleys. The successful songwriters were often working with a number of different artists, producers, and labels at the same time, and consequently could hope to have several hits on the charts simultaneously; the regular work at a stable location and the promise of considerable royalty income made this type of work seem both more reliable and more potentially lucrative than that of

The Shirelles (Beverley Lee, Doris Kenner-Jackson, Shirley Alston, and Addie "Micki" Harris) in 1961. Photo by Gilles Petard/Redferns.

performers. Some of the Brill Building songwriters did perform occasionally on records, playing instruments, providing background vocals, and sometimes even doing a lead vocal, but this was not a regular practice. In the early 1960s the only one of this group to have a name as a recording artist was Neil Sedaka, who generally performed his own material. By the 1970s, as the culture of rock began to focus on more personal statements, many of these songwriters—such as Carole King and Neil Diamond—had stepped out from the shadows and began to perform their own material.

Like Phil Spector, a large proportion of the Brill Building songwriters tailored their output toward vocal groups, and many of the resulting records remain classics of their period. The Drifters performed "Save the Last Dance for Me" by Doc Pomus and Mort Shuman (Number 1, 1960), "Up on the Roof" by Goffin and King (Number 5, 1963), and "On Broadway" by Mann and Weil and Leiber and Stoller (Number 9, 1963); the Shirelles—one of the first successful girl groups—recorded "Will You Love Me Tomorrow?" by Goffin and King (Number 1, 1961); the Dixie Cups sang "Chapel of Love" by Barry and Greenwich and Spector (Number 1, 1964); and the list could go on and on. Talented hopefuls flocked to the Brill Building.

Phil Spector retired from steady writing and production work in 1966, periodically resurfacing to work on special projects that attracted his interest. The best known of these involved the Beatles; he worked on the last album released by the group, *Let It Be* (1970), and then assisted individual members with solo albums in the early 1970s. Unfortunately, his subsequent history suggests that his drive for control was as much psychological as musical. After living as a recluse for the better part of three decades, two events brought him back to the public consciousness. In the spring of 2003, the surviving Beatles announced that they were so dissatisfied with Spector's production choices on *Let It Be* that they were taking the unprecedented step of re-releasing the album that fall with Spector's contributions removed. On February 3, 2003, actress Lana Clarkson was found shot to death at Spector's Los Angeles mansion, reviving longstanding rumors of Spector's reckless use of firearms (including in the recording studio). In April 2009, he was found guilty of second-degree murder and sentenced to 19 years to life in prison.

Personal failings aside, Phil Spector's career represents one of the most successful attempts to combine rock 'n' roll with Tin Pan Alley. Not only did

Spector merge the rock 'n' roll feel with a Tin Pan Alley business model, he also combined the role of the songwriter (responsible for the words, chords, and melody of a song) with that of the producer (responsible for the way that a song sounds on a recording). The significance of this fusion cannot be overstated: The idea that making a recording is actually *part* of the songwriting process is a concept that is fundamental to popular music to the present day. Spector's rise also represents the final conceptual shift in the transition from sheet music to records. People bought his records as much for their *sound* as for the songs themselves. This is a shift in sensibility that could not have happened until the technology existed to support it: The idea of realizing a personal vision through the recording process requires a recording process that contains enough options to make those choices significant. In short, the rise of Phil Spector represents the coming together of the cultural changes that rock 'n' roll exemplified with the business concerns that it raised and the technological opportunities to address both.

BERRY GORDY AND MOTOWN

Meanwhile, in Detroit, Berry Gordy Jr. (b. 1929) was experimenting with his own blend of the rock 'n' roll and Tin Pan Alley, by creating a songwriting/ producing/marketing organization that was based on the production lines that defined the city's auto industry: a self-described "hit factory." But Motown (named after the "Motor Town" or "Motor City"—i.e., Detroit, the automobile production capital of America) came to be the most stunning success story in the entire history of African American businesses in this country. Though Motown was not the first black-owned record company, the intensity and duration of its commercial success (it is still an important market presence at the time of this writing) may be attributed to the distinctive dual thrust of Gordy's vision.

First of all, he was determined to keep all of the creative and financial aspects of the business under African American control—which effectively meant under his control. This worked because Gordy had an uncanny ability to surround himself with first-rate musical talent in all areas of the record-making process, and to maintain the loyalty of his musicians for substantial periods of time. It also worked, of course, because Gordy had a shrewd head for business as well as for music, and this leads us to the second element of his visionary plan. Unlike the music of earlier black-owned record companies, Motown's music was not directed primarily at black audiences. Gordy unapologetically sought to make an African American pop music addressed to the widest possible listening public. The only segregation Gordy permitted his product was geared to age; like rock 'n' roll itself, Motown's music was designed to cut across divisions of race, region, and class, but it definitely was—as the label itself proclaimed— "the sound of young America."

It is almost as if Gordy launched his enterprise as a kind of counteroffensive against the expropriation of African American music and the exploitation of African American musicians that had been as much a part of the early history

LISTENING TO TWO PHIL SPECTOR PRODUCTIONS: "BE MY BABY" AND "UPTOWN"

"Be My Baby," composed by Phil Spector, Ellie Greenwich, and Jeff Barry, performed by the Ronettes (Number 2, 1963); "Uptown," composed by Barry Mann and Cynthia Weil, performed by the Crystals (Number 13, 1962)

"Be My Baby" was one of the biggest hits among the many produced by Spector, and it remains a favorite to this day on oldies radio. With its employment of a full orchestral string section, pianos, an array of rhythm instruments, and a background chorus behind the lead vocal, it is an opulent "teenage symphony" and a fine illustration of Spector's "wall of sound" at full tilt. It is certainly the arrangement and production that gives this record its individual and enduring character. As a composition, the song itself is a simple if effective vehicle, expressing the most basic romantic sentiments in a straightforward verse-chorus framework. But the listener is hooked from the first, as an aggressive, distinctive rhythmic pattern on the solo drum gives the record its beat from the get-go and draws us immediately into the song. (Notice also the spectacular effect achieved by the surprise recurrence of this drum introduction just before the final repetitions of the song's chorus; this sudden crack in the wall of sound has an explosive impact!)

"Uptown" is an earlier, very different Philles record (one of the first to be issued) that serves well to illustrate another aspect of Spector's production talents. "Uptown" is a song quite unlike "Be My Baby," and Spector appropriately provided it with a highly individual arrangement and production. Although "Uptown" uses orchestral strings and percussion effects in as sophisticated a manner as "Be My Baby," the earlier song conveys a much more open, spacious feeling, as if illustrating in sound the relief experienced by the protagonist when he leaves work each evening and goes uptown.

"Uptown" deals with class inequalities and economic injustice; the fact that it does this gently makes it no less remarkable for 1962, when pop songs on such subjects were virtually nonexistent. (These subjects would have been regarded as appropriate for urban folk music at this

of rock 'n' roll as it had been of other periods in the development of American popular music. And the unique genius of Gordy—and of his entire Motown organization—was the ability to create a black music aimed right at the commercial mainstream that somehow never evoked the feeling, or provoked the charge, of having sold out. With remarkably few exceptions, Motown recordings avoided direct evocations of earlier rhythm & blues forms and styles; twelve-bar blues patterns are strikingly rare, as are the typical devices of doo-wop or anything suggestive of the 1950s sounds of Chuck Berry, Fats Domino, or Little Richard. Yet a generalized blues or gospel manner remained a defining characteristic of Motown's performers; sometimes it could be very subtle, as is often the case with William "Smokey" Robinson, and sometimes much more overt, as is the case with Martha Reeves. And this manner proved sufficient to give a definite African American slant to the pop-structured, pop-flavored songs that were characteristic of Motown.

At this point, you may be wondering why Motown—an African American-owned record label that featured African American music performed almost time, but not for the pop market; see Chapter 5.) The hero of the song works downtown, where he "don't get no breaks," and it is only when he comes uptown in the evening to his lover's "tenement," where they "don't have to pay much rent," that he can feel like a "king" with the world "at his feet." The contrast between downtown and uptown is captured in the music's harmony as well. The downtown sections are in a **minor** key (also unusual for this period), while the uptown sections move to a **major** key. Note also the striking effect of the flexible tempo of the opening section on the record, which helps establish the unusual atmosphere and functions as a kind of atypical hook, by setting up a high degree of anticipation in the listener. The suspense is relieved when a steady tempo is established at the first occurrence of the word "uptown."

Spector recorded "Uptown" in New York. Given his own New York background, which he shared with the songwriters Mann and Weil, it is hard to escape the conviction that "Uptown" is indeed about New York, where uptown and downtown Manhattan exemplify the economic and class distinctions depicted in the lyrics. Furthermore, given the many "Spanish"-sounding features of this recording, one suspects that the specific uptown location is probably New York's Spanish Harlem, a largely Puerto Rican enclave that had gained pop music notoriety just a year before the release of "Uptown" through a song actually called "Spanish Harlem"—a Top 10 hit for Ben E. King that was cowritten by Phil Spector himself.

Several factors contribute to the general Latin feeling of "Uptown." (Like so much pop music, "Uptown" is concerned with the general evocation of an "exotic" locale, not with any kind of ethnomusicological accuracy. The "exotic" stylistic effects in "Uptown" are actually not specifically characteristic of Puerto Rican music at all.) The ornate guitar figures heard as accompaniment to the opening verse are obviously reminiscent of flamenco guitar style. The prominent use of castanets (also present in "Be My Baby," but just as part of the wall of sound, not as a specifically evocative presence) for percussion, and the general rhythmic feeling of Latin American dance throughout the record (aspects of *baion* rhythm in the accompaniment, and aspects of Cuban *bolero* rhythm in the song's melody) also contribute strongly to the exotic coloration of "Uptown." We dwell on this because "Uptown" serves as an example here of an important trend—the incorporation of Latin American elements into the fabric of 1960s rock 'n' roll. The trend is also clearly evident in "Spanish Harlem" and in many records of the early 1960s by the Drifters (the most famous of which is "Save the Last Dance for Me").

exclusively by African American singers and musicians—should be considered rock 'n' roll music. This is an important question, because it leads directly to a deeper issue: What *is* rock 'n' roll anyway? In reality, there is no single definition, only a series of opinions that are associated with different moments and different situations. Rather than ask whether something *is* or *is not* rock, we find it more useful to ask *who* considered it rock and *why* did they hold that opinion? The answers to these questions can tell us a lot about the evolving relationship between rock and American culture generally.

In this case, the idea of African American artists directing their work toward a mainstream audience was still central to most people's definition of rock 'n' roll in the early sixties. In fact, as we have seen, the idea of merging black and white audiences into a single community was actually one of the main themes of rock 'n' roll culture at the time. In other words, contrary to the way it may look in retrospect, the music that Motown produced was not just an influence on rock 'n' roll—it *was* rock 'n' roll. This was not an accident. As we noted, Berry Gordy was—and remains—very forthright that his intention was to capture the rock 'n' roll audience, which he defined along generational lines rather than racial ones. In addition to the obvious financial wisdom of this approach, it was also very much in keeping with the politics of the era, particularly those of the Civil Rights Movement. Though Gordy resisted the use of explicit political references in Motown's music well into the seventies, he was a strong supporter of the Civil Rights Movement, both politically and financially. And the sound of the music itself sent the message loud and clear. For many, the Motown sound embodies the promise of the movement even to the present day: a music that brought black and white together through song.

Like Phil Spector, Berry Gordy Jr. started his career as a songwriter (he cowrote a number of pop and rhythm & blues hits performed by Jackie Wilson in the late 1950s), although unlike Spector he did not perform on records.

The Supremes (with Diana Ross in the middle) in the 1960s. RB/Redferns/Retna, Ltd.

Motown, which began its operations in 1959 but at first grew very slowly, was reaching its commercial peak just at the point when Spector folded Philles in 1966. The Motown model was strikingly similar to that employed by Philles: tight quality control on all levels of creation and production, and the concentration on a small number of records to yield a high proportion of hits. It is impossible to determine direct influence, one way or the other, between the Philles and Motown organizations; it seems to be a case of two remarkable talents having similar ideas, and similar success, at around the same time. However, Gordy's organization was noticeably larger in its scope and ambition than Spector's.

From the beginning, Gordy planned a group of labels rather than just one: records under the Motown, Tamla, Gordy, and Soul names were all issued from his Detroit headquarters, and each label boasted its own roster of hitmakers. Furthermore, whereas Spector was essentially interested only in the records themselves, Gordy specifically chose and developed his recording artists to be charismatic and sophisticated live performers, complete with characteristic modes of dress and distinctive stage choreography—not to mention strict codes of conduct on and off stage that apparently were enforced quite vigorously. There were complaints about the iron hand with which Gordy ruled his roost, just as there were complaints about Spector's passion for control. But there can be no doubt that Gordy's active encouragement of his artists to be more than just recording acts made it possible for both individuals and groups from the organization to develop long-term careers. It is no accident that groups like the Supremes and the Temptations are significantly better known to a wide public than are the Crystals or the Ronettes—or that individuals like Smokey Robinson and Diana Ross were able to win the kind of name recognition that enabled them eventually to branch off from the groups with which they initially were associated (the Miracles and the Supremes, respectively) and to forge hugely successful solo careers. (The musical *Dreamgirls*, successful first as a Broadway show and then as a movie, presented a fictionalized account of the career of a Supremes-like singing group while capturing effectively the behind-the-scenes environment of a Motown-like organization.)

The Motown records of the early 1960s exemplify the rock 'n' roll trends of their time. Among the biggest of Motown's early hits were "Please Mr. Postman" by the Marvelettes (Number 1, 1961), a quintessential girl group record, and "Do You Love Me" by the Contours (Number 3, 1962), a hard-driving dance record that linked success in romance to the ability to perform currently popular dance steps, such as the twist and the mashed potatoes. (The Contours' "Do You Love Me" found renewed chart success in 1988, on the strength of its prominent employment on the soundtrack of the movie *Dirty Dancing*, which is set in the early 1960s.) By the mid-1960s a more complex, occasionally lush sound came to characterize Motown's productions. Surely the Temptations' "My Girl" (see the Listening To section) is as much a "teenage symphony" as any of Phil Spector's most elaborate offerings. Just like Spector, however, Motown never lost touch with a danceable beat, and although the Supremes' "You Can't Hurry Love" (see the Listening To section) has a much more sophisticated sound and arrangement than "Please Mr. Postman" from five years earlier, both records share an irresistible groove. Gordy's touch seemed never to falter, and his organization steadily increased its share of the hit record market throughout the 1960s; in the year 1970 alone, Motown and its affiliated labels placed sixteen records in the Top 10 and scored seven Number 1 records (out of the year's total of twenty-one Number 1 songs)!

Motown's headquarters in Detroit (which Gordy named "Hitsville, USA") served as a magnet for a spectacular array of talented individuals, some of whom did session work or even office work until they finally managed to get the attention of Gordy. Among performers, Gordy—like so many other producers—tended to favor vocal groups, although he did have important solo acts from early on, such as Marvin Gaye, Mary Wells, and Stevie Wonder, and did eventually wean some solo performers from the groups that they fronted. Important Motown groups not yet mentioned include Martha (Reeves) and the Vandellas, Junior Walker and the All Stars, the Four Tops, Gladys Knight and the Pips, and the Jackson Five; the last-named group made their first record for Motown in 1969, when lead singer Michael was all of eleven years old, and their string of hits for the label helped assure Motown's fortunes well into the 1970s. Gordy's organization was also blessed with remarkable songwriting and production talent, and Gordy would often have his teams of songwriting producers compete for the privilege of working with particular hot recording acts. Among the most famous of these Motown writing/production teams were (Eddie) Holland–(Lamont) Dozier–(Brian) Holland, Norman Whitfield and Barrett Strong, and Nickolas Ashford and Valerie Simpson. Smokey Robinson was unusual among the earlier Motown artists in being both a performer and a songwriter-producer; he furnished material not just to his own group, the Miracles, but also to Mary Wells, the Marvelettes, and the Temptations. Later on, in the 1970s, Marvin Gaye and Stevie Wonder also took on writing and production responsibilities for their own records.

Finally, but certainly not least in importance, Motown had a sterling house band, the so-called Funk Brothers, in every sense a match for Phil Spector's Wrecking Crew in assuring that the highest level of instrumental musicianship was always present to back up and inspire the vocal performers. Bass player James Jamerson, drummer

Smokey Robinson (second from right) **and the Miracles** in the 1960s. Michael Ochs Archives/Corbis.

Benny Benjamin, and keyboardist Earl Van Dyke were among the most important contributors to the Motown sound. Much like Phil Spector, Gordy used his studio musicians to build what would now be thought of as a "brand identity" for Motown. Since, in a sense, virtually all Motown songs were by the same band (only with different vocalists), fans could confidently buy a record by a Motown artist that they had never even heard of, knowing that it would sound similar to other Motown music that they already knew. The documentary film *Standing in the Shadows of Motown* (2002) offers a fine, ultimately sobering history of these insufficiently celebrated musicians.

In 1971 Berry Gordy moved the Motown headquarters to Los Angeles, at last joining the "westward migration" that had been playing an important role in American pop music, and in American culture generally, since the early 1960s. Next we turn our attention specifically to California, to surf music, and to Brian Wilson—who did more than any other single person to make California the new focus of America's rock 'n' roll mythology.

THE CALIFORNIA SOUND

Brian Wilson and the Beach Boys

The Beach Boys represent a different take on the commercial hybrids of the early sixties. Rather than starting with a Tin Pan Alley business model and adding a rock 'n' roll sound, the Beach Boys started with a rock 'n' roll approach and

The Beach Boys, with Brian Wilson on bass guitar, second from right, in 1964. Michael Ochs Archives/Corbis.

🎧 LISTENING TO THE MOTOWN SOUND: "MY GIRL" AND "YOU CAN'T HURRY LOVE"

"My Girl," composed and produced by Smokey Robinson and Ronald White, performed by the Temptations (Number 1, 1965); "You Can't Hurry Love," composed by Holland-Dozier-Holland, produced by Brian Holland and Lamont Dozier, performed by the Supremes (Number 1, 1966)

"My Girl" is a moderate-tempo love ballad. As a composition, it is a song of sweetly conventional romantic sentiment in a straightforward verse-chorus form. But as a recording, it is lifted emphatically beyond the ordinary by virtue of the Temptations' thoroughly engaging performance and by virtue of Motown's spectacular production values.

From the outset, the arrangement hooks the listener: A repeating solo bass motive establishes the beat, over which a lead guitar enters with a memorable melodic figure. (Both of these instrumental hooks are also used later on in the recording, so that they are firmly fixed in the listener's mind after one hearing of the song.) Then the drums and lead voice enter, followed subtly by background vocals; by the time the first chorus is reached, brass instruments are present in the accompaniment, to which are then added orchestral strings. The cumulative layering of sounds gives a sense of steadily increasing passion and intensity to the song, as the singer's words metaphorically detail his feelings for his "girl." The second verse brings new brass fanfares in response to the lead vocalist's calls. There is a sumptuous instrumental interlude before the third (last) verse, dominated by the strings, which play a new melodic figure over the song's characteristic chord progressions. Then, as a final intensifying gesture, a dramatic upward key change takes place just before the concluding verse and chorus.

If "My Girl" showcases the brilliance of Motown's arranging and producing staff, "You Can't Hurry Love" demonstrates that Motown's writers could also come up with clever, innovatively structured pop songs. The outline that follows conveys the intricacies of this Holland–Dozier–Holland composition, although the most casual hearing of the record will affirm that—as with so much of the finest pop music—catchiness was absolutely not sacrificed to the cause of sophistication.

The opening A section of "You Can't Hurry Love" is extremely short, just half the length of each of the ensuing B and C sections. The function of this A is at first unclear, both because of its brevity (Is it a kind of introduction? Or is it a very short verse?) and because of its similarity to the music of B; the basic chord progressions underlying both A and B are virtually identical, even though their vocal melodies differ. C brings a striking chord change and another change of melody, which might initially suggest a kind of bridge section. But when A fails to return after C, and instead B and C alternate with one

LISTENING CHART "YOU CAN'T HURRY LOVE"		
FORM		**LYRICS**
Instrumental intro		
A	0.07	*I need love . . .*
B: b	0.17	*You can't . . .*
b	0.27	*You can't . . .*
C	0.37	*But how many . . .*
B: b	0.57	*(You can't—) no . . .*
b	1.07	*How long . . .*
C	1.17	*No, I can't . . .*
B: b	1.37	*(You can't—) no . . .*
b	1.47	*You can't . . .*
Brief instrumental break	1.57	
A	2.00	*No, love, love . . .*
A	2.09	*for that soft . . .*
A or B?	2.19	*I keep waitin' . . .*
B: b	2.29	*You can't . . .*
b	2.39	*You can't . . .*

another, we seem to be in an unorthodox verse-chorus type of situation, in which we hear the first verse (C) after the chorus (B), and in which the words of the chorus aren't always exactly the same. Just when a pattern seems to have been established, A unexpectedly returns with a vengeance. Instead of proceeding right to B, it is played twice through, creating a composite section that is now as long as B or C. Then, in the most clever formal maneuver of all in this already complex song, an ambiguous section is inserted, as the composers take advantage of the chord progression shared by A and B; with minimal melodic activity from the voice, which keeps "waitin'," we can't tell for sure which of the two sections we're actually hearing! The instruments tease us briefly here by playing the melodic motive associated with B, "you can't hurry love." But the voice holds back until we're at the top of the chord progression again, at which point it finally begins a proper, full repetition of B, toward the end of which the record fades out.

All this play with form would be just so much intellectual busywork if it didn't reflect on the meaning of the song.

"You Can't Hurry Love" is a song about the importance of waiting. Formally, the song keeps us guessing—waiting for clarification of the functional relationships among the different sections. When the A section at last returns, it keeps us waiting extensively for B and its restatement of the song's essential message. On the level of detail, notice also in the second and third B sections how the lead vocalist avoids or postpones singing the words "you can't hurry love," again forcing the listener to wait. This makes the final B that much more of a release of tension, as it behaves in an expected manner at last.

Like all the great Motown hits, "You Can't Hurry Love" submerges its many subtleties beneath an irresistible pop-friendly surface. Maybe this is why you don't tend to find it, or other Motown records, the subject of discussion when matters turn toward innovative aspects of 1960s music. Still, any list of the significant music of this period that omits a record like "You Can't Hurry Love" is surely missing something important.

expanded it to include pop elements. Ultimately, this allowed them to bring the production innovations of Phil Spector squarely into the rock world, where they have resided ever since.

Brian Wilson (b. 1942) formed the Beach Boys with his two brothers, a cousin, and a friend in Hawthorne, California, in 1961. The band was achieving national chart hits within a year and thrived right through the period of the "British Invasion" to become not only the bestselling American group of the 1960s but probably the most nationally and internationally celebrated American rock group ever—and certainly the one with the longest history of chart success. (They scored a Number 1 hit as late as 1988, with "Kokomo.") As songwriter, arranger, producer, and performer, Brian Wilson was the guiding spirit of the Beach Boys during the first decade of the group's existence, when their artistic and commercial importance and influence were at a peak. Wilson's clear, and stated, model was Phil Spector, and Wilson worked regularly in the Los Angeles recording studios with many of the same musicians who graced Spector's productions. Unlike Spector, however, Wilson was always an essential performing presence on the records he wrote, arranged, and produced for the Beach Boys. Even after he stopped touring with the group in 1964, the sound of Wilson's clear, intense falsetto remained a defining element of the Beach Boys' studio recordings.

By participating significantly in the creation of beautifully produced "teenage symphonies" featuring vocal groups, Wilson and the Beach Boys obviously contributed to one of the central trends of the early 1960s. But if we wish to understand why their importance and influence went well beyond this, we have to look at even broader issues.

If we were to conceptualize a defining model for the career of a self-sustaining, trend-setting rock group of the 1960s, it would look something like this:

- Start out by demonstrating a mastery of the basic early rock 'n' roll ballad and up-tempo styles.
- Create original material based on, and extending, those styles.
- Eventually branch out totally beyond the traditional forms, sounds, and lyric content of rock 'n' roll to create something truly different and unique.

The reference point that most people would use for constructing a model like this would probably, and understandably, be the career of the Beatles—the shape of their career is surely encapsulated in the preceding description—or possibly one of the other "British Invasion" groups. But the group that first established this model, and did so with outstanding success, was the Beach Boys. The Beach Boys were in fact a clear, and stated, model for the Beatles, especially during the remarkably productive and innovative years (for both groups) of 1965–67.

In a sense, Brian Wilson represented a new generation of rock 'n' rollers. By this we mean two things. First, that Wilson explicitly acknowledged his reliance on, and reverence for, his predecessors in the rock 'n' roll field—by covering, and quoting from, their records. In other words, he did not begin with musical material from other genres like rhythm & blues or country. Musically and culturally, rock itself was his starting point and his ongoing touchstone. Second, that at the same time, Wilson carved out distinctive new ground—by deliberately moving the lyrics, and eventually the music, of his own songs beyond the territory carved out by his predecessors, into novel areas that were of particular meaning to him, to his time, and to his place in America. (The Beatles, the Rolling Stones, and other bands were also self-conscious new-generation rock 'n' rollers in this sense, but it is important to realize that Brian Wilson was, in all essential respects, the first fully realized representative of this type of pop musician.)

Brian Wilson's place in America was, of course, southern California, and that land of sun and surf was celebrated in song after song by the Beach Boys. These songs enshrined Wilson's somewhat mythical version of California indelibly in the consciousness of young Americans—to such an extent that still, for legions of pop music fans, merely the titles are sufficient to summon an entire state of mind: "Surfin' Safari," "Surfer Girl," "The Warmth of the Sun," "California Girls," and so forth. Wilson's vision was appealingly inclusive, even as it remained place-specific; "I wish they all could be California girls," he sang.

(One also thinks of the opening lines of "Surfin' USA": "If everybody had an ocean, across the USA, then everybody'd be surfin' like Californ-i-ay.") Motor vehicles retained their importance to status and young romance in Wilson's California mythology, the models suitably modernized and spruced up to serve the new time and place, as in "409," "Little Deuce Coupe," and other songs.

A few examples may suffice to trace Wilson's journey from imitation, through emulation, to innovation. The Beach Boys' first Top 10 hit, the famous "Surfin' USA" (Number 3, 1963), simply borrows the music of Chuck Berry's 1958 hit "Sweet Little Sixteen" as a setting for Brian Wilson's paean to California's—and America's—new beach craze. While the words are all new, they also embody an indirect homage to Berry's original lyrics, insofar as Wilson adopts Berry's idea of national celebration while changing its mode of expression from dancing to surfing. The many listeners who knew "Sweet Little Sixteen" encountered in "Surfin' USA" an unusual hybrid: musically a cover record that shortened and simplified the form of Chuck Berry's original, lyrically a tribute to the spirit of Berry that reworked and updated his approach to writing rock 'n' roll anthems to suit the requirements of a new time and place. The B-side of "Surfin' USA," "Shut Down," was a substantial hit as well. In "Shut Down," Wilson employed an established rock 'n' roll hybrid song form, the AABA pattern in which the A sections are twelve-bar blues structures, to tell the story of a drag race between two high-powered automobiles. Needless to say, it is the singer's car that wins!

The Beach Boys' next hit, "Surfer Girl" (Number 7, 1963), reinvigorated the sound and spirit of the doo-wop ballad (and the AABA song form) by infusing it with California beach content. "Fun, Fun, Fun," the group's first hit of 1964, evoked Chuck Berry again, in an initially overt but ultimately more subtle way. The solo guitar introduction cops its twelve-bar blues licks directly from Berry's "Roll Over Beethoven" and "Johnny B. Goode." But after paying its respects (or its dues?) to Berry in this way, the main body of the song pursues an original path. It's a strophic form, with newly composed music and words, whose sixteen-bar strophes have nothing to do with the structure of the blues—but everything to do with what Brian Wilson learned from Chuck Berry about how to write and perform rock 'n' roll anthems. That is to say, after acknowledging Berry by quoting his signature manner of beginning a record, Wilson surprises his listeners and proceeds to pay his mentor the best possible tribute: not by copying him, but by revealing how well his lessons have been absorbed. "Fun, Fun, Fun" turns imitation into emulation. With its rapid-fire, clearly articulated lyrics, that manage to compress a remarkable number of deeply resonant references to youth culture (fancy cars, car radios, fast driving, hamburger stands, schoolwork, parents, the pursuit of romance and—naturally—fun) into two minutes' time, and its eminently catchy and danceable music, "Fun, Fun, Fun" is the kind of song Chuck Berry might have written had he been born sixteen years later, in Southern California. (In the song "Do You Remember?"—an album track from the Beach Boys' *All Summer Long* [1964]—Berry is mentioned as "the greatest" of the early rock 'n' rollers to whom Brian Wilson pays tribute.)

By mid-1964 Wilson had moved past obvious emulation into a period of aggressive experimentation with his inherited styles and forms. "I Get Around," the Beach Boys' first Number 1 record, turns the up-tempo rock 'n' roll anthem into a thoroughly individual kind of expression; the song's adventurous chord changes and quirky phrase structure take it well beyond the boundaries of 1950s rock 'n' roll, without ever sacrificing the immediate appeal and accessibility so essential to the genre. On the other hand, an album track like "The Warmth of the Sun" (from *Shut Down, Volume 2*, released in 1964), while clearly a descendent of the doo-wop ballad in sound, rhythm, and vocal parts, presents lyrics that probe the dissolution of young romance in a newly poignant and personal way, set to music that so enlarges the melodic and harmonic boundaries of the style that one quickly forgets the song's antecedents and focuses instead on its remarkable individuality. While it is questionable whether a song like "Warmth of the Sun" would have been successful as a single, it is unquestionable that songs like this were heard and appreciated, both by listeners and by those involved in the making of pop music, and thus contributed significantly to the evolution of musical style. We can also see here the beginnings of a significant trend: namely, the increasing importance of album tracks, and eventually of albums themselves, in the development of adventurous popular music. Rock 'n' roll was on its way to becoming rock.

By 1965 Brian Wilson was achieving international acclaim as a composer and recording studio wizard who produced brilliant singles and albums, and the Beach Boys were being viewed as the most serious creative and commercial threat—in America and in England—to the dominance of the Beatles, whose American triumph in 1964 had turned the entire world of pop music upside down. In the next chapter we will catch up with the Beatles, whose music in its turn was providing Brian Wilson, and many, many others, with creative stimulation and challenges.

Other "Surf Music"

The Beach Boys were not the only representatives of a distinctive "California sound" in the early 1960s. The popular duo Jan (Berry) and Dean (Torrence) worked with Brian Wilson and the Beach Boys on a number of mutual projects; Wilson in fact cowrote Jan and Dean's biggest hit, "Surf City" (Number 1, 1963). In addition, a highly influential style of guitar-dominated instrumental rock 'n' roll was pioneered in Southern California by Dick Dale (b. 1937), who performed with his band, the Del-Tones. Dale employed a solid-body guitar, a high-wattage Fender amplifier, and lots of reverb to achieve the "wet" sound of what came to be known as "surf guitar." A characteristic device was Dale's rapid, descending **tremolo**—borrowed by a group called the Chantays to open their recording of what became the most famous surf instrumental, "Pipeline" (the title is a surfing term for the curl of a wave before it breaks). Sustained national recognition eluded Dick Dale in the 1960s, but it finally became his in the 1990s, when his recording of "Misirlou," from 1962, was used as opening music for the hit film *Pulp Fiction*. The most successful instrumental group associated with surf rock was, paradoxically, a Seattle-based ensemble, the Ventures, who adopted aspects of the style after it became popular in California.

CONCLUSION

The early 1960s saw both the expansion of the commercial market for rock 'n' roll music, and the application by record companies of business strategies and production techniques ultimately modeled on the Tin Pan Alley era of popular song. New York's Brill Building tunesmiths and Motown Records' formidable songwriting teams, situated in the industrial capital of Detroit, created music that producers and record label owners such as Phil Spector and Berry Gordy turned into multi-million-selling hit singles, promoted across the nation on Top 40 radio and the increasingly powerful medium of television. At the same time, the emergence of a vibrant stream of African American popular music, including the commercially successful "crossover" recordings of Ray Charles and Sam Cooke, influenced the development of rock 'n' roll and marked the bifurcation of popular music into distinctive, though complexly related, streams that would come to be known and marketed as "soul" and rock." Out on the West Coast, the Beach Boys' Brian Wilson absorbed the style and sensibility of the quintessential rock 'n' roll musician/songwriter Chuck Berry, creating a string of hit singles that celebrated southern California's surf culture and pointed in the direction of the more experimental and iconoclastic achievements of the latter half of the 1960s.

In the next chapter we trace the transformation of rock 'n' roll into rock music, focusing on the seminal contributions of musicians such as the Beatles, the Rolling Stones, Brian Wilson, and Bob Dylan.

5
THE BRITISH INVASION
AND AMERICAN RESPONSES

The early 1960s was a time of consolidation, formalization, and re-evaluation for rock 'n' roll. As its first wave receded, new ideas arose for where the music should go next. There was an attempt to re-absorb rock 'n' roll into the mainstream of popular music by integrating its sound into traditional Tin Pan Alley approaches to music production, in the form of the Brill Building songwriters, Phil Spector's "wall of sound" production techniques, and new dance trends. While some historians of American popular music have argued that the mainstream of early 1960s pop music was bland and shallow—a virtual retreat from the freshness and brash energy of the "golden age" of early rock 'n' roll—we have seen that the situation was actually much more complicated and diverse. The continued evolution of popular styles grounded in African American traditions, the application of "industrial" mass-production techniques to pop music, the increasing cultural influence of television, and the rise of vigorous regional variants of rock 'n' roll such as California surf music indicate a situation that was at least somewhat in flux and full of interesting musical, and social, possibilities.

However, no one could have foreseen what must be regarded as the epochal musical event of 1960s America—the mid-decade arrival on American shores of four charismatic young musicians from the English port town of Liverpool. Americans generally regarded England as a bastion of regal traditions and cultural conservatism—even stuffiness—and certainly not as the locus of a musical movement that would challenge the American music industry, reenergize rock 'n' roll, and pull together many of the diverse strands of 1960s popular music into a powerful whole. Meet the Beatles.

THE BEATLES AND THE BRITISH INVASION

By the time the Beatles had their first Number One record in America—"I Want to Hold Your Hand," which topped the charts at the beginning of February 1964—they were established stars in Great Britain and were widely known throughout Europe. Already in 1963, spurred by the mass adulation surrounding the group across the Atlantic that had come to be known as "Beatlemania," some small American indie companies had licensed Beatles recordings for stateside release—but the group's British hits did not catch on here at first.

Much ink has been spilled over conjectures regarding the timing of the Beatles' remarkable success on American shores. Many historians of pop culture point to the impact of the assassination of President John F. Kennedy on November 22, 1963, claiming that, as a new year began, young people were hungry for a change in the prevailing national mood of solemnity, and that the Beatles provided just the ticket in the form of something novel, "exotic," uplifting, and fun. This seems a convenient but facile explanation. A more practical, if also more cynical, one might be that the Beatles really "hit" in America only when a major label, Capitol (the American label officially linked to the Beatles' British label, EMI), launched a major promotional campaign behind the first Beatles single they chose to release here, "I Want to Hold Your Hand," and its accompanying album, *Meet the Beatles*. But outpourings of mass enthusiasm for entertainers were nothing new in the America of 1964; one thinks of the manias for Frank Sinatra in the 1940s and for Elvis Presley in the 1950s. Arguably the chief common element in these and other related phenomena in the entertainment business is their unpredictability.

Still, although America has retained a cultural fascination with things British throughout its history, American Beatlemania does represent the first time this degree of adulation was bestowed on non-native rock musicians. America had been exporting its popular music to Great Britain, to Europe, and increasingly throughout the industrialized world with enormous success for a long time, but the impact of the Beatles in this country marked the significant beginning of an aggressively reciprocal process. Of course, the reciprocities involved here are deep and complex. American popular music, especially that of the twentieth century, is built on a complex amalgam of influences that may be traced to a variety of world sources. And the most direct, formative influences on the music of the Beatles themselves—and of countless other British bands of the 1960s—

The Beatles on *The Ed Sullivan Show*. Left to right: Paul McCartney, George Harrison, John Lennon, Ringo Starr. CBS/Landov.

were those of 1950s American rock 'n' roll. But their British heritage was far from the only thing that distinguished the Beatles from other artists of their era.

In contrast to the previous model of a rock 'n' roll ensemble that focused on a featured singer and their (often anonymous and interchangeable) backup musicians, the Beatles were arguably the first important rock 'n' roll *group*, in the sense that each member was of equal importance. On the most basic level, this allowed potential fans to view the band from no less than *five* different perspectives, depending on whether they identified with a specific band member or the whole group. A George Harrison fan may have had very different tastes from a Ringo Starr fan, but they were both ultimately Beatles fans.

Moreover, every member of the group sang, played at least one instrument, *and* wrote songs, a situation that had numerous implications. By merging writing, playing, and singing into a single job, the Beatles clearly aligned themselves with the rock 'n' roll tradition rather than the Brill Building/Tin Pan Alley approach, where these roles would have been separated. This also meant that the Beatles constituted a self-contained autonomous musical unit; they were not necessarily dependent on songwriters, producers, and backup musicians (or the people who hired them) for their success. This, in turn, allowed them to present themselves less as show-business professionals and more as a group of friends making music together who *just happened to have become famous.*

For this reason, the Beatles were also quite possibly the first rock 'n' roll musicians that the majority of their audience actually identified with, a quality that was reinforced by their big-screen debut, *A Hard Day's Night.* This film presented a backstage view of the life of a rock 'n' roll musician, which (according to the film) consisted mainly of joking around with friends, playing music, and running away from mobs of affectionate female fans. By sharing their offstage experiences in this way (or at least appearing to), the Beatles treated their fans as peers rather than as customers. Fan and musician became partners in crime, both resisting an uptight conformist society symbolized by virtually all of the older characters in the film. For many of the Beatles' fans, this apparent rejection of the paternalistic advice of an older generation of music business operatives echoed their own attempts to break away from parental control. After watching *A Hard Day's Night,* many young viewers could say to themselves "Hey, those guys are just like me and my friends!" This is not a reaction that most would have had after seeing Little Richard or Elvis Presley, even if they were fans of their music.

This type of identification also allowed rock fandom itself to become a road to self-definition. It has been noted that the liberating potential of this change was particularly strong for the Beatles' young female fans. While much commentary was devoted at the time to the screaming and crying crowds of young women in the Beatles' presence, it was not until later that feminist writers began to point out that such activities were actually a form of performance on the fans' part, not something that they suffered against their will. This, then, raised the question of what it was about the Beatles that young women were responding to: ". . . [W]hen we watched these joyful, androgynous young men, we saw not just a newly feminized, distinctly friendlier form of manhood," recalls feminist scholar Susan J. Douglas, "We also saw our own reflection" (Douglas 1995: 119). As the sixties wore on, the act of identifying as a fan of a particular group or style of rock 'n' roll would increasingly become a lifestyle choice as much as a musical one.

These factors not only contributed to the Beatles' popularity, but as the Beatles became the dominant group in rock 'n' roll, they came to define rock 'n' roll itself. Rock went from being something performed *for* middle-class youth to something performed *by* middle-class youth. This is the model that has more or less applied ever since.

The idea that the Beatles not only represented a musical style but also a *life* style led them to achieve a level of popularity that was unmatched before and has remained unmatched. In 1964 alone, they managed to land thirty hit singles on the *Billboard* Hot 100—on average, that's one hit song every twelve days for an entire year! On the week of April 4 alone, they had twelve singles in the Hot 100, including all of the top five, a feat that's never been equaled since.

Another, somewhat less celebrated, aspect of the Beatles' success was their understanding of the importance of publishing rights; they clearly saw themselves as songwriters as much as performers. Unlike the previous generation of rock 'n' roll musicians, who almost always sold their rights to an existing publisher, the Beatles formed their own publishing company in 1963, at the very beginning of their career. Called "Northern Songs Ltd.," it was jointly owned by the Beatles, their manager Brian Epstein, and Dick James, an established music publisher. In February of 1965, the company went public, offering 1.2 million shares of stock for sale, along with a promise to continue to register any new songs through the company until 1973. Almost a half-century later, this collection of songs, having been folded into a larger company called Sony/ATV, and jointly owned by the estate of Michael Jackson, remains one of the most valuable properties in the music business. The exact value of the Beatles' publishing rights is unknown, but as of 2004, these rights were estimated to generate approximately thirty to forty-five million dollars per year, every year, or almost a half *billion* dollars per decade.

One immediate result of the Beatles' popularity in America was to unleash a flood of recordings by British bands on the American market, an astoundingly large number of which were successful. Although the impact of many of these "British Invasion" bands was short-lived, other groups have retained substantial, long-term importance in the pop culture of this country; one thinks particularly of the Rolling Stones, the Who, and the Kinks. Another immediate result was the formation—or adaptation—of American groups to mimic distinctive aspects of "British" style, which of course included fashion (particularly Beatles-style, "mop-top" haircuts) and pseudo-English accents along with the musical characteristics that were supposed to evoke the Beatles or their countrymen. This trend found its ultimate expression in 1966 with the Monkees, a "made-for-television" band lambasted by many rock music critics because they initially didn't write most of their own material or play all of the instruments on their records. (The band, which has actually garnered increasing respect over the years, deftly satirized the judgment of rock critics in their 1968 song "Ditty Diego (War Chant)": *Hey hey, we are the Monkees, you know we love to please; A manufactured image, with no philosophies.*) An earlier and even more extreme example of the effect of the British Invasion may be found in the career of the Walker Brothers, an American group that actually went to England in 1964 to record. They became popular in England and achieved some American hits—after being marketed here as a British Invasion band! (They weren't really brothers, either!)

The close interconnections between American and British pop music that were established in the wake of the Beatles' stateside success continue to this day; among the most successful artists on the American charts in the 1990s, for example, were British acts like Eric Clapton, Elton John, Sting, and the group Oasis. Even more significantly, the British Invasion was the first of many developments that may be seen as indicative of an accelerating receptivity in America to overt pop music influences from all over the world. The Beatles themselves modeled such receptivity in their own embrace of influences from Indian music—first heard as a surface element in their employment of an Indian instrument, the sitar, in "Norwegian Wood" (a track from the album *Rubber Soul*, 1965), and later heard as a more profound influence on both the sound and structure of "Within You Without You" from *Sgt. Pepper's Lonely Hearts Club Band* (1967; see the discussion of this album in Chapter 6).

At present, "world music" is important enough in the culture of American pop to represent a distinctive marketing category, a category responsible for the sale in this country of increasing numbers of albums from international sources. And the mingling of American and world popular musics, with all their attendant reciprocal influences, continues to accelerate.

This may seem a rather elaborate heritage to trace ultimately to one group, a group that had an American chart run of just over six years before they announced their disbandment. But the remarkable thing about the Beatles is that they proved truly worthy of the early adulation heaped upon them: Up to the end of their career as a group, they continued to evolve in new and unexpected directions and to challenge themselves and their wide audience. They altered the character of pop music profoundly and bequeathed to popular culture a remarkably rich, and complex, inheritance.

We can trace the evolution of the Beatles by using the model advanced for describing the career of the Beach Boys. They started out as a performing band modeled on Buddy Holly's group, the Crickets (see Chapter 3); after some initial shifts in personnel, the Beatles achieved a stable lineup by 1962 consisting of John Lennon and George Harrison (lead and rhythm guitars and vocals), Paul McCartney (bass and vocals), and Ringo Starr (drums and occasional vocals). During their extended apprenticeship period, the Beatles played at clubs in their hometown of Liverpool and elsewhere—most famously in Hamburg, Germany—performing an imitative repertoire that centered on covers of songs by the American rock 'n' roll artists they most admired, such as Chuck Berry, Little Richard, Carl Perkins, and, naturally, Buddy Holly. (The country/rock 'n' roll duo the Everly Brothers also exercised a significant influence on the Beatles' group singing style.) Several such covers found their way onto early Beatles albums, once their manager Brian Epstein managed, after much difficulty, to get them a recording contract (in 1962). A few of these cover recordings were also eventually chart hits for the Beatles in America, among them "Matchbox," a Carl Perkins tune (Number 17, 1964) and the Beatles' best-known cover record, "Twist and Shout" (Number 2, 1964), a rhythm & blues dance number composed by Phil Medley and Bert Russell that the Beatles doubtless learned from the 1962 hit recording by the Isley Brothers.

LISTENING TO FOUR SONGS BY THE BEATLES, 1962–1966: "PLEASE PLEASE ME," "A HARD DAY'S NIGHT," "YESTERDAY," AND "ELEANOR RIGBY"

"Please Please Me" was recorded in late 1962. It was the Beatles' first Top 10 hit in Britain and was one of the songs unsuccessfully released in America in 1963. But indie label Vee-Jay re-released the single when "I Want to Hold Your Hand" began its rapid ascent on the American charts in early 1964, and before long "Please Please Me" was up in the Top 3 along with "I Want to Hold Your Hand" and another Beatles hit, "She Loves You," which had also initially been released in this country in 1963. (During a now-famous week in early April 1964 the Beatles achieved the unprecedented and still unique feat of having all of the top five records on the American charts for the week—an index of the intensity of American Beatlemania at the time.)

"Please Please Me," a fine example of the early Beatles' songwriting and performing, is a straightforward up-tempo love song in a typical AABA form. The group sings and plays it crisply, energetically, and efficiently—once through the song, and it's over, in just two minutes' time.

Still, individualistic features in the song already point to the creative energy at work in the group. The lyrics contain some clever internal rhymes, as when "complainin" is rhymed with "rain in [my heart]" at the beginning of the B section. The title itself plays with the word "please," using it both as adverb and verb. Effective rhymes and wordplay would become two trademarks of the Beatles' songwriting.

Musically, as shown in the Listening Chart, the A sections have their own distinctive internal form that proves a source of considerable interest. First, there are two identical phrases (a, a) to set the poetic couplets that open these sections. These a phrases have a basically descending melodic motion over minimal chord changes. In the rather unexpected third phrase, b, where the text consists simply of the repeated words "Come on, come on," the music becomes the focus of interest, with continuous chord changes and a steadily ascending melodic line depicting the intensity that underlies the unchanging lyrics. With the final phrase, c, a melodic

LISTENING CHART "PLEASE PLEASE ME" (1962)
Written by John Lennon and Paul McCartney; performed by the Beatles

FORM		LYRICS	DESCRIPTIVE COMMENTS
Instrumental intro			As a hook, the lead guitar and harmonica play the melody of the first two phrases of A.
A: a	0.08	*Last night . . .*	Same melody line, new words.
a	0.15	*I know . . .*	Note steady chord changes, ascending melody.
b	0.21	*Come on . . .*	High point of melody comes on words of the title.
c	0.27	*Please please me . . .*	
A: a	0.35	*You don't . . .*	Same music as before, with new words for the first two lines of the stanza.
a		*Why do I . . .*	
b		*Come on . . .*	
c		*Please please me . . .*	
B: d	1.02	*I don't . . .*	Bridge section; new music.
d′	1.09	*I do . . .*	Note change and extension at the end of this phrase, leading back to the final A.
A	1.20	*Last night . . . (etc.)*	Exact repetition of the opening A, with brief extension at the end.

high point is reached as the lyrics arrive at the words of the song's title, "Please please me," after which the melody descends once again and the harmony presents a conclusive cadence. The musical form of the A sections, a-a-b-c, also delineates the rhyme scheme in the four-line stanzas of the lyrics.

"A Hard Day's Night," a Number 1 hit in 1964, was the title song from the Beatles' first movie. It shares a few surface characteristics with "Please Please Me." The name of the song once again demonstrates wordplay, in characterizing the work experience of those who do their "hard day's work" at night—like members of a rock band. The overall form of the song is once again AABA. But the considerably more subtle and elaborate playing with formal characteristics and expectations clearly demonstrates the increasing sophistication of the Beatles' songwriting. And while the performance of the song is fully as energetic and engaging as that of "Please Please Me," some novel touches reveal the group's increasing attention to details of sound and arrangement.

In a sense, "A Hard Day's Night" may be heard as the Beatles' updating of the subject matter of the 1920s Tin Pan Alley classic "My Blue Heaven": the delights of returning home to a rewarding domestic relationship. (It is not at all unthinkable that the Beatles knew "My Blue Heaven," especially since Fats Domino had revived it and made it a hit again, in rock 'n' roll style of course, in 1956. Domino was very popular in Britain, and the Beatles eventually created an implicit tribute to his New Orleans style by writing and recording "Lady Madonna" in 1968. Domino appreciated the compliment and returned it by recording the song himself the same year.) Musically, "A Hard Day's Night" is clearly modeled on those AABA song forms in which the A sections are twelve-bar blues stanzas. But while these A sections are indeed twelve bars in length, have three four-bar phrases, and incorporate blue notes, they are not exactly traditional twelve-bar blues structures. In the *lyrics*, the Beatles begin by making a reference to the a-a-b poetic stanza common in many blues, by having the second line begin with the same words as the first (see Listening Chart). But that second line ends with different words, and the following A stanza features three completely independent lines. In the *music* of these A sections, the Beatles do not

LISTENING CHART "A HARD DAY'S NIGHT" (1964)
Written by John Lennon and Paul McCartney; performed by the Beatles

FORM		LYRICS	DESCRIPTIVE COMMENTS
Introductory guitar chord, then pause			Dissonance followed by open space creates anticipatory tension.
A	0.03	It's been a . . . It's been a . . . But when . . .	Music and lyrics of A sections are modeled on twelve-bar blues patterns but introduce significant variations.
A	0.24	You know . . . And it's . . . So why on earth . . .	Same music, new lyrics.
B	0.44	When I'm home . . .	Bridge section; new music, consisting of two similar phrases.
A	0.58	It's been a . . .	Exact repetition of the first A section.
A	1.20	[Instrumental interlude] So why on earth . . .	Guitar solo for the first eight bars, then voices return for the last phrase (four bars) of the section.
B	1.40	When I'm home . . .	As before.
A	1.54	It's been a . . .	As before.
Instrumental coda	(2.21)		Fades out.

follow the traditional chord structure of twelve-bar blues. There are chords used in addition to the traditional three (tonic, subdominant, and dominant—see the discussion of twelve-bar blues in Chapter 1), and the traditional chords do not always occur in the expected places. In particular, the usual chord change at the start of the second phrase (the move to the subdominant chord) is postponed to the start of the third and final phrase of the twelve-bar section. This yields an interesting result: although the *lyrics* to the A sections do not conform to the a-a-b pattern, the *musical* phrases do.

These musical alterations are not merely technical details, for they serve the meaning of the lyrics. It is the third line in each of the A stanzas that describes the trip home from work and the actual reuniting with the loved one. Thus it is entirely appropriate that the harmony should wait until this point to make its own anticipated move. (The harmony does return to the tonic at the expected point—in the eleventh bar—as the singer settles down with his lover at home and feels "all right," or "okay.")

Lastly, we may mention three aspects of the song's arrangement. The song begins literally with a bang: a loud, isolated guitar chord whose unexpected harsh **dissonance** is permitted to ring in the air before the song actually gets going. This is the most effective and efficient of hooks, and it also perfectly prepares the tense feelings described in the opening words of the song. Notice also the unique guitar timbre employed for the instrumental solo in the middle of the record, which allows this solo on the twelve-string guitar to stand out from the many other guitar sounds heard elsewhere throughout the performance. The very end brings an unexpected instrumental conclusion, or **coda,** as a solo guitar gently strums a repeating figure that fades out. The abrupt cessation of drums and accompanying chords underlines the relaxed character of this ending, which creates an effective counterbalance to the song's unnerving opening and surely signifies the final lifting of tension after the "hard day's night" and the settling in to the delights of being home.

"Yesterday," which reached the Number 1 position on the pop charts in 1965, may be the Beatles song with the most wide-ranging and enduring popularity; certainly it has been the one most performed by other artists, and its appeal cuts across generational and stylistic divides. The song comes across with a remarkable directness and simplicity, so natural in its verbal and melodic expression that it seems hardly to have been consciously composed. But, as we know from many previous examples of fine popular music, such an effect is difficult to achieve and almost invariably conceals much art.

As a composition, "Yesterday" obviously evokes Tin Pan Alley models. Musically, it employs a standard AABA form. Its lyrics approach the time-honored theme of broken romance in a gentle, general, and straightforward

LISTENING CHART "YESTERDAY" (1965)
Written by John Lennon and Paul McCartney; performed by the Beatles (actually Paul McCartney, vocal solo, accompanied by guitar and string ensemble)

FORM		LYRICS	DESCRIPTIVE COMMENTS
Brief intro: acoustic guitar vamp			
A	0.05	*Yesterday . . .*	Guitar accompaniment continues.
A	0.22	*Suddenly . . .*	String ensemble joins the guitar; fuller sound.
B	0.40	*Why she . . .*	Bridge section; new music, consisting of two similar phrases.
	(0.49)	*I said . . .*	
A	0.59	*Yesterday . . .*	
Repetition of B and final A sections, followed by brief coda, in which the voice hums the closing melodic phrase of A accompanied by the strings.			

manner, such that virtually anyone could understand and empathize, and virtually nobody could take offense. (One aspect of the song's appeal is that the feelings involved are utterly clear, whereas the specific situation remains vague enough to stimulate the imagination of many different listeners.) But the song may assert its kinship with Tin Pan Alley most tellingly in its emphasis on a distinctive and expressive melodic line, a line that fits the words beautifully. The melody is accompanied by equally expressive harmonies, which explore a wider range of chords than was typical for rock music at this time. The moderate tempo, and the general avoidance of any intense rhythmic effects, also distance "Yesterday" from the rock mainstream and edge it closer in spirit to Tin Pan Alley.

The Beatles' recording of "Yesterday" underlines the song's unexpected character in every way. The use of a solo voice throughout, the similarity of Paul McCartney's lyrical and unaffected style of delivery to Tin Pan Alley–style crooning, the choice of acoustic (rather than electric) guitar, the employment of orchestral string instruments to augment the accompaniment, the lack of any drums or percussion instruments, the prevailing softness of the recording—all these elements set the record apart from others of its time, including other records by the Beatles, as if to emphasize that this song is a deliberate venture into new musical territory. While anyone who had been listening carefully to the Beatles knew by 1965 that they were capable of writing beautifully melodic love ballads (such as "And I Love Her" and "If I Fell," both from the Beatles' 1964 movie *A Hard Day's Night*), "Yesterday" was designed to—and did—make listeners really sit up and take notice. Maybe the Beatles were more than just a good old rock 'n' roll band, or even more than a good new rock band. Maybe they were just something else entirely.

As you listen to "Yesterday," try to notice some of the artistry that went in to the creation and performance of this famous song. Each of the A sections begins with an isolated, essential word that serves as a decisive hook into the story (see Listening Chart); these single opening words are set to foreshortened musical phrases (one bar in length, as opposed to the standard two bars) that function equally as focusing hooks. The ascending gestures in the melody always depict the receding past ("all my troubles . . ."), while the immediately following

descending gestures always bring us back down to earth in the present ("Now it looks . . ."). The lyrics to the bridge section reveal again the Beatles' adeptness at internal rhyming ("go" and "know," "wrong" and "long"). And the final word in the bridge, "yesterday," links this B section effectively to the final A, which begins with the same word. In terms of the arrangement, we can admire how withholding the entrance of the orchestral strings until the second A section makes their arrival a wonderfully rich, intense surprise that goes splendidly with the word "suddenly."

"Eleanor Rigby," a Number 11 pop hit in 1966, was not quite the smash hit the preceding three songs were. Actually, it was issued as the B-side of "Yellow Submarine," a novelty number that went to the Number 2 position on the charts; it is a tribute to the impact of "Eleanor Rigby" that it made the charts at all, let alone that it reached nearly as high as the Top 10.

"Eleanor Rigby" is a startling song right from the outset. Without any preparation, the voices enter with a high, loud cry of "Ah," accompanied by an active string ensemble (violins, violas, and cellos). Orchestral strings are traditionally associated with soothing music—an association exemplified by a song like "Yesterday"—but here they are confined to steady, repeated chords and brief rhythmic figures, assuming functions much like those of the rhythm guitar and drums in a more typical rock configuration. The harmony is equally dislocating. The song opens on a big major chord, but after the initial vocal phrase it settles onto an unexpected minor chord. These two chords alternate throughout the song, and they are in fact the only two chords used. The restriction of the chordal vocabulary (which beautifully suits the story of repression told by the song), the oscillation between two chords that do not share a traditional harmonic relationship, and the fact that it is the second, minor chord (rather than the opening major chord) that proves to be the central focus (or tonic) of the song as a whole are all factors contributing strongly to the unique atmosphere of "Eleanor Rigby."

The subject matter of the song, loneliness, is not in itself an unusual one in pop music, but "Eleanor Rigby" looks at loneliness and the lack of human connection from a uniquely philosophical, even spiritual, viewpoint rather than from a romantic viewpoint. Eleanor Rigby and

LISTENING CHART "ELEANOR RIGBY" (1966)

Written by John Lennon and Paul McCartney; performed by the Beatles, with accompanying string ensemble

FORM		LYRICS	DESCRIPTIVE COMMENTS
Introduction		*Ah, look at . . .*	Voices and strings enter at once.
	(0.07)	*Ah, look at . . .*	Exact repetition.
Verse 1: a	0.14	*Eleanor Rigby . . .*	Solo voice, accompanied by strings marking each beat with
		Lives in . . .	a chord; unusual phrase structure creates a striking effect.
a	0.23	*Waits . . .*	
Chorus: b	0.31	*All the lonely . . .*	
b'	0.39	*All the lonely . . .*	Second phrase of chorus changes the melody to go higher than the first phrase.
Verse 2: a	0.45	*Father McKenzie . . .*	As before.
		No one . . .	
	0.54	*Look at him . . .*	
Chorus: b	1.03	*All the lonely . . .*	
b'	1.10	*All the lonely . . .*	
Introduction recurs	1.17	*Ah, look at . . .*	As before.
	(1.24)	*Ah, look at . . .*	
Verse 3: a	1.31	*Eleanor Rigby . . .*	As before.
		Nobody came.	
a	1.39	*Father McKenzie . . .*	
Chorus: b	1.48	*All the lonely . . .*	As a conclusion, the melody and lyrics of the introduction
b'	1.55	*All the lonely . . .*	are sung in counterpoint against the melody and lyrics of the chorus, then strings bring the song to an abrupt ending.

Father McKenzie, introduced in two separate verses of the song, remain isolated from one another—and from other people—in their lives. And even in death! Only Father McKenzie is even aware of Eleanor's passing; they "meet" in the third and final verse only in a graveyard that finalizes their nonrelationship, and the "good" Father can only wipe dirt from his hands as he walks away from the site of Eleanor's burial. As the lyrics say, so succinctly and eloquently, "No one was saved." This is somber stuff indeed, and it is to the Beatles' credit that the song conveys its despairing message in an efficient and utterly unsentimental way, which of course maximizes the effect.

Apart from the striking introduction, the form of the song suggests that of the traditional folk **ballad,** with verses that tell a developing story alternating with a repeated chorus (see Listening Chart). By the mid-1960s the urban folk revival had already been in full swing for years (see the next section of this chapter), so it was not surprising to see the Beatles laying claim to the folk ballad

form as they continued to expand their musical horizons. What was, and remains, surprising is their unique take on this tradition. The ballad form was conventionally used as a means of telling a large-scale, dramatic, often tragic story. And many of the urban folk performers, such as Bob Dylan, adapted the form in their original songs to serve the same kind of dramatic purpose. In "Eleanor Rigby," on the other hand, *nothing* happens in the lives of the protagonists. And that, the Beatles tell us, is the source of this tragedy.

The bowed strings take over the role of a strumming guitar in the "ballad" of "Eleanor Rigby," paradoxically giving the song a much harder edge. As you listen, notice the slight variations in the string parts from verse to verse and even in the repetitions of the chorus; they help maintain interest in the emerging story.

A few more musical details deserve mention here. The phrase structure of the verses is distinctive: a long initial phrase (of four bars): "Eleanor Rigby . . ." is answered by a very short (one-bar) phrase: "Lives in a dream." The consistent, atypical, extreme asymmetry of these paired phrases gives the song an unquiet quality of continual incompletion—especially since the shorter phrases are left to hang melodically at a relatively high point, without any conventional feeling of resolution. This is a perfect musical illustration of the incompleteness that characterizes the lives being described. (In a sense, this kind of phrase structure is the reverse of that used in "Yesterday," where the opening phrase of each section is foreshortened while the ensuing phrases blossom out to traditional lengths.) Also, in the chorus, notice how the second phrase goes higher than the first, making the question it asks even more intense and insistent.

Finally, the Beatles find extremely imaginative uses for their introductory material later on in the song, demonstrating again their originality and mastery of form. Just at the point when two successive verse-chorus sections have us convinced that we are listening to a straightforward strophic form, the introduction is unexpectedly brought back. This underlines the song's theme and helps set off the crucial third verse. Then, at the very end, the final chorus is rendered climactic rather than simply repetitive because the introduction's words and melody are sung simultaneously with it in **counterpoint**. This brings the song full circle; there is nothing left to say, and the strings bring "Eleanor Rigby" to a quick, brusque conclusion.

"Twist and Shout" was on the Beatles' first album, *Please Please Me*, released in Great Britain in 1963. By the time of this recording the Beatles were entering a period of emulation by writing some of their own songs; *Please Please Me* contains six covers and eight original selections. The Beatles' chief songwriters were Lennon and McCartney, who, at least at first, worked as a team, but eventually Harrison began to contribute songs as well, and by the end of the Beatles' career even Starr had emerged occasionally as a songwriter. The Beatles were also blessed with a sympathetic and encouraging producer in George Martin. Martin was sometimes called "the fifth Beatle" in acknowledgment of his increasingly essential role in the recording studio in the later 1960s, as the Beatles came to attempt more and more sophisticated arrangements and electronic engineering effects on their recordings.

We have chosen four representative songs to chart the Beatles' career as songwriting performers from 1962 to 1966, the year that they quit touring, gave up live performance, and went on to become the world's first famous studio rock band. (See detailed discussion pp. 116–121.) These four songs demonstrate their development from emulators to innovators; the final phase of their career is discussed in the next chapter. From very early on, the Beatles' original songs showed considerable individuality and creativity in dealing with the inherited materials of rock 'n' roll. By 1965, with the appropriately titled "Yesterday," they were revealing an ability to emulate Tin Pan Alley as well as American rockers. And with "Eleanor Rigby" in 1966, the Beatles achieved a song that was—and is—truly "beyond category," a song that helped certify their new status as not only the most popular band in the history of rock 'n' roll but also the most innovative one.

The Beatles and their music have been discussed in such detail in this book simply because the impact of their popularity and originality on American popular music has been incalculable; the group was *the* central fact of American pop culture in the 1960s. Brian Wilson viewed them as his principal rivals in the creation of innovative pop music, and even Motown's Temptations acknowledged, in their own hit song "Ball of Confusion," that "the Beatles' new record's a gas"! Thus the Beatles are an essential part of the history of American pop; or, put another way, with the arrival of the Beatles on our shores and on our charts, the history of American pop becomes unavoidably international.

THE ROLLING STONES AND OTHER BRITISH INVADERS

It was not only the Beatles' immense popularity but also the wide-ranging and eclectic character of their musical output that made their influence on American pop so great. No other 1960s band—British or American—had the range or reach of the Beatles. The other British Invasion acts that did make a long-term impact in America started as the Beatles did: with firm roots in American rhythm & blues and rock 'n' roll. But bands as diverse as the Rolling Stones, the Animals, the Who, the Kinks, Gerry & the Pacemakers, the Hollies, and Herman's Hermits all remained closer to these roots, on the whole, during their careers

The Rolling Stones on *Thank Your Lucky Stars*, a British variety show, in 1964. Photo by David Farrell/Redferns.

🎧 LISTENING TO "(I CAN'T GET NO) SATISFACTION"

The Rolling Stones excelled in presenting cover versions and original songs of an intense, gritty, and often dark character. They cultivated an image as "bad boys," in deliberate contrast to the friendly public image projected by the Beatles. Perhaps their most famous hit record is "(I Can't Get No) Satisfaction" (Number 1, 1965, composed by band members Mick Jagger and Keith Richards); with its memorable buzzing guitar "hook," its unrelenting beat, and its unabashedly self-oriented and ultimately sexual lyrics, the song perfectly exemplifies the distinctive low-down, hard-rocking essence both of the Rolling Stones themselves and of their music.

"(I Can't Get No) Satisfaction" also exemplifies the extent to which multicultural influences have always been central to rock 'n' roll, as well as the extent to which this has been forgotten. As Ned Sublette writes:

> Almost all the Stones' sixties hits, the Jagger–Richard compositions, are in Latin time. There's no better example than that "hey-hey-hey" drum break of "Satisfaction," when everything else falls away but the unvarying *1-2-cha-cha-cha* that's been going on from the first bar; it's exactly the same part that Earl Palmer played on woodblock throughout "La Bamba." The difference is that the Stones weren't playing for dancers who were actually doing the cha-cha-chá. But that insistent rhythm still had its effect, making listeners want to move, even if they no longer knew how. (Sublette 2007: 90)

than did the Beatles. Indeed, it was just at the point that the Beatles became a studio band and began producing music that was essentially uncategorizable, like "Eleanor Rigby" and many of the songs on the album *Sgt. Pepper's Lonely Hearts Club Band* (see Chapter 6), that the Rolling Stones—who to this day play international live tours—began to call themselves the "World's Greatest Rock 'n' Roll Band." Regardless of one's feelings about that claim, there is no doubt that, of all the British Invasion acts other than the Beatles, the Rolling Stones have had the greatest cumulative influence in America.

The Stones experimented occasionally in the later 1960s with unusual instrumentation and unconventional forms, as did virtually every other major British and American group—one had, after all, to keep up with the Beatles in some sense. While a record like "As Tears Go By" (Number 6, 1966) is undeniably affecting and effective, its gently somber atmosphere and employment of orchestral strings render it a highly atypical Stones opus. The core of the Rolling Stones' repertoire and of their popular appeal was, and remains, hard-driving rock music. We revisit their career in Chapter 6.

MEANWHILE, BACK IN CALIFORNIA . . .

While the other Beach Boys were out on tour, Brian Wilson was preparing his response and challenge to the Beatles, whose late 1965 album *Rubber Soul* had particularly inspired him, in the form of an elaborately produced and strikingly unconventional album called *Pet Sounds*. Less a work of rock 'n' roll than a nearly symphonic cycle of songs, *Pet Sounds* charts a progression from youthful optimism ("Wouldn't It Be Nice" and "You Still Believe in Me") to philosophical and emotional disillusionment ("I Just Wasn't Made for These Times" and "Caroline, No"). Released in mid-1966, *Pet Sounds* was arguably rock's first concept album—that is, an album conceived as an integrated whole, with interrelated songs arranged in a deliberate sequence. (The listening sequence was easier to mandate, obviously, in the days of long-playing records with two numbered sides, played on phonographs without remote controls, than in today's world of listener-programmed digital sound.) *Pet Sounds* was a modest seller compared to some other Beach Boys albums, but it had an enormous impact on musicians who heard it. With its display of diverse and unusual instrumentation, including orchestral wind instruments as well as strings; its virtuosic vocal arrangements, showcasing the songs' advanced harmonies; and its occasional formal experiments, exemplified by the AA′BCC′ form of the remarkable instrumental "Let's Go Away for Awhile," the album was state-of-the-art pop music in every sense, designed to push at the boundaries of what had been considered possible. Its historical importance is certified by Paul McCartney's affirmation that *Pet Sounds* was the single greatest influence on the Beatles' landmark 1967 album *Sgt. Pepper's Lonely Hearts Club Band* (see next chapter).

Wilson furthered his experimentation with the late 1966 single "Good Vibrations," which reached Number 1 on the charts and has remained probably the Beach Boys' most famous song (see the "Listening to" section, pp. 126–128). By this time, Wilson was also at work on an album to be called *Smile*. Eagerly anticipated for many months, *Smile* was abandoned in 1967, and the collapse of what was evidently a strikingly novel and ambitious project—even by Wilson's exceptionally high standards—marked the onset of a decline in his productivity and achievement from which he has only recently recovered. Material from the *Smile* sessions occasionally surfaced on later albums and CD compilations by the Beach Boys, hinting at how unprecedented and stunning the album was intended to be. The promise of *Smile* was finally fulfilled when Wilson returned to and completed the project in 2004.

URBAN FOLK MUSIC: BOB DYLAN

In the early 1960s, rock 'n' roll was seen primarily as dance music for teenagers, with little to offer fans as they moved into their twenties. This would probably have been true had rock 'n' roll appeared in any historical era, but the times made it particularly glaring. The rise of the Civil Rights Movement, the election of the youthful John F. Kennedy as president of the United States, and America's growing involvement in the Vietnam War made social change, civic participation, and politics in general increasingly relevant to the lives of young adults, particularly those who were going off to college for the first time. Many college students felt that it would be inconsistent to spend the day discussing sophisticated political and philosophical ideas, but then come home and listen to the "The Twist" or "Be My Baby." As a result, many of the people who were rock 'n' roll's most fervent fans when they were teenagers felt that the music no longer spoke to them by the time they turned twenty-one. Many moved on to jazz, folk music, or both.

Folk music is, by definition, the music of "the people." In this case, it was associated with working-class, rural, southerners (white and black) and their social and political struggles. It was also a people's music in the sense that its artists were not expected to be professional musicians, the chords and melodies were not technically sophisticated or difficult to learn by ear, and the contexts in which it was heard tended to be informal and noncommercial. The acoustic guitars favored by folk musicians were portable, readily accessible, and presented no elaborate barrier between performers and audiences. It was a relatively simple matter to bring an acoustic guitar along to a political meeting or demonstration, and to set it up and play it there when and if the occasion presented itself, which surely cannot be said of rock 'n' roll band equipment. The use of acoustic guitars—in contrast to the raucous, amplified sound of rock—also allowed the lyrics to be heard clearly. The words were of paramount importance in folk music, and often carried with them a subtext of political identification—with labor, with the poor, with minority groups and other peoples seen as oppressed, with a movement for international peace and understanding—depending on the nature and origins of the particular songs chosen.

Within the context of the times, then, folk music carried exactly the right connotations for college students: It was anti-commercial, concerned with social and political issues, self-consciously artistic (due to both its anti-commercialism and its lyric-heavy form), "authentic," and often even scholarly. In fact, it was not uncommon for folk performers to introduce a song with a brief speech detailing its history and social context. All of these elements stood in stark contrast to the rock 'n' roll that could be heard on the radio. It is perhaps ironic, then, that the man who was considered the embodiment of the folk movement would make his greatest contribution not by rejecting rock 'n' roll, but by embracing it.

Bob Dylan (born Robert Zimmerman, 1941) first established himself as an acoustic singer-songwriter in New York City's burgeoning urban folk scene. The early 1960s was a period of explosive growth for acoustic urban folk music. The baby boomers were reaching college age, demonstrating increasing cultural and political interests and awareness, and they represented an expanding audience both for traditionally based folk music and for newly composed "broadsides" on the issues of the day (such as the Cold War with the Soviet Union, the testing and stockpiling of nuclear arms, and racial bigotry). Encouragement and a sense of history were provided by elder statesmen of the urban folk scene, such as Pete Seeger and the Weavers (see Chapter 1), whose careers in turn were reinvigorated by the thawing of the political climate after the blacklisting days of the 1950s and by the enthusiasm of younger folk performers and their audiences. By 1962

🎧 LISTENING TO "GOOD VIBRATIONS"

"**G**ood Vibrations" may well be the most thoroughly innovative single from the singular decade of the 1960s. Virtually every aspect of the record is unusual, from the vocal arrangement to the instrumentation, from the chordal vocabulary to the overall form. Beginning with a gentle, unaccompanied sigh in a high solo voice right at the outset (which might be an anticipation of the opening word, "I," but could also be just the sighing sound "ah"), "Good Vibrations" establishes a unique world of sounds, textures, and feelings.

Probably the only remotely conventional thing about the song is its lyrics, with their admiring references to the beloved's "colorful clothes," hair, perfume, smile, and eyes. But there is something otherworldly about the lyrics as well—at least when they claim, "I don't know where, but she sends me there," or when they refer to "a blossom world," not to mention the "good vibrations" themselves. Notice also the extensive periods on the recording where lyrics are of secondary importance, or of no importance at all: the C section, the following instrumental transition, and the concluding "variations on B" section (see Listening Chart). These are in no sense secondary or unimportant portions of the record itself; it is just that here *sound* becomes more significant than *sense* (literally speaking)—or better, here the sound *becomes* the sense of the song. The sound is the way in which Wilson musically communicates the sensuous experience that is the essential subject matter of "Good Vibrations."

Form

There is no name for the form of "Good Vibrations"; it is as individual and distinctive as everything else about this recording. The best way to follow it is with the Listening Chart. The formal freedom is that much more effective because Wilson sets the listener up at first to expect a straightforward, predictable verse-chorus form with his initial ABAB pattern—since the lyrics to A change but those to B remain the same—and then goes on to present the unexpected. The C section could seem at first like a bridge, but instead of any return to A we get totally new material in D. In fact, the A music never returns at all, which is probably the second most surprising thing about this formal structure. The most surprising thing is that

Wilson somehow manages to make this unconventional form work so effectively.

It works because of subtle interconnections that are established among the different musical sections. The C section has overlapping vocal figures that are reminiscent of the vocal sounds in B sections, even though the specific music and the words are different. In the unexpected D section, the organ and percussion accompaniment maintains a kinship with the A sections, which also prominently feature those instruments. In addition, the clear presence of the words "good vibrations" in the D section provides a textual link between it and the preceding B sections, and also ties D to the concluding section, which we are calling "variations on B."

This final section requires a few comments. Its relationship with the earlier B sections is textually and musically obvious, but it is also clear that this is not a literal repetition, nor is it the kind of slight modification that would mandate a B' label. Rather, Wilson is taking verbal, musical, and vocal sound ideas from his B material and arranging them in new ways to create a section that sounds evolutionary rather than stable. We could borrow a term from classical music and call this a kind of "development" of the ideas; "development" is a term rarely if ever needed to describe formal sections of popular songs, but then most popular songs do not behave like "Good Vibrations." (Wilson employs one particularly sophisticated music device here. At the beginning of the "variations on B" he plays the characteristic chord progression of the earlier B sections, but in *reverse* order, starting on the final chord and ending on the opening chord. This allows him to proceed by then taking the opening chord again and playing the chords in the original order—but with new, textless vocal parts. The material is constantly in flux.) Remarkably, the song fades out while immersed in this development section, never having returned to its point of origin or to any other stable reference point. In a way, this is a perfect ending for a record so thoroughly liberated from traditional formal constraints.

The Song/The Recording

Anyone who would question the extent to which Brian Wilson was influenced by Phil Spector need only examine

LISTENING CHART "GOOD VIBRATIONS"
Music by Brian Wilson; lyrics by Mike Love; produced by Brian Wilson; as performed
by the Beach Boys with instrumental accompaniment; recorded 1966

FORM		LYRICS	DESCRIPTIVE COMMENTS
A		*I love the colorful clothes . . .*	High solo voice, with delicate, high-range accompaniment of organ, flutes, and eventually percussion; minor key.
B	0.26	*I'm pickin' up good vibrations . . .*	Bass voice enters, accompanied by cello, theremin, and percussion, then rest of group comes in with overlapping vocal parts; major key.
A	0.51	*Close my eyes, she's somehow closer now . . .*	As before.
B	1.16	*I'm pickin' up good vibrations . . .*	As before; formal structure up to this point suggests verse-chorus form.
C	1.42	*[soft humming at first, then more vocal activity, then:]*	Steadily building tension; no stable key.
		I don't know where, but she sends me there . . .	
Brief instrumental transition: organ and percussion	2.14		New key established (major)
D	2.22	*Gotta keep those lovin' good vibrations happenin' with her.*	Solo voice, then group, with organ accompaniment; the line of text repeats, then fades out while organ finishes the section.
Transition	2.54	*[Aah!]*	
Variations on B	2.57	*I'm pickin' up good vibrations . . .*	Full group texture, with overlapping vocal parts; major key; then voices drop out, leaving cello and theremin, which are joined by percussion before fading out; no stable key.

this recording. Beyond his general philosophy of recording and specific studio techniques, Wilson *actually used many of the same musicians* that played on Spector's biggest hits, the Wrecking Crew. Indirectly, this is also an example of the Beatles' influence. The Beatles' sudden popularity abruptly led to an expectation that rock groups should play their own instruments, a standard that many preexisting groups were not prepared to meet. As a result, for much of the late sixties, it was common practice to hire professional studio musicians for recording purposes, but to deny or downplay that fact to the public.

As a composition, "Good Vibrations" boasts memorable melodic hooks and a wide and colorful palette of chords. Both the high opening minor-key melody of the A section (which first ascends, and then descends) and the major-key bass line "I'm pickin' up good vibrations" of the B section (which first descends, and then ascends) are instantly memorable tunes—and beautifully contrasting ones. Consequently, they serve as effective landmarks for the listener who is journeying for the first time through this complex musical landscape. The D section offers a new but equally memorable melody. Some details of the harmony are indicated on the Listening Chart, for those who may wish to follow them.

The instrumentation of "Good Vibrations" is perhaps the most unusual ever employed on a hit record. Organ, flutes, solo cello, and colorful percussion instruments are all in evidence, clearly differentiating the sound of this recording from anything commonly associated with rock 'n' roll. But the ultimate exotic touch is provided by the *theremin*—the whirring, sirenlike, otherworldly instrument that appropriately illustrates the "good vibrations" in the B sections. (There is some question about whether the recording actually employed a theremin or a somewhat different instrument that sounds very much like one. But such questions are not of great significance to listeners; the exotic effect is certainly achieved!) Notice how Wilson also uses the voices of the Beach Boys as an additional choir of sound colors, pitting solo against group sounds, high voices against low, and so forth. Some prominent details of both the instrumental and vocal parts are indicated in the descriptive comments on the listening chart.

"Good Vibrations" was an extremely costly recording to produce, in terms of both time and money. Wilson tried out many different instrumental and vocal arrangements and a number of different formal schemes, committing hours and hours of rehearsal time to tape before he finally settled on the version we can hear today on record—which is actually a composite of several tapes made at various times. Thus, "Good Vibrations," which Brian Wilson called his "pocket symphony," is an important milestone in the developing history of rock production, as well as a landmark hit record of the 1960s.

even the extremely popular Kingston Trio—whose acoustic folk repertoire almost always stayed within the bounds of safe traditional material or the occasional novelty number—ventured to record Pete Seeger's poignant antiwar song "Where Have All the Flowers Gone?," unexpectedly scoring a pop hit with it (Number 21). This attests to the increasing politicization of the urban folk movement and its audiences at this time; the success of "Where Have All the Flowers Gone?" doubtless helped pave the way for that of "Blowin' in the Wind" the following year.

Bob Dylan's contemporaries in the urban folk scene included such gifted performers as Joan Baez and Judy Collins, and such talented songwriters as Tom Paxton and Phil Ochs. But Dylan stood out early for two basic reasons. First was the remarkable quality of his original songs, which reflected from the beginning a strong gift for poetic imagery and metaphor and a frequently searing intensity of feeling, sometimes moderated by a quirky sense of irony. (His interest in poetry was manifest in the choice of his new last name, borrowed from the Welsh poet Dylan Thomas.) Second was Dylan's own style of performance, which eschewed the deliberate and straightforward homeliness of the Weavers, the smooth and pop-friendly approach of the Kingston Trio and Peter, Paul, and Mary, and the lyrical beauty of Joan Baez and Judy Collins, in favor of a rough-hewn, occasionally aggressive vocal, guitar, and harmonica style that demonstrated strong affinities to rural models in blues and earlier country music. Dylan's performance style was sufficiently idiosyncratic in the context of the urban folk scene to keep him from being truly pop-marketable for years; his early songs were introduced to Top 40 audiences by other, smoother performers. Still, it may be claimed that Dylan's own performances serve the distinctive intensity of his songs more tellingly than the inevitably sweeter versions of other singers.

Bob Dylan the songwriter was introduced to many pop fans through Peter, Paul, and Mary's recording of his "Blowin' in the Wind," and to this day the song remains probably Dylan's best-known work. The opening strophe clearly reveals Dylan's gift for concise, evocative, and highly poetic lyric writing, the ability to suggest much with a few finely tuned images:

> *How many roads must a man walk down*
> *Before you call him a man?*
> *Yes, 'n' how many seas must a white dove sail*
> *Before she sleeps in the sand?*
> *Yes, 'n' how many times must the cannon balls fly*
> *Before they're forever banned?*
> *The answer, my friend, is blowin' in the wind,*
> *The answer is blowin' in the wind.*

Joan Baez in the March on Washington in 1963. ©1963 Ivan Massar/Take Stock/The Image Works.

The three successive questions build in specificity and intensity. The first question could imply many different things having to do with maturity and experience, though it was widely viewed as a criticism of America's lack of respect for African Americans. The image of the "white dove" in the second question is one traditionally associated with the idea of peace. With the third question, the subject of war becomes inescapable, and it becomes clear that Dylan is asking, in three different ways, just what it will take, and how long it will take, before humankind develops the maturity to put a stop to wars. What makes the song so poignantly effective, though, is that Dylan leaves the answer—and even the issue of whether there is an answer—up to us, and in our hands: the phrase "The answer is blowin' in the wind" returns to the deliberate, thoroughgoing ambiguity of the opening question. This effectively sets up the two additional strophes of the song, which are similarly structured as three increasingly pointed questions followed by the same ambiguous answer. Dylan's avoidance of any specific political agenda in "Blowin' in the Wind" is typical of many of his best "protest songs" and is actually a source of strength, as it helps assure their continuing relevance despite changes in the political climate. In any case, the questions posed in "Blowin' in the Wind" surely—if unfortunately—ring with a resonance not limited by the time and place of the song's creation.

As is the case with many of the finest folk songs, whether traditional or newly composed, the melody of "Blowin' in the Wind" provides a simple, functional, and immediately memorable setting for the words. In this **strophic** form, notice how Dylan's melody makes each of the three questions hang unresolved; a final feeling of **cadence** in the melody is delayed until we reach the "answer" on the last word of each strophe.

In addition to writing impressive topical songs like "Blowin' in the Wind," Dylan quickly distinguished himself as a composer of more intimate but highly original songs about human relationships. One hesitates to call a song like "Don't Think Twice, It's All Right" (also a Top 10 single for Peter, Paul, and Mary—their follow up hit to "Blowin' in the Wind") a "love song," however. Dylan himself is quoted in the liner notes to *The Freewheelin' Bob Dylan* album concerning this song: "A lot of people make it a sort of a love song—slow and easy-going. But it isn't a love song. It's a statement that maybe you can say to make yourself feel better." Dylan's gift for irony, to which we have previously referred, is exemplified memorably in the lyrics of "Don't Think Twice, It's All Right," which are basically an itemized list of his partner's faults and transgressions, with each complaint ending with the passive-aggressive assurance, "but don't think twice, it's all right." Clearly, this situation is not "all right" at all, and the blunt realism underlying Dylan's view of romantic relationships, as expressed in this song and in many others, sounded a refreshingly original note in a pop landscape where the typical treatment of relationships was still that reflected in a song like "Be My Baby," and where a relationship crisis might be represented by a date's inability to do the twist or the mashed potatoes. Dylan's own performance of "Don't Think Twice, It's All Right" does the song full justice by conveying a deep, underlying sense of personal injury—not exactly the most common sentiment among earnest folk musicians, but one that would soon become typical of rock 'n' roll. It was not for nothing that the critic Janet Maslin once described Dylan's songs about love as being of the "you-can't-fire-me-I-quit" variety (Maslin 1980: 223).

We have been stressing the innovative character of Dylan's songwriting, but he maintained important ties with folk traditions as well. Many of his original compositions were modeled, implicitly or explicitly, on the musical and poetic content of preexisting folk material. The melody of "Blowin' in the Wind" is adapted from a traditional African American anti-slavery spiritual, "No More Auction Block," which Dylan had previously recorded and copyrighted under his own name. The practice of using traditional melodies was common in folk music, and was not considered stealing. For those who even noticed, it was viewed as an additional sign of authenticity and insider knowledge. One of Dylan's most famous "protest" songs, "A Hard Rain's A-Gonna Fall," is clearly based on the old English ballad "Lord Randall"; both employ a strophic pattern, in which each strophe opens with a pair of questions addressed by a mother to her son, followed by the son's answer or answers, ending always with the same concluding line. While the melodic lines of "Lord Randall" and "A Hard Rain's

A-Gonna Fall" are distinctly similar, Dylan is never merely a mimic, and "A Hard Rain's A-Gonna Fall" introduces a highly original structural device that has no parallel in "Lord Randall": Its strophes are of widely varying lengths, depending on the number of times the third melodic phrase is repeated to changing words. (The son offers anywhere from five to twelve answers to the individual questions posed by his mother.) The concept of the "variable strophe," as we might call it, is found in a number of Dylan's finest songs, notably "Mr. Tambourine Man" and—as we shall see shortly—"Like a Rolling Stone."

Bob Dylan was important to the folk movement for many reasons. He was one of a relatively small number of folk singers that wrote their own songs, and one of an even smaller number that performed them in a style intended to make them feel as deeply authentic as the centuries-old ballads, blues songs, and spirituals that made up much of the folk repertoire. In this way, he offered the best of both worlds: the legitimacy and power of the ancient folk tradition combined with the topicality of current music. In fact, Dylan often wrote songs, such as "The Lonesome Death of Hattie Carroll," that sounded like they could have been hundreds of years old, but which in fact commented on events that had only occurred a few months earlier. He was also a member of an intimate community of young New York-based folk singers, who played in small noncommercial venues such as coffee houses and parks, where it was relatively easy for fans to interact with them on a person-to-person basis. When Bob Dylan became famous, many people in the folk scene saw him as one of their own friends—and for many, he was! Even for those who did not know him personally, his creativity was seen as representing the creativity and sincerity of the entire community, as a way of showing an older generation that—despite what rock 'n' roll may have led them to believe—the youth were capable of making great artistic and political statements in their music.

It was largely for this reason that, when Bob Dylan transformed himself into a rock 'n' roll musician in 1965, it was seen by the folk music community as a deep betrayal. From their perspective, Dylan was rejecting the social, political, and artistic principles of folk music in order to embrace the silly teen pop of rock 'n' roll. He was also viewed as rejecting the sincere and principled folk community that had supported him in order to pursue a broader audience . . . and their money. But the picture looked quite different from the perspective of rock 'n' roll: from that side of the fence, he was not rejecting the politics, poetry, maturity, sincerity, and artistic potential of folk; he was bringing those qualities *into* rock 'n' roll.

The year 1965 was the pivotal one in Bob Dylan's career, the year in which he moved from being the most distinctive songwriter among American urban folk artists to being an epochal influence on rock music. We may cite four major events that proved decisive in this extraordinary development, involving the release of an album, two hit singles (one by the Byrds and one by Dylan himself), and a live performance.

Bob Dylan as urban folk singer (1963) and as folk rocker, (1966). Getty Images.

Early in 1965 Dylan released his fifth album, *Bringing It All Back Home*, in which acoustic numbers demonstrating Dylan's now-familiar style shared disc space with songs using electric guitar and drums. In addition to adumbrating a radical shift in Dylan's sound, the album featured several songs that carried Dylan's flair for intense and unusual poetic imagery into the realm of the surreal. One such song, "Mr. Tambourine Man," which was not one of those performed by Dylan in a rock-oriented style, was covered by the fledgling California rock group the Byrds; their truncated version of "Mr. Tambourine Man," adapted to fit the customary length for radio play, soared remarkably to Number 1 in June 1965, thus becoming the first landmark *folk-rock* hit. The Byrds' combination of Dylan's lyrics and melody with a musical accompaniment that included tambourine (naturally), drums, and their own trademark electric Rickenbacker twelve-string guitar sound was unique, memorable, and—obviously, if unexpectedly—marketable. The lesson was not lost on Dylan himself, who returned to the recording studio early in the summer with a rock band to cut his own breakthrough single, "Like a Rolling Stone." This six-minute, epic pop single, which made it to Number 2 on the charts, certified that a sea change was taking place in American popular culture. (See the detailed discussion of this song on pp. 134–136.) As if to affirm that there would be no turning back, Dylan then appeared at the famous Newport Folk Festival in late July with an electric band. Many folk purists were appalled by this assault on their home turf, and Dylan was booed off the stage (returning later to do an acoustic set). But he had the last laugh, of course, as it was not long before many urban folk artists had followed his lead into the electric wonderland of rock music.

From our latter-day vantage point, all the fuss about Dylan's "going electric" can seem quite silly. The entire history of American popular music has been a story of influences, interactions, and syntheses among its various streams, and the history of rock has been no different. The steadily increasing popularity of both urban folk music and rock 'n' roll in the early 1960s made it inevitable that these two supposedly independent styles would eventually interact with one another, and even fuse to some extent. But the boost given to this fusion by the fact that the most individual and creative of the young urban folk artists, Bob Dylan, was the first to promote it—and to promote it aggressively and enthusiastically at that—should not be underestimated.

From Dylan's own point of view, he was probably just following a model already well established by performers in the genres of blues and country music, genres to which his personal performing style had always demonstrated obvious ties. Rural blues artists like Muddy Waters and Howlin' Wolf had long ago made their way to the city and developed electric blues, just as country artists like Bob Wills and Hank Williams had developed the western swing and honky-tonk styles (see Chapter 1). And these newer blues- and country-based styles had themselves played an essential role in the 1950s synthesis that is called rock 'n' roll.

By the mid-1960s changes within rock 'n' roll were already in the wind, as we have seen in previous discussions of music by the Beatles and the Beach Boys. But Bob Dylan's electric style and other manifestations of folk rock had the effect of an enormous injection of growth hormones into the pop music scene. Suddenly, it was all right—expected, even—for rock 'n' roll to be as "adult" as its baby boomer audience was now becoming itself, and rock 'n' roll abruptly grew up into rock. Pop records on serious subjects, with political and poetical lyrics, sprang up everywhere; before long, this impulse carried over into the making of ambitious concept albums, as we shall see. The later 1960s flowered into a period of intense and remarkable innovation and creativity in pop music. (Of course, the pressure to be adult and creative also inevitably led to the production of a lot of pretentious music as well.)

Dylan was, naturally, the main man to emulate. In the summer and fall of 1965 it seemed that almost everybody was either making cover records of Dylan songs or producing imitations of Dylan's songs and style. For example, both the Byrds and the pop singer Cher were on the charts during the summer with competing versions of Dylan's "All I Really Want to Do," and the first Number 1 pop hit of the fall was the politically charged, folk-rock "Eve of Destruction"—composed by the Los Angeles songwriter P. F. Sloan in an obviously Dylanesque style, complete with variable strophes, and sung in a gruff Dylanesque voice by Barry McGuire, who had been a member of the acoustic urban folk group the New Christy Minstrels. Beyond covers and imitations, Dylan's influence extended even to a group as independently established and distinctive as the Beatles. Dylan was an artist the Beatles knew and admired. The new maturity and seriousness found in the Beatles' lyrics beginning around the summer of 1965 (for examples, see "Help!" and "You've Got To Hide Your Love Away" from the soundtrack of their 1965 movie *Help!*), as well as the poetic surrealism of songs like "Strawberry Fields Forever" (1967) and "Lucy in the Sky with Diamonds" from *Sgt. Pepper's Lonely Hearts Club Band* all seem to point clearly

🎧 LISTENING TO "LIKE A ROLLING STONE"

"Like a Rolling Stone" is one of a handful of watershed recordings in the history of American popular music. It effectively put an end to previous restrictions on length, subject matter, and poetic diction that had exercised a controlling influence on the creation of pop records. Although surely other recordings had mounted some challenges to these restrictions before Dylan cut "Like a Rolling Stone," no other pop record had attacked them so comprehensively or with such complete success. After the huge acceptance of "Like a Rolling Stone," literally nothing was the same again.

In discussing the impact of this recording, its sheer *sound* must not be neglected. "Like a Rolling Stone" has an overall timbre and a sonic density that were unique for its time, owing to the exceptional prominence of *two* keyboard instruments—organ and piano—that dominate the texture even more than the electric guitars, bass, and drums. And the distinctive sound of Dylan's vocal cuts aggressively through this thick instrumental texture like a knife. It is difficult to say which was more influential on the future sound of rock: the keyboard-dominated band, or Dylan's in-your-face vocal style, which was positioned on the cutting edge between rhythmic speech and pitched song.

The density of sound and the aggressiveness of the vocal style are clearly suited to this fierce song about a young woman's fall from a state of oblivious privilege into one of desperation. The lyrics range from the bluntest realism

> You've gone to the finest school—all right,
> Miss Lonely, but you know you only used
> to get—
> juiced in it.
> Nobody's ever taught you how to live
> out on the street,
> and now you're gonna have to get—
> used to it.

to the kind of novel surrealistic imagery that Dylan was pioneering in many of his lyrics at this time:

> You used to ride on a chrome horse with

> your diplomat,
> Who carried on his shoulder a
> Siamese cat.

The chorus that concludes each strophe is typical of Dylan insofar as it provides no resolution or answers; instead, it hurls a defiant question at the song's protagonist—and at the listener:

> How does it feel
> To be without a home
> Like a complete unknown,
> Like a rolling stone?

Doubtless for many of those in Dylan's audience, reaching adulthood and venturing out on their own for the first time, this question possessed a profound and pointed relevance.

Form

"Like a Rolling Stone" reveals its antecedents in Dylan's acoustic folk style in a number of ways, the most obvious of which relate to form. Like "Blowin' in the Wind" and many of Dylan's other early compositions, "Like a Rolling Stone" falls into a strophic verse-chorus pattern (see the Listening Chart). But the strophes in "Like a Rolling Stone" are extremely long; it is as if every formal aspect present in "Blowin' in the Wind" has been enlarged to create an effect of great intensity and expansion. In the strophes of "Blowin' in the Wind," each verse consists of three questions, which are followed by the "answer" of the chorus. Each of the questions, as well as the "answer," is eight bars long; the result is a rather typical thirty-two bar formal unit. In "Like a Rolling Stone," however, the verse portions alone are forty bars in length. In the chorus portions, Dylan employs his "variable strophe" idea on a small scale but to considerable effect: The chorus in the first strophe is twenty bars long (five four-bar phrases), while in succeeding strophes the chorus expands to twenty-four bars in length (*six* four-bar phrases, the result of an additional repetition of a musical phrase, accompanying added words).

This formal expansion is necessary to accommodate the song's poetic content. The remarkable thing is that "Like a Rolling Stone" feels denser, not looser, than

LISTENING CHART "LIKE A ROLLING STONE"
Composed and performed by Bob Dylan (with unidentified instrumental accompaniment); recorded 1965

FORM		LYRICS	DESCRIPTIVE COMMENTS
[Instrumental introduction]			Note the double-keyboard sound: organ and piano.
Strophe 1: Verse	0.12	Once upon a time . . .	
Chorus	1.00	How does it feel . . .	
Strophe 2: Verse	1.34	You've gone to the finest school . . .	
Chorus [expanded]	2.23	How does it feel . . .	Note the additional phrase, which makes the chorus even longer than in strophe 1.
Strophe 3: Verse	3.02	You never turned around . . .	
Chorus [expanded]	3.51	How does it feel . . .	As in strophe 2.
Strophe 4: Verse	4.31	Princess on the steeple . . .	
Chorus [expanded]	5.19	How does it feel . . .	As in strophe 2.
[The record fades out.]			

"Blowin' in the Wind"; compare a typical phrase in the lyrics of the latter:

> How many roads must a man walk down
> Before you call him a man?

with the opening phrase of the former:

> Once upon a time you dressed so fine; you
> threw the bums a dime in your prime
> Didn't you?

Obviously, the lyrics are packed more tightly in an eight-bar phrase of "Like a Rolling Stone" than they are in a comparable eight-bar phrase of "Blowin' in the Wind." The combination of greater verbal density (note the internal rhymes in the line just quoted, which are not atypical of "Like a Rolling Stone" and add considerably to the effect) with overall formal expansion creates an ongoing, coiled-spring intensity. This is the more marked because Dylan's choruses in "Like a Rolling Stone" don't even afford the listener the comfort of an ambiguous "answer"; they only ask questions. Poetically, "Like a Rolling Stone" takes the question–answer format of "Blowin' in the Wind" and in effect turns it on its head. Finally, the attitude expressed in the lyrics is quite different from that of most other rock 'n' roll songs up to that point—the narrator not only describes the downfall of the song's subject, but he actually seems to be delighting in it.

The Song/The Recording

In a strophic form, it is obviously the lyrics that must supply a sense of continuing development. Each succeeding strophe of "Like a Rolling Stone" widens its focus, as the alienation of the protagonist from her earlier realm of privilege becomes more and more marked and painful. The opening strophe basically describes the protagonist and her behavior. The second strophe mentions the school she used to attend; the third refers to "the jugglers and the clowns" who entertained her and the "diplomat" with whom she consorted. With the final strophe, we are given a wide-angle picture of "all the pretty people" who are "drinkin', thinkin' that they got it made"—a party at which the protagonist is no longer welcome.

Dylan's music serves its purpose of reinforcing the tension embodied in the content of the lyrics. We have already discussed this in terms of the overall sound of the recording. Notice also how every phrase in the verses ends with a sense of melodic incompletion, keeping the tension alive. This is another structural similarity to "Blowin' in the Wind." And, again as in the earlier song, a cadence is reached only in the chorus portions—although this arguably has an ironic effect in "Like a Rolling Stone," since the words offer no sense of completion whatsoever at these points. (Dylan's recording of "Like a Rolling Stone" fades out rather than actually concluding—like a typical rock 'n' roll song—while his "Blowin' in the Wind" comes to a formal ending, like a typical acoustic folk song.)

One further connection with acoustic folk traditions in the recording of "Like a Rolling Stone" lies in the fact that this record is, for all intents and purposes, simply a document of a live studio performance—with minimal, if any, editing or obvious "production" effects. Dylan has remained true to this kind of sound ideal throughout his recording career, eschewing the highly produced sound typical of so much 1960s (and later) rock.

At a duration of six minutes, "Like a Rolling Stone" was by far the longest 45 r.p.m. pop single ever released up to that time. Dylan's record company knew they were making history; the time "6:00" was emblazoned on the label in huge black numerals, demanding as much attention as the title of the song and the name of the artist! At first, some record stations pared the record down to conventional length by playing only the first two of the song's four strophes. But before long the complete single was being heard widely on national radio, and an important barrier in pop music had been broken. By the end of the 1960s, pop singles lasting over seven minutes had been made—the Beatles' "Hey Jude" (1968), the biggest chart hit of the entire decade, clocked in at seven minutes, eleven seconds.

to Dylan's impact on the group. The generalized influence of urban folk music, in addition to that of Dylan specifically, on the Beatles may be heard in the basically acoustic sound of songs like "You've Got To Hide Your Love Away" and "Norwegian Wood" (from *Rubber Soul*, 1965).

Despite the popularity of "Like a Rolling Stone" and of a few singles that followed, Bob Dylan never really established himself as primarily a "singles artist." Rather, he was the first important representative of yet another pop phenomenon: the rock musician whose career was sustained essentially by albums. (Among many prominent figures who followed in these particular footsteps of Dylan, we could cite Frank Zappa, Joni Mitchell, Led Zeppelin, and the Grateful Dead.) Every single Bob Dylan album except his very first one has appeared on *Billboard* magazine's Top Pop Albums chart. Although his influence was at its peak in the 1960s—and one way to measure that peak is to remember that Dylan was the choice of the then-new *Rolling Stone* magazine for president of the United States in 1968!—Dylan has continued to be a widely admired and closely followed artist into the new century. Never content to be pigeonholed or to fall into a predictable role as elder statesman for any particular movement or musical style, Bob Dylan has over the course of his career produced a distinctive, heterogeneous, and erratic output of albums that, taken together, represent a singular testament to the spirit of pop music invention. Among these albums may be found examples of country rock (*Nashville Skyline*, 1969), what would later be termed Christian rock (*Slow Train Coming*, 1979), and even latter-day forays back into traditional acoustic folk material (*Good as I Been to You*, 1992)—along with many examples of the folk-rock approach that initially sealed his place in the pantheon of American music. As of this writing, Dylan is still touring and recording tirelessly and challenging his audiences to guess what his next move might be.

Bob Dylan's significance to rock culture cannot be overstated. He vastly expanded the acceptable subject matter for rock 'n' roll lyrics, and in so doing changed the role that rock itself played in people's lives. He raised the possibility that rock 'n' roll could be art, which in turn made it suitable for adults. By bringing the culture of folk music into rock's orbit, he provided an alternative source of identity for rock that was not primarily African American, thus implicitly resolving the question of whether white people could be authentic rock artists. The rise of a folk sensibility in rock allowed the music to be more inclusive and experimental, as ideas of professionalism were rejected in favor of a spirited amateurism. This was particularly the case with regard to singing technique, as Dylan's ragged vocal quality was far from the standard of many previous singers. In the post-Dylan era, the lack of a conventionally "good" singing voice was no longer a bar to success in rock. This, in turn, helped to shift the focus of rock 'n' roll from singing to other areas, including instrumental skill, lyrical content, and general attitude.

When the folk mentality was combined with the rock approach, a new door was opened for the future of rock: a politically engaged, intellectually mature, self-consciously artistic musical style that—not incidentally—had its roots in the same cultural heritage as many of its fans. At the same time, this development tended to marginalize African American rock 'n' roll artists. Ironically, Bob Dylan—who was unintentionally responsible for this development—was also one of the development's most vocal critics, often citing contemporary African American artists such as Smokey Robinson and Sam Cooke as influences on his songwriting.

CONCLUSION

As the first generation of rock 'n' roll fans moved into their mid-twenties, their music changed to accommodate them. Artists like the Beatles, Brian Wilson, and Bob Dylan introduced fundamental conceptual and practical innovations into rock 'n' roll music, and in so doing expanded the boundaries of the genre itself. They extended the idea, already present in the careers of pioneering performer/songwriters like Chuck Berry and Ray Charles, of the rock musician as artist, an independent and distinctive creative force that exerted control over multiple facets of the process of composing, performing, and producing music. In addition, these musicians began experimenting with both the musical form and the lyrical content of rock 'n' roll, pointing the way toward new styles and more provocative and socially engaged subject matter. In the late sixties, these trends continued, as rock became a more experimental, mature, and influential musical form, a far cry from what it had been even a few years earlier.

In the next chapter we follow this important stage in the evolution of rock music, including the work of pathbreaking artists such as the Beatles, Jimi Hendrix, and the Doors, the development of hybrid subgenres like "folk rock" and "country rock," and the emergence of influential music "scenes" in Los Angeles and San Francisco. At the same time, we consider the flowering of soul, a harder-edged, more culturally assertive genre of African American popular music, which was to cross paths with rock in the work of musicians like Otis Redding and Sly Stone.

6
FROM ROCK 'N' ROLL TO ROCK: 1965–1970

As the first generation of rock 'n' roll fans moved into their mid-twenties, their music changed to accommodate them. Artists like Bob Dylan and the Beatles introduced fundamental conceptual and practical innovations into rock 'n' roll music, and in so doing expanded the boundaries of the genre itself. In the late sixties, these trends continued, as rock became a more experimental, mature, and influential musical form, a far cry from what it had been a decade earlier.

The implications of this redefinition were reflected in a shift of terminology, from "rock 'n' roll" to "rock." The term "rock 'n' roll" had two major connotations in the mid-sixties. On one hand, it spoke of a musical genre that was primarily associated with teenagers and their concerns, and especially with dancing and young love. At the same time, as noted earlier, the phrase also reflected a strong connection to its sister genre, rhythm & blues, and by extension to African American culture generally. By the late sixties, both of these associations were being drastically rethought.

Bob Dylan's lyrics reflected maturity in both style and content, while the self-consciously artistic approach to songwriting and recording pioneered by the Beatles and the Beach Boys reflected a worldview that was more concerned with making a serious cultural statement than with getting teenagers to dance in a gymnasium. The perceived frivolity of a term like "rock 'n' roll" no longer seemed to fit. At the same time, rock's newfound experimentalism opened the door for hybrid genres that mixed elements of rock with ideas from other musical forms, including folk, classical music, and jazz. This led to the coining of increasingly precise terms for each new style. But a four-syllable term like "folk rock 'n' roll" was just difficult to say, and it was quickly shortened to "folk rock." Soon other terms followed, including "jazz rock," "country rock," "acid rock," "raga rock," and later "hard rock," "soft rock," "punk rock," and many others. The result was far-reaching: It created a sense that "rock" was the root tradition from which many new genres were suddenly branching off. And the idea that there could even be such a thing as a "rock tradition" itself represented a newfound maturity for the genre. At the same time, this sudden influx of new influences—intentionally or not—continued to de-center African American cultural values as the primary standard by which musical authenticity and quality were to be judged.

The rise of the term "rock," then, encapsulates many of the changes that rock was undergoing in the late sixties and early seventies: an increased sense of its own maturity and cultural value, a growing appreciation of its vast artistic potential, an acknowledgment of its fragmentation into distinct subgenres, and a diminishing association with African American culture. As the sixties turned to the seventies, these changes would become the foundation for a new approach to the business of popular music. In particular, the association of different genres of rock with different lifestyles, which originated as a cultural orientation in the sixties, would soon open up new opportunities for marketing and advertising that would eventually circle back to influence the music itself.

In retrospect, the late sixties were an almost perfect storm of social and musical experimentation. The baby boomers, born after World War II, now ranged in age from their late teens to mid-twenties, a time of experimentation in most people's lives. The birth control pill, approved by the United States Food and Drug Administration in 1960, separated sex from reproduction, introducing a more open attitude toward sexuality in American society. The civil rights movement brought the idea of activism and political participation into America's living rooms. And the Vietnam War was becoming an increasingly dominant factor in the lives of many Americans, especially young men. The draft associated with the war meant that millions of young men did not know whether or not they would be at war the following year, a factor that undoubtedly pushed many to take a more immediate and experimental attitude toward life in general, and toward music in particular.

There is a tendency to stereotype the late sixties as a time of "peace and love," but for many it was also time of deep uncertainty. The war, changing attitudes toward politics and culture, and the assassination of many of the era's most significant political figures (including John F. Kennedy, Malcolm X, Dr. Martin

Luther King Jr., and Robert Kennedy, among others) led to a general sense of social—and often personal—instability. The Rolling Stones' song "Gimme Shelter" (1969), often cited as an anthem of this era, reflects this idea with its repeated insistence that "war," "rape," and "murder" were "just a shot away," before concluding with the more comforting notion that "love . . . is just a kiss away." The implication that both the best and worst aspects of life were close at hand—and that either could manifest itself at any moment—is reflective of the spirit of the times.

Musically, the paradoxes of the era were first exemplified by the merging of folk and rock sensibilities in the mid-sixties, creating a musical approach that was simultaneously mature and youthful, thoughtful and energetic, wild and serious. At the same time, while the folk attitude was moving into the rock world, the rock world was exploring new technological and artistic possibilities. The former phenomenon, as we've discussed, was embodied by Bob Dylan. The latter was exemplified by the Beatles, particularly their 1967 album, *Sgt. Pepper's Lonely Hearts Club Band*. In addition, new social and cultural movements were developing that gave these technological and artistic experiments an even deeper context. The emergence of the so-called counterculture and the widespread use of psychedelic drugs led artists and fans alike to adopt a very broad view of culture's potential value.

THE INFLUENCE OF THE COUNTERCULTURE

The **counterculture** is a now-famous, but slippery, phenomenon. It was never the kind of systematic, highly organized movement that many liked to claim it was at the time (and later on). Although the mythic typical member of the counterculture was a young rock music fan who supported the civil rights movement and opposed the Vietnam War, it is important to remember that many older folks opposed the Vietnam War, and many of these probably had no special fondness for the new rock music; that many young rock music fans were apolitical, or even supporters of conservative political agendas; and that many of the same movements that promulgated utopian visions of a new, more just social order excluded most women and people of color from leadership positions. In other words, the notion of a counterculture, while it provides us with a convenient label for the more innovative, rebellious, and radical aspects of 1960s musical, political, and social culture taken all together, is inevitably a simplification, and, unless we are careful, it may involve us in a number of dubious historical fictions. What is probably most significant here, for our purposes, is to note that rock music—the 1960s descendant of 1950s rock 'n' roll—was an essential part of the definition of the counterculture, which demonstrates once again the remarkable degree of identification between the baby boomer generation and the music they chose to make and hear.

Along with rock music and radical politics, the counterculture developed its own characteristic jargon, fads, and fashions: long hair for both women and men; beards; beads; "peasant," "Eastern," and tie-dyed shirts; and blue jeans. The slang terms most often associated with hippies—"groovy," "far out," "stoned," and so on—were mainly derived from black English, a continuation of a historical pattern that goes back to nineteenth-century minstrelsy. In addition, the counterculture's fascination with "exotic" cultures—as reflected in the popularity of Indian classical music, Nehru jackets, and African dashikis—also has deep historical roots. At the same time, a distinctive openness and sense of freedom regarding sexual activity also emerged, encouraged to no small extent by the aforementioned development and marketing of the first birth-control pills for women.

Many members of the counterculture were members of the American middle class, born into families that were predominantly white, Christian or Jewish, and financially solvent. It is thus understandable that the rebellious attitude of young people during the late 1960s—as during earlier periods—focused as much on a critique of the values and social habits of the middle-class family as they did on resistance to government policies or the operations of big industry. This critical attitude toward bourgeois values and attitudes was

The Woodstock festival ushered in an era of large rock gatherings in which the communal culture was as much of a draw as the music itself. © Henry Diltz/Corbis.

perhaps quintessentially embodied in the concept of communal living, regarded as an antidote to the psychological pathologies of the nuclear family. (Some prominent San Francisco rock bands, including the Grateful Dead and the Jefferson Airplane, actually *were* communes.) These communitarian values were embodied in large, loosely bounded public events called "be-ins," which emphasized informal musical performance, spontaneity, and camaraderie. Such events were conceived as an answer to the "sit-ins" and "teach-ins" of the civil rights and anti-war movements, making an implicit argument that just "being" a countercultural person was a form of activism. This mentality was clearly reflected in the rock music of the era: If expressing a new cultural outlook was a form of activism, and rock music was the best way to express that outlook, then rock musicians were almost automatically political leaders. This communal, "let it all hang out" ethos spilled over into the large concert venues where rock music was typically played in the late 1960s, including San Francisco's Avalon Ballroom and the Fillmore West. The countercultural commitment to anti-establishment values included a variety of anarchist and libertarian philosophies. This commitment was correlated with a rejection of the romanticism of mainstream pop music, and a rejection of the commercial motivations of the big corporations that marketed pop music. (Ironically, some rock bands associated closely with the counterculture—including the Jefferson Airplane—had enough business savvy to secure lucrative contracts with major labels. Some of the biggest record corporations—for example, Columbia Records—actually promoted themselves as specializing in countercultural music.)

It is worth noting that the vast majority of countercultural rock musicians of the late sixties were veterans of the folk movement of the early sixties. Many of the values—and musical techniques—of the psychedelic music movement clearly drew from that well. The folk movement's anti-commercial attitude could be found in the many musicians of the late sixties who were in open rebellion against the mainstream music industry. The folk movement's informal approach to performance was manifested in the common practice of musicians sitting in with members of other bands, and "jamming" in the spirit of musical experimentation. Its "all for one" approach to life in general was manifested on a practical level in such things as bands living together in communal households and on a business level by equally sharing songwriting credits regardless of each individual's contribution. The connection with the folk movement could also be found in specific musical techniques, including vocal style, song structure, and even the songs themselves, which were often traditional folk songs performed in newly electrified arrangements.

The issues surrounding free love—or liberated sexuality—in the 1960s have become so controversial and mythologized (especially in light of our more recent, ongoing crises with AIDS) that straightforward discussion of them is still nearly impossible. In fact, the sexual mores of the period had surprisingly little direct effect on the style or substance of pop music. Surely there was much intricate and newly poetic probing of the *emotional* nature of relationships in the song lyrics of the era, owing chiefly to the influence of Dylan and other folk rockers. But apart from isolated, and slightly later, examples (one could cite "Love the One You're With," a hit for both Stephen Stills and the Isley Brothers in 1971, or "The Pill," a 1975 recording by country star Loretta Lynn), the sexual revolution of the 1960s seems not to have been significantly documented in the music of the time. Of course, it could also be claimed that sexuality has been at least an implicit subject in most of the popular love songs of any period and that consequently there was little need to change the basic character of love song lyrics in the 1960s to accommodate a new generation. Presumably, everybody who needed to know knew what was being sung about when a singer pleaded "I want you," whether that singer was Elvis Presley in the culturally conservative 1950s ("I Want You, I Need You, I Love You," 1956) or Bob Dylan in the culturally radical 1960s ("I Want You," 1966).

Similarly, the contemporary dilemma of drug use in American society—including the abuse of drugs by very young people—makes it hard to provide a simple, unambiguous evaluation of the counterculture's relationship to intoxicants and recreational chemicals. The catchphrase was "sex, *drugs*, and rock and roll"; and instead of (or in addition to) the alcohol of their parents' generation many young people in the 1960s came to favor psychedelic substances, particularly marijuana and LSD (lysergic acid diethylamide, or "acid"). Unquestionably there was lots of drug use, both by musicians and by their audiences, in the later 1960s. Many recordings and concerts were experienced by "stoned" young people; at least some of those recordings and concerts were probably intended by the musicians to be experienced in that way; and some of the musicians involved made the music while stoned themselves. There is, for example, no possible dispute about the subject matter of a song with a title like "Don't Bogart That Joint." But when questioned about the Beatles' song "Lucy in the Sky with Diamonds," whose title and psychedelic imagery was widely assumed to be connected to LSD, John Lennon replied that the song had been inspired by a picture drawn by his four-year-old son that the little boy had himself called "Lucy in the sky with diamonds," and Lennon disclaimed any connection between the song and drugs. (Of course, one could choose to be skeptical about Lennon's statement as well; the point is that there is no absolute "truth" that can be determined here.) Certainly the flamboyant, colorful visual effects used on rock music posters and record jackets and in the light shows at rock concerts were to some degree modeled on the experience of tripping. In the end, however, it is not easy to determine to what degree the characteristic open-endedness of many rock music performances—including the hours-long musical explorations of bands like Jefferson Airplane and the Grateful Dead—is directly attributable to drug use.

In order to put the drug culture of the 1960s into perspective, it is necessary to remember a number of things. The use and abuse of alcohol, marijuana,

cocaine, heroin, and other drugs has formed a part of the culture of musicians and their audiences in this country for a very long time. The pressures and doldrums of a performer's life have led many musicians to use stimulants, depressants, and intoxicants of various kinds, and unhealthy dependencies have naturally resulted all too frequently, prematurely snuffing out some of the brightest lights in America's musical history. (A partial list would include jazz great Charlie Parker, Hank Williams, Elvis Presley, Janis Joplin, Jerry Garcia, and Jimi Hendrix, among many others.) Furthermore, the venues in which pop music is heard live are most commonly those in which the legal—and sometimes illegal—consumption of intoxicants forms an essential aspect of the audience's "good time." In this connection, it is important to recall that during the era of Prohibition (1919–1933) the manufacture and sale of alcoholic beverages were illegal in the United States. Thus many adults who were nonplussed by younger people's consumption of illegal marijuana and LSD in the 1960s had doubtless themselves enjoyed the new pop music and jazz of the 1920s and early 1930s to the accompaniment, in speakeasy clubs or at home, of illegal bootleg liquor.

An appropriate perspective on the drug use of the 1960s would also take into account that many participants in the counterculture, including musicians and members of the rock audience, were not involved with drugs. Furthermore, along with the pleasure seekers who sought only to enjoy themselves and follow fashion while repeating the slogans of the time about "mind expansion" and "turning on," there were those who were quite seriously seeking alternatives to the prevailing American bourgeois lifestyle, who may have employed hallucinogens such as peyote, psilocybin mushrooms, and LSD carefully and sparingly as an aspect of spiritual exploration (in a manner akin to that found in certain non-Western cultures—there was, for example, a good deal of interest in Indian culture among members of the counterculture, some of it superficial and trendy but some of it assuredly serious). In the end, it appears that the value of psychoactive substances depends on the context and manner of their use; and that the drug culture of the 1960s was, at various times, both an enabler and a destroyer of musical creativity. Interviews with rock musicians of the late 1960s—now in their fifties and sixties—are notable for their lack of nostalgia in relation to drug use.

It was, and is, easy to poke fun at stereotypical images of the counterculture. Frank Zappa, assuredly a participant in the counterculture (and reportedly a non–drug user), wrote a savagely satirical song in 1967 called "Who Needs the Peace Corps?" that targeted "phony hippies" and their "psychedelic dungeons." Yet the greatest virtue of the 1960s counterculture, for all its naïveté and excesses, may be that it gave birth to and encouraged some innovative and remarkable creative manifestations, among which are certainly the works of Zappa himself. We will now look at a few of these creative reflections of, and influences on, the "age of psychedelia," beginning with the most celebrated rock album of that (and possibly all) time.

Sgt. Pepper's Lonely Hearts Club Band

Summer 1967 was the so-called Summer of Love, when many young participants in the newly self-aware counterculture were following the advice of a pop hit (actually called "San Francisco") that told them to head for San Francisco, where the Haight-Ashbury district was already a legendary center of countercultural activity, wearing flowers in their hair; see the discussion of "The San Francisco Scene" following this section. But the group celebrations called "love-ins" were not limited to San Francisco. In fact, a sense of participation in the counterculture was readily available that summer to anyone who had a phonograph and the spending money to purchase the Beatles' new album, *Sgt. Pepper's Lonely Hearts Club Band*, as revolutionary a work of pop musical art as had ever been made.

The countercultural ambience of *Sgt. Pepper* was obvious in a number of ways. The unprecedented and now-famous album cover, a wild collage of faces and figures surrounding the four Beatles dressed in full formal band regalia, pictured a number of people from many different time periods who were associated with aspects of the counterculture: Karl Marx, Oscar Wilde, Marlon Brando, and James Dean, not to mention Bob Dylan. (The figure of a young girl off to the side was dressed in a sweater that read "Welcome the Rolling Stones"!) The song that opened the second side of the record, "Within You Without You," was the most thoroughgoing of the Beatles' attempts to evoke the sound and spirit of Indian music; it featured Indian instruments (sitar and tabla, in lieu of guitars and Western drums), unusual meters and phrase structures, and deeply meditative, philosophical lyrics. The lyrics to a number of other songs had what could easily be interpreted as drug references, for those so inclined. We have already mentioned "Lucy in the Sky with Diamonds," but among other examples well noted at the time were "A Little Help from My Friends," which features the repeated line "I get high with a little help from my friends," and the concluding song "A Day in the Life," which ends the album with the famous line "I'd love to turn you on." Furthermore, the record had many musical sounds and sound effects that could be—and were—interpreted as psychedelic in inspiration. Among the most celebrated of these were the electronically distorted voices in "Lucy in the Sky with Diamonds" and the chaotic orchestral sweep upward that occurs twice in "A Day in the Life."

Arguably more important than any specific countercultural references in *Sgt. Pepper* was the way in which the album was structured to invite its listeners' participation in an implied community. The record is a clearly and cleverly organized performance that reflects an awareness of, and actually addresses, its audience. The opening song, "Sgt. Pepper's Lonely Hearts Club Band," formally introduces the "show" to come and acknowledges the listener(s) with lines like "We hope you will enjoy the show," and "You're such a lovely audience, we'd love to take you home with us." This song is reprised, with different words ("We hope you have enjoyed the show") as the penultimate selection on the album, after which the "performance" ends and the performers return to "reality" with "A Day in the Life" ("I read the news today, oh boy"). Yet even in this final song, the continued presence of the listener(s) is acknowledged, at least implicitly, with the line "I'd love to turn you on."

The Beatles' brilliant conceit of *Sgt. Pepper* as a "performance" is evident even before the music begins: the opening sounds on the record are those of a restless audience. Audience sounds of laughter and applause are heard at schematic points in both the initial presentation and the reprise of the song "Sgt. Pepper's Lonely Hearts Club Band." Yet this is clearly not a recording of an actual live performance. Virtually every song on the album features a unique instrumental arrangement significantly different from that of the songs that precede and follow it—in other words, the songs are arranged to provide maximum variety and contrast on a record album, not as a practical sequence for a live performance situation. Even more obviously, the album is full of studio-produced effects,

The *Sgt. Pepper*–era **Beatles.** Everett Collection.

the most spectacular of which are the sound collage that actually overlaps the ending of "Good Morning Good Morning" with the reprise of "Sgt. Pepper's Lonely Hearts Club Band," and the explosively distorted final chord of "A Day in the Life," which very gradually fades out over a duration of about forty-five seconds. In the employment of these effects, and in many other aspects of the album, the hand of the producer George Martin is clearly evident.

There is a profound irony in the fact that the first album made by the Beatles after they decided to abandon live performing and assume an identity solely as a recording act is an album that, in effect, mimics and creatively re-imagines the concept of performing before an audience. This irony would, of course, not be lost on Beatles fans, who were well aware of the group's highly publicized decision, and who had to wait longer for this album than for any previous one by the group. (More than nine months separated the release of *Sgt. Pepper* from that of the Beatles' immediately preceding album, *Revolver,* and that was a long time in those days.) But *Sgt. Pepper* in turn so widened and enriched the idea of what a rock album could be that, it could be argued, the gain at least somewhat balanced the loss of the Beatles as a touring group.

Rock 'n' roll had always communicated to its widest audience by means of records. *Sgt. Pepper* simply turned that established fact into a basis for brilliantly self-conscious artifice. When the Beatles sang "We'd love to take you home with us" in the opening song of the album, they must have done so with ironic recognition of the fact that it was actually their audience that takes *them* home—in the form of their records. As we have already suggested, everything about *Sgt. Pepper* is inclusionary; the rock album becomes the creator of an audience community, a community for which that album also serves as a means of communication and identity. And in fact the album achieved unprecedented success in reaching a large community, even by the Beatles' standards: It sold eight million copies and remained on *Billboard*'s album charts for more than three years.

The most historically significant fact about *Sgt. Pepper* is the way in which it definitively redirected attention from the single-song recording to the record album as the focus of where important new pop music was being made. That *Sgt. Pepper* was conceived as a totality, rather than as a collection of single songs, is apparent in many ways, but most indicative perhaps was the unprecedented marketing decision not to release any of the songs on the album as singles. (The singles gap was filled by the Beatles' release of "All You Need Is Love" in the summer of 1967, a song that would only later be collected on an album.) *Sgt. Pepper* was not the first concept album, but it was the first album to present itself to the public as a complete and unified marketing package, with a distinctive and interrelated collection of parts, all of which were unavailable in any other form: not just the songs on the record itself, but also the cover art and the inside photograph of the Beatles in their band uniforms, the complete song lyrics printed on the back of the album jacket (a first, and a precedent-setting one), the extra page of "Sgt. Pepper cut-outs" supplied with the album, and even (with the earlier pressings) a unique inner sleeve to hold the record that was adorned with "psychedelic" swirls of pink and red coloring!

Sgt. Pepper did for the rock album what Dylan's "Like a Rolling Stone" had done for the rock single. It rewrote all the rules, and things were never the same again. Countless albums appearing in the wake of *Sgt. Pepper* imitated aspects of the Beatles' tour de force, from its cover art to its printed lyrics to its use of a musical reprise, but few could approach its real substance and achievement. To their credit, the Beatles themselves did not try to imitate it but went on to other things, continuing to produce innovative music on albums and singles until they disbanded early in 1970. As of the present writing, interest in the Beatles continues unabated; their three *Anthology* collections (on discs and videos) of previously unreleased material have all been best-sellers, and in 2000 a new compilation of their top-selling singles, entitled simply *1*, was released and proved extremely popular. In November 2010, the entire Beatles catalog was made available on iTunes for the first time, bringing the Fab Four fully into the age of digital commerce.

SATANIC MAJESTIES: THE ROLLING STONES AFTER *SGT. PEPPER*

The relationship between the public images of the Beatles and the Rolling Stones—initially a marketing strategy pitting the adorable, witty mop-tops against their rougher, more street-wise cousins—took on an added dimension in December 1967 when the Stones released their "answer" to *Sgt. Pepper*, the album *Their Satanic Majesties Request*. *Satanic Majesties* reached Number 2 on the album charts, but was widely panned as a pretentious and overambitious attempt to outdo the Beatles. In the years that followed, the Stones turned more and more to their ultimate inspiration—the blues and rhythm & blues they had heard and attempted to master as youths—while continuing to cultivate the dark image suggested by the album's title.

The thick, guitar-centered sound texture that fans now associate with the Rolling Stones—and that was a template for hard rock bands to follow—wasn't fully realized until the late 1960s. In 1968 the band's guitarist, Keith Richards, began to use "open tunings," in which a guitar is tuned so that a chord may be played without fretting, or pressing down, any of the strings. This technique—used most commonly in blues and folk music—contributed greatly to the sound of hit singles like "Honky Tonk Women" and "Brown Sugar" (Number One singles in 1969 and 1971, respectively). The morally ambiguous, even malevolent image of the Rolling Stones was intensified by the release of songs like "Street Fighting Man" and "Sympathy for the Devil" (both on the 1968 album *Beggars Banquet*). And the association between the Stones and rock 'n' roll, violence, and Satanism was reinforced by the film *Gimme Shelter* (1970), which documented a free concert at the Altamont Speedway in California the

The Rolling Stones in 1967. Left to right: Charlie Watts, Mick Jagger, Bill Wyman, Keith Richards, Brian Jones. Photo by Popperfoto/Getty Images.

previous December, where members of the Hell's Angels motorcycle gang, who had been hired to provide security for the concert, killed a young black man, Meredith Hunter. Mick Jagger's desperate pleas to the audience to "keep cool" and "relax," captured in the film, did nothing to dispel the impression that the Rolling Stones were ultimately responsible for the outbreak of violence at Altamont, and for putting a definitive end to the era of Peace and Love, symbolized by the Woodstock Festival just four months earlier.

The controversy surrounding *Gimme Shelter,* and the subsequent convictions of Mick Jagger and Keith Richards on drug charges, seem only to have increased the appetite of Rolling Stones fans. Between 1971 (*Sticky Fingers*) and 1981 (*Tattoo You*) all eight of the Stones' studio albums reached the top of the American charts. In 1986, the group achieved a Top 10 hit with "Harlem Shuffle," their faithful remake of a neglected American rhythm & blues hit from 1964 by Bob and Earl.

However, while both their new releases and back catalog continue to sell well in the age of the digital download, the Rolling Stones remain, first and foremost, a live band. The album *Steel Wheels* (1989) reached Number Three on the charts, but the record was far overshadowed in economic terms by its supporting tour, which grossed over 140 million dollars and set a new watershed for box office records. The international *A Bigger Bang Tour* (2005–2007) was the highest grossing rock tour of all time, generating well over half a billion dollars in receipts. The huge concert earnings that have been generated by the Stones over the last two decades were a harbinger of the increasing importance of live performance revenues over sales of recordings, and attendance at a Rolling Stones concert today remains a badge of honor for many rock fans.

THE SAN FRANCISCO SCENE

During the late 1960s an "alternative" rock music scene, inspired in part by the Beatles' experimentalism, established itself in San Francisco. The city had already long been a center for artistic communities and subcultures, including the "beat" literary movement of the 1950s, a lively urban folk music scene, and a highly visible and vocal gay community. "Psychedelic rock," as the music played by San Francisco bands was sometimes called, encompassed a variety of styles and musical influences, including folk rock, blues, "hard rock," Latin music, and Indian classical music. In geographical terms, San Francisco's psychedelic music scene was focused on the Haight-Ashbury neighborhood, center of the counterculture. The Haight, which bordered on Golden Gate Park, was a working-class neighborhood where large groups of young people discovered they could pool their money to rent old Victorian-style homes relatively inexpensively. This led to a general spirit of youthful communalism that almost immediately began to reinforce itself once word got out to the rest of the country.

The foremost promoter of the new rock bands—and the first to cash in on the music's popularity—was Bill Graham. Like the youth who were quickly renting out older homes, Graham also took advantage of a unique economic opportunity. In the first half of the twentieth century, ballroom and swing dancing had been popular pastimes, and an earlier generation of entrepreneurs had built ballrooms across San Francisco to meet the demand. But by the late sixties, these forms of dancing had been out of fashion for decades, leaving ballroom owners desperate to rent their venues out at cheap prices, even to idealistic young people whose knowledge of the concert business was questionable at best. Graham, along with other San Francisco concert promoters such as Chet Helms, realized that these venues were perfect for the new music that was emerging. The ballrooms usually accommodated about one thousand people, featured a bar from which drinks and food could be sold, and of course had a stage suitable for dance bands. But their most distinctive feature was something they *didn't* have: seats. The ballrooms were dominated by large wooden dance floors, designed for dancers.

The open dance floor created an atmosphere where patrons could not only dance but also wander around and socialize with each other during the show, thus creating a more free and vibrant social setting than that of a theater, where they would be expected to simply sit and listen. At the same time, since the venues were inexpensive to rent, the promoters could afford to charge low admission prices. And since the audience had paid a minimal price to get in—usually less than the cost of seeing a movie—they had relatively low expectations, giving the musicians tremendous freedom to experiment. Together, these factors allowed the community to create a context in which the scene itself was almost more important than any particular musicians. In fact, it was common for people to attend shows at Graham's Fillmore Auditorium, Chet Helms' Avalon Ballroom, or the Carousel Ballroom (a venue that was actually run by the Grateful Dead) without even knowing who was playing that night! Graham in particular took advantage of this opportunity to introduce young fans to older musicians from other genres like jazz, blues, and folk by putting them on bills with established rock acts, a practice he compared to making children eat their vegetables before getting dessert. This practice served to influence both the fans and the musicians themselves to be more musically open-minded, an attitude that was quickly reflected in the integration of diverse influences into the music of the era. This is a good example of how economic, cultural, and even physical factors such as the layout of the venue can profoundly influence musical development; the locations *where* music is played can sometimes be almost as important as *what* is played.

In addition to Graham, a number of musical entrepreneurs and institutions supported the growth of the San Francisco rock music scene. Tom Donahue, a local radio DJ, challenged the mainstream Top 40 AM pop music format on San Francisco's KYA and later pioneered a new, open-ended, and eclectic broadcasting format on FM station KMPX. (Donahue is the spiritual forefather of today's alternative FM formats, including many college stations.)

Supported by both Graham and Donahue, Jefferson Airplane was the first nationally successful band to emerge out of the San Francisco psychedelic scene. Founded in 1965, the Airplane was originally a folk-rock band, performing blues and songs by Bob Dylan. Eventually they began to develop a louder, harder-edged style with a greater emphasis on open forms, instrumental improvisation, and visionary lyrics. Along with the Quicksilver Messenger Service and the Grateful Dead, Jefferson Airplane was one of the original triumvirate of San Francisco "acid rock" bands, playing at the Matrix Club (center of the San Francisco alternative nightclub scene), larger concert venues such as the Avalon Ballroom and Fillmore, and at communal outdoor events such as happenings and be-ins. In late 1965 the Airplane received an unprecedented twenty-thousand-dollar advance from RCA, one of the largest and most powerful corporations in the world. (Despite the anti-commercial rhetoric of the counterculture, this event was responsible for sparking off the formation of dozens of psychedelic bands in the Bay Area eager to cash in on the Airplane's success. Parallels to this seemingly paradoxical link between countercultural values and the good old profit motive may sometimes be observed in connection with today's "alternative" music movements.) The Airplane's 1967 LP (long-playing record album) *Surrealistic Pillow* sold over one million copies, reaching Number 3 on the pop album charts and spawning two Top 10 singles. The biggest celebrity in the group was vocalist

Grace Slick (b. 1939), who—along with Janis Joplin—was the most important female musician on the San Francisco scene.

Jefferson Airplane was introduced to a national audience by their recording of "Somebody to Love," which reached Number 5 on the national pop charts in 1967. "Somebody to Love" exemplifies the acid rock approach, including a dense musical texture with plenty of volume and lots of electronic distortion. (The process of making hit singles encouraged the band to trim its normally extended, improvised performances down to a manageable—and AM radio–friendly—three minutes.) The song itself, which originated in an act of familial composition by Grace Slick, her husband, and her brother-in-law, exemplifies the tendency of late 1960s rock musicians to compose their own material. (Another paradox of the psychedelic rock movement was that it combined the urban folk musicians' emphasis on communal creativity with the influential rock-musician-as-artist ideology represented in the work of the Beatles, Bob Dylan, and Brian Wilson.)

Grace Slick's only serious competition as queen of the San Francisco rock scene came from Janis Joplin (1943–70), the most successful white blues singer of the 1960s. Born in Port Arthur, Texas, Joplin came to San Francisco in the mid-1960s and joined a band called Big Brother and the Holding Company. Their appearance at the Monterey Pop Festival in 1967 led to a contract with Columbia Records, eager to cash in on RCA's success with Jefferson Airplane, and on the growing national audience for acid rock. Big Brother's 1968 album

Jefferson Airplane on *The Smothers Brothers Show* in 1967. A psychedelic light show was projected onto the blue screen for the television audience. © Michael Ochs Archives/Corbis.

Janis Joplin performing at the Monterey Pop Festival, 1967. Ted Streshinsky/Corbis.

Cheap Thrills—graced with a cover design by the underground comic book artist Robert Crumb—reached Number 1 on the pop charts and included a Number 12 hit single (the song "Piece of My Heart," a cover version of a 1960s R&B hit by Erma Franklin, the older sister of soul icon Aretha Franklin).

Joplin's full-tilt singing style and directness of expression were inspired by blues singers such as Bessie Smith, and by the R&B recordings of Big Mama Thornton. (Joplin rediscovered Big Mama in the late 1960s and helped to revive her performing career.) She pushed her voice unmercifully, reportedly saying that she would prefer a short, exceptional career to a long career as an unexceptional performer. Although her growling, bluesy style made her an icon for the mainly white audience for rock music, Joplin was not a success with black audiences, and she never managed to cross over to the R&B charts.

One of Joplin's most moving performances is her rendition of the George and Ira Gershwin composition "Summertime," written in 1935 for the American folk opera *Porgy and Bess*. Although this recording was criticized for the less-than-polished accompaniment provided by Big Brother and the Holding Company, Joplin's performance is riveting. She squeezes every last drop of emotion out of the song, pushing her voice to the limit, and creating not only the rough, rasping tones expected of a blues singer but also multipitched sounds called "multiphonics." The impression one retains of Janis Joplin—an impression reinforced by listening to her recordings—is actually that of a sweet, vulnerable person, whose tough exterior and heavy reliance on drugs functioned as defense mechanisms and as armor against life's disappointments.

No survey of the 1960s San Francisco rock scene would be complete without mention of the Grateful Dead, a thoroughly idiosyncratic band—actually as much an experience or institution as a band in the usual sense—whose career spanned more than three decades. "The Dead," as they are known to their passionately devoted followers, grew out of a series of bands involving Jerry Garcia (1942–95), a guitarist, banjoist, and singer who had played in various urban folk groups during the early 1960s. This shifting collective of musicians gradually took firmer shape and in 1965 was christened the Grateful Dead (a name that was extremely disturbing by the standards of the day). The Dead helped to pioneer the transition from urban folk music to folk rock to acid rock, adopting electric instruments, living communally in the Haight-Ashbury district, and participating in public LSD parties ("acid tests") before the drug was outlawed. (These experiences are chronicled in Tom Wolfe's book *The Electric Kool-Aid Acid Test*.)

In musical terms, it is hard to classify the Grateful Dead's work. For one thing, their records do not for the most part do them justice. The Dead were the quintessential "live" rock band, specializing in long jams that wander through diverse musical styles and grooves and typically terminate in unexpected places. The influence of folk music—prominent on some of their early recordings—was usually just below the surface, and a patient listener may expect to hear a kind of "sketch-map" of American popular music—including folk, blues, R&B, and country music, as well as rock 'n' roll—with occasional gestures in the direction of African or Asian music. Their repertoire of songs was huge; in any given live performance, one might have heard diverse songs from different periods in the band's existence. (This means that each performance was also a unique musical version of the band's history, at least for those who had studied it.)

The Grateful Dead (Jerry Garcia at far left) performing ca. 1980. Photo by Waring Abbott/Michael Ochs Archives/Getty Images.

If the Grateful Dead were a unique musical institution, their devoted fans—"Deadheads"—were a social phenomenon unparalleled in the history of American popular music. Traveling incessantly in psychedelically decorated buses and vans, setting up camp in every town along the tour, and generally pursuing a peaceful mode of coexistence with local authorities, hardcore Deadheads literally lived for their band. And the band reciprocated: In retrospect, one of the Grateful Dead's lasting legacies was the creation of a business model that accommodated itself to the needs of their fans, rather than forcing the fans to accommodate to them.

Somewhat ironically, this approach—which at the time was viewed as hopelessly naïve—is now seen as an important prototype for the contemporary, Internet-based music business. Relatively early in their career, it became apparent that the Grateful Dead's primary appeal lay in their highly improvisational live performances and not in the more constrained music of their records. As a result, fans began to smuggle tape recorders into venues to capture each performance, and quickly built social networks with which to trade the tapes. Although the Grateful Dead initially resisted this development, they eventually came to realize that—even from a purely economic standpoint—these tapes were actually helping them more than they were hurting them. Since their records were so different from their live performances (and record sales were minimal anyway), the tapes did not significantly detract from their recording income. On the other hand, the tapes helped to create a fan base that appreciated the nuances of the different concerts, and who would therefore want to attend many more live performances than the average rock fan. At one point in the eighties, the Grateful Dead even began to sell the rock equivalent of season tickets, called "tour packs," which granted admission to *every show* on a given tour! It is extremely unlikely that there would have been demand for such a thing had the tapes not helped to create such a devoted and knowledgeable audience. Around the same time, the band even went a step further, creating a "tapers' section" in the audience, from which fans could legally record the concerts.

Ultimately, this all led to a business model in which recordings—both those made by fans and those made by the band themselves—were viewed more as accessories to live performances than as sources of income. During the seventies and eighties, when most rock bands made the majority of their money from record sales, the Grateful Dead were virtually alone in taking this approach. More recently, however, as Internet file-sharing and other economic factors have made it increasingly difficult to profit from record sales, the Grateful Dead approach has come to look much more attractive to other artists.

Jerry Garcia died in 1995—partly as a result of longtime drug use—and the remaining members of the band have gone their separate ways. Periodically, however, the survivors assemble to hit the road together, with their huge entourage in tow. And although in the span of more than three decades the band placed only one single in the Top 40 ("Touch of Grey," a Number 9 pop hit in 1987), the thirty-odd albums recorded by the Grateful Dead continue, year by year, to sell hundreds of thousands of copies to one of the most loyal audiences in the history of American popular music.

The Doors

One of the most controversial rock bands of the sixties, the Doors, was formed in Los Angeles in 1965 by keyboardist Ray Manzarek and singer Jim Morrison (both film students at UCLA), with the addition of John Densmore on drums, and guitarist Robby Krieger. The Doors adopted their name from philosopher Aldous Huxley's 1954 book, *The Doors of Perception*, which detailed Huxley's experiences with the hallucinogen mescaline, derived from the peyote cactus.

The group never added a bass player, and their sound was dominated by Manzarek's ornate electric organ playing and Morrison's deep baritone voice and poetic, often obscure lyrics.

The Doors soon landed a steady gig as the house band at the Whisky A Go-Go nightclub on Sunset Boulevard, where they opened for acts such as Buffalo Springfield and the Turtles. They were signed by Elektra Records in 1966 and recorded their eponymous first album, featuring the hit single "Light My Fire," the following year. (Elektra, an independent label specializing mainly in folk acts, also signed a number of important rock bands, including Detroit-based proto-punk bands the MC5 and the Stooges.) *The Doors* went to Number 2, where it got stuck behind the immovable *Sgt. Pepper*.

The Doors (Jim Morrison, right) pose for their first album cover, 1967. Photo by Mark and Colleen Hayward/Getty Images.

So much attention has been focused on the persona of "Lizard King" Jim Morrison—whose Dionysian lifestyle, controversial lyrics, and early demise reinforced his potency as a symbol of countercultural rebellion—that it is easy to overlook the strictly musical impact of the group's early recordings. Although other songs on *The Doors* more explicitly challenged prevailing norms of content and taste—including "The End," a psychedelic, introspective twelve-minute meditation on the end of a romance that squeezes in an explicit reference to the Oedipal myth—it was "Light My Fire," cowritten by Krieger and Morrison, and distinguished by Ray Manzarek's classically inspired introduction and solo on the Vox electric organ, that had the greatest impact on the way that rock music was experienced and consumed in the late 1960s.

At six minutes and fifty seconds in length, the original version of the song was deemed too long for AM radio airplay, which was then still largely limited to three-minute singles (despite the success of Dylan's six-minute "Like a Rolling Stone." Elektra Records issued the original single with part of the instrumental break excised, and it shot to Number 1 on the pop charts, staying there for three weeks. Once "Light My Fire" was established as a hit, a number of Top 40 stations began to play the longer version of the song from the album, figuring that it made sense to use a hit record to hold a listener's attention for almost seven minutes of airtime. As more AM stations put the long version of "Light My Fire" into their top-three rotation, sales of *The Doors* album took off. From the perspective of the record industry, this was a potential goldmine, since albums were much more profitable than singles. The record companies began to more actively promote rock albums on radio, particularly on the still-emerging progressive FM stations, which were willing to experiment with playing extended material by emerging artists. This was a crucial development in the economy of rock music.

FOLK ROCK AND COUNTRY ROCK

The developmental trajectories of folk rock—a mixture of urban folk music and rock—and country rock—a blend of rock with country and western music, particularly the honky-tonk or "hard country" style (discussed in Chapter 1)— were closely intertwined. Folk rock emerged in the mid-1960s, as Bob Dylan's individualism, creativity, and rock 'n' roll spirit inspired young urban folk musicians to experiment with the use of electronically amplified instruments and rock style. The first and most influential of these groups was The Byrds, who followed their chart-topping version of Dylan's "Mr. Tambourine Man" (1965) with a cover of "Turn! Turn! Turn!" (Number 1, 1965), Pete Seeger's adaptation of a biblical text from the book of Ecclesiastes. (The only part of the song's lyrics composed by Seeger himself— besides "Turn, turn, turn"—was the final line, "a time for peace, I swear it's not too late," often interpreted as a plea for world peace.) The Byrds' last Top 20 hit was the psychedelic folk-rock hybrid "Eight Miles High" (Number 14 in 1966), which featured hallucinatory lyrics, ethereal vocal harmonies, and a striking guitar solo by Roger McGuinn, inspired by Indian classical music (introduced to the rock music community by the Beatles at about that time). "Eight Miles High" might well have risen even higher on the charts had many radio stations not banned it for its supposed drug-oriented lyrics.

The Byrds (Roger McGuinn, far right; David Crosby, far left) performing on British television in 1965. Photo by CA/Redferns.

The Byrds' 1968 album *Sweetheart of the Rodeo*, featuring the pianist, guitarist, and songwriter Gram Parsons (1946–73), was the first serious and effective exploration of country and western music by rock musicians during the late 1960s, and signaled a kind of revival of one of the main southern roots of rock 'n' roll, which had grown weaker as an influence during the early 1960s. *Sweetheart of the Rodeo* included songs by country music legends Merle Haggard and the Louvin Brothers, alongside country-tinged original songs, and compositions by Bob Dylan and Woody Guthrie. Members of the Byrds went on to found some of the most important rock groups of the early 1970s. Chris Hillman and Gram Parsons became members of the Flying Burrito Brothers, whose 1969 debut album, *The Gilded Palace of Sin*, forged a blend between psychedelic rock and honky-tonk country music that would have seemed utterly impossible just a few years earlier.

Another major force in the development of the folk rock and country rock genres was the band Buffalo Springfield, formed in Los Angeles in 1966. Although the band only scored one hit single ("For What It's Worth [Stop, Hey What's That Sound]," Number 7 in 1967), their three albums exerted a strong impact, and the band served as a springboard for the careers of Stephen Stills and Neil Young, who later joined Byrds' alumnus David Crosby to form the folk rock "supergroup," Crosby, Stills, Nash, and Young. (We return to the extraordinarily long and varied career of the Canadian musician Neil Young, which has spanned over forty years and thirty-four studio albums, later in our narrative.)

The Lovin' Spoonful and the Turtles represent another branch of folk rock, groups also inspired by the Byrds but tending toward a more mainstream pop sound. Led by the singer and songwriter John Sebastian, a veteran of the Greenwich Village folk music scene in New York City, the Lovin' Spoonful were among the first American groups to challenge the domination of the British Invasion bands. Between mid-1965 and the end of 1967, the group recorded one hit single after another, including "Do You Believe in Magic?" (1965), "Daydream" (1966), and "Summer in the City"—an uncharacteristically hard-edged and gritty song that topped the singles charts in 1966. The Turtles, led by vocalists Howard Kaylan and Mark Volman, started out as a California surf-rock band, but soon rebranded themselves as a folk-rock group, the Tyrtles (a tongue-in-cheek reference to the Byrds that didn't last long). Like the Byrds, the Turtles achieved their first popular success with a cover version of a Bob Dylan song, "It Ain't Me Babe," which reached Number 8 on the charts in the summer of 1965. The peak of their commercial success came two years later with the jaunty love song "Happy Together," which topped the charts in 1967. (The only thing that distinguishes "Happy Together" in a musical sense is the fact that its verses are in a minor key and its chorus in a "parallel" major key, both built upon the same tonic note, a relatively unusual approach in popular songs of the time.) In later years Kaylan and Volman joined Frank Zappa's rock-satire band The Mothers of

Invention—under the stage names "Phlorescent Leech and Eddie"—and sang backup vocals on hit records as diverse as T. Rex's "Get It On (Bang a Gong)" (1971) and Bruce Springsteen's "Hungry Heart" (1980).

ROCK AND SOUL

As rock musicians of the sixties continued to explore new stylistic influences, they no longer saw the African American tradition as their primary source of musical standards and expectations. A black musical perspective still shaped rock in certain ways, but it was no longer definitive, as it had been in the fifties. Rather than take it for granted, the rock artists of the sixties made a conscious choice to draw upon elements of African American culture (or not) in specific areas, particularly performance style and repertoire. Soul artists such as James Brown and Aretha Franklin influenced the stagecraft of rock singers like Mick Jagger and Janis Joplin, while bands drew upon the songs of artists like Wilson Pickett and Otis Redding as a rich source of exciting covers. On the surface, this phenomenon may seem similar to early rockers' cover versions of R&B songs in the fifties, and in some ways it was. But in other ways, things had changed considerably.

James Brown

Of all the stars of late sixties' soul music—including luminaries such as Aretha Franklin, Otis Redding, and Marvin Gaye—James Brown (1933–2006), the "Godfather of Soul," exerted the most profound and long-lasting influence on descendent genres such as funk and hip-hop, and on the wider field of popular music. Brown is the most frequently **sampled** artist in the history of hip-hop, and his influence has been celebrated by rock musicians such as David Byrne and Led Zeppelin guitarist Jimmy Page, who described Brown as "almost a musical genre in his own right." The film *T.A.M.I. Show*, which documents a 1964 rock 'n' roll revue in Santa Monica, California, presents the image of the still-young, and obviously somewhat terrified, Rolling Stones put in the exceedingly uncomfortable position of following James Brown's group, the Famous Flames, onstage immediately after Brown's devastatingly effective, emotionally charged performance of "Please, Please, Please." In later years Stones' guitarist Keith Richards said that choosing to follow James Brown was the biggest mistake of their careers. Certainly it was the ultimate baptism by fire for a young rock band, and it is clear in retrospect that Mick Jagger's trademark energetic onstage performing style—still in evidence nearly half a century later in his performance at the 2011 Grammy Awards show—was initially forged as a defensive response to the reigning master of soulful stagecraft, a.k.a. the "Hardest Working Man in Show Business."

James Brown's style was maximalist in its expression of emotion, and minimalist in its reliance on stripped-down, highly disciplined rhythmic structures, or grooves. His first record, "Please, Please, Please" (Number 5 R&B,

James Brown, the "Godfather of Soul," on stage in Los Angeles in 1969. Time Life Pictures/ Getty Images.

1956), which Brown wrote himself, is indicative of this approach: While the song is in the general format of a strophic 1950s R&B ballad, Brown's vocal clings obsessively to repetitions of individual words (the title "please," or even a simple "I") so that sometimes the activity of an entire strophe will center around the syncopated, strongly accented reiterations of a single syllable. The result is startling and hypnotic. Like a secular version of a transfixed preacher, Brown shows himself willing to leave the traditional notions of verbal grammar, and even meaning, behind, in an effort to convey a heightened emotional condition through the effective employment of rhythm and vocal timbre, animating repetitive ideas.

Later on, Brown would leave the structures of 1950s R&B far behind and eventually would abandon chord changes entirely in many of his pieces. By the later 1960s a characteristic Brown tune like "There Was a Time" (Number 3 R&B, Number 36 Pop, 1968) offered music focused almost exclusively on the play of rhythm and timbre, in the instrumental parts as well as in the vocal. While the singer does tell a story in this song, the vocal melody is little more than informal reiterations of a small number of brief, formulaic pitch shapes; the harmony is completely static, with the instrumental parts reduced to repeating riffs or held chords. But this description does the song scant justice—when performed by Brown and his band, its effect is mesmerizing. James Brown's fully developed version of soul is a music of exquisitely focused intensity, devoted to demonstrating the truth of the saying "less is more."

As influential as his recordings were and are, Brown was, above all, an artist who exulted and excelled in live performance, where his acrobatic physicality and extraordinary personal charisma added great excitement to the vocal improvisations he spun over the ever-tight accompaniment of his band. A typical Brown show ended with the singer on his knees, evoking once again the intensity of the gospel preacher as he exhorted his "congregation," "Please, please, please!" Although he was not the first pop artist to release a "live" album, Brown's *Live at the Apollo*, recorded in concert at the famed Apollo Theater in Harlem in late 1962, proved an important pop breakthrough both for him and for the idea of the concert album, as it reached the Number 2 position on the *Billboard* chart of bestselling albums in 1963 and remained on that chart for well over a year. In particular, the album allowed the listener to experience without interruption an example of one of Brown's remarkable extended "medleys," in which several of his songs would be strung directly together, without dropping a single beat, to produce a cumulative effect of steadily mounting excitement. Many pop artists since have released "live" albums—in fact, the "live" album has become virtually an expected event in the recording career of any artist with a significant following—but few have matched the sheer visceral thrill of James Brown's *Live at the Apollo*.

Aretha Franklin

Beginning with "I Never Loved a Man (The Way I Love You)" (Number 1 R&B, Number 9 Pop, 1967), Aretha Franklin (b. 1942) produced an exceptional and virtually uninterrupted stream of hit records over a five-year period that included thirteen million-sellers and thirteen Top 10 pop hits. Unlike artists such as Ray Charles and James Brown, Franklin literally grew up with gospel music; her father was the Reverend C. L. Franklin, the pastor for a large Baptist congregation in Detroit and himself an acclaimed gospel singer. Aretha Franklin's first recordings were as a gospel singer, at the age of fourteen, and she occasionally returned to recording gospel music even in the midst of her career as a pop singer—most spectacularly with the live album *Amazing Grace* (1972), which was actually recorded in a church. *Amazing Grace* built on Franklin's established popularity to introduce legions of pop music fans to the power of gospel music. The album was a Top 10 bestseller and the most successful album of Franklin's entire career; it sold over two million copies.

Aretha Franklin performing on television, 1967. Courtesy Library of Congress.

What is most important about Aretha Franklin is the overwhelming power and intensity of her vocal delivery. Into a pop culture that had almost totally identified female singers with gentility, docility, and sentimentality, her voice blew huge gusts of revisionist fresh air. When she demanded "respect" (in her cover of Otis Redding's song of the same name), or exhorted her audience to "think about what you're trying to do to me" (in the hit recording "Think" of 1968, which she cowrote), the strength of her interpretations arguably moved her songs beyond the traditional realm of personal intimate relationships and into the larger political and social spheres. Especially in the context of the late 1960s, with the civil rights and black power movements at their heights, and the movement for women's empowerment undergoing its initial stirrings, it was difficult *not* to hear large-scale ramifications in the records of this extraordinary African American woman. Although Aretha Franklin did not become an overtly political figure in the way that James Brown did, it may be claimed that she nevertheless made strong political and social statements just through the very character of her performances.

Directly tied to this issue is the fact that Franklin was not only a vocal interpreter on her records but also—like Charles and Brown—a major player in many aspects of their sound and production. She wrote or cowrote a significant portion of her repertoire (this involvement goes back to her early days at Columbia Records). In addition, Franklin is a powerful keyboard player; her piano is heard to great advantage on many of her recordings. And she also provided vocal arrangements, which were colored by the call and response of the gospel traditions in which she was raised.

In other words, Franklin not only symbolized female empowerment in the sound of her records but also actualized female empowerment in the process of making them. By the time she recorded a tune called "Sisters Are Doin' It for Themselves" (with Eurythmics) in 1985, she was, in effect, telling a story that had been personally true of her for a long time. But in the 1960s female empowerment was something quite new and important in the history of pop music, and it influenced rock in several ways. One was in the rise of female singers, such as Janis Joplin, whose vocal style and stage personae presented them as active agents of their own romantic fate rather than passive recipients of male desire. Joplin openly cited Franklin as an inspiration, and—as previously mentioned—one of her biggest hits was her defiant cover of "Piece of My Heart," a song originally recorded by Aretha Franklin's sister, Erma Franklin.

By participating in the arrangement and production of her songs, Franklin also inspired a rising generation of female singer-songwriters, such as Laura Nyro, Joni Mitchell, and Carole King. King, who began her career as a Brill Building songwriter and later became a performer in her own right, presents an especially interesting example of the complex interactions of gender, race, and musical genre in this era. As we discuss in the next chapter, Carole King's solo debut *Tapestry* (1971) was the most successful album of the singer-songwriter era, ultimately selling over twenty-five million copies worldwide. A major selling point of the album was King's cover version of "(You Make Me Feel Like) A Natural Woman," a song that had previously been a Top 10 pop hit for Aretha Franklin in 1967. At this point this may seem like a typical case of a white artist covering a song that had been a hit a few years earlier for an African American artist, but the story is different in two ways. First, the vast majority of King's listeners were familiar with the original recording of the song, and thus interpreted her version in comparison to Franklin's version, rather than in place of it. And second, the song's original author was Carole King herself; she had written it specifically for Aretha Franklin. The questions of whose relationship to the song was more personal (the original writer's or the original singer's?), which of each artist's stylistic choices influenced the other's, and even which genre the song "really" belongs to, defy simple answers.

Otis Redding, Stax Records, and the Relationship of Rock and Soul

Though in many ways "A Natural Woman" was a unique case, the overall relationship between rock artists and the soul repertoire was far more complex in the late sixties than such relationships had been even ten years earlier. Largely as a result of the folk music culture of the early sixties, rock's sense of authenticity increasingly became tied to its influences, and the role of cover versions was reinterpreted in this light. Like folk singers, rock artists of the late sixties tended to use cover versions as statements of cultural solidarity with the original artists, which made them more likely to celebrate the song's origins than to obscure them. The rockers' knowledge and appreciation of the original artists was also intended to serve as a testament to the sophistication and diversity of their own musical tastes. In fact, many of the rock musicians who covered soul songs in the sixties not only acknowledged the original artists, they actively worked to get them recognition and performance opportunities (the Rolling Stones were particularly active in this regard, advocating on behalf of such African American musicians as Howlin' Wolf, Ike and Tina Turner, and Stevie Wonder, among many others). As a result of this advocacy, it was not uncommon in this era for a soul artist essentially to have two parallel audiences—among soul and rock listeners.

A particularly striking example of this was Memphis-based soul singer <u>Otis Redding</u> (1941–67), who not only performed at the Monterey Pop Festival (considered one of the most important concerts of the psychedelic rock era), but also at the Fillmore Auditorium, the epicenter of the San Francisco counterculture. "Every artist in the city asked to open for Otis," remembered the venue's owner, Bill Graham. "The first night, it was the Grateful Dead. Janis Joplin came at three in the afternoon the day of the first show to make sure that she'd be in front. To this day, no musician ever got everybody out to see them the way he did" (Graham & Greenfield 1992: 174). Significantly, while many rock artists covered Otis Redding's songs, Otis Redding was also known to cover songs by such rock artists as the Rolling Stones ("Satisfaction") and the Beatles ("Day Tripper").

Otis had emerged from Memphis, Tennessee's Stax Records, a company that in many ways exemplified the southern soul sound. Founded in 1957 as Satellite Records, the label initially specialized in country music and pop recordings. By the early 1960s the company had changed its name, established a national distribution deal with New York–based Atlantic Records, and undergone a thorough stylistic transformation, propelled by a formidable "house band" that included pianist Booker T. Jones, bassist Donald "Duck" Dunn, guitarist Steve Cropper, and drummer Al Jackson, Jr. (These four musicians formed the core of the band Booker T. & The MGs, a racially integrated instrumental soul combo that scored a series of hit singles in the 1960s; Cropper and Dunn went on to anchor the band in the 1980 comedy film *The Blues Brothers*.) This core group, with the addition of musicians like Isaac Hayes (more recently the voice of the character Chef on *South Park*), accompanied a rising generation of soul music stars, including Aretha Franklin, Wilson Pickett, and Otis Redding, and was responsible for producing almost all of the Stax label's output from about 1962 through 1969. The Stax recording studio, housed in a converted movie theater, was the primary birthplace of "southern soul," a style that blended aspects of rhythm & blues and rock 'n' roll.

The use of the term "soul" to describe this genre was no accident. An important social aspect of the civil rights movement of the early sixties was its embrace of African American cultural norms as being distinctive and worthy of celebration, in much the same way that other ethnicities celebrated the cultures of their nations of origin. The term "soul" eventually became a general term for manifestations of African American culture in various areas of life. Characteristically African

American food preferences, for example, were termed "soul food," just as music that emphasized its African American roots had become "soul music."

In the mid-sixties, Stax played up its southern soul orientation by becoming involved in a rivalry with Motown records that allowed each label to accentuate its distinctive approach by contrasting it with that of the other. While Motown had proclaimed its mainstream aspirations by adopting the slogan "the Sound of Young America," Stax emphasized its southern roots, "down-home" aesthetic and commitment to African American audiences with the slogan "the Sound of Black America." In contrast to Motown's pursuit of mainstream audiences for both its recordings and live performances, Stax sought more traditional outlets, focusing on both African American radio and traditionally African American performance venues. Somewhat ironically, this emphasis on African American racial identity may have been precisely the element that made Stax music attractive to white rock musicians in the late sixties. Influenced by the folk ideal, these musicians were already comfortable with the idea of music as a marker of "authentic" ethnic identity, especially when—as noted previously—it could be used to bolster their own musical credibility. It is interesting to note that it was a Stax artist that played the Monterey Pop Festival and not a Motown artist. In another layer of irony, it is also worth mentioning that Motown, the supposed "crossover" label, was black-owned and operated, and almost all of the musicians and songwriters they employed were also African American. Meanwhile, Stax, the label that emphasized its commitment to the African American community, was white-owned, and (as noted earlier) many of the musicians that helped to create their proudly African American sound were not themselves African American. These contrasts serve to remind us that race, perceptions of racial authenticity, and *performances* of racial authenticity are rarely, if ever, clear-cut; in fact, this is arguably why music is such a powerful tool for addressing such issues, since it is capable of carrying multiple, sometimes ambiguous meanings. Regardless of how one chooses to interpret these relationships, however, one thing is certain: Though the specific racial issues of the late sixties were in some ways quite different from those of the fifties, the *concept* of race—and the complexities it engendered—remained central to rock music.

Sly Stone and Santana: The Rebirth of Rock Multiculturalism

Two bands that emerged from the San Francisco Bay Area—Sly and the Family Stone and Santana—reveal a nascent trend within rock music toward multicultural engagement. By bringing African American and Latin American perspectives, respectively, back to rock, they cleared new paths for all rock musicians.

Sly Stone (Sylvester Stewart) was born in Dallas, Texas, in 1944, and moved to Vallejo, California, with his family in the 1950s. He began his musical career at the age of four as a gospel singer, went on to study trumpet, music theory, and composition in college, and later worked as a disc jockey at both R&B and rock-oriented radio stations in the San Francisco Bay area. Sly formed his first band (the Stoners) in 1966 and gradually developed a style that reflected his own diverse musical experience: a blend of jazz, soul music, San Francisco psychedelia, and the socially engaged lyrics of folk rock. The Family Stone's national popularity was boosted by their fiery performance at the Woodstock Festival in 1969, which appeared in the film and soundtrack album *Woodstock*.

Between 1968 and 1971 Sly and the Family Stone recorded a series of albums and singles that reached the top of both the pop and soul charts. Recordings like "Dance to the Music" (Number 8 Pop and Number 9 R&B

Sly and the Family Stone in New York City (ca. 1975). David Redfern/Redferns/Retna, Ltd.

in 1968), the double-sided hit singles "Everyday People"/"Sing a Simple Song" (Number 1 Pop and R&B in 1969) and "Thank You (Falletinme Be Mice Elf Again)"/"Everybody Is a Star" (Number 1 Pop and R&B in 1970), and their last big crossover hit, "Family Affair" (Number 1 Pop and R&B, 1971) exerted a big influence on funk music. The sound of the Family Stone was anchored by the electric bass of Larry Graham—positioned prominently in the studio mix—and by an approach to arranging that made the whole band, including the horn section, into a collective rhythm section.

Sly Stone's contributions to rock and soul music are manifold, not the least of which was simply the fact that he was considered to be a central figure in both genres simultaneously. This was no accident: A major part of Stone's agenda was to combine the influences—and audiences—of rock, soul, and later funk music. This agenda can even be seen in the assembly of the group itself. Stone intentionally chose men and women from diverse backgrounds—including a white drummer and female trumpet player—as a symbolic statement of the ability of people from different backgrounds to overcome their differences and work together. Beyond the visual and symbolic nods to integration, the instrumentation of the group also reflected a similar outlook, mixing a horn section typical of soul music with distorted electric guitars typical of San Francisco rock, and complex lyrics that showed a strong influence from Bob Dylan. Another aspect of Sly Stone's appeal that is often overlooked is his extensive use of a Beatles-influenced approach to studio recording, using the studio itself to create art, rather than just capture a performance. His work in this area was tremendously influential on soul and funk music and can be heard in the later work of artists like Marvin Gaye, Stevie Wonder, and the Jackson Five.

Santana was led by guitarist Carlos Santana (b. 1947, in Mexico), who began his musical career playing guitar in the nightspots of Tijuana. As a kid he was exposed to the sounds of rock 'n' roll, including the music of Mexican American musicians such as Ritchie Valens, whose version of the folk song "La Bamba" had broken into the *Billboard* Top 40 in early 1959. (See Chapter 3.) Santana moved to San Francisco at age fifteen, where he was exposed to other forms of music that were to play a profound part in shaping the style and sensibility of his music: jazz, particularly the experimental music of John Coltrane and Miles Davis; salsa, a New York–based style of Latin dance music strongly rooted in Afro-Cuban traditions; and, in the late 1960s, San Francisco rock, including artists as diverse as Janis Joplin, Jimi Hendrix, and Sly and the Family Stone. Around 1968 Santana put together a group of middle- and working-class Latino, black, and white musicians from varied cultural backgrounds. Interestingly, one of Santana's biggest supporters was the promoter Bill Graham, who had grown up in New York City listening to Latin music, and who felt that Santana was the perfect group to bring these influences into rock. In fact, Graham felt so strongly about this that he pressured the organizers of the Woodstock festival to put Santana on the bill, despite the fact that the group had not yet released its first record and was largely unknown. Their performance, which can be seen in the film *Woodstock*, was considered one of the highlights of the festival, and is credited with introducing Santana to the world. The band's eponymous first album, *Santana*, released later in 1969, reached Number 4 on the Top LPs chart.

In 1970 Columbia Records released Santana's second LP, which firmly established both the band itself and a strong Latin American substream within rock music. *Abraxas* held the Number 1 position on the LP charts for six weeks, spent a total of eighty-eight weeks on the charts, and sold over four million copies in the United States alone. The album also produced two Top 40 singles: "Black Magic Woman" (Number

Carlos Santana performing at Woodstock. Photo courtesy Warner Bros/ Photofest.

4 Pop in 1970), originally recorded by the English blues rock band Fleetwood Mac; and the infectious "Oye Como Va" (Number 13 Pop, Number 32 R&B in 1971), composed by New York Latin percussionist and dance music king Tito Puente. These two singles, which had a great deal to do with the success of the album, were shorter versions of the tracks found on the LP. (This was a typical strategy, given the duration of tracks on many rock LPs.) Tying blues, rock, and salsa together in one multicultural package, *Abraxas* also featured less commercial tracks such as "Gypsy Queen" (composed by the jazz guitarist Gabor Szabo), and the impressionistic "Singing Winds, Crying Beasts." We will take a closer look at the LP version of "Oye Como Va," since it allows the band to stretch out a bit and best illustrates certain features of Santana's style.

In thinking about how the boundaries of the rock genre have continuously been redefined over the years, it is interesting to note that most observers at the time cited the performances of Santana, Sly and the Family Stone, and Jimi Hendrix (see the next section of this chapter) as the most impressive of the Woodstock festival. The fact that the three most acclaimed performances at the most important festival in the history of rock were all by nonwhite musicians stands in stark contrast to the widespread perception of rock as a form of music that tends to exclude these communities. So how can we account for this apparent contradiction?

First and foremost, of course, was the general celebration of multiculturalism in the immediate post–civil rights era, and particularly in the counterculture of the late sixties. This is reflected in the fact that all three of these acts—though fronted by musicians of color—had members from a

🎧 LISTENING TO "OYE COMO VA"

To appreciate what goes into a recording like "Oye Como Va," we must consider not only the instrumentation—essentially a guitar-bass-keyboards-drums rock band plus Latin percussion—but also the recording's "mix," that is, the precise tonal quality, balancing, and positioning of sounds recorded on various tracks in the studio. (*Abraxas* was coproduced by the band and Fred Catero, whose straightforward approach to studio production can also be heard on early LPs of the jazz rock band Chicago.) Santana's instantly recognizable sound focused on the fluid lead guitar style of Carlos Santana and the churning grooves created by the drummer (Mike Shrieve), the bass player (Dave Brown), and two Latin percussionists (José Areas and Mike Carabello). The rhythmic complexity of "Oye Como Va"—essentially an electrified version of an Afro-Cuban dance rhythm—required that the recording be mixed to create a "clean" stereo image, so that the various instruments and interlocking rhythm patterns could be clearly heard. Listening over headphones or good speakers, you should be able to hear where the various instruments are positioned in the mix. The electric bass is in the middle, acting as the band's rhythmic anchor; the guitar and keyboards are placed slightly to the left and right of center, respectively, and thus kept out of each other's way; and the percussion instruments (including *güiro*, a ridged gourd scraped with a small stick; *timbales*, a set of two drums played with flexible sticks; *agogo*, a metal bell; and *congas*, hand-played drums) are positioned even farther out to the left and right.

The track opens with the electric bass and Hammond B-3 organ—one of the most characteristic sounds of 1970s rock music—playing the interlocking pattern that functions as the core of the groove throughout the recording. (In a salsa band, this two-measure pattern would be called the *tumbao*.) In the background we hear someone say "Sabor!" ("Flavor!"), and at the end of the fourth measure the *timbales* and *agogo* enter, bringing in the rest of the instruments at the beginning of the fifth measure. At this point all of the interlocking repeated patterns—bass, organ, bell, scraper, and congas—have been established. The signature sound of Carlos Santana's guitar enters in the ninth measure, as he plays a two-measure melodic theme four times. This is followed by the first of four sections in which the whole band plays a single rhythmic and melodic pattern in unison (see the Listening Chart, where we call these sections B and B9, respectively). Throughout the track, the rhythm functions as the heart of the music. As if to remind us of the importance of this deep connection with Afro-Latin tradition, all of the other layers are periodically stripped away, laying bare the pulsing heart of the music.

At the most general level, we can make a few observations about how the four minutes and seventeen seconds of "Oye Como Va" are organized. The whole arrangement is 136 measures in length; out of that total only 16 measures (about 12 percent of the total) is devoted to singing, which in this context seems almost a pretext for the instrumental music. In general, song lyrics are less important than the musical groove and texture in most of Santana's early recordings. (The lyric for this song consists of a short phrase in Spanish, repeated over and over, in which the singer boasts about the potency of his "groove" to a brown-skinned female dancer.)

Taking away the other obviously precomposed elements—the guitar melody (phrase A), unison figures played by the whole band (B, B9, and the call-and-response figure after the first guitar solo), and the other interlude sections—we find that nearly half of the recording (66 measures) is devoted to improvised solos by the guitar and organ. The other elements of the arrangement—including the dramatic group crescendos (increases in volume) that lead into the last two solos—seem designed to support improvisation. In essence, then, "Oye Como Va" is a vehicle for instrumental soloing, more like a jazz performance than a Top 40 pop song. (Of course, it is precisely the solos that Columbia Records chose to cut when they edited the track for AM radio airplay.) In particular, Carlos Santana's solos on "Oye Como Va" provide us with a good example of the work of a talented rock improviser. Rather than playing torrents of fast notes to show off his guitar technique (which was and remains considerable), Santana uses the electric guitar's ability to sustain notes for long periods of time to create long, flowing melodic lines that gradually rise in intensity, lifting the whole band with him. In live performance, of course, Santana and other instrumental soloists could stretch out for much more than four and a half minutes.

		LISTENING CHART "OYE COMO VA"	
		Music and lyrics by Tito Puente; performed by Santana; recorded 1971	
FORM		**LYRICS**	**DESCRIPTIVE COMMENTS**
Groove (8)		Instrumental	The basic rhythm is established on organ, electric bass, and (from the fifth measure) percussion.
A (8)	0.16			The guitar states a two-measure melodic phrase four times (with minor embellishments).
B (4)	0.31			A unison figure, played by the whole band.
C (8)	0.38	*Oye como va . . .*	Vocals (two four-measure phrases)
B9 (2)	0.53	Instrumental	The unison figure again (first half only).
Guitar solo (20)	0.57			Extended solo by Carlos Santana.
Interlude (6)	1.34			Call-and-response exchange between guitar and band.
Groove (4)	1.45			Stripped down to the basics again.
Interlude (8)	1.53			Suddenly quieter; organ and guitar play chord pattern; gradual crescendo.
Organ solo (22)	2.08			
Groove (4)	2.48			One more time!
B9 (2)	2.56			The unison figure again (first half only).
C (8)	3.00	*Oye como va . . .*	Vocals (two four-measure phrases)
Interlude (4)	3.14	Instrumental	Suddenly quieter, then crescendo.
Guitar solo (24)	3.22			Another solo by Carlos Santana.
B (4)	4.06			The unison figure again, functioning as a tag.

variety of ethnicities, something that would actually become *less* common as the seventies wore on. In the late sixties, however, rock culture was particularly open to diverse cultural influences, a position that made rock itself more attractive to listeners—and musicians—from those cultures. Stone, Santana, and Hendrix were all *fans* of rock as well as rock musicians. This then made them more likely to see their own destiny as being within rock, rather than in other genres. This development was also facilitated by the rise of FM radio, which provided a medium for music that (initially) rejected the strict genre conventions of an earlier era (see next chapter).

GUITAR HEROES: JIMI HENDRIX AND ERIC CLAPTON

The 1960s saw the rise of a new generation of electric guitarists who functioned as culture heroes for their young fans. Their achievements were built on the shoulders of previous generations of electric guitar virtuosos—Les Paul, whose innovative tinkering with electronic technology inspired a new generation of amplifier tweakers; T-Bone Walker, who introduced the electric guitar to R&B music in the late 1940s; urban blues musicians such as Muddy Waters and B.B. King, whose raw sound and emotional directness inspired rock guitarists; and early masters of rock 'n' roll guitar, including Chuck Berry and Buddy Holly. Beginning in the mid-1960s, the new guitarists—including Jimi Hendrix, Eric Clapton, Jimmy Page, Jeff Beck, and the Beatles' George Harrison—took these influences and pushed them farther than ever before in terms of technique, sheer volume, and improvisational brilliance.

Jimi Hendrix (1942–70) was the most original, inventive, and influential guitarist of the rock era, and the most prominent African American rock musician of the late 1960s. His early experience as a guitarist was gained touring with rhythm & blues bands. In 1966 he moved to London, where, at the suggestion of the producer Chas Chandler, he joined up with two English musicians, bassist Noel Redding and drummer Mitch Mitchell, eventually forming a band called the Jimi Hendrix Experience. The Experience was first seen in America in 1967 at the Monterey Pop Festival, where Hendrix stunned the audience with his flamboyant performance style, which involved playing the guitar with his teeth and behind his back, stroking its neck along his microphone stand, pretending to make love to it, and setting it on fire with lighter fluid and praying to it. (This sort of guitar-focused showmanship, soon to become commonplace at rock concerts, was not unrelated to the wild stage antics of some rhythm & blues performers. Viewing the Hendrix segment of the documentary film *Monterey Pop*, it is clear that some people in the self-consciously hip and mainly middle-class white audience found themselves shocked and therefore delighted by Hendrix's boldness.)

Jimi Hendrix's creative employment of **feedback**, **distortion**, and sound-manipulating devices like the wah-wah pedal and fuzz box, coupled with his fondness for aggressive dissonance and incredibly loud volume, all represented important additions to the musical techniques and materials available to guitarists. Hendrix was a sound sculptor, who seemed at times to be consciously exploring the borderline between traditional conceptions of music and noise, a pursuit that links him in certain ways to composers exploring electronic sounds and media in the world of art music at around the same time. (One of the most famous examples of Hendrix's experimentation with electronically generated sound was his performance of the American national anthem at the Woodstock Festival in 1969. Between each phrase of the melody, Hendrix soared into an elaborate electronic fantasy, imitating

Jimi Hendrix in performance. Henry/Corbis.

"the rockets' red glare, the bombs bursting in air," and then landing precisely on the beginning of next phrase, like a virtuoso jazz musician. This was widely taken as an anti-war commentary, though Hendrix had himself served in the U.S. Army paratroopers.) All of these cited characteristics, along with any number of striking studio effects, may be heard on the first album by the Experience, *Are You Experienced?* (1967), and particularly on its famous opening cut, "Purple Haze."

In one limited sense, "Purple Haze" is a strophic song with clear roots in blues-based melodic figures, harmonies, and chord progressions. But to regard the extraordinary instrumental introduction, the guitar solo between the second and third strophes, and the violently distorted instrumental conclusion all as mere effects added to a strophic tune is really to miss the point. In fact, it could be argued that the strophic tune serves as a mere scaffolding for the instrumental passages; but at the least, the effects are equal in importance to the elements of the tune itself. The radical character and depth of Hendrix's contribution may be seen in the extent to which he requires us to readjust our thinking and terminology in the effort to describe appropriately what constitutes the real essence of his song. When we add in the impact of the lyrics, with their reference to "blowin' my mind" and lines like "'scuse me while I kiss the sky," it is easy to see why Hendrix became an iconic figure for the counterculture, as well as a role model for rock musicians.

It is emblematic of how far Hendrix had strayed from his rhythm & blues roots in music like "Purple Haze" that neither this song, nor any other released by Hendrix as a single, ever made a dent in the in the R&B charts. Hendrix was not a singles artist in any case, and his real kinship was with the new rock audience that viewed the record album as its essential source of musical enlightenment. In a sense, this made him a new kind of crossover artist. His audience rewarded him by elevating all of the five albums he designed for release in his all-too-brief lifetime into the Top 10.

We have noted that Hendrix's notoriety as a creative force first developed in England, and this was no accident. On one hand, it was difficult for an African American musician who neither fit into nor cared much about popular definitions of black musical style to find acceptance in the American popular music scene. And the way toward Hendrix's success in London was also paved by a thriving British pop culture scene, including boutiques, nightclubs, and youth movements such as the "mods"—who wore elaborate clothing reminiscent of centuries-old fashions and listened to American soul music—and the "rockers"— leather-jacketed rock 'n' roll fans. As we have seen, British youth seized upon American popular music with a passion during the 1960s, and an important part of this fascination was focused on the electric guitar.

At the same time, however, Hendrix's acceptance by British youth may have actually facilitated his acceptance by American youth. In a sense, Hendrix offered the best of both worlds to his American audiences: in terms of his age, sensibility, immediate history, and band (composed of white British musicians), he functioned essentially as a British Invasion artist. But, unlike other blues-influenced British musicians who were openly imitating African American music and culture, Jimi Hendrix *really was* African American. Even at the time, this raised a number of complex issues of race and authenticity, most of which were dodged with generic observations that Hendrix "transcended" race. Exactly what that was supposed to mean is still debated to the present day. On a more general level, it is significant that in 1967 just the *idea* of an African American rock musician was viewed as unusual, when only ten years earlier

Archetypal power trio **Cream** rocks out at the Cafe Au Go Go in New York City (1967). Michael Ochs Archives/Getty Images.

rock 'n' roll itself was viewed as a genre with deep connections to the African American community.

Finally, Jimi Hendrix was one of the first rock musicians to build his own studio, Electric Lady Studios, which is still in operation to this day. This reflects a conception of the recording process as an organic and ongoing part of the rock musician's lifestyle, as opposed to an occasional professional obligation. Although this view has subsequently become widespread, particularly with the rise of inexpensive home recording, it was highly unusual in Hendrix's day.

Eric Clapton (b. 1945) was the most influential of the young British guitarists who emerged during the mid-1960s. Influenced by the blues recordings of Robert Johnson and B.B. King, he first attracted notice as a member of the Yardbirds, a band that had little pop success but served as a training ground for young guitarists, including Clapton, Jeff Beck, and Jimmy Page (later a member of Led Zeppelin). Clapton soon began to attract the adulation of young blues and R&B fans, largely as a result of his long, flowing blues-based guitar solos. (The most common graffiti slogan in mid-1960s London was "Clapton is God," an index of his popularity.) From 1966 to 1968 Clapton played in a band called Cream, featuring the drummer Ginger Baker and bassist Jack Bruce. Cream, the first in a line of rock "power trios" that formed during the late 1960s and early 1970s, exerted a major influence on early heavy metal music. Their performances were more akin to avant-garde jazz than to pop music, using "songs" as quickly discardable excuses for long, open-ended improvised solos. Cream took the United States by storm in the late 1960s, selling millions of albums in the space of three years and placing two singles in the Top 10.

🎧 LISTENING TO "CROSS ROAD BLUES" AND "CROSSROADS"

Written and performed by Robert Johnson; recorded 1936. Adapted and performed by Cream; recorded 1968

In order to understand the aesthetics of rock, it is instructive to listen to cover versions by rock groups of earlier recordings in the ancestral genres that preceded rock. The recordings of Mississippi Delta bluesman Robert Johnson (1911–38) had a greater influence on later generations of blues and rock musicians than those of any other country blues artist. His work was especially revered by the British guitarist Keith Richards of the Rolling Stones, and by Eric Clapton, whose band Cream released a celebrated cover of Johnson's "Cross Road Blues" in 1968. Eventually, Johnson's posthumous reputation was such that when his complete output was reissued on compact discs in 1990, the set quickly became a surprise million-seller.

Robert Johnson's brief life is shrouded in mystery and legend, much like the history of the blues itself; it is the stuff of which myths are made. Little is known of his early years. His guitar playing was so remarkable and idiosyncratic that stories circulated claiming Johnson had sold his soul to the devil in order to play that way; when performing for an audience, he apparently turned in such a position as to conceal his hands so that nobody could see what he was doing to produce his sounds. Only eleven records (twenty-two songs) by Johnson were released during his lifetime. Yet by late 1938 his fame had spread sufficiently that the American music talent scout and promoter John Hammond sought him out to appear with major African American folk and jazz artists in a "Spirituals to Swing" concert in New York City's celebrated Carnegie Hall—only to discover that Johnson had very recently died, apparently a victim of poisoning by a jealous husband.

"Cross Road Blues" serves as a fine example of Johnson's artistry. Johnson's acoustic guitar playing is forcefully rhythmic, and there is a strong feeling of regular pulse throughout "Cross Road Blues." Johnson uses his unamplified guitar principally as a chordal instrument, and his aggressive, rapid strumming of chords gives his work a flavor that anticipates the electric guitar styles of rock music. This modern feeling is abetted by the wide range of timbres Johnson obtains from his acoustic guitar; note his effective alternations of high-pitched, strained chordal sounds with low-pitched, fuller chordal sounds. He also makes use of the *bottleneck* technique, common among Mississippi Delta blues guitarists. To achieve this effect, the guitarist slips the sawed-off neck of a glass bottle over a finger on his left hand, which allows him to produce smooth glides between individual pitches. In the hands of a great guitarist like Johnson, the bottleneck technique can even be used to imitate the sound of the human voice. Johnson's creative use of guitar timbres is mirrored in his singing, which also veers eerily from high to low, from strained to gruff colors, as if depicting through sound itself the desperation expressed in the words of the song. The expressive intensity of the performance is given shape by the form of the blues, which is heard in the basic chord sequences as well as in the poetic structure of the piece.

Like many rural blues songs, the lyrics to "Cross Road Blues" are highly personal. Just where the "crossroad" is, what its special significance might be for the singer, and whether it even refers to a specific place at all or functions just as a metaphor—these are all unknowable mysteries. (The image probably represents a continuity with West African mythologies, in which the crossroad figures as a place of uncertainty, danger, and opportunity, and as a symbol of destiny.) Even in 1936 the name Willie Brown in the last stanza would have been recognized only by those who really knew their country blues (he was a mentor of Johnson's). In terms of narrative technique, "Cross Road Blues" hardly tells a story at all. Like some of the greatest lyric poetry, it uses words to evoke an emotional and spiritual condition, in this instance a condition of harrowing darkness and despair.

Although it is difficult to summarize the work of a musical improviser in a single recording, Cream's version of "Cross Road Blues," retitled "Crossroads," recorded live at the Fillmore West in San Francisco, does convey a sense of the power and passion of Eric Clapton's guitar playing. While this song represents the deep respect that many rock guitarists held for Robert Johnson, the 1936 and 1968 recordings are in many ways light-years apart in sound and sensibility. Cream was the original rock "power trio," consisting of electric guitar, electric bass, and drums, and Johnson's complex solo guitar accompaniment has been reduced to a single powerful riff, played in unison by the electric guitar and bass guitar, and projected by a veritable wall of amplifiers. Cream's use of stripped-down rock instrumentation, combined with the loud volumes and thick textures made possible by amplification (and demanded by the huge performance venues in which rock bands played), meant that the expressive nuances of a performance like Robert Johnson's "Cross Road Blues" could not be reproduced even if that had been the musicians' aim. Clearly, while the recordings of Robert Johnson were an inspiration for young guitarists like Clapton, the application of rock aesthetics and technology yielded a very different end product.

Still, there is at least one similarity between the musical challenges faced by the two master guitarists, playing some thirty years apart: both men's performances are highly exposed, Johnson playing solo and Clapton with only bass and drum set accompaniment. This has the effect of focusing attention on the guitarist and requiring that he play more or less constantly to keep the performance moving. Clapton's approach to this task involves not only the application of highly developed technical skills but also the use of electronic feedback, which allows him to sustain long notes and create flowing streams of shorter notes. The performance opens with Clapton singing a few strophes of Johnson's song, then launching into an escalating series of improvised twelve-bar choruses. This is "busy" music, designed to showcase the virtuosity of the performers, and Baker and Bruce play constantly throughout, driving Clapton along to higher and higher emotional peaks. Although some rock critics regard Cream as an example of the self-indulgence and showiness of some late-1960s rock music, there can be no disputing that Clapton, Baker, and Bruce both upped the technical ante for rock musicians and paved the way for later guitar-focused bands. And they, along with the Rolling Stones, the Grateful Dead, and the Doors, also helped to establish the importance of the concert as a venue for experiencing rock music—hardcore fans argued that unless you heard Clapton play live, you hadn't really heard him at all.

CONCLUSION

The late sixties was an era of great change, but it was not removed from what came before. From a purely musical standpoint, the rock of the late sixties clearly built upon earlier styles, from folk to blues to early rock 'n' roll itself. At the same time, many new cultural, political, and economic influences flooded into the rock scene and were met with a general climate of openness and experimentation. New recording technology enabled artists to explore sonic textures and techniques that could not have even been conceived ten years earlier. And musicians took on political and social roles that went far beyond those of the simple "entertainers" of an earlier era. The association of rock music with the counterculture—though often taken for granted in retrospect—was something that had to be intentionally forged by musicians and others. In fact, some countercultural figures, particularly those who were most political, felt that rock was more of a distraction from important cultural work than a part of it. For those who did make this association, however, rock took on a new importance as a vital forum for artistic innovation, not only for its own sake but in hopes of making a better world. In a related development, artists developed newer, more humane business models that reflected their new worldviews. As attitudes toward both music and business changed, artists from a variety of cultural traditions found a new openness to diverse cultural and social perspectives in rock—not just as influences but as part of the genre itself.

7

THE 1970s:
ROCK BECOMES ESTABLISHED

In this chapter, we discuss the rise of rock as a mainstream cultural form, exploring several different ways that this trend manifested itself. We also address the reactions against this development, which for the first time largely came from within rock itself. While these responses were often ideologically motivated, in the sense that they represented different views of what rock should be, in many cases they were also generational. Rock had now been around long enough that its own earliest forms and attitudes had begun to seem old-fashioned to young fans. Whether it was playfully dismissed or reverently embraced, rock now had a history.

One of the most pervasive stereotypes about the 1970s—famously captured in novelist Tom Wolfe's epithet, "the Me decade"—has to do with a shift in the values of young adults, away from the communitarian, politically engaged ideals of the 1960s counterculture, toward more materialistic and conservative attitudes. While this generalization should be taken with a large grain of salt, it is undeniable that the early 1970s did see a kind of turning inward in American culture. The majority of Americans had grown weary of the military conflict in Vietnam, which drew to a close with the U.S. withdrawal from Saigon in 1975. Around the same time, popular attention was focused on domestic problems, including the oil crisis (1973) and economic inflation, which threatened the financial security of millions of Americans. If the assassination of President Kennedy in 1963 had robbed many Americans of a certain political idealism, the Watergate hearings—viewed by millions on television—and the subsequent resignation of President Nixon (1974) occasioned a growing cynicism about politics.

Meanwhile, the ideological polarization of the late 1960s continued unabated, and popular music remained a favorite target of conservative politicians and commentators, much as it had been during the jazz and rock 'n' roll "scares" of the 1920s and 1950s. It is interesting that in 1970, just as America was taking a conservative turn, hippie dress and slang, psychedelic imagery, and rock music had begun to enter the cultural mainstream of AM radio, network television, and Hollywood movies. (This suggests an analogy to the 1920s, when the "jazz age" was born in a period of strong political conservatism.) In the early 1970s the market for popular music became focused on two main categories of consumers: a new generation of teenagers, born in the late 1950s and early 1960s; and adults aged twenty-five to forty, who had grown up with rock 'n' roll and were looking for more mature (i.e., more conservative) material. Nostalgic fare such as the film *American Graffiti* (1973), the Broadway musical and film *Grease* (1972 and 1978, respectively), and the popular television series *Happy Days* used early rock 'n' roll—now nearly twenty years old—to evoke the so-called Golden Age of 1950s America, before the Kennedy assassination, the invasion of the Beatles, the rise of the counterculture, and the escalating social conflicts of the late 1960s.

If many Americans wished that the 1960s would just go away, others mourned the decade's passing. For rock fans, the end of the counterculture was poignantly symbolized by the deaths of Jimi Hendrix (1970), Janis Joplin (1970), and Jim Morrison of the Doors (1971), and by the breakup of the Beatles, who, more than any other group, inspired the triumphs (and excesses) of rock music. On December 31, 1970, Paul McCartney filed the legal brief that was to formally dissolve the business partnership of the Beatles. For many rock fans, the demise of the Fab Four was incontrovertible proof that the 1960s were dead and gone. But this certainly didn't mean that rock music itself was moribund. If in the late 1960s rock was the music of the counterculture, defined by its opposition to the mainstream of popular music, by the 1970s it had helped to redefine the popular mainstream, becoming the primary source of profit for an expanding and ever more centralized entertainment industry.

During the 1970s the music industry reached new heights of consolidation. Six huge corporations—Columbia/CBS, Warner Communications, RCA Victor, Capitol-EMI, MCA, and United Artists–MGM—were responsible for over 80 percent of record sales in the United States by the end of the decade. Total profits from the sale of recorded music reached new levels—two billion dollars in 1973 and four billion dollars in 1978—in part owing to the increasing popularity of prerecorded tapes. (The eight-track cartridge and cassette tape formats had initially been introduced during the mid-1960s, and their popularity expanded rapidly during the early 1970s. By 1975 sales of prerecorded tapes accounted for almost one-third of all music sales in the United States.)

ROCK COMES OF AGE

During the 1970s rock music, the brash child of rock 'n' roll, diffused into every corner of the music industry. Influenced by the Beatles, Bob Dylan, Brian Wilson, and Jimi Hendrix, many progressive rock musicians had come to view themselves as artists, and their recordings as works of art. While this occasionally led to the production of self-indulgent dross, some musicians used the medium of the long-playing record album to create innovative and challenging work. At the same time, the music industry moved to co-opt the appeal of rock music, creating genres like "pop rock" and "soft rock," designed to appeal to the widest possible demographic and promoted on Top 40 radio and television. Musicians as diverse as Led Zeppelin; Stevie Wonder; Elton John; Carole King; Pink Floyd; Paul Simon; Neil Diamond; Crosby, Stills, and Nash; the Rolling Stones; Frank Zappa and the Mothers of Invention; Blood Sweat & Tears; and Santana were promoted by record companies under the general heading of rock music. Even Frank Sinatra, scarcely a rock musician, tried his hand at a Beatles song or two.

There were, however, some important exceptions to the general popular appeal of rock music. Record sales in black communities, as reflected in the *Billboard* soul charts during the 1970s, do not suggest much interest in rock music. (The Rolling Stones managed to get only one of their singles into *Billboard*'s soul Top 40 chart during the decade, and multiplatinum rock acts such as Led Zeppelin, Deep Purple, and Pink Floyd made no dent whatsoever.) While the Monterey and Woodstock rock festivals had featured performances by African American artists, the promise of rock music as a zone of interracial interaction seemed to have largely vanished by the early 1970s. Many of the white rock stars who had formed their styles through exposure to earlier styles of blues and R&B seemed to have little interest in contemporary black popular music of the 1970s. As one critic put it in 1971, "Black musicians are now implicitly regarded as precursors who, having taught the white men all they know, must gradually recede into the distance" (Morse 1971, p. 108).

As always, however, one's position on this issue depends on how the boundaries of rock itself are defined. In terms of both its sound and its audience, rock was clearly continuing to grow away from the mainstream of African American popular music. But at the same time, many of the conceptual innovations of rock—in terms of culture, business, and lifestyle—were becoming integrated *back into* African American music. This was largely the result of the fact that rock culture itself was becoming a well-defined tradition.

As we have discussed in previous chapters, the changes in rock's sound were a result of the interactions among musical innovation, social change, and economic opportunity over the course of its entire history. By the seventies, these interactions had begun to organize themselves into a self-sustaining system, in which the cultural and artistic principles of the style were aligned with its economic needs, and each reinforced the other. One part of this cultural system was the new idea that rock musicians should be artists, unencumbered by issues of commerce (the extent to which this was actually the case, of course, depended on the artist). This new role soon led to musicians beginning to see the album format as a more suitable outlet for their creativity than individual singles, since by virtue of its length it could contain more complex and profound artistic statements.

At the same time, this shift was supported by a changing radio landscape that was also increasingly album-oriented, thereby increasing the album's commercial viability. Radio served simultaneously to reinforce the *cultural* idea of the album-as-artistic-statement and support the *economic* idea of the album-as-product. In fact, the relationship between the business of radio and the culture of rock was particularly close in the early seventies. The rise of FM radio, and its association with rock music, opened new opportunities in both arenas.

Until the seventies, a "Top 40" model associated with AM radio had dominated the radio business. Under this model, radio stations competed to win the largest number of listeners ("market share") by playing the most popular songs of the day. A large listenership would then allow the station to charge high advertising rates to businesses, on the grounds that their ads would reach a large number of potential customers. This system had a logic that was well understood by rock artists and their record companies. If musicians wanted to sell their record, people had to know about it. In order for people to know about it, it had to be played on the radio. In order to be played on the radio, the radio station had to feel that the song would attract a wide range of listeners, in order to justify their advertising rates. This meant that record companies were naturally interested in rock artists with mass appeal, such as the Beatles.

The new FM radio model was somewhat different, as it was based on what would now be called "niche marketing." Under this model, the appeal to advertisers was not that a radio station could reach the *most* listeners, but that they could target *specific kinds* of listeners. The logic here was that a smaller number of listeners who were actually interested buying in your product could be more valuable than a large number who were not. The result of this new thinking was the fragmentation of radio into different "formats"—album-oriented rock, soft rock, urban contemporary—that were each designed to appeal to a specific advertising demographic. Rather than encouraging their artists to seek the broadest possible audience, record labels began to encourage them to match certain styles and attitudes that would appeal to specific radio formats. This was not difficult to do, since, as we discussed in the previous chapter, rock itself was undergoing a similar fragmentation anyway, and these two influences naturally reinforced each other.

It is useful at this point to think about how far the concept of the rock musician had come in just fifteen short years. At the birth of the rock era, the rock musician was a working-class outsider, whose appeal largely stemmed from *not* being a part of the middle-class popular music world, or even the culture that it reflected. By the early seventies, rock musicians were not only considered part of mainstream culture, in many ways they were its leaders! And, as such, they were felt to be entitled to both the respect and the economic rewards that went along with this position. The idea of the "rock star" developed in this era, and—as we shall see—it was a reflection of both the economic and cultural changes that were afoot in rock music. More to the point, it reflects an evolving relationship *between* the economics and culture of rock that continues to the present day.

As we noted, FM radio opened up a space for a more "free-form" approach to broadcasting that reflected the emerging rock culture. There were two major reasons for this. First, since FM had been a relatively unused radio band in the sixties, even many people who owned radios did not own radios that could receive FM broadcasts. Since few people were listening, those who produced FM broadcasts were largely left to their own devices. At the same time, unlike AM radio, FM radio could broadcast in high-quality stereo, which allowed many of the more subtle and "artistic" aspects of rock recordings to be appreciated. This fit perfectly with the emerging view of the rock album as an innovative work of art and not simply a compilation of radio-friendly singles.

In a previous era, even rock musicians that took themselves seriously as artists were expected to express that artistry in the form of singles that were suitable for Top 40 radio. This would then serve to promote their album as a whole. But the rise of FM radio in the seventies gave deejays the freedom to play any song they liked from the album, not just the single. As this practice took hold, radio stations began consciously to embrace this freedom as a selling point, designating themselves as "album-oriented rock" stations, a term that was soon abbreviated as "AOR." The rise of the AOR format—a mass medium that promoted whole albums rather than individual songs—made the album-as-artistic-statement commercially viable. This in turn gave record companies an economic incentive to support more self-consciously "artistic" acts that had little interest in crafting traditional pop singles. And this, among other things, gave rise to a new ideology of rock stardom in which the pursuit of commercial success and the desire to express a deeply personal artistic vision were no longer considered mutually exclusive.

Though it is now such a part of our cultural landscape that we may take it for granted, the concept of the rock star was deeply tied to the specific character of rock in the seventies. At its foundation, the concept was based on the newly emergent idea that you could actually get rich as a rock musician. Beyond that, there was a growing feeling that wealth and fame could *contribute* to the quality of one's art, rather than detract from it, a position that would have been viewed with suspicion even five years earlier. There are several reasons for the change in attitude. First, there was a sense that wealth was the best path to the artistic independence that artists had been seeking since the 1960s. Simply stated, rich rock stars could do what they wanted. Even if what they wanted was no longer political revolution but just "sex, drugs, and rock 'n' roll," that could still represent a kind of cultural revolution. And if rock was supposed to be about the liberating potential of self-indulgence, then who better to perform it than a rich outlaw? At the same time, part of what made this kind of indulgence acceptable was the belief that artists had earned it through their cultural output. In other words, the persona had an aspirational quality that the average person could relate to, much like winning the lottery. Rock stars, almost by definition, were working-class or middle-class kids with an almost religious commitment to the ideals of rock 'n' roll, who had struggled, paid dues, and finally seen their dreams come true. From this point of view, the rock stars enjoyed wealth and debauchery almost on behalf of their fans.

The "rock star," then, was an almost perfect embodiment of rock in the seventies, a salt-of-the-earth, hardworking, artistically gifted individual who had achieved financial success beyond anyone's wildest dreams, which then gave him or her the freedom to express personal artistic vision without compromise. It is not difficult to see why this narrative would have an appeal that went far beyond the boundaries of rock. In the seventies the general rock star profile, and the musical approach associated with it, became the norm in many musical styles, from funk to country music to reggae.

The idea of the rock star was also connected to new performance opportunities. The seventies are known as an era of flamboyance, hedonism, and—for lack of a better term—partying. To a large degree, this was simply the spirit of the era, but there was also a specific practical influence on this trend that has been largely forgotten in retrospect: the lowering of the legal drinking age. As a result of the Vietnam-era draft, which sent eighteen-year-olds to war, a movement developed to lower the federal voting age from twenty-one to eighteen. After that happened in 1971, it began to seem strange that eighteen-, nineteen-, and twenty-year-olds would be considered old enough to vote and go to war, but not to drink. As a result, thirty states lowered their drinking age from twenty-one to eighteen or nineteen in the seventies, thus suddenly allowing millions of eighteen- to twenty-year-olds to patronize clubs and bars. This enormous new clientele created an economic incentive for the opening of thousands of new performance venues, most of which were looking to hire rock bands to play several nights a week. For young musicians, the dream of a career as a working rock musician suddenly became infinitely more plausible, and the rock scene blossomed.

Another major change during the seventies was in the nature of the venues that were available to play. Until the late sixties, rock performances had largely been limited to bars, theaters, and ballrooms. Larger venues, such as sports

Elton John shows how "stadium rock" got its name as he performs at Dodger Stadium in 1975. Terry O'Neill/Hulton Archive/Getty Images.

arenas and stadiums, had been off-limits for two major reasons. First, rock artists were simply not popular enough to fill such venues. And, second, in the days before giant video screens and high-quality sound systems, the sound and view available to the average stadium concertgoer was so poor that promoters assumed that no self-respecting music fan would be willing to pay for the experience. The Beatles, however, had challenged both of those assumptions. Their groundbreaking concert in New York City's 55,600-seat Shea Stadium in 1965 showed that not only were there enough fans to fill such a venue, but also that the *overall experience* of the concert was more important to fans than either the sound or the view. The Beatles—as rock stars—were so beloved that fans were willing to pay just to be in their presence, regardless of whether they could even see or hear them. And the music industry took notice; after all, ten times the audience meant ten times the money. The idea that rock was suitable for large venues was reinforced by the huge rock festivals of the late sixties, such as Monterey (1967) and Woodstock (1969). These festivals emphasized cultural experience as much as they emphasized performance; you were there to participate in the counterculture as much as to listen to the music. This attitude—though surely sincere—also conveniently excused poor views, lackluster sound systems, and, in many cases, mediocre performances.

By the early 1970s, these festivals had mutated into highly profitable mass-audience concerts, held in civic centers and sports arenas across the country. In 1973 the British hard rock group Led Zeppelin toured the United States, breaking the world record for live concert attendance set by the Beatles during their tours of the mid-1960s. A whole series of bands that sprang up in the 1970s—Grand Funk Railroad, Kansas, Electric Light Orchestra, Journey, Heart, Pink Floyd, and others—tailored their performances to the concert context, touring the country with elaborate light shows, spectacular sets, and powerful amplification systems, transported in caravans of semi trucks. For most rock fans, the live concert was the peak of musical experience—you hadn't really heard Led Zeppelin, it was said, until you'd heard and seen them live (and spent a little money on a poster or T-shirt, imprinted with the band's image). Of course, the relationship between rock stars and their devotees at these concerts was anything but intimate. Nonetheless, the sheer grandiosity, the sound and spectacle of a rock concert, helped to create a visceral sensation of belonging to a larger community, a temporary city formed by fans.

THE ROCK ALBUM

As rock stars began to see themselves as artists, and were commercially supported in that change, they increasingly began work in the form of albums rather than single songs. In the 1960s recordings such as the Beach Boys' *Pet Sounds* (1966), the Beatles' *Sgt. Pepper's Lonely Hearts Club Band* (1967), and the Who's "rock opera" *Tommy* (1969) established the idea of the record album as a thematically and aesthetically unified work and not simply a collection of otherwise unrelated cuts. By the early 1970s the twelve-inch high-fidelity LP had become established as the primary medium for rock music.

What makes a rock album more than a mere collection of singles? Let's start with a basic fact about the medium, its capacity: a twelve-inch disc, played at 33⅓ r.p.m., could accommodate more than forty minutes of music, over twenty minutes per side. In the 1950s and early 1960s little creative use was made of this additional real estate; most rock 'n' roll-era LPs consisted of a few hit singles, interspersed with a lot of less carefully produced filler. During the second half of the 1960s rock musicians began to treat the time span of the LP as a total entity, a field of potentiality akin to a painter's canvas. They also began to put more effort into all of the songs on an album, and to think of creative ways to link songs together, creating an overall progression of peaks and valleys. (Of course, old habits die hard, and most rock albums still used songs, each approximately three to six minutes in length, as basic building blocks.) Even in cases where the songs were not explicitly linked, the order in which they appeared on the album—known as "sequencing"—was still extremely important, since it created a distinct emotional curve to the listening experience. This curve mixed pure artistic concerns with technological and economic concerns. For one thing, the first single—the song that was believed to have the most immediate appeal—would almost always appear as the first song on the first side of the record, while the second single would be the first song on the second side. This was done for practical reasons: It made the most popular songs easily accessible to anyone who wanted to play them, either fans or radio deejays. But this expectation also tended to set an emotional tone for rock albums, creating a general format where the record would begin with an upbeat, engaging song before delving into more complex and experimental songs (known as "deep album cuts" because they were "buried" in the albums' interior). Then the first side would end, and there would be a period of silence—not unlike an intermission—until the listener got up and flipped the record. Next, the second side would begin with a similarly upbeat tune and the process would continue through the second side. As cassettes became popular as a medium, they were similarly sequenced in a two-sided format. In this way, records became somewhat like plays in the way they unfolded for listeners. Recent changes in technology, listening habits, and mass media, however, have led to a renewed focus on individual songs, making the album format largely obsolete. The result is that even when modern listeners listen to rock recordings from the seventies, we almost never hear them in the form in which they were meant to be heard.

The development of studio technology also encouraged musicians to experiment with novel techniques. High-fidelity stereo sound, heard over good speakers or headphones, placed the listener in the middle of the music (and the music in the middle of the listener!) and allowed sound sources to be "moved around." The advent of 16-, 24-, and 32-track recording consoles and electronic sound devices allowed musicians—and the record producers and studio engineers with whom they worked—to create complex aural textures, and to construct a given track on an LP over a period of time, adding and subtracting (or "punching in" and "punching out") individual instruments and voices. Innovations in the electronic synthesis of sound led to instruments like the Melotron, which could imitate the sound of a string orchestra in the studio and at live performances.

The musical response to the opportunities provided by these technological changes varied widely. Some rock bands became famous for spending many months (and tons of money) in the studio to create a single rock "masterpiece." A few multitalented musicians, such as Stevie Wonder and Edgar Winter, took advantage of multitracking to play all of the instruments on a given track. Other musicians reacted against the dependence on studio technology, recording their albums the old-fashioned way, with little overdubbing. (As we shall see, when punk rock arose in the late 1970s as a reaction against the pretentiousness of studio-bound progressive rock, musicians insisted on doing recordings in one take to create the sense of a live performance experience.) Studio technology could even be used to create the impression that studio technology was not being used, as in many folk rock albums.

Although the idea of creating some sort of continuity among the individual tracks, and of creating an inclusive structure that could provide the listener with a sense of progression, was shared widely, rock musicians took a range of approaches to this problem. One way to get a sense of this range is to listen to a handful of classic rock LPs from the early 1970s.

Some rock albums are centered on a fictitious character whose identity is analogous to that of one or more musicians in the band. Perhaps the best-known example of this strategy is *The Rise and Fall of Ziggy Stardust and the Spiders from Mars* (1972), the creation of "glam rock" pioneer David Bowie. (Glam—short for *glamour*—rock emphasized the elaborate, showy personal appearance and costuming of its practitioners.) In this case, the coherence of the album derives more from the imaginative and magnetic persona of the singer and his character than from the music itself. As Bowie put it, "I packaged a totally credible plastic rock star," an alien who comes to visit Earth and becomes first a superstar and finally a "Rock 'n' Roll Suicide," perishing under the weight of his own fame. Much of the LP's effect was connected with the striking image of Bowie playing the role of Ziggy, decked out in futuristic clothing and heavy facial makeup, a sensitive rocker, sexy in an androgynous, cosmic way. The *Ziggy Stardust* concert tour was a theatrical tour de force, with special lighting effects and spectacular costumes, and it set the standard for later rock acts, ranging from "new wave" bands like Talking Heads to hard rockers like Kiss. Bowie's unique ability to create quasi-fictional stage personae, and to change them with every new album, was a precedent for the image manipulation of 1980s stars like Michael Jackson, Prince, and Madonna.

Other successful rock albums were held together not by a central character or coherent plotline, but by an emotional, philosophical, or political theme.

David Bowie performing as **Ziggy Stardust**, 1973. Debi Doss/Hulton Archive/Getty Images.

The album *Blue* (1971), composed and performed by the singer-songwriter Joni Mitchell (b. 1943 in Canada), consists of a cycle of songs about the complexities of love. The album is carefully designed to create a strong emotional focus, which is in turn clearly related to the autobiography of the singer herself. In some ways *Blue* is a culmination of the tendency inherent in the folk rock and singer-songwriter genres toward self-revelation. Even the most optimistic songs on the album—"All I Want," "My Old Man," and "Carey"—have a bittersweet flavor. Some—such as "Little Green," about a child given up for adoption, and the concluding track "The Last Time I Saw Richard"—are delicate yet powerful testimonials to the shared human experience of emotional loss. The sound of the LP is spare and beautiful, focusing on Mitchell's voice and acoustic guitar. This is a case where studio technology is used to create a feeling of simplicity and immediacy.

Dark Side of the Moon (1973), an album by the British rock band Pink Floyd, is based on the theme of madness and the things that drive us to it—time, work, money, war, and fear of death. The LP opens with the sound of a beating heart, then a ticking clock, a typewriter, a cash register, gunfire, and the voices of members of Pink Floyd's stage crew, discussing their own experiences with insanity. The album's feeling of unity has something to do with its languid, carefully measured pace—most of the songs are slow to midtempo—as well as its musical texture and mood. In terms of style, the progression moves from spacey, neo-psychedelic sound textures to jazz and blues-influenced songs and then back to psychedelia. The sound of the record, produced by Alan Parsons, is complex but clear, and interesting use is made of sound effects, as in the song "Money," with its sampled sounds of clinking coins and cash registers, treated as rhythmic accompaniment. (This achievement is particularly impressive when we recall that 1973 was before the advent of digital recording techniques.)

If there was ever an antidote to the notion that popular music must be cheerful and upbeat in order to be successful, *Dark Side of the Moon* is it. This meditation on insanity stayed on the *Billboard* Top LPs charts for over fourteen years, longer than any other LP in history, and sold twenty-five million copies worldwide. In recent years, various mythologies have grown up around *Dark Side of the Moon*. For example, it is claimed that the album can be synchronized with the 1939 film *The Wizard of Oz*. Many people maintain that if you start the album up after the MGM lion's third roar there are some amazing synchronicities. (For example, the song "Brain Damage" begins playing just as the Scarecrow starts to sing "If I Only Had a Brain"). Whatever the merit of these claims, it is clear that Pink Floyd's *Dark Side of the Moon* continues to exert a powerful, if somewhat dark, fascination upon millions of rock fans.

A final example of the "theme album" is Marvin Gaye's bestselling LP *What's Going On* (1971), which fused soul music and gospel influence with the political impetus of progressive rock. The basic unifying theme of this album is social justice. The title track, inspired by the return of Gaye's brother from Vietnam, is a plea for nonviolence, released during the peak of anti-war protests in the United States. Other songs focus on ecology, the welfare of children, and the suffering of poor people in America's urban centers. Gaye (1939–84) cowrote the songs and produced the album himself, supporting his voice—overdubbed to sound like an entire vocal group—with layers of percussion, strings, and horns. Once again, the producer's consideration of the overall sound texture of the album had a great deal to do with its aesthetic effect and commercial success.

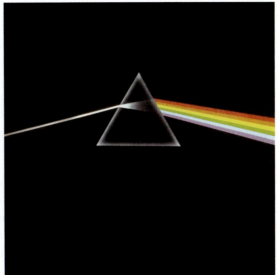

Motown owner Berry Gordy initially didn't want to release *What's Going On*, because he thought it had no commercial potential. This was a rare case of misjudgment on Gordy's part; the album reached Number 2 on the LP charts and generated three Number 1 singles on the soul charts, all of which crossed over to the pop Top 10: the title song, "Mercy Mercy Me (The Ecology)," and "Inner City Blues (Make Me Wanna Holler)." Two other tracks, "Wholy Holy" and "Save the Children," inspired hit cover versions by Aretha Franklin and Diana Ross. But the significance of this album, and of Marvin Gaye's commitment to a socially responsible aesthetic vision, surpasses any measure of commercial success. Along with Stevie Wonder and Sly Stone, Marvin Gaye showed that soul and R&B albums could provide artistic coherence that transcended the three-minute single; managed to bridge

(a) *Blue,* Joni Mitchell album cover, 1971 (Michael Ochs Archives/Getty Images);(b) *Dark Side of the Moon,* Pink Floyd album cover, 1973; (c) *Exile on Main Street,* Rolling Stones album cover, 1972.

the divides among AM Top 40, FM album-oriented radio, and the soul music market; and held open the possibility that popular music might still have something to do with social change, as well as money making and artistic self-expression. As Gaye himself acknowledged, this was an example of ideas about artistry that had largely been developed within a rock context being integrated back into African American popular music.

A strategy that was fairly unusual in rock music was the adoption of elements of large-scale structure from European classical music. The live album *Pictures at an Exhibition* (1971), recorded by the "art rock" band <u>Emerson, Lake, and Palmer</u>, adopts its main themes and some of its structural elements from a suite of piano pieces by the Russian composer Modest Mussorgsky (1839–81). This was a canny choice, since Mussorgsky's composition—inspired by a walk through an art gallery—consists of a sequence of accessible, reasonably short, easily digestible "paintings," a parallel with the song format of much popular music. Some sections of the LP are adaptations of the original score (making prominent use of Keith Emerson's virtuosity on organ and synthesizer), while others are improvisations on the borrowed materials, and still others new songs by the band, musing on ideas in the music. The album concludes with "Nutrocker," a rock 'n' roll version of Tchaikovsky's *Nutcracker Suite*.

In the end, however, rock music is less centrally concerned with large-scale, architectural structures than with the immediate experience of musical sound, rhythmic momentum, and emotional intensity. Many of the most effective rock albums do not have an overarching structural logic, a story to tell, or a single organizing image; rather, they find their unity in a visceral cohesion of musical style, sound, and attitude. *Exile on Main Street* (1972), now often cited as the best album ever recorded by the Rolling Stones, had decidedly mixed reviews when it first came out, because of its impenetrable sound and the inaudibility of its lyrics. The cover art for the LP—a photographic collage of freaks and misfits—represented a new trend away from standard photos of artists or groups. It seemed designed to repel many in the Stones' loyal audience, who had followed the band since their early days as the slightly nasty counterpart of the Beatles. In *Exile on Main Street* we have an album—actually a double album, containing two LPs and eighteen songs—that is held together by its texture (dense, dark, guitar-based rock 'n' roll), its rough, unpolished studio sound (reminiscent on some tracks of Elvis Presley's early work with Sun Records), and its bad attitude (personified by the sneering, mumbling Mick Jagger). The material is strongly oriented toward the Stones' musical roots, as it consists mainly of blues-based rockers like "Rocks Off," "Shake Your Hips," and "Tumbling Dice," with a few examples of country and folk music influence ("Sweet Virginia" and "Sweet Black Angel").

Exile on Main Street was recorded in the basement of guitarist Keith Richards's home in France—where the Stones were living in tax exile at the time—and Jagger's voice is purposefully buried in the mix, under the gritty guitars, bass, and drums, and the occasional horn section. (The producer Jimmy Miller was largely responsible for creating the LPs cohesive sound palette.) The overall impression is one of bleakness and desolation, a reflection of the Stones' state at the time. The band's abuse of drugs and alcohol was so intense that members of the band have since wondered aloud how they ever got the record made. *Exile on Main Street* is at once an apotheosis of the Stones' image as bad boys, and a tip of the hat to the influences that formed their style, including urban blues, soul, and country music.

ROCK CULTURE

In the sixties, new attitudes toward rock had stood alongside new approaches to politics, spirituality, drugs, sexuality, and art as part of a larger countercultural movement. In the seventies, as the counterculture declined and rock became more culturally dominant, that relationship essentially turned inside out. If in the sixties rock was part of the counterculture, in the seventies the counterculture was part of rock. This change opened up new opportunities to define and express a distinctive "rock" culture, and each of these new areas would cycle back to influence the music itself. Three of the most prominent expressions of the new rock culture were album art, merchandising (such as T-shirts and posters), and an independent rock press.

If the rock LP was a container for music, it was also an art object in its own right. LP dust jackets often featured a printed version of the lyrics and a range of highly imaginative designs. Covers conveyed a lot, not only about a rock group's physical appearance, but also about their aesthetic aims and personality. Some showed concert photos of the artists at work; Jimi Hendrix's *Band of Gypsys* (1970) and Deep Purple's *Made in Japan* (1973) were bestselling examples. Others revealed some aspect of the musicians' private lives; the eponymous LP *Crosby Stills and Nash* (1969) has a cover photo of the three folk rock musicians lounging on an old sofa on the front porch of a house, while the inside of Marvin Gaye's *What's Going On* (1971) contains a photo collage of his family. The cover art for Joni Mitchell's album *Blue* (1971) reflects the introspective mood of her songs. The sexuality of rock stars was often emphasized, as on the Rolling Stones' quadruple-platinum LP *Sticky Fingers* (1971), which featured a close-up photograph of the crotch of a pair of blue jeans widely (though mistakenly) believed to belong to Mick Jagger, complete with a working zipper! Other covers, particularly of hard rock and heavy metal albums, tapping into the sexual fantasies of the young male audience for rock music, featured scantily clad women in suggestive poses. Alternative models of sexuality also found their way onto album covers, the most notorious example being David Bowie's *Diamond Dogs* (1975), which featured an androgynous Bowie-canine creature with its genitals exposed. (The cover created a furor and was soon yanked from the shelves of record stores and replaced with a tamer alternative.)

Record companies often gave dust-jacket artists wide latitude to invent visual analogues to the music inside. The cover of *Brain Salad Surgery* (1973), a Top 10 LP by the art rock band Emerson, Lake, and Palmer, was designed by the Swiss artist H. R. Giger, who went on create the nightmarish creature in the film *Alien*. The Latin rock band Santana's second LP, *Abraxas* (1970), presented a colorful surrealistic rendering of the fusion of European and African cultural influences (a reproduction of the 1961 painting *Annunciation* by artist Marti Klarwein). Even reissues of oldies from the 1950s and 1960s were given imaginative treatments, as on the Drifters' *Greatest Recordings* album cover (1971), which took an old publicity photo and turned it into a psychedelic image. Finally, some album designs featured a minimalist approach, the prototypical example being *The Beatles* (1968), whose stark monochromatic cover (designed by the British pop artist Richard Hamilton) earned it the nickname "the White Album."

Other material expressions of rock culture and attitude included what would now be called "lifestyle accessories": T-shirts, posters, mirrors embossed with band logos, and other souvenirs. These items reflect the developing idea that one's personality could be expressed through one's taste in consumer goods. While this was not a new idea in American culture, the growing relationships among rock subgenres, radio formatting, and niche marketing led to an environment in which this concept was increasingly applied to rock music. A Led Zeppelin fan was no longer just someone who happened to like Led Zeppelin, but a *type of person*. By wearing a band's T-shirt you were not only proclaiming your taste in music, but your whole attitude toward life. And from a business standpoint, the sale of rock music paraphernalia at concerts, record stores, and "head shops" became an increasingly profitable sideline.

A third important aspect of the expanding rock culture was the rise of rock media, and particularly a thriving rock press. Before the late sixties, those who wrote about rock were primarily older music critics who had grown up listening to other styles of music, and who were often suspicious of, or misinformed about, rock's values. It was only as the first generation of rock fans came to maturity in the late sixties that rock could be written about from an insider's perspective. But even then, the majority of these writers were working for mainstream publications, and thus still had to write for an audience that was unlikely to be very sympathetic or informed when it came to rock. This began to change when the counterculture developed an "alternative press," written by and for audiences with a countercultural sensibility. Rock culture constituted a major part of these magazines' subject matter and became even more so as other aspects of counterculture began to fade away in the early seventies. The establishment of magazines that were specifically devoted to rock music and culture, such as *Rolling Stone* and *Creem*, had a profound effect on the development of rock in the seventies. The rock press served to unify the rock audience around a common set of standards and values. If an artist appeared on the cover of *Rolling Stone* magazine, that alone could establish their significance to rock music. (There was even a song to this effect, "The Cover of *Rolling Stone*," written by the poet Shel Silverstein and performed by Dr. Hook and the Medicine Show.) By the same token, criticisms from the rock press could no longer be dismissed as the opinions of out-of-touch older writers who didn't understand rock. The new rock journalism was critiquing rock music from *within*, and in so doing, it defined a set of expectations and standards that still largely hold to the present day.

LED ZEPPELIN AND HARD ROCK

By the early 1970s the British hard rock band Led Zeppelin, formed in London in 1968, was well on its way to becoming the most profitable and influential act in rock music. "Zep," as its fans called it, was made up of Jimmy Page, a brilliant guitarist who had honed his skills as Eric Clapton's successor in the pioneering British band called the Yardbirds; John Bonham, who established the thunderous sound of heavy metal drumming; John Paul Jones, who provided the band's solid bottom, doubling on electric bass and organ; and Robert Plant, whose agile high tenor voice established the norm for subsequent heavy metal singers. Zeppelin's sledgehammer style of guitar-focused rock music drew on various influences, including urban blues, San Francisco psychedelia, and the virtuoso guitar playing of Jimi Hendrix. Although Led Zeppelin is usually associated with the heavy textures and extremely loud volume of their hard rock repertoire, their recordings also included another important stream—an interest in folk music, particularly the traditions of the British Isles.

"Stairway to Heaven" is Led Zeppelin's most famous recording, and it reflects certain unique features of the band's musical approach, as well as its position

Robert Plant and Jimmy Page of **Led Zeppelin** in 1975. © Neal Preston/Corbis.

🎧 LISTENING TO "STAIRWAY TO HEAVEN"

What accounts for this recording's tremendous commercial success and its ability to ignite the imaginations and inspire the loyalty of millions of fans? To begin with, "Stairway" skillfully juxtaposes two dimensions of Led Zeppelin's musical persona—the bone-crushing rock band, known for inspiring riots and dismantling hotel rooms, and the folk music aficionados, steeped in a reverence for ancient English and Celtic mythology. While these two sensibilities might seem diametrically opposed, the twin musical threads of sonic aggression and acoustic intimacy run through the entire history of heavy metal. (Most heavy metal albums include at least one "ballad," a term that in this context usually implies the use of acoustic guitar.) For many fans in Zeppelin's predominantly young, male audience, the combination of rock physicality and folk mysticism in "Stairway to Heaven" created something akin to a sacred experience. The somewhat inscrutable song text, composed by singer Robert Plant during a rehearsal, was also an important

source of the recording's attraction. Both Plant and Jimmy Page were at the time exploring the writings of the noted English mystic Aleister Crowley—into whose house Page eventually moved—and reading scholarly tomes like *Magic Arts in Celtic Britain*, which Plant later said influenced the lyrics for "Stairway." The text's references to mythological beings—the May Queen and the Piper—and rural images—paths and roads, rings of smoke through the forest, a songbird by a brook, the whispering wind—helped to create a cumulative mood of mystery and enchantment.

Although the basic building blocks of "Stairway to Heaven" are straightforward four- and eight-bar phrases, the overall arrangement is quite complex in formal terms (see the Listening Chart). There are three main sections. Section One alternates two eight-measure phrases, which we are calling A and B. The basic form of Section One is ABABAA' (the last section being an abridged version of A). Section Two reverses the order of the phrases and inserts a brief one-measure linking

LISTENING CHART "STAIRWAY TO HEAVEN"
Music and lyrics by Jimmy Page and Robert Plant; performed by Led Zeppelin; recorded 1971

FORM		LYRICS	DESCRIPTIVE COMMENTS
Section One (0:00)			
A (8 measures)		Instrumental	Six-string acoustic guitar; double-tracked recorder (flute) duet enters in measure 5; Slow tempo (72 beats per minute).
B (8)	0.26		Guitar and recorders continue.
A (8)	0.53	*There's a lady . . .* *When she gets there . . .*	Vocal enters.
B (4)	1.21	*Ooo . . .* *And she's buying . . .*	
A (8)	1.33	*There's a sign . . .* *In a tree . . .*	
A' (4)	2.01	Instrumental	Six-string guitar and recorders continue.
Section Two (2:14)			Twelve-string guitar, soft electric guitar, electric piano; intensity increases, tempo slightly faster (80 b.p.m.).
B (8)		*Oooo, It makes . . .* *Oooo, It makes . . .*	

A (8)	2.38	There's a feeling . . . In my thoughts . . .	
X (1)		Instrumental	One-measure linking section; electric guitar becomes more dominant.
B (8)	3.07	Oooo, It makes . . . Oooo, really makes . . .	Texture thickens, volume and tempo increase slightly.
A (8)	3.29	And it's whispered . . . And a new day . . .	
X (1)		Instrumental	Linking section.
B (8)	3.57		Slight crescendo, slight tempo increase. Drums enter at end, leading us into next section.
Section Three (4:19)			
C (8)		If there's a bustle . . . Yes there are . . .	New minor chord progression; electric guitar, twelve-string acoustic guitar, plus electric bass and drum set; tempo faster (84 b.p.m.).
X (1)		Instrumental	Linking section.
B (8)	4.45	And it makes . . .	
C (8)	5.07	Your head . . . Dear lady . . .	
X—(2)		Instrumental	Linking section, plus one measure pause.
D (8)	5.35	| |	Instrumental fanfare using chords from C; Tempo speeds up, leading us into next section.
Guitar solo (20)	5.56	| | |	Chord pattern continues; tempo faster (ca. 98 b.p.m.); multitracked guitar plays supporting pattern under solo (last 8 measures).
C (18)	6.44	And as we . . . (4) There walks . . . (4) How everything . . . (4) The tune . . . (4) To be a rock . . . (2)	
C (8)	7.27	Instrumental	Tempo slows down, intensity decreases.
B (3)	7.46	And she's buying . . .	Solo voice (tempo rubato).

phrase (which we are calling X). The form of Section Two is BAXBAXB. Section Three, which takes up almost half of the total eight minutes of recording time, introduces a new (though closely related) chord progression and melody, which we are calling C.[1] The first part of Section Three has the form CXBCX. After a one-measure pause, this is followed by an instrumental fanfare that propels us into Jimmy Page's guitar solo. Robert Plant's voice then re-enters, and there is an extended vocal section, using the harmonies from phrase C. The arrangement concludes with an instrumental phrase, slowing down and becoming much quieter in the last two measures.

1. Throughout "Stairway to Heaven," the harmonies circle around a set of closely related chords, giving the performance an additional sense of continuity.

The track concludes quietly, with Robert Plant repeating the key line of the text: *And she's buying a stairway to heaven*. The arrangement of "Stairway to Heaven" is constructed to create a continual escalation in density, volume, and speed. (The tempo increases from around 72 beats per minute at the opening of the recording to 84 beats per minute at the beginning of Section Three, and peaking at around 98 b.p.m. during the guitar solo. This substantial, though gradual, increase in speed is crucial to the overall impact of the recording.)

If "Stairway" seems complex in purely structural terms, this may be because the logic of its organization is fundamentally emotional and metaphoric. The recording can itself be seen as an analogue of the heavenly stairway, springing from the rural, mythological past (symbolized by acoustic instruments), soaring on jet-powered wings of metal, and finally coming to rest on a high, peaceful plateau. Similarly, the outer cover of the original album juxtaposes the sepia image of a peasant with that of a modern skyscraper rising over the formerly rustic landscape. The inner jacket portrays a mysterious hooded figure standing atop an icy peak with a staff and a lantern, looking down at a bell-bottomed seeker of knowledge who struggles to reach the top. Also included inside the album's dust jacket are the lyrics to "Stairway to Heaven" and a set of mystical symbols, or runes, one of which inspired the informal name for the album, "zoso." In seeking to understand what a recording like "Stairway" meant to its fans, the analysis of musical form must be coupled with a consideration of its other expressive dimensions, including the song text and the graphic design of the album on which it appeared.

vis-à-vis the commercial mainstream of pop music. To begin with, the song presents us with a fascinating marketing strategy, at first glance perverse but actually quite brilliant. Although "Stairway to Heaven" was the most frequently requested song on FM radio during the 1970s, the eight-minute track was never released as a single. In other words, to own a copy of "Stairway to Heaven," you had to buy the album. Of course, that could prove difficult for the uninitiated consumer, since the band insisted on an album cover that bore neither the name of the album, nor the name of the band, nor the name of the record company. (Atlantic Records was horrified by this design, but the band held the master tapes for the album hostage, and the record company had no choice but to go along.) Driven in part by the popularity of "Stairway to Heaven," the LP *Led Zeppelin IV* reached the Number 2 position on the *Billboard* Top LP charts and stayed on the charts for five years, eventually selling fourteen million copies.

STADIUM ROCK

The growing popularity of groups like Led Zeppelin allowed rock music to move from small clubs and theaters to arenas and stadiums. Over time, this change in venue began to alter the music itself. When presented with the opportunity to play larger venues, musicians began to design their music and general performance style to work well in that environment, an approach that would come to be known as "stadium rock" or "arena rock." Stadium rock is not really a genre in the conventional sense, but more an approach to music making that became prominent in the mid-seventies. Its defining characteristic was grandiosity in every regard, from song structure to attitude to general stagecraft. Its goal was to present an exciting audiovisual experience to a huge crowd; everything else was secondary. Two of the most successful exponents of stadium rock were Peter Frampton and Kiss.

Peter Frampton had been a moderately successful blues-rock guitarist, primarily known as a minor figure of the British Invasion of the sixties as part of the groups the Herd and Humble Pie. In the seventies he went solo, eventually achieving success with the album *Frampton Comes Alive* (1976), which was the biggest selling live album to that time. It was no accident that Frampton's breakthrough would come in the form of a live album; the stadium rock form was built for the live concert environment and would not have worked nearly as well in the studio. "Do You Feel Like We Do," the album's most popular song, emphasized this orientation in several ways. Like most stadium rock songs, the song built to a rousing, sing-along chorus. Though ostensibly a love song, the "you" of the title was widely understood to refer to the *audience*, rather than to an individual lover. Thus, not only did it serve as a love song from band to audience, but it was one that explicitly demanded a participatory response from the listener (Frampton: *Do you feel like we do?* Audience: *YES!*), making the band–audience relationship a central theme of the song itself.

The song also made extensive use of the Heil Talk Box, a machine that routed the sound of the guitar through a plastic tube into Frampton's mouth, thus allowing him to essentially "talk" using the sound of the guitar rather than his own vocal cords. On the recording, the audience can be heard loudly cheering about twenty-five seconds before the effect can be heard, presumably because they could see that he was preparing to use it. In other words, the audience was cheering more for the *existence* of the effect, than for how it was used. Such mythologizing of rock technology was part of a larger trend in stadium rock (and rock in general) during this era. If rock stars were like gods on Earth, then their tools were to be treated as relics. This can be seen not only in the Talk Box, but also in the treatment of guitars (e.g. Jimmy Page's distinctive double-neck guitar) and amplifiers. In fact, the widespread use of so-called "dummy cabs"—large walls of fake guitar speakers that served no musical purpose—was a hallmark of stadium rock. This would have made no sense in an earlier era of rock, when equipment served in a primarily utilitarian capacity. In the seventies, by contrast, sound equipment was now viewed as part of a theater set, as a visual symbol of rock's power.

The foremost exponents of stadium rock were the members of Kiss. Founded in 1973, Kiss was primarily known for its circus-like stage show that featured the spitting of blood (fake) and fire (real), a complex hydraulic stage set, and multiple explosions and smoke bombs. Their personae were equally theatrical, with each musician taking on a character that was expressed through elaborate costumes and iconic makeup. Bassist Gene Simmons was "The Demon," lead guitarist Ace Frehley was "The Spaceman," rhythm guitarist Paul Stanley was "The Star Child," and drummer Peter Criss was "The Cat." More than a

Kiss, with Gene Simmons up front, in 1979. Photo by Steve Jennings/WireImage.

performance choice, the makeup soon became a marketing tool as well. The members were never seen in public without their makeup, creating a sense of mystery about their true identities. Kiss was candid about their intention to exploit this mystique to the fullest, and they did. In addition to the standard records and posters, Kiss fans could buy such products as action figures, costumes, makeup kits, and even a comic book about the band that was rumored to be printed in their own blood. Like Peter Frampton, Kiss's musical breakthrough also came in the form of a live album, *Kiss Alive* (1975). The album featured their first Top 40 single "Rock 'n' Roll All Nite," which—like other stadium rock hits—directly addressed the audience in the second person.

SOUTHERN ROCK

The sound and sensibility of what came to be called Southern Rock drew upon regional traditions such as the blues, boogie-woogie piano music, Louisiana Cajun music, and the big-band swing music of "territory bands" that roamed the South and Southwest during the 1930s and 1940s. This reassertion of the southern "roots" of rock took many forms, and was arguably pioneered by a group from the San Francisco Bay area, rather than the Deep South. In 1969, a year when the influence of the counterculture seemed to be at a new height— what with domestic political turmoil on one hand, and the Woodstock music festival attracting nearly half a million fans on the other—the pop charts were ruled by <u>Creedence Clearwater Revival</u>. This seems initially like another of pop music's great historical ironies. Creedence was a deliberately old-fashioned rock 'n' roll band, consisting of two guitarists, a bass player, and a drummer, performing both original material and some old 1950s rock 'n' roll tunes in a musical style essentially untouched by the trappings of the psychedelic era: no exotic instruments, no unusual or extended guitar solos, no studio effects, no self-conscious experimentation with novel harmonies, rhythms, or song forms. Creedence was one of the all-time great singles bands, turning out a spate of incredibly catchy, up-tempo two- to three-minute pop records that cut right through all the psychedelic haze of the San Francisco scene and scored major hits for the group, one after the other. Given these songs' lack of pretension, they were as effective as live performance vehicles as they were as pop recordings. In addition, the albums put out by Creedence were all huge sellers, despite—or perhaps we should say because of—the fact that they were essentially just old-fashioned collections of great singles.

In terms of the subcategories of rock music that we are discussing here, Creedence is not easily classifiable. Despite their origins in the Bay Area, they positioned themselves as Southern rock stylists, singing about bayous, Mississippi riverboats, catfish and bullfrogs, and other popular elements of Southern iconography. Their sound was influenced by early rock 'n' rollers such as Chuck Berry and Elvis Presley, the honky-tonk music of Hank Williams, and the studio sound of Memphis's Sun Records. Creedence Clearwater Revival restored to rock music a sense of its roots at precisely the point when the majority of important rock musicians seemed to be pushing the envelope of novel possibilities as far and as rapidly as they could. Creedence was in no sense a reactionary phenomenon, however; the group's choice of the word "revival" was an astute one. The many original songs in their repertoire, all written by lead singer and guitarist John Fogerty, possessed solid musical virtues, and several of them also reflected a decidedly up-to-date political awareness (such as "Bad Moon Rising"

Creedence Clearwater Revival takes it to the streets in 1970. Michael Ochs Archives/Getty Images.

Allman Brothers Band in 1970. GAB Archive/Redferns.

and "Fortunate Son") that nevertheless was not tied to any specific agenda (much like the kind of awareness found in Bob Dylan's lyrics). In fact, Creedence's best songs have arguably stood the test of time better than a lot of other music from the 1960s that might have seemed much more adventurous and relevant at the time. Creedence Clearwater Revival was the first widely successful "roots" rock 'n' roll band. Perhaps owing to their extraordinary popularity, many other roots artists have appeared as rock has continued to evolve. But Creedence set the standard in this realm, and it is one that has yet to be approached by anyone else.

A very different though no less brilliant group, the <u>Allman Brothers Band</u>, helped to reconnect the generative power of southern music, particularly the blues, to the mainstream of rock music and to the open-ended instrumental improvisations of modern jazz and of San Francisco "jam bands" such as the Grateful Dead. The Allman Brothers Band is still regarded as the quintessential southern rock group, and for a brief time in the early 1970s, led by the brilliant and regrettably short-lived guitarist Duane Allman (1946–71), they truly lit up the southern sky.

The Florida-born brothers Duane and Gregg Allman had been gigging with various bands since the early 1960s. In 1969 they joined with guitarist Dickey Betts, bassist Berry Oakley, and drummers Butch Trucks and Jai Johanny (Jaimoe) Johanson to form the Allman Brothers Band, featuring Duane on lead guitar and Gregg on organ, piano, and lead vocals. A sought-after session musician both before and during his tenure with the band, Duane Allman recorded with soul music stars such as Aretha Franklin and Wilson Pickett, and he collaborated with Eric Clapton on the celebrated 1970 album *Layla and Other Assorted Love Songs*. Working out of Macon, Georgia, the Allman Brothers Band achieved their artistic and commercial breakthrough in 1971 with the release of *At Fillmore East*, often cited by critics as one of the best live rock albums ever made. We will take a closer look at the Allman Brothers' version of the song "Statesboro Blues" from that album in order to familiarize ourselves both with their unique style and with Duane's mastery of the electric guitar, particularly his use of a blues-derived technique called "bottleneck."

The Allman Brothers Band's performances in the leading concert venues of the day, their use of rock music technology, and their celebrity status marked them as contemporary artists; their use of traditional songs, rhythms, and textures derived from African American folk and popular music, and of

🎧 LISTENING TO "STATESBORO BLUES"

"Statesboro Blues" was composed and originally recorded by the Georgia-born blues musician Blind Willie McTell (1898–1959), and it became one of the Allman Brothers Band's signature tunes, often used to open their concerts. This song is an example of the twelve-bar blues form that we discussed in Chapter 1 in connection with Louis Jordan's "Choo Choo Ch'Boogie." In this recording the twelve-bar musical structure is combined with a traditional form for blues lyrics consisting of three lines of text, in which the singer performs an opening line, repeats it more or less exactly, and then concludes the verse with a contrasting line (a version of the "call-and-response" form that appears so frequently in African American folk, popular, and sacred music).

The performance begins with a riff (repeated pattern), played four times in unison by the band, and answered each time by Duane Allman's bottleneck guitar. The band then plays through the twelve-bar form once with Duane soloing on bottleneck guitar, and Gregg enters singing:

> Wake up Mama, turn your lamp down
> low
> Wake up Mama, turn your lamp down
> low
> You got no nerve, baby, to turn Uncle
> John from your do[or]
> I woke up this morning, had them
> Statesboro Blues
> I woke up this morning, had them
> Statesboro Blues
> Well, I looked over in the corner, baby,
> and grandma seemed to have them,
> too.

Following the second verse, Duane Allman plays a soaring, almost continuous guitar solo over two iterations of the twelve-bar blues structure. This is followed by the third sung verse, which during the first four bars of the form uses a technique called "stop-time," in which the band plays the same riff that opened the recording and stops abruptly on the first beat of each bar, leaving an open space for the singer:

> (RIFF) Well, my mama died and lef' me
> (RIFF) My papa died and lef' me

> (RIFF) I ain't good looking, baby
> (RIFF) But I'm somewhat sweet and
> kind
> I'm goin' to the country, baby do you
> want to go?
> If you can't make it, baby, your sister
> Lucille said she wanna go.

The next two iterations of the blues form feature a guitar solo by the band's second guitarist, Dickey Betts, and the performance concludes with two additional sung verses.

The twelve-bar blues form is relatively easy to hear on this recording, but no formal analysis can capture the power of the performance itself: Gregg Allman's gritty, Ray Charles-influenced singing; the flexibly coordinated rhythmic relationship between the two drummers; and, most importantly, the soaring, expressive, voice-like presence of Duane Allman's guitar. The unique sound of Duane's guitar was achieved by running the signal from his electric guitar (a Gibson Les Paul) through a distortion unit called a "fuzzbox" and then through two powerful bass amplifiers, which allowed him to create loud, sustained tones of potentially infinite length. This use of the cutting-edge technology of the time was combined with a guitar technique derived from the country blues tradition discussed in Chapter 6 in connection with Robert Johnson's 1936 recording of "Cross Road Blues": the use of a "bottleneck"—sometimes literally the severed neck of a bottle, sometimes a substitute made of plastic or metal—which when slid over a finger on the guitarist's left hand, allows him to glide smoothly over the individual tones of the scale, and thus to create long, swooping melodic lines. (The track's second guitar solo, by Dickey Betts, does not use a bottleneck—see if you can hear the difference between the two.) *At Fillmore East* established Duane Allman's stature as a rock guitarist; in 2003, *Rolling Stone* magazine ranked him Number 2 in their list of the 100 greatest guitarists of all time, second only to Jimi Hendrix.

instruments such as bottleneck guitar and harmonica ("blues harp") rooted them in the rich soil of Southern folk music. "Statesboro Blues" is in fact one of the most musically conventional tracks on the *At Fillmore East* album, which also features relatively lengthy, open-ended improvisations on original compositions such as "In Memory of Elizabeth Reed" and "Whipping Post." For the first half of the 1970s, and despite the tragic deaths of Duane Allman (1971) and bassist Berry Oakley (1972) in eerily similar motorcycle accidents, the Allman Brothers Band was among the most influential rock groups in America. Their incorporation of elements of blues, rhythm & blues, and jazz (and, increasingly, country music), and their powerful, extended live "jams," helped to alter the norms of concert performance. While other rock groups, such as the Grateful Dead and Cream, were known for their on-stage jamming, when the Allman Brothers stretched a song out for a half hour or more, they were capable of achieving peaks of collective musical creativity that surpassed any band of their era. At the same time, they established the genre of Southern Rock, paving the way for other bands from the Deep South, including the Marshall Tucker Band, Lynyrd Skynyrd, and the Charlie Daniels Band.

Before moving on, it is important that we address the political implications of a genre that defined itself as proudly—and often defiantly—"Southern." In expressing this pride, many Southern rock bands, intentionally or unintentionally, presented a view of the South that was, at best, insensitive to African American history and, at worst, simply racist. Such sentiments could be seen in everything from the use of Confederate iconography in album packaging and stage sets, to a general conflation of the idea of the rock rebel with that of the southern rebel, to specific song lyrics. Perhaps the most famous instance of this association is a musical exchange between the southern rock band Lynyrd Skynyrd and Canadian-born rock musician Neil Young, whose song "Southern Man" (Number 4 in 1970) evokes the racist treatment of blacks in the American South ("I saw cotton and I saw blacks, tall white mansions and little shacks. Southern Man, when will you pay them back?"). Lynyrd Skynyrd's response, "Sweet Home Alabama" (Number 8, 1974), was a direct rejoinder:

> *Well I heard mister Young sing about her (Alabama)*
> *Well, I heard ol' Neil put her down*
> *Well, I hope Neil Young will remember*
> *A Southern man don't need him around, anyhow*

While Lynyrd Skynyrd's lead singer, Ronnie Van Zant, has argued that the lyrics of "Sweet Home Alabama"—which also make reference to segregationist governor George Wallace—are more ambiguous than is generally recognized, there can be little doubt about the association of much Southern rock with a specifically white Southern heritage. At the same time, it is equally true that, musicologically speaking, Southern rock is built almost entirely on a foundation of African American tradition, from the blues and soul apparent in its lead vocals and musical forms, to the gospel influence on its backup vocals, to the impact of jazz on its harmonized guitar lines and long, improvised solos.

In fact, the Allman Brothers Band—arguably the definitive representative of the Southern rock genre—openly declared their indebtedness to and admiration for black musicians as varied in approach as Willie Dixon, Ray Charles, and jazz great John Coltrane. And, as previously mentioned, before forming the band Duane Allman had recorded extensively with many of the major African American soul artists of the era, as had drummer Jai Johanny Johanson, who was himself African American. Ultimately, the simple fact is that, when it comes to race, Southern rock contains many contradictions. Regardless of how—or even if—one chooses to resolve those contradictions, one thing is clear: The stereotypical association of certain genres of music with certain social values and attitudes (and certain "kinds of people") rarely tells the whole story.

JAZZ ROCK

Jazz Rock was a loosely defined category that included commercially successful collaborations between jazz and rock musicians—such as the two groups Blood, Sweat & Tears and Chicago Transit Authority (later simply Chicago)—along with a variety of hybrid styles that melded rock aesthetics and instrumentation with the harmonic and rhythmic complexity and improvisational virtuosity of contemporary jazz (as in the work of the Flock, the Mahavishnu Orchestra, and Weather Report). Some of these groups and their recordings are most often mentioned in the context of jazz history, while others are typically included in discussions of the development of rock music.

The most influential, and for many listeners, startling example of a fusion between jazz and rock music was Miles Davis's album *Bitches Brew*, released in 1970. Miles Davis (1926–91) began his career in the late 1940s playing trumpet with modern jazz pioneers such as Charlie Parker, and had for much of the 1950s and 1960s played a critical role in the evolution of jazz—leading a variety of bands, pushing the evolution of the music along at critical junctures, and helping to bring to prominence younger musicians who themselves became leading innovators of modern jazz (including the brilliant saxophonist John Coltrane).

Somewhat parallel to the reaction of traditionalist folk music fans to Bob Dylan's embrace of rock music in the mid-1960s, many jazz aficionados were confounded, even alienated, by *Bitches Brew*, which combined the exploratory spirit of avant-garde jazz with sonic textures and funky grooves inspired by the music of Jimi Hendrix and Sly Stone. The double album made a vivid visual impression, designed around a surrealistic Afrocentric painting by German artist Mati Klarwein, whose work also adorned Santana's *Abraxas* album (released the same year). To make *Bitches Brew*, Miles Davis assembled a roster of thirteen musicians, including the pianists Joe Zawinul and Chick Corea, drummers Jack DeJohnette and Lenny White, bassist Dave Holland, saxophonist Wayne Shorter, guitarist John McLaughlin, and the Brazilian percussionist Airto Moreira. (Most of these musicians went on to play major roles in the evolution of jazz rock, performing in bands such as Weather Report, Mahavishnu Orchestra, and Return to Forever.) The ensemble for *Bitches Brew* was larger than the norm for contemporary jazz groups or rock bands and was centered on a rhythm section of two drummers, two keyboardists, and two bassists (electric and acoustic), who created shifting rhythmic grooves and textures.

The musicians were brought together for three days in the studio and were given only minimal instructions: an indication of the tempo that Davis wanted, a musical gesture or melody, or impressionistic suggestions of the desired mood or tone. As Davis himself described the process:

> I would direct, like a conductor, once we started to play, and I would either write down some music for somebody or would tell him to play different things I was hearing, as the music was growing, coming together. While the music was developing I would hear something that I thought could be extended or cut back. . . . After it had developed to a certain point, I would tell a certain musician to come in and play something else.[2]

Davis worked closely on *Bitches Brew* with record producer and composer Teo Macero, who kept the tape running continuously throughout the recording sessions, and worked with the trumpeter to shape the final product by cutting, splicing, and rearranging the music and adding post-production studio effects. (It has been suggested that Macero's decades-long creative relationship with Miles Davis was not unlike producer George Martin's work with the Beatles.) This fluid process—akin to "free jazz" improvisation and the open-ended jamming of the Grateful Dead, but with two "authors" firmly in charge of the final recorded product—yielded a recording that didn't fit either the jazz or the rock paradigms of the time, and that still sounds fresh and challenging today. Extraordinarily, for a double album that contained more than 100 minutes of highly experimental music, *Bitches Brew* reached Number 4 on the R&B Album chart and Number 35 on the Pop Album chart, and was Miles Davis's first recording to be certified a gold record (indicating sales of half a million units).

Of the various bands that inhabited the rock-oriented, AM-radio-friendly side of Jazz Rock in the early 1970s, Chicago (who changed their name from Chicago Transit Authority in response to threatened legal action by the real CTA) achieved the greatest long-term popularity and commercial success. According to *Billboard* chart statistics, Chicago is second only to the Beach Boys as the most successful American rock band of all time, in terms of both albums and singles. In 2002, Chicago's hit singles were assembled together on a two-

---

2. See "The making of Bitches Brew," by Paul Tingen. *Jazz Times* 31(4), May 2001, p. 49.

Chicago in 1977. Rex USA.

disc set, and the album debuted in the Top 40, giving the band the distinction of having had chart albums in five consecutive decades.

Today Chicago is best known for anthemic love songs such as "If You Leave Me Now" (1976), "Hard to Say I'm Sorry" (1982), and "Look Away" (1988), all of which reached Number 1 on both the Pop and Adult Contemporary charts. But in their early days the band specialized in a harder-edged style that fused the guitar-centered sound of rock with a three-piece horn section that could play R&B-style riffs and improvise in the manner of jazz musicians. They honed their chops as the house band at Los Angeles's Whisky A Go-Go nightclub, following in the footsteps of the Doors. In 1968 they were heard by Jimi Hendrix, who, on the strength of guitarist Terry Kath's playing, hired them to open for him and Janis Joplin on a European tour. The band was signed by Columbia Records in 1969, and their first album (*Chicago Transit Authority*) reached the Top 20, without benefit of a hit single.

"25 or 6 to 4" (Number 4 Pop in 1970), was the highest-charting track from Chicago's second album (*Chicago II*), and is a good example of their earlier, more rock-oriented approach. "25 or 6 to 4" is part of a twelve-song suite entitled *Ballet for a Girl in Buchannon*, an indication of the band's artistic ambitions, very much in tune with rock albums of the time. The track opens with guitarist Terry Kath playing the song's signature riff, a series of five descending chords. (The muffled, distorted sound of the chords was created with the use of the foot-operated electronic device called a fuzzbox.) This chord sequence is repeated with the addition of drums, followed by the entry of the horn section, playing a tightly organized sequence of unison and contrapuntal melodic lines, dominated by the trombone sound of James Pankow. The song consists of a series of verses sung by bassist Peter Cetera (the voice on many of Chicago's later hit singles), and a chorus sung in harmony. The sound and the attitude of this recording place it clearly within the category of rock music; whether this music is more accurately described as "jazz rock" or as "rock music with horns" is in the end an academic matter. Two features appear to have commanded the attention of fans at the time the song was released: the lyrics, written by the band's organist, Robert Lamm; and Terry Kath's extraordinary guitar solo, which places him among the most virtuosic rock guitarists of the era.

There is a tradition among rock fans of debating the meaning of the enigmatic (or supposedly enigmatic) lyrics of songs—certain compositions by Bob Dylan, the later Beatles, and Led Zeppelin rank high in this regard. Chicago fans' interpretations of the meaning of "25 or 6 to 4" included the suggestions that the title is a drug reference (the number of joints that can be rolled from a bag of marijuana) or a poetic, mystical invocation of a spiritual revelation. For his part, Robert Lamm has said that the song is about the experience of staying up all night writing a song, and that the title phrase refers to the time of day (25 or 26 minutes before 4:00 A.M.).[3] But the continuing delight of puzzling over lines such as "flashing lights against the sky" and "staring blindly into space" appears to have rendered this mundane interpretation unpalatable for many fans.

It has been argued that the rock sound of Chicago's early recordings is primarily attributable to the presence of the guitarist and singer Terry Kath, who died of an accidental self-inflicted gunshot wound in 1978. Kath was a talented musician, admired by contemporaries such as Hendrix and Eric Clapton, and his solo on the album version of "25 or 6 to 4" provides an example of his virtuosic technique, his command of scales not commonly used by rock guitarists, and his adept use of a device called a wah-wah pedal, which approximates the acoustic characteristics of a human voice saying "wah." (One of the most popular wah-wah pedals of the early 1970s was called "Cry Baby," an evocation of the sound of an infant wailing.) Kath's playing is melodically inventive and unpredictable, and uses the continuous sound created by electronic distortion to soften and blur the attack of his guitar pick, so that the notes form a smooth, flowing chain of sound that builds gradually in intensity. In a parallel to the Doors' "Light My Fire," which was initially edited for AM airplay by cutting out Ray Manzarek's organ solo, Terry Kath's solo on the album version of "25 or 6 to 4," which is about 76 seconds in length (accounting for over one-quarter of the duration of the entire track), was truncated drastically in the single version that received the most airplay on AM Top 40 radio. (Singing is almost invariably favored over instrumental improvisation in the creation of three-minute pop singles. The

3. See "Chicago History, Chapter VI," *Official Site of Chicago the Band*. http://chicagotheband.info/chapters68.cfm.

album version of "25 or 6 to 4" was, however, favored on the more free-form format of FM radio.) Terry Kath's death was a watershed moment for Chicago, which in the years to follow achieved commercial success by moving away from rock music toward a smoother, "adult contemporary" sound.

SINGER-SONGWRITERS AND SOFT ROCK

The rise of singer-songwriters in the early seventies reflected the confluence of several largely unrelated factors that were emerging at the time. Perhaps the most central was the idea that a relaxed, mature musical style that focused on intimacy in both its sound and lyrical content could still be considered rock. This was a direct result of the expanding of rock's boundaries in the mid-1960s. Another important factor was that not only was it *possible* for rock to relax, but that a substantial number of listeners actually *wanted it to*. This reflected both a change in the national mood and also the maturing of rock's baby boomer audience into their late twenties and early thirties. As their concerns shifted from revolution to personal growth and domesticity, rock could now accommodate them. This change was also facilitated by the rise of a new radio format, called "Soft Rock," a term that would have seemed like a contradiction only a few years earlier. While not all singer-songwriters were considered soft rock and not all soft rock consisted of singer-songwriters, there was a substantial overlap between the two fields. But perhaps the most fascinating implication of the rise of soft rock was that it represented a merging of two branches of the rock family tree that had been directly opposed to each other only a decade earlier: folk musicians and Brill Building songwriters.

The concept of the singer-songwriter was based on the idea of sincerity, in the form of a professional singer who wrote and performed songs about his or her own emotional life. Folk musicians, such as Simon and Garfunkel, kept their acoustic guitars, song style, and emphasis on lyrical sophistication but added commercial hooks and highly personal subject matter. Brill Building songwriters such as Carole King and Neil Diamond simply began to perform their own music, rather than farming it out to slick "teen idols." While in the early sixties, these professional songwriters may have been excluded from the world of pop performance by their plain looks, workmanlike vocal style, or ethnicity (both King and Diamond were Jewish), all of these considerations had been made obsolete by the rise of Bob Dylan. On every level, then, the singer-songwriter genre of the 1970s thus represents a middle ground—reconciliation between opposing camps after the conflicts of the sixties. The folk side of the equation is well represented by <u>Simon and Garfunkel</u>.

Perhaps nothing illustrates the changes wrought by the phenomenon of folk rock as well as the story of Simon and Garfunkel's first hit record, "The Sounds of Silence." In early 1965 Paul Simon and Arthur Garfunkel were an urban folk duo with a fine acoustic album to their credit, *Wednesday Morning, 3 A.M.*, that was causing no excitement whatsoever in the marketplace. When

Folk rockers **Paul Simon** (left) and **Art Garfunkel** performing in 1966. David Redfern/Redferns/RDA/Getty Images.

folk rock hit the scene in midyear and Bob Dylan went electric, Simon and Garfunkel's producer, Tom Wilson—who was also the producer for Bob Dylan's records at the time—had a "bright idea." He took one of Simon's original compositions from the *Wednesday Morning* album, a highly poetic song about urban alienation called "The Sound of Silence," overdubbed a rock band accompaniment of electric guitars, bass, and drums onto the original recording, speeded it up very slightly, changed the title for some reason to "The Sounds of Silence," and released it as a single—all without Simon or Garfunkel's prior knowledge or permission! The duo found little to complain about, however, as they found themselves with a Number 1 pop hit on New Year's Day 1966. Needless to say, they never looked back. Simon and Garfunkel became one of the most enduringly popular acts ever to perform in a folk-rock style. Although the duo broke up in 1970 (they have occasionally reunited for special occasions), their songs and albums continue to be popular to this day.

Paul Simon is among the few singer-songwriters to come to prominence in the 1960s who arguably achieved his creative peak considerably later on. To say this is not to denigrate Simon's work with Simon and Garfunkel, which includes such memorable and varied songs as "A Hazy Shade of Winter," "America," and "Bridge Over Troubled Water"; it is simply to claim that these earlier compositions would probably not lead one to suspect that Simon would eventually go on to produce such adventurous works of world music as *Graceland* and *The Rhythm of the Saints* (see Chapter 10).

The career of <u>Carole King</u> in the 1970s represents the Brill Building side of the singer-songwriter equation, and illustrates, perhaps better than any other example could, the central prominence of singer-songwriters during this period. King had been an important songwriter for more than a decade (in the 1960s, she wrote many hits with Gerry Goffin, her husband at that time), but was virtually unknown as a performer until she released the album *Tapestry*, from which the single "It's Too Late" was drawn, in 1971. The astounding popularity of both the single and album established Carole King as a major recording star. In the aftermath of King's success as a performer, relatively few songwriters were content to remain behind the scenes; it came to be expected that most pop songwriters would want to perform their own material and, conversely, that most pop singers would want to record material that they had written themselves.

Just the same, few singer-songwriters at this time were able to achieve the degree of success won by King. "It's Too Late" held the Number 1 spot for five weeks, and even its flip side, "I Feel The Earth Move"—also a cut from *Tapestry*—proved popular in its own right and was frequently played on the radio. (Both songs remained long-term favorites of King's fans.) *Tapestry* itself was an unprecedented hit. It was the Number 1 album for fifteen weeks, remained on the charts for nearly six years, and sold in excess of twenty-four million copies worldwide, making it one of the best-selling albums of all time.

Carole King was approaching the age of thirty when she recorded "It's Too Late." Clearly she was far from being the teenager who had written such songs as "Will You Love Me Tomorrow?" and "Take Good Care of My Baby" for a market consisting primarily of other teenagers. King had matured, and her audience had matured along with her. "It's Too Late" is clearly an adult relationship song, written from the point of view of someone who has long left behind teenage crushes, insecurities, and desperate heartbreak. The singer describes the ending stage of a significant relationship with a feeling of sadness, but also with a mature philosophical acceptance that people can change and grow apart, and an understanding that this does not represent the end of the world for either of them.

The music of "It's Too Late" also reflects King's maturity. Her acoustic piano is the song's backbone, and it leads us through a sophisticated progression of relatively complex chords that portray a music world far removed from the harmonic simplicity of early rock 'n' roll. When, toward the end of the substantial instrumental interlude preceding the final verse of the song, the saxophone enters to play a melody, the context evokes a kind of light jazz, rather than earlier rock. (The recording as a whole epitomizes the kind of sound that came to be known—fortunately or otherwise—as "soft rock.") Like the words of the song, the sound of its music was clearly geared toward an audience of maturing young adults. It is equally clear that the audience was out there and more than ready to appreciate a recording like this one.

The emotions that King's music evoked were emblematic of the seventies: Her songs spoke of a mature re-evaluation of the choices made by her generation in the sixties, and in some cases even a longing for simpler times. Such attitudes were not unique to singer-songwriters, and in fact could also be found in the work of other kinds of mainstream rock artists, such as the Eagles and Bruce Springsteen.

THE EAGLES

By the early 1970s, a network of Los Angeles–based artists such as Poco (founded by Buffalo Springfield alumni Richie Furay and Jim Messina), Linda Ronstadt, and the <u>Eagles</u> (founded by members of the Flying Burrito Brothers and Linda Ronstadt's band) were specializing in a smooth, laid-back variant of country rock that achieved commercial success on the pop and, to a lesser extent, the country charts. (Perhaps the best example of this trend is Linda Ronstadt's single "When Will I Be Loved," which peaked at Number 1 Country and Number 2 Pop in 1974.)

California in the 1970s retained the central position in American popular culture that it had attained during the 1960s, and if the Beach Boys epitomized the culture of Southern California in the earlier decade, then the Eagles were the group that most obviously inherited that distinction. Indeed, the close association of this Los Angeles–based group with the Golden State was so well established at the time of their peak popularity (1975–80) that it lent particular authority to their ambitious saga of "Hotel California" (1976)—the million-selling single from the extraordinarily successful album of the same name (which has sold in excess of sixteen million copies).

The Eagles serve as an excellent case in point to illustrate the accelerating ascendancy in importance of albums over singles during the 1970s. When the Eagles issued their first compilation of singles in album form, *Eagles/Their Greatest Hits, 1971–1975,* the album achieved sales far beyond those of all its hit singles taken

The Eagles in the early 1970s. Michael Ochs Archives/Getty Images.

🎧 LISTENING TO "HOTEL CALIFORNIA"

Starting out in 1971 with feet firmly planted in country rock, the Eagles had moved from laid-back tunes like "Take It Easy" and "Peaceful Easy Feeling," and songs that evoked traditional Western imagery like "Desperado" and "Tequila Sunrise," to harder-hitting material like "One of These Nights" by 1975. "Hotel California" was the fourth of their five Number 1 singles, and it introduced a new, complex, poetic tone into the Eagles' work. Indeed, compared with many rock recordings of the 1970s, "Hotel California"—which reportedly took a full eight months to record—sounds much more like an ambitious late-1960s record. This is due to several factors: Its length, its minor-key harmonies, and its rather unusual overall shape (with extended guitar solos at the *end* of the record) all contribute to the effect, but surely it is the highly metaphoric lyrics that establish the most obvious kinship with the songwriting trends of the 1960s.

The tone of "Hotel California," however, is pure 1970s. The sense of loss and disillusionment is intense here, assuming a desperate, almost apocalyptic, character.

When the visitor to "Hotel California" asks the hotel captain to bring up some wine, he is told, that that "spirit" hasn't been available at the hotel since 1969, a dark pun indicating that the California of the late '60s is long gone. Finally, as the last verse ends, the fleeing visitor is told by the "night man" at the door that "... you can never leave." As if to illustrate all the implications of this memorable line, the song neither proceeds to the now-expected chorus ("Welcome to the Hotel California," whose pop-friendly major-key music assumes an increasingly ironic edge as the record progresses) nor fades out quickly. Instead, those words become the final words we hear, and the Eagles launch into lengthy guitar solos—over the chords of the verses, not those of the chorus—as if to underline our "stuck" situation and to eliminate anything that remotely suggests "welcoming." California, that sun-blessed beacon to the generation of "peace and love" in the 1960s, has here become a sinister trap for those who have no place left to go.

together; it was, in fact, the first recording to be certified by the Recording Industry Association of America (RIAA) as a million-selling ("platinum") album, and it went on to sell more than forty-two million copies worldwide.

CONCLUSION

In the seventies, rock became solidly established both as a cultural force and as a business enterprise. The profits generated by recordings, mass media, and live performances were brought into a self-perpetuating relationship that would last for decades. The "rock star" ideology flourished; stadium concerts, platinum albums, and mega-tours became commonplace; and a cultural infrastructure developed to support (and to critique) the genre. At the same time, the massive expansion of rock and its audience opened the door for the music's fragmentation into specialized subgenres, a trend that would continue with even greater intensity in the decades to follow.

In the next chapter we examine various offshoots of (and reactions to) mainstream rock music that rose to prominence during the second half of the seventies. Punk rock and its more cerebral cousin, new wave, emerged as a rejection of commercialism, and a self-conscious return to rock 'n' roll roots. Reggae music, a creolized Afro-Caribbean genre that incorporated American rhythm & blues, entered the U.S. market via a popular movie, and, with the rise of Bob Marley, became both an alternative for rock fans and a predecessor of worldbeat music. Funk emerged as another kind of back-to-basics movement, focused on social dance and drawing on the wellsprings of R&B and soul, while disco took the "gotta dance" impulses of funk and transformed them into a slicker, more studio-dependent, and pop-friendly style of social dance music, a kind of "anti-rock." Finally, hip-hop arose, in the impoverished South Bronx neighborhood of New York City, as an intensely local urban genre that simultaneously reasserted African American expressive values and made new uses of existing technologies.

8

THE 1970s: ROCK OFFSHOOTS AND RESPONSES

In the seventies, rock became identifiable not only as a genre of music, but also as a whole ideology about what a musician should be and do. The idea of the "rock star" in particular had an obvious appeal for musicians in other genres, including reggae and funk. Musicians in these genres were of course interested in living the life of a rock star, but they were equally—if not more—interested in applying the *ideology* of rock stardom to their work. The idea of a musician as a hard-living rebel—whose art emerges from a combination of self-indulgence, spirituality, and a unique point of view (often from the margins of society)—was not necessarily new, but its celebration by rock culture gave it a broad and consistent appeal that it had never had before.

At the same time, a new generation of musicians, working within the basic stylistic framework established by rock 'n' roll in the 1950s, reacted against what they saw as the artifice and excess of corporate rock music, symbolized quintessentially by glamorous rock stars wearing designer sunglasses and riding in limousines. These young musicians articulated a "back-to-basics" ideology that drew upon the rebellious energy and informality of early rock 'n' roll, and in so doing laid the groundwork for the rise of alternative rock in the 1980s.

PUNK ROCK AND NEW WAVE

During the 1970s the first "alternative" movements emerged within rock music. While rock had begun as a vital part of the 1960s counterculture, by 1975 it had come perilously close to occupying the center of popular taste, a development that left some young musicians feeling that its rebellious, innovative potential had been squandered by pampered, pretentious rock stars and the major record companies that promoted them. The golden age of *punk*, a "back to basics" rebellion against the perceived artifice and pretension of corporate rock music, lasted from around 1975 to 1978, but both the musical genre and the sensibility with which it was associated continue to exert a strong influence today on alternative rock musicians.

As its name suggests, punk was as much a cultural style—an attitude defined by a self-consciously bratty rebellion against authority and a deliberate rejection of middle-class values—as it was a musical genre. The contrarian impulse of punk culture is evoked (and parodied) in the song "I'm Against It," recorded by the Ramones in 1978.

> I don't like sex and drugs
> I don't like waterbugs
> I don't care about poverty
> All I care about is me
> I don't like playing Ping-Pong
> I don't like the Viet Cong
> I don't like Burger King
> I don't like anything
> Well I'm against it, I'm against it

In its automatic gainsaying of everything from sex and drugs to the Viet Cong and Burger King, this song evokes the motorcycle gang leader played by Marlon Brando in the archetypal teen rebellion film *The Wild One* (1954). When asked by a young woman, "What are you rebelling against?" the Brando character responds, "Whaddaya got?" It also—possibly unintentionally—echoes the song "Whatever It Is, I'm Against It," sung by Groucho Marx in the movie *Horsefeathers* (1932), suggesting ties to the rebellious humor of an earlier era.

Punk was in fact both the apotheosis and the ultimate exploitation of rock 'n' roll as a symbol of rebellion, a tradition that began in the 1950s with white teenagers gleefully co-opting the energy and overt sexuality of black rhythm & blues to annoy their parents, and continued through the 1960s with songs like the Who's 1966 youth anthem "My Generation" ("Why don't you all just f-f-fade away?"). To many of its fans, punk rock represented a turn toward the authentic, risk-taking spirit of early rock 'n' roll and away from the pomposity and self-conscious artistry of album-oriented rock. On the other hand, like all alternative styles of popular music, punk rock was riven with contradictions.

To begin with, if punk was explicitly against the standards of traditional commercial fashion, it was also a fashion system in its own right, with a very particular look: torn blue jeans, ripped stockings, outfits patched with ragged bits of contrasting materials, and perhaps a safety pin through the cheek. If some punk musicians framed their challenge to established authority in terms of progressive social values, others flirted with fascist imagery, attaching Nazi swastikas to their clothing and associating with the racist "skinhead" movement. Many in the punk movement—including musicians, fans, and those rock critics who championed the music—saw punk as a progressive response to the conservatism of the record industry. Yet the nihilism of much punk rock—the music's basic "I don't give a f____" stance—posed a crucial question that still resonates in today's alternative rock music: Is it possible to make music that is "authentic" or "real" while at the same time loudly proclaiming that you don't care about anything?

In musical terms, punk rock turned progressive rock—with its artistic aspirations and corporate backing—on its head. As Tommy Ramone, drummer for the archetypal punk band the Ramones, put it:

> We took the rock sound into a psychotic world and narrowed it down into a straight line of energy. In an era of progressive rock, with its complexities and counterpoints, we had a perspective of nonmusicality and intelligence that took over from musicianship. (Laing 1985, p. 23)

Punk was a stripped-down and often purposefully "nonmusical" version of rock music, in some sense a return to the wildness of early rock 'n' roll stars like Jerry Lee Lewis and Little Richard, but with lyrics that stressed the ironic or dark dimensions of human existence—drug addiction, despair, suicide, lust, and violence. As David Byrne, the leader of the new wave band Talking Heads, put it (on the PBS television series *Rock & Roll*, 1995, Episode 9):

> Punk . . . was more a kind of do-it-yourself, anyone-can-do-it attitude. If you only played two notes on the guitar, you could figure out a way to make a song out of that, and that's what it was all about.

Punk rock and its more commercial cousin, new wave, took shape in New York City during the mid-1970s. One of the predecessors of punk rock was an American musical institution called the *garage band*, typically a neighborhood operation, made up of young men who played mainly for themselves, their friends, and the occasional high school dance. A few of these local groups went on to enjoy some commercial success, including the Los Angeles–based Standells (whose "Dirty Water" was a Number 11 Pop hit in 1966); ? and the Mysterians, from the industrial town of Flint, Michigan (who took "96 Tears" to the top of the charts in the same year and are generally considered to be the first Latino rock band to have a Number 1 hit); and, from Portland, Oregon, the Kingsmen, best known for their cover version of the 1950s R&B song "Louie, Louie" (Number 2 Pop in 1963). The rough-and-ready, do-it-yourself attitude of the garage bands—something akin to a rock 'n' roll–based folk music movement—paved the way for punk rock.

Three groups, none of them very successful in commercial terms, are frequently cited as ancestors of 1970s punk music, and of later genres such as new wave, hardcore, industrial, and alternative rock: the Velvet Underground, the Stooges, and the New York Dolls. The <u>Velvet Underground</u>, a New York group, was promoted by the pop art superstar Andy Warhol, who painted the famous cartoonlike image of a banana on the cover of their first LP. Their music was rough-edged and chaotic, extremely loud, and deliberately anti-commercial, and the lyrics of their songs focused on topics such as sexual deviancy, drug addiction, violence, and social alienation. The leaders of the Velvet Underground were singer and guitarist <u>Lou Reed</u>—who had worked previously as a pop songwriter in a Brill Building–style "music factory"—and <u>John Cale</u>, a viola player active in the avant-garde art music scene in New York, who introduced experimental musical elements into the mix, including electronic noise and recorded industrial sounds.

If the Velvet Underground represented the self-consciously experimentalist roots of 1970s new wave music, the <u>Stooges</u>, formed in Ann Arbor, Michigan, in 1967, were the working-class, motorcycle-riding, leather-jacketed ancestors of punk rock. The lead singer of the Stooges, Iggy Stooge (a.k.a. <u>Iggy Pop</u>,

The Velvet Underground (Lou Reed, right) in 1967. © Jeff Albertson/Corbis.

James Osterburg), was famous for his outrageous stage performances, which included flinging himself into the crowd, cutting himself with beer bottles, and rubbing himself with raw meat. Guitarist Ron Asheton described the Stooges' approach:

> Usually we got up there and jammed one riff and built into an energy freak-out, until finally we'd broken a guitar, or one of my hands would be twice as big as the other and my guitar would be covered in blood. (Palmer 1995, p. 263)

The Stooges' eponymous first album (1969), produced by the Velvet Underground's John Cale, created a devoted if small national audience for the Stooges' demented "garage band" sound. A good example of the sensibility that underlay much of the Stooges' work—the depression of unemployed Michigan youth caught in the middle of a severe economic recession—is the song "1969," which evokes a world light-years distant from the utopianism of the hippie movement and the Woodstock festival, held that same summer.

Another band that exerted a major influence on the musical and visual style of the punk rock movement was the New York Dolls, formed in New York City in 1971. Dressed in fishnet stockings, bright red lipstick, cellophane tutus, ostrich feathers, and army boots, the all-male Dolls were an American response to the English glam rock movement, typified by the reigning master of rock gender bending, David Bowie (see Chapter 7). Their professional career began inauspiciously—at a Christmas party in a seedy welfare hotel in Manhattan—but by late 1972 they had built a small and devoted following. Although the New York Dolls soon succumbed to drug and alcohol abuse, they did establish certain core features of punk antifashion and helped to create a new underground rock music scene in New York City.

The amateur energy of garage band rock 'n' roll, the artsy nihilism of the Velvet Underground, the raw energy and abandon of the Stooges, and the antifashion of the New York Dolls converged in the mid-1970s in New York City's burgeoning club scene. The locus of this activity was a converted folk music club called CBGB & OMFUG ("Country, Bluegrass, Blues & Other Music for Urban Gourmandizers"), located in the run-down Bowery area of Manhattan. The first rock musician to perform regularly at CBGBs was Patti Smith (b. 1946), a New York–based poet, journalist, and singer who had been experimenting with combining the spoken word and rock accompaniment. In 1975 Smith began a stint at CBGBs, establishing a beachhead for punk and new wave bands, and signed a contract with Arista, a new label headed by Clive Davis, the former head of Columbia Records. (Her critically acclaimed album *Horses* reached Number 47 on the *Billboard* charts in 1976.) Beyond her artistic output, Patti Smith also helped to redefine gender roles in rock culture, refusing to make concessions to traditional notions of femininity in her appearance,

The New York Dolls make a fashion statement. Bob Gruen.

attitude, language, or clothing. She is often cited as a direct influence by women in rock to the present day.

Other influential groups who played at CBGBs during the mid-1970s included Television—whose lengthy instrumental improvisations were inspired by the Velvet Underground and avant-garde jazz saxophonist Albert Ayler— Blondie, and the Voidoids, featuring the alienated lyrics and howling voice of lead singer Richard Hell, one of the original members of Television.

The first bona fide punk rock band was the <u>Ramones</u>, formed in 1974 in New York City. The Ramones' high-speed, energetic, and extremely loud sound influenced English punk groups such as the Sex Pistols and the Clash and also became a blueprint for 1980s Los Angeles hardcore bands. Although they projected a street-tough image, all of the band's members were from middle-class families in the New York City borough of Queens. The band—not a family enterprise, despite their stage names—consisted of Jeffrey Hyman (a.k.a. Joey Ramone) on vocals; John Cummings (Johnny Ramone) on guitar; Douglas Colvin (Dee Dee Ramone) on bass; and Tom Erdelyi (Tommy Ramone) on drums. The band's first manager, Danny Fields, had previously worked with the Stooges and Lou Reed and thus had a good sense of the Ramones' potential audience.

Taking the stage in blue jeans and black leather jackets—a look calculated to evoke the sneering, rebellious ethos of 1950s rock 'n' rollers—the Ramones began playing regularly at CBGBs in 1975. By the end of the year they had secured a recording contract with Sire Records, an independent label that signed a number of early punk groups. Their eponymous debut album was recorded in 1976 for just over six thousand dollars, an incredibly small amount of money in an era of expensive and time-consuming studio sessions. The album gained some critical attention and managed to reach Number 111 on the *Billboard* album charts.

Later that year the Ramones staged a British Invasion in reverse. Their concerts in English cities, where their records had already created an underground sensation, were attended by future members of almost every important British punk band, including the Sex Pistols (see Box, page 224), the Clash, and the Damned. In 1977 the Ramones scored a U.K. Top 40 hit with the song "Sheena Is a Punk Rocker" (Number 81 U.S.), which announced that the center of the rock 'n' roll universe had shifted from the beaches of Southern California to the Lower East Side of Manhattan.

The Ramones' music reflected their origins as a garage band made up of neighborhood friends. As the guitarist Johnny Ramone phrased it in an interview with the popular music scholar Robert Palmer:

> I had bought my first guitar just prior to starting the Ramones. It was all very new; we put records on, but we couldn't figure out how to

The Ramones in 1977. Jan Persson/Getty Images.

play the songs, so we decided to start writing songs that were within our capabilities. (Palmer 1995: 274)

These songs had catchy, pop-inspired melodies, were played at extremely fast tempos, and generally lasted no more than two and a half minutes. (In live performances, the Ramones managed to squeeze twelve or thirteen songs into a half-hour set.) The band's raw, hard-edged sound was anchored by a steady barrage of notes, played on drums, bass, and guitar. Johnny Ramone rarely if ever took a guitar solo, but this makes sense when you consider the band's technical limitations and the aesthetic goal of the music: a rejection of the flashy virtuosity of progressive rock music, with its extended and sometimes self-indulgent solos.

The song "I Wanna Be Sedated," from the band's fourth album, *Road to Ruin* (1978), is a good example of the Ramones' style and of their mordant—one is tempted to say twisted—sense of humor:

> *Twenty-twenty-twenty-four hours to go, I wanna be sedated*
> *Nothin' to do and nowhere to go-o-o, I wanna be sedated*
> *Just put me in a wheelchair, get me to the show*
> *Hurry hurry hurry, before I gotta go*
> *I can't control my fingers, I can't control my toes*
> *Oh no no no no no*
> *Ba-ba-bamp-ba ba-ba-ba-bamp-ba, I wanna be sedated*
> *Ba-ba-bamp-ba ba-ba-ba-bamp-ba, I wanna be sedated*

The song text's images of drug-induced insanity (and its putative antidote, drug-induced paralysis) are juxtaposed with a catchy pop melody and Beach Boys–like chorus, a combination that affirms Joey Ramone's early description of the band's style as "sick bubblegum music." The Ramones' connection to sixties rock, though expressed in a totally different way, was based on many of the same impulses as that of their famous contemporary Bruce Springsteen (see Chapter 9): a re-evaluation of the sixties that took note of what had been lost as much as what had been gained. This trend reached its peak on their 1980 album *End of the Century*, which featured such evocations of early-sixties teendom as "Rock 'n' roll High School," the openly nostalgic "Do You Remember Rock 'n' roll Radio?" and a surprisingly straightforward cover of the Ronettes' 1963 hit "Baby, I Love You." But perhaps the clearest connection to the Brill Building sound is that the Ramones actually hired Phil Spector—who had been living in seclusion for almost a decade at that point—to produce the album.

It is, in fact, hard to know how seriously to take the Ramones. Although they played alongside self-consciously "cutting-edge" bands like the Patti Smith Group and Television, the Ramones identified themselves as a band that was "able to just play and be song-oriented and sound great, people who play real rock 'n' roll." Nonetheless, some of their recordings did provide grim "news flashes" on the facts of life in many working-class and middle-class homes during a period of severe economic recession. The song "I Wanted Everything" (1978), the stark and gritty tale of a good boy gone wrong, is in fact reminiscent of the work of Springsteen, who is often regarded as a working-class rock 'n' roll hero, and this realism suggests that American punk rock was not a totally nihilistic movement.

If the Ramones and the Sex Pistols epitomized punk rock's connections to the rebellious energy of early rock 'n' roll, another band, Talking Heads, represented the more self-consciously artistic and exploratory side of the alternative rock scene of the mid-1970s. Talking Heads was formed in 1974 by David Byrne (born in Scotland in 1952), Chris Frantz, and Tina Weymouth, who met as art students at the Rhode Island School of Design. They first appeared at CBGBs in 1975 as the opening act for the Ramones, though they attracted a somewhat different audience, made up of college students, artists, and music critics. In 1976 they were signed to a recording contract by Sire Records, and their first album, *Talking Heads: 77*, achieved critical acclaim and broke into the Top 100 on the *Billboard* album charts. The band's style reflected their interest in an aesthetic called minimalism, which stresses the use of combinations of a limited number of basic elements—colors, shapes, sounds, or words. This approach was popular in the New York art music scene of the 1960s and 1970s, as represented in the work of composers such as Steve Reich, Terry Riley, and Philip Glass, who made use of simple musical patterns, repeated and combined in various ways. Talking Heads' instrumental arrangements fused this approach with the interlocking, riff-based rhythms pioneered by African American popular musicians, particularly James Brown. In fact, Bernie Worrell, a keyboardist and core member of the groundbreaking funk group Parliament-Funkadelic, was even a member of Talking Heads for several years (see the discussion of funk music later in this chapter). Clarity is another important aspect of the minimalist aesthetic, and Talking Heads' songs were generally quite simple in structural terms, with strong pop hooks and contrasting sections marked off by carefully arranged changes in instrumental texture.

In their visual presentation and stage demeanor, Talking Heads were from another universe than the other CBGBs bands—they dressed in slacks, sweaters, and vests, projecting the image of cerebral but nerdy college students. David Byrne's stage demeanor was described by reviewer Michael Aron for *Rolling Stone* magazine (11/17/77):

Everything about him is uncool: his socks and shoes, his body language, his self-conscious announcements of song titles, the way he wiggles his hips when he's carried away onstage (imagine an out-of-it kid practicing Buddy Holly moves in front of a mirror).

"THE END OF ROCK 'N' ROLL": THE SEX PISTOLS

We have already mentioned the impression made by the Ramones on musicians in the United Kingdom, an "American Invasion" that began some twelve years after the Beatles stormed New York City. The English stream of punk rock bubbled up during the summer of 1976, an unusually hot summer and a high point of unemployment, inflation, and racial tension in cities like London, Birmingham, Manchester, and Liverpool. In England, more than the United States, punk rock was associated with a mainly white working-class youth subculture. More explicitly political and less artsy than some of the New York bands, groups like the Sex Pistols, the Clash, and the Damned succeeded in outraging the British political establishment and the mainstream media while at the same time achieving a modicum of commercial success in the late 1970s.

The most outrageous—and therefore famous—punk band was the Sex Pistols, formed in 1975 in London. They were the creation of Malcolm McLaren, owner of a London "antifashion" boutique called Sex, which specialized in leather and rubber clothing. (McLaren had begun his career in the music business in 1974, when he managed unsuccessfully the short-lived New York Dolls.) Upon his return to London, McLaren conceived the idea of a rock 'n' roll band that would subvert the pop music industry and horrify England's staid middle class. Glen Matlock (bass), Paul Cook (drums), and Steve Jones (guitar) were regular customers at the shop, and they were looking for a singer. McLaren introduced them to John Lydon, a young man who hung around listening to the jukebox at Sex and had never sung in public before. A famous rock anecdote states that the rest of the band immediately respected Lydon due to the fact that he happened to be wearing a T-shirt for the band Pink Floyd (known for their elaborate and very serious concept albums), with the words "I hate" scrawled above the band's name. Whether true or not, this story fairly accurately sums up punk's attitude toward what rock had become in the seventies. (Lydon's inconsistent approach to personal hygiene led Steve Jones to christen him *Johnny Rotten*, a stage name that stuck.) The Sex Pistols got their first gigs by showing up and posing as

The Sex Pistols. © INTERFOTO/Alamy.

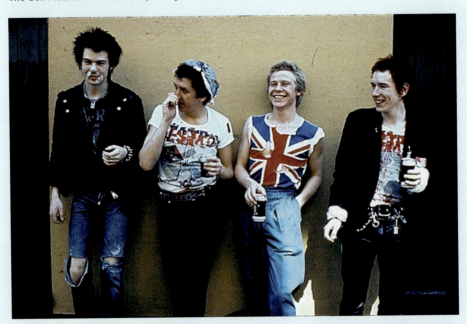

the opening band. Given the nature of Johnny Rotten's stage act—sneering and screaming obscenities at the audience, commanding them to applaud, and throwing beer on them when they didn't—it is perhaps not surprising that they were banned from many nightclubs.

The trajectory of this band's rapid ascent and implosion is complex, and we can present only a summary here. EMI Records, England's biggest and most conservative label, signed the Sex Pistols for around sixty thousand dollars in 1976, releasing their first single, "Anarchy in the UK," in December. The single was a Top 40 hit in the U.K. but was withdrawn from record shops after Rotten uttered an obscenity during a television interview. At an annual meeting of shareholders in December 1976, the chairman of EMI, Sir John Read, made the following statement (as recorded in the Report of the EMI General Meeting, 12/7/76):

> Sex Pistols is the only "punk rock" group that EMI Records currently has under direct recording contract and whether EMI does in fact release any more of their records will have to be very carefully considered. I need hardly add that we shall do everything we can to restrain their public behavior, although this is a matter over which we have no real control.

The resulting uproar caused EMI to terminate the Sex Pistols' contract in January 1977, and all but five out of twenty-one dates on a planned concert tour of the U.K. were promptly canceled. In March the bassist Glen Matlock was replaced by John Ritchie, a nonmusician friend of John Lydon, who went by the stage name *Sid Vicious*. The American label A&M Records then signed the Pistols for over $200,000, only to fire them the very next week. In May Virgin Records signed them and released their second single, "God Save the Queen (It's a Fascist Regime)." Despite being banned from airplay, the song went to Number 2 (cited as a blank on the U.K. charts). The band was featured in a 1978 film called *The Great Rock 'n' Roll Swindle*, a title that some critics thought captured perfectly the essence of the band's exercise in manipulation. The Sex Pistols broke up that same year, during their only U.S. tour, a tour undertaken to support the release of their only studio album, *Never Mind the Bollocks, Here's the Sex Pistols* (1977). In 1979 Sid Vicious was imprisoned in New York on charges of stabbing his girlfriend to death, and he died of a heroin overdose while out on bail. In 1986 the surviving members of the group sued Malcolm McLaren for cheating them of royalties and were awarded around $1.5 million. John Lydon in particular has remained a relevant voice in rock to the present day, exhibiting a surprisingly sophisticated and multicultural approach to rock with his post–Sex Pistols group Public Image Ltd., as well as a rebelliously sarcastic attitude that was highly influential on later rockers, particularly those in the Seattle alternative rock scene of the early nineties.

Just as the punk rockers' antifashion became a new kind of fashion, so David Byrne's studied awkwardness established a new, nerdy variety of cool, one still much in evidence on college campuses today.

Rather like David Bowie's Ziggy Stardust, the character projected in "Psycho Killer"—tongue-tied, nervous, emotionally distant, and obsessively intellectual—provided David Byrne with a durable stage persona. In a review of the 1984 Talking Heads concert film *Stop Making Sense,* one critic remarked on Byrne's ability to project "a variant on his basic 'Psycho Killer' self for each song; he demonstrates over and over that a public self is a Frankenstein self, a monster put together from bits and pieces of image tissue." Throughout the late 1970s and 1980s Talking Heads recorded a series of critically acclaimed albums, most of which reached *Billboard's* Top 40 and achieved either gold

Talking Heads (David Byrne, front) in 1976. Photo by Richard E. Aaron/Redferns.

or platinum status. The commercial success was linked to the accessibility of Talking Heads' music, which mixed in influences from rhythm and blues and funk music, and from West African music, with its complexly interlocking but catchy polyrhythmic patterns. David Byrne went on to become a major figure in the worldbeat movement of the 1980s and 1990s, introducing American audiences to recording artists from Africa, Brazil, and the Caribbean.

Though many of the more pop-oriented bands to emerge at this time, such as Talking Heads and Blondie, continued to view themselves as punk rock musicians, they were often grouped by others under the umbrella of "New Wave." This use of a genre name to create a safe version of a rebellious musical form can be seen as paralleling the birth of the term "rock 'n' roll" itself in the 1950s.

REGGAE MUSIC—ROCK IN THE DIASPORA

Reggae—a potent mixture of Caribbean folk music and American rhythm & blues—was the first style of the rock era to originate in the so-called Third World. The popularity of reggae in America may be related both to earlier "exotic" music crazes—the Argentine tango and the Cuban rumba—and to the coming world beat movement of the 1980s and 1990s. Born in the impoverished shantytowns of Kingston, Jamaica, reggae first became popular in the United States in 1973, after the release of the Jamaican film *The Harder They Come* and its soundtrack album. (This is yet another example of the importance of film as a medium for promoting popular music, exemplified by the Hollywood musicals of the 1930s and rock 'n' roll films of the 1950s.) During the 1970s a handful of Jamaican musicians, notably Bob Marley and Jimmy Cliff, achieved a measure

🎧 LISTENING TO "PSYCHO KILLER"

The center of attention on most Talking Heads recordings was David Byrne's trembling, high-pitched voice and his eclectic songwriting. Byrne often delivered his lyrics in a nervous, almost schizophrenic stream-of-consciousness voice, like overheard fragments from a psychiatrist's office. A good example of this approach—as well as the only single from the group's first LP to appear on the singles charts (peaking at Number 92)—was the song "Psycho Killer," inspired by Norman Bates, the schizophrenic murderer in Alfred Hitchcock's film *Psycho*. Although it now seems like an ironic commentary on mass media portrayals of "the serial killer," this song had a darker, more immediate resonance when it was released in 1977, during the Son of Sam killing spree, in which a deranged man shot thirteen people in New York City.

The recording opens with Tina Weymouth's electric bass, playing a simple riff reminiscent of mid-1970s funk or disco music (see the sections on funk and disco later in this chapter). She is soon joined by two guitars, playing crisply articulated, interlocking chord patterns. David Byrne's voice enters in the thirteenth bar, enunciating the lyrics in a half-spoken, half-sung style, over a simple melody that uses only a few pitches and stays mainly on the tonic note. The first verse (A^1) gives us a glimpse into the psychosis of the narrator:

> I can't seem to face up to the facts
> I'm tense and nervous and I can't relax
> I can't sleep 'cause my bed's on fire
> Don't touch me I'm a real live wire

This verse is followed by two statements of the chorus (B), which references the title of the song, dips abruptly and somewhat schizophrenically into a second language (French), and ends with a stuttered warning to the listener:

> Psycho Killer, Qu'est-ce que c'est
>   [What is it?]
> Fa fa fa fa fa fa fa fa fa far better
> Run run run run run run run away

The chorus blends into a four-bar vocal interlude, with Byrne's voice leaping up an octave and emitting a distressed "Ay yai yai yai," and a two-bar instrumental section that reestablishes the basic groove. In the second verse (A^2), Byrne shifts from singing to speech, becoming more agitated as he expresses his anger at people who talk a lot, despite having nothing to say, and at his own inability to communicate with others:

> You start a conversation, you can't
>   even finish it.
> You're talking a lot, but you're not
>   saying anything.
> When I have nothing to say, my lips
>   are sealed.
> Say something once, why say it again?

The chorus (B) is heard two more times, followed by the interlude, and then by a new section (C), in which Byrne struggles to confess his crime in an awkward, strangled variant of French:

> Ce que j'ai fais, ce soir la [The things I
>   did on that night]
> Ce qu'elle a dit, ce soir la [The things
>   she said on that night]
> Réalisant mon espoir [Achieving my
>   hope]
> Je me lance vers la gloire . . . Okay
>   [I hurl myself toward glory . . .
>   Okay]

The last line—*Je me lance vers la gloire*—is a cultural reference that would likely have been obscure to all but a small segment of the Talking Heads' audience. These were reputedly the final words spoken by the American dancer and choreographer Isadora Duncan (1877–1927) before she accidentally strangled herself by catching the end of her long scarf in the wheel of a car. For those in the know, the indirect reference to this ghastly incident no doubt reinforced the foreboding tone of the lyrics.

Eventually Byrne switches back into English, focusing obsessively on a single pitch and revealing more of his character's motivation for committing an unspecified though presumably horrific act:

> We are vain and we are blind
> I hate people when they're not polite

LISTENING CHART "PSYCHO KILLER"

Music and lyrics by David Byrne, Chris Frantz, Tina Weymouth; performed by Talking Heads; recorded 1977

FORM		LYRICS	DESCRIPTIVE COMMENTS
Intro (12)		Instrumental	Bars 1–4: The electric bass plays a simple two-bar pattern two times. Bars 5–8: The bass drum enters with a steady pulse, and electric guitar plays sustained chords. Bars 9–12: The second electric guitar enters, completing the basic groove—the two guitars play choppy, rhythmically interlocking chords (à la James Brown).
A¹ (8)	0.24	*I can't seem to face up* *I'm tense and nervous . . .* *I can't sleep . . .* *Don't touch me . . .*	Vocal enters; simple melody, centered on tonic pitch; instrumental accompaniment is based on interlocking riffs.
B (8)	0.40	*Psycho Killer, Qu'est-ce que c'est?* *Fa fa fa fa fa fa fa fa fa far better* *Run run run run run run run away* *Oh-oh-oh-oh . . .*	New harmonies, sustained chords on guitar mark beginning of chorus; bass and drums continue pulse.
B (8)	0.55	Lyric repeats	
Interlude (6)	1.10	*Oh . . . Ai yai yai yai yai (4)* Instrumental (2)	Byrne sings nonsense syllables, makes muffled vocal sounds in background. Bass, drums, and guitars play basic groove for last two bars.
A² (8)	1.22	*You start a conversation . . .* *You're talking a lot . . .* *When I have nothing to say . . .* *Say something once . . .*	Byrne moves from singing into speech mode; uses vocal quality to evoke psychotic persona.
B (8)	1.38	*Psycho Killer, Qu'est-ce que c'est?* *Fa fa fa fa fa fa fa fa fa far better* *Run run run run run run run away* *Oh-oh-oh-oh . . .*	
B (8)	1.54	Lyric repeats	
Interlude (2)	2.09	*Oh . . . Ai yai yai yai yai*	First part only.
C (20)	2.13	*Ce que j'ai fais, ce soir la* *Ce qu'elle a dit, ce soir la* *Réalisant mon espoir*	Rhythm section plays marchlike pulse in unison for first eight bars, while Byrne speaks the lyrics. Guitar plays sustained chords (four bars).
		Je me lance, vers la gloire . . . Okay *Ya ya ya ya ya ya ya* *We are vain and we are blind* *I hate people when they're not polite*	Rhythm section reestablishes basic groove (four bars). Groove continues (four bars).

B (8)	2.52	Psycho Killer, Qu'est-ce que c'est? Fa fa fa fa fa fa fa fa fa far better Run run run run run run run away Oh-oh-oh-oh . . .	
B (8)	3.07	Lyric repeats	
Interlude (4)	3.23	Oh . . . Ai yai yai yai yai	Byrne sings nonsense syllables, makes vocal sounds in background.
Coda (3 × 8 = 24)	3.30	Instrumental	Bass, drums, and guitars elaborate on basic groove for last twenty-four bars, building in intensity. Last eight bars feature stereo effect, guitar moving back and forth from left to right speaker.

After final repetitions of the "Psycho Killer" chorus (B) and interlude, the band moves into a concluding twenty-four-bar instrumental section (or coda), in which the basic groove is elaborated with distorted textures, wavering pitches on the guitars, strange vocal sounds from Byrne, and the panning of one guitar back and forth from left to right speaker, like the unanchored movement of a madman's thoughts. The last sound we hear is the squeal of feedback from one of the microphones, fading into silence and darkness.

of commercial success in the United States, while numerous American and British rock musicians—including Eric Clapton, Paul Simon, the Police, and Elvis Costello—found inspiration (and profit) in the style. In addition, rap music of the 1980s was strongly influenced by Jamaican "dub," a branch of the reggae tradition in which verbal performances are improvised over prerecorded musical accompaniments.

Reggae music was itself a complex composite of influences, some of them from the United States. The history of reggae thus gives us an opportunity to examine not only the burgeoning interest of American musicians in "world music" but also the influence of American forms on local music elsewhere, a fascinating story that mainly lies outside the scope of this book. The roots of reggae lie in the Jamaican equivalent of country music, a genre called *mento*. Mento—a mixture of Jamaican folk songs, church hymns, sailor's shanties, and Cuban influences—arose in rural Jamaica during the late nineteenth century. By World War II, mento had lost its popularity among the thousands of young Jamaicans who were migrating to the capital city of Kingston. (Today's tourist resorts on Jamaica's north coast are among the last places where mento can be heard.) During the 1940s and early 1950s swing bands from the United States—including those of Benny Goodman, Count Basie, and Glenn Miller—became popular in the dance halls of Kingston. Jamaican musicians formed what they called "road bands," local swing bands that toured from town to town, playing public dances.

Starting in the 1950s, American rhythm & blues—broadcast by powerful radio stations in Miami and New Orleans—became popular among youth in Kingston. Migrant Jamaican workers in Costa Rica, Panama, Cuba, and the United States brought back the hit recordings of American artists such as Louis Jordan and Fats Domino, and local entrepreneurs set up portable sound systems to play R&B records for dances and parties, driving the road bands out of business. In the 1960s a shortage of U.S. records encouraged some sound system operators to set up their own recording studios in Kingston. Some of these men—including Coxsone Dodd and Leslie Kong—became leading producers in the Jamaican popular music business.

During the 1960s a succession of new popular genres emerged out of the intersection of Jamaican folk music and American rhythm & blues. The first of these was *ska* (an onomatopoeic term derived from the style's typical sharp, offbeat accents). The instrumentation of ska bands was derived from

Bob Marley. Hulton Archive/Getty Images.

R&B, with a rhythm section of piano, bass, guitar, and drums and a horn section including some combination of brass instruments and saxophones. Ska music was usually played at fast tempos, with the bass playing a steady four-beat pattern and the piano, guitar, and drums emphasizing the backbeats. The singing on ska records was strongly influenced by R&B, ranging from rougher blues-influenced styles to romantic crooning. The biggest star of Jamaican ska was Don Drummond, a trombonist and leader of a band called the Skatalites. The Skatalites also worked as a studio band, backing many of the most popular singers of the time and exerting a substantial influence on the youth culture of Kingston, particularly when several members of the band joined the Rastafarian religious movement.

The Rastafarian Movement

It is worth taking a moment here to discuss the Rastafarian movement, since it is such a prominent theme in reggae music. Rastafarianism drew heavily on the work of Marcus Mosiah Garvey (1887–1940), a Jamaican writer and political leader who inspired a "Back to Africa" repatriation movement among black Americans in the 1920s. Before leaving Jamaica for the United States in 1916, Garvey wrote, "Look to Africa for the crowning of a black king; he shall be the redeemer," a phrase that was taken quite literally as prophecy by Garvey's followers. In 1930, when Haile Selassie ("Power of the Trinity") was crowned king of the African nation of Ethiopia, preachers in Kingston saw this as confirmation of Garvey's prediction and proceeded to scrutinize the Old Testament in search of passages that supported the authenticity of Selassie's divinity. The Rastafarians' reinterpretation of the Bible focused on passages that dealt with slavery, salvation, and the apocalyptic consequences that would eventually be visited upon the oppressors (collectively referred to as Babylon). Rastafarianism became associated with a unique set of cultural practices, including special terminology (for example, "I-and-I" is substituted for "we"), the use of marijuana (*ganja*) as a sacramental herb, and the wearing of a distinctive hairstyle called "dreadlocks."

The Rastafarian movement spread rapidly, through an extensive network of neighborhood churches and informal prayer meetings, where music and dance were used to "give praise and thanks" (*satta amassanga*) and to "chant down Babylon." In the mountainous interior of Jamaica, where communities of escaped slaves called "maroons" had been living since the nineteenth century, Rastafarian songs and chants were mixed with an African-derived style of drumming called *burru*, creating a heavier, slower sound. This style in turn fed back into urban popular music, resulting around 1966 in an updated version of ska called *rock steady*. Rock steady was considerably slower in tempo than ska, reflecting the aforementioned influence of burru drumming, and some of its leading exponents—notably Alton Ellis, who had the first big rock steady hit in 1966—began to record songs with social and political content.

The main patrons of rock steady were the Rude Boys, a social category that included anyone against "the system": urban Rastas, thugs hired by competing political parties, and lower-class youth generally. An informal and unruly Jamaican youth movement, Rude Boys increasingly came into conflict with the Jamaican police, and media coverage of their exploits helped to create the image of romantic outlaw heroes. The film that initiated reggae music's popularity in the United States, *The Harder They Come* (1972), was in fact a thinly disguised biography of one such ghetto hero (Vincent Martin, a.k.a. Rhygin', a Jamaican outlaw of the early 1960s). Bob Marley's song "I Shot the Sheriff" is about a young man who is persecuted by the local sheriff and then accused of murdering both the sheriff and his deputy in cold blood.

Under the influence of Rastafarian religiosity and Rude Boy street politics, a new genre called reggae took shape in Kingston during the late 1960s. (The word "reggae" is derived from "raggay," a Kingston slang term meaning "raggedy, everyday stuff.") In musical terms reggae was a further extension of the evolution from ska to rock steady. In reggae music the tempo was slowed down even further, creating wide spaces between notes, allowing the music to breathe and emphasizing the polyrhythmic heritage of Afro-Jamaican traditions. Each instrument in a reggae band has its own carefully defined role to play. The heart of reggae music consists of "riddims," interlocking rhythmic patterns played by the guitar, bass, and drums. The guitar often plays short, choppy chords on the second and fourth beat of each measure, giving the music a bouncy, up-and-down feeling. The bass-drum combination is the irreducible core of a reggae band, sometimes called the "riddim pair." (The most famous of these are the brothers Aston and Carlton Barrett, who played in Bob Marley's band, and Sly Dunbar and Robbie Shakespeare, who have appeared on literally hundreds of reggae recordings, and on the LPs of rock artists such as Bob Dylan, Mick Jagger, and Peter Gabriel.) This musical mixture was further enlivened by the influence of contemporary black American popular music, particularly the soul recordings of James Brown and Aretha Franklin. Political messages were central to reggae music—while ska musicians of the early 1960s, like their American R&B counterparts, sang mainly about love and heartbreak, the most popular reggae artists focused their attention on issues such as social injustice and racism.

Jimmy Cliff and Bob Marley

The film *The Harder They Come* featured reggae songs by a number of the most popular Jamaican musicians. The star of the film, and the vocalist on the title track of the soundtrack LP, was Jimmy Cliff (b. 1948). Like Ivan, the outlaw character he portrayed in the film, Cliff was only a teenager when he left the rural Jamaican town of St. James for the city of Kingston. Cliff arrived in Kingston in 1962 and made his first record within a year. Working with the Chinese-Jamaican producer Leslie Kong, he recorded a series of Jamaican

Top 10 hits during the mid-1960s. While performing at the 1964 World's Fair in New York City, Cliff met Chris Blackwell of the English independent label Island Records, who convinced him to move to London. After working as a backup singer and scoring a few hits on the European charts, he returned to Jamaica in 1969 and recorded the song "Many Rivers to Cross," which inspired the director Perry Henzel to offer him the lead role in *The Harder They Come*. Although the film did not reach the mass audience commanded by many Hollywood movies, it did create a devoted audience for reggae music in the United States, particularly among young, college-educated adults, who were attracted by the rebellious spirit of the music and its associations with Rastafarianism and *ganja* smoking. (The film played for seven years straight at a movie theater in Boston, Massachusetts, sustained mainly by the enthusiasm of that city's large student population.)

Jimmy Cliff in the film *The Harder They Come*, 1972.

Jimmy Cliff's 1972 recording of "The Harder They Come" exemplifies the reggae style of the early 1970s: a moderate tempo; strong guitar chords on the second and fourth beats of each measure; R&B-influenced singing; and a gritty lyric about the individual's struggle against oppression.

> *I keep on fighting for the things I want*
> *Though I know that when you're dead you can't*
> *But I'd rather be a free man in my grave*
> *Than living as a puppet or a slave*
> *So as sure as the sun will shine*
> *I'm gonna get my share now what is mine*
> *And then the harder they come, the harder they fall*
> *One and all*

Although Cliff was the first Jamaican musician to gain recognition in the United States, his contemporary Bob Marley (1945–81), leader of the Wailers, quickly surpassed Cliff in popularity. A national hero in his native Jamaica, Marley was reggae's most effective international ambassador. His songs of determination, rebellion, and faith, rooted in the Rastafarian belief system, found a worldwide audience that reached from America to Japan and from Europe to Africa. The son of a British naval officer who deserted his family when

Bob was six years old, Marley migrated to Kingston from the rural parish of St. Ann at the age of fourteen. His early career reflects the economic precariousness of the music industry in a Third World country. After making a few singles for producer Leslie Kong, Marley formed the Wailers in 1963 and signed with Coxsone Dodd's studios. Following a long period with little financial success (including a year of factory work for Marley in Wilmington, Delaware), the Wailers signed with the producer Lee Perry, who added Aston and Carlton Barrett, a masterful bassist-and-drummer "riddim pair."

In 1972 Chris Blackwell, who had launched Jimmy Cliff's international career, signed Bob Marley and the Wailers to Island Records and advanced them the money to record at their independent Tuff Gong studio in Jamaica. Marley's recognition abroad was boosted by the success of Eric Clapton's cover of "I Shot the Sheriff," from the Wailers' second LP for Island Records (see "The Popularization of Reggae," following). The Wailers' first major concert in the United States took place in 1974 in Boston, where for a year and a half over a thousand young people a day had been viewing *The Harder They Come*. Between 1975 and 1980 Marley recorded six best-selling LPs for Island Records, including *Rastaman Vibration*, which reached Number 8 on the *Billboard* Top LPs charts in 1976. Wounded in a politically motivated assassination attempt in 1976, Marley died of cancer in 1981, at the age of thirty-six. His appeal and popularity, both in America and worldwide, has only grown in the years since his death: The 1984 LP compilation *Legend* has sold over eight million copies in the United States alone.

The Popularization of Reggae in the United States

Although the majority of American listeners became conscious of reggae as a distinctive musical style only in the mid- to late 1970s, with the steadily increasing popularity in this country of Bob Marley and the Wailers, there are individual instances long before this of Jamaican music appearing on the American charts. In fact, among the many imported hits during the British Invasion year of 1964 was a ska-flavored recording by the Jamaican teenager Millie Small called "My Boy Lollipop," which climbed all the way up to Number 2 on *Billboard's* list of top singles. In 1968 Johnny Nash, an African American pop singer who established a recording studio in Jamaica, had a Top 5 hit with the reggae-influenced "Hold Me Tight," and 1969 saw the American success of two reggae records by Jamaican artists: "Israelites" by Desmond Dekker and the Aces (Number 9 Pop), and "Wonderful World, Beautiful People," by Jimmy Cliff (Number 25 Pop).

Both Johnny Nash and Jimmy Cliff went on to bigger things in the early 1970s. Nash hit the Number 1 spot for four weeks in 1972 with another reggae-flavored tune, "I Can See Clearly Now." Nash wrote this song himself (as was also the case with "Hold Me Tight"), but he assured a sense of Jamaican authenticity by arranging for members of the Wailers to provide his instrumental support on the track. He then followed this up with a cover of Bob Marley's "Stir It Up" (Number 12 Pop, 1973). As for Jimmy Cliff, his starring role in the 1972 movie *The Harder They Come* introduced both him and the Jamaican music scene to a significant American audience previously unaware of both. (We might recall here the significance of another movie, *Blackboard Jungle,* in popularizing another music from the margins, rock 'n' roll, in 1955; see the discussion of "Rock Around the Clock" in Chapter 2.) In a fine illustration of the reciprocal relationships that tend to characterize so much of pop music history, Cliff returned to the charts for the first time in many years, and hit the American Top 20 for the first time, in the early 1990s with nothing other than his own cover of Nash's "I Can See Clearly Now" (Number 18 Pop, 1994), which was also featured in a movie, *Cool Runnings.*

Surely the best-known cover version of any reggae number is Eric Clapton's million-selling recording of Bob Marley's "I Shot the Sheriff," a Number 1 hit in 1974, which appears on Clapton's Number 1 album from the same year, *461 Ocean Boulevard.* Clapton's name on the label, along with his easygoing vocal delivery, doubtless helped to propel the single to the top of the charts; considered in terms of the song's lyrics and music, "I Shot the Sheriff" seems an unlikely 1970s hit. It is clearly a political song, but for anyone not thoroughly versed in contemporary Jamaican politics, its precise significance is difficult to grasp. This is an example of a "coded" lyric, reminiscent of coded blues lyrics that communicate something extra to members of a specific group who are attuned to its message. Furthermore, the music of the song is appropriately dark in color, with a predominance of minor chords.

It is instructive to compare Clapton's version with Bob Marley's own recording of "I Shot the Sheriff," which may be found on the 1973 album *Burnin'* and on compilations issued after Marley's death in 1981. Marley's version sounds much more insistently rhythmic and intense than Clapton's. Actually, Marley's tempo is only a hairbreadth faster than Clapton's, but the greater prominence of both bass and percussion in Marley's recording emphasizes the distinctive "riddims" of Jamaican reggae and creates the illusion of a considerably faster performance. (The recording closes with just the bass guitar and drums—the heartbeat of reggae—played by the riddim pair of Aston and Carlton Barrett.) In addition, the high range of the Wailers' voices creates a strong element of urgency that is lacking in the Clapton recording. Marley and the Wailers add small but effective, and apparently spontaneous, variations in the vocal lines of the successive verses of the song, giving a sense of familiarity and freedom with the material that also has no real counterpart in the cover version. And there is, of course, no substitute for the Jamaican patois (a dialect of English with strong African influence) in Marley's original ("Ev'ry day the bucket a-go-a well; one day the bottom a-go drop out"). It is to Clapton's credit, however, that he doesn't try to mimic Marley's rendition of a Jamaican proverb about the eventual triumph of the oppressed (he sings "Every day the bucket goes to the well, but one day the bottom will drop out"). Interestingly, after Clapton's version of the song became popular, Bob Marley began to perform the song with Clapton's version of the lyrics rather than his own.

This is only one of several factors that indicate Bob Marley's awareness of the rock audience and its expectations. Another is the format of his band, the Wailers. Originally, the Wailers were a vocal group, modeled after African American soul ensembles like the Temptations and the Four Tops. In the seventies, the Wailers transformed themselves into a self-contained group that played their own instruments, something that was virtually unheard of in Jamaica at that time (Garnette Cadogan, personal communication). Marley himself even began to play a classic rock guitar—the Les Paul—while he was singing. At the same time, his albums began to take on many of the characteristics of rock albums, from their elaborate covers to their extended rock guitar solos to their sequencing into larger works of art.

FUNK MUSIC

Funk music represented yet another back-to-basics impetus, the impulse to dance. Most album-oriented rock music was aimed at a predominantly white male audience and was designed for listening rather than dancing. (While rock fans certainly engaged in free-form movement, the idea of organized social dancing was anathema to the "do your own thing" ethos of the counterculture and to the "high art" aspirations of some rock musicians.) In urban black communities across America, however, dance remained a backbone of social life, a primary means for both transmitting traditional values and for generating a sense of novelty and excitement. And for the first time since the twist craze of the early 1960s, funk music—and its commercial offspring, disco—brought this intensive focus on dancing back into the pop mainstream.

The word "funky"—probably derived from the (central African) BaKongo term *funki,* meaning "healthy sweat"—was already in wide use by New Orleans jazz musicians during the first decade of the twentieth century. Today "funky" carries the same ambivalent meaning that it did a century ago—strong body odors (particularly those related to sex), and a quality of earthiness and authenticity, quintessentially expressed in music. If the concept of soul symbolized the spiritual, uplifting side of black consciousness, then funk was its profane and decidedly down-to-earth counterpart.

By the early 1970s the term "funk" was being used as a label for a genre of popular music characterized by strong, dance-oriented rhythms, catchy melodies, call-and-response exchanges between voices and instruments, and heavy reliance on repeated, rhythmically interlocking patterns. Most funk bands echoed the instrumentation and style of James Brown's soul music hits of the 1960s, records such as "Papa's Got a Brand New Bag" (1965), "I Got You (I Feel Good)" (1965), "Cold Sweat—Part 1" (1967), and "Say It Loud—I'm Black and I'm Proud" (1968), all of which had crossed over to the pop Top 20. Brown's band, the Famous Flames, consisted of a rhythm section (guitar, keyboards, electric bass, and drums) and a horn section, which effectively functioned as part of the rhythm section and occasionally supplied jazz-influenced solos, and this format was adopted as the core of 1970s funk bands. In terms of musical style, James Brown's characteristic and most influential recordings emphasized rhythmic patterns over chord changes or melodic lines. (See the discussion of "There Was a Time" in Chapter 6.)

During the early 1970s James Brown continued to score successes with dance-oriented hits, including "Super Bad" (1970), "Hot Pants (She Got to Use What She Got to Get What She Wants)" (1971), "Get on the Good Foot" (1972), and "The Payback" (1974). His ranking on the pop charts declined gradually throughout this period, however, in large part owing to competition from a new generation of musicians who played variations on the basic style he had established the decade before. This approach—the core of funk music—centered on the creation of a strong rhythmic momentum or groove, with the electric bass and bass drum often playing on all four main beats of the measure, the snare drum and other instruments playing equally strongly on the second and fourth beats (the backbeats), and interlocking repeated patterns distributed among other instruments, including guitar, keyboards, and horns.

Although funk music was initially targeted mostly at the predominantly urban black audience for soul music, by 1973 funk music had burst onto the pop music scene, pushed to the top of the charts by a large and heterogeneous audience, united by their thirst for rhythmically propulsive dance music. Crossover million-selling records such as Kool and the Gang's "Jungle Boogie" (Number 4 Pop and Number 2 R&B in 1973) and "Hollywood Swinging" (Number 6 Pop and Number 1 R&B in 1974), and the Ohio Players' "Fire" (Number 1 Pop and R&B, 1974) and "Love Rollercoaster" (Number 1 Pop and R&B in 1975)—along with the multimillion-selling "Play That Funky Music" (Number 1 Pop and R&B in 1976) by the *white* funk band Wild Cherry were played constantly on AM radio and in nightclubs and discotheques. Funk represented a vigorous reassertion of African American musical values, and it paved the way for the more commercialized sounds of disco music in the mid-1970s.

Funk bands kept the spirit and style of James Brown and Sly Stone alive, albeit in a commercialized and decidedly nonpolitical manner. The image of black musicians dancing in Afro hairdos, sunglasses, and brightly colored clothing on television shows like *American Bandstand* and *Soul Train* occasionally came uncomfortably close to racial stereotyping. Certainly, the record industry's packaging of black "authenticity"—as symbolized by strongly rhythmic, body-oriented music—had a great deal to do with the sudden crossover success enjoyed by bands such as Kool and the Gang and the Ohio Players (who had struggled for success as an R&B band since 1959). However, if the success of funk music in the mainstream pop market capitalized to some degree upon long-standing white American fantasies about black culture, white funk bands such as Wild Cherry and the Average White Band were also able to place records in the R&B Top 10. ("Pick up the Pieces" and "Cut the Cake," Top 10 R&B hits for the Average White Band in 1974 and 1975, respectively, offer the only example known to us of a Scottish band exerting mass appeal in the African American community with funk-derived music.)

Although they did not share the apolitical orientation and huge commercial success of the groups just mentioned, the apotheosis of 1970s funk music was a loose aggregate of around forty musicians (variously called Parliament or Funkadelic), led by George Clinton (a.k.a. Dr. Funkenstein). Clinton (b. 1940), an ex-R&B vocal group leader and songwriter, hung out with Detroit hippies, listened to the Stooges, and altered his style (as well as his consciousness) during the late 1960s. Enlisting some former members of James Brown's band (among them bassist William "Bootsy" Collins and saxophone player Maceo Parker), he developed a mixture of compelling polyrhythms, psychedelic guitar solos, jazz-influenced horn arrangements, and R&B vocal harmonies. Recording for the independent record company Casablanca (also a major player in the field of disco music), Parliament/Funkadelic placed five LPs in the *Billboard* Top 40 between 1976 and 1978, two of which went platinum.

The band's reputation was in substantial measure based on their spectacular concert shows, which featured wild costumes and elaborate sets (including a huge flying saucer called "the Mothership"), and their innovative concept albums, which expressed an alternative black sensibility, embodied in a patois of street talk, psychedelic imagery, and science-fiction-derived images of intergalactic travel. George Clinton took racial and musical stereotypes and played with them, reconfiguring black popular music as a positive moral force. On his albums, Clinton wove mythological narratives of a primordial conflict between the "Cro-Nasal Sapiens" (who "slicked their hair and lost all sense of the groove") and the "Thumpasorus People," who buried the secret of funk in the Egyptian pyramids and left Earth for the Chocolate Milky Way, under the wise leadership of "Dr. Funkenstein." Parliament concerts featured a cast of characters such as "Star Child" (a.k.a. "Sir Lollipop Man"), the cosmic defender of funk, and "Sir Nose D'VoidOfFunk," a spoof of commercialized, soulless, rhythmically challenged pop music and its fans. Clinton's blend of social criticism, wacky humor, and psychedelic imagination is perhaps best captured in his revolutionary manifesto for the funk movement: "Free Your Mind, and Your Ass Will Follow."

"Give Up the Funk (Tear the Roof off the Sucker)," from the million-selling LP *Mothership Connection*, was Parliament's biggest crossover single (Number 5 R&B, Number 15 Pop in 1976). It exemplifies the band's approach to

George Clinton in 1977. Michael Ochs Archives/Getty Images.

ensemble style, known to fans as "P-Funk": heavy, syncopated electric bass lines; interlocking rhythms underlain by a strong pulse on each beat of each measure; long, multisectioned arrangements featuring call-and-response patterns between the horn sections and keyboard synthesizer; R&B-styled vocal harmonies; and verbal mottoes designed to be chanted by fans ("We want the funk, give up the funk; We need the funk, we gotta have the funk"). Arranged by Clinton, bass player Bootsy Collins, and keyboardist Bernie Worrell, the recording is constructed out of these basic elements, alternated and layered on top of one another to create a series of shifting sound textures, anchored in the strong pulse of bass and drums.

Clinton and other former Parliament/Funkadelic musicians continued to tour and record throughout the 1980s, but public and critical disdain for 1970s popular culture—especially disco and the dance-oriented music that preceded and inspired it—had a negative impact on the band's fortunes. During the early 1990s the rise of funk-inspired rap (e.g., Dr. Dre) and rock music (e.g., Red Hot Chili Peppers) established the status of George Clinton and his colleagues as one of the most important—and most frequently sampled—forces in the recent history of black music. Discovered by a new generation of listeners, Clinton is still performing as of this writing.

THE RISE OF DISCO

No overview of rock music in the seventies would be complete without a discussion of disco. Although few would consider disco music to be part of rock—in fact, most at the time considered it the exact *opposite* of rock—that is precisely the reason why it is important. Disco was a form of popular music that did not accept many of rock's cultural assumptions, but which achieved tremendous popularity in the late seventies. As the first real threat to rock's dominance since its inception, disco raised a number of important questions for rock artists and fans.

The *disco* era—roughly 1975 to 1980—represented the rise of a massively popular alternative to rock music. Unlike most rock music, disco was centrally focused on social dancing, including couple-based dances such as the hustle and choreographed line dances that hearkened back to nineteenth-century ballroom dances such as the quadrille. Disco music also represented a reaction against two of the central ideas of album-oriented rock: the LP as art and the rock group as artists. Disco de-emphasized the importance of the band—which, in disco music, was usually a shifting concatenation of professional session musicians—and focused attention on the producers who oversaw the making of recordings, the DJs who played them in nightclubs, and a handful of glamorous stars, who sang with the backing of anonymous studio musicians and often had quite short-lived careers. Disco also rejected the idea of the rock album as an architecturally designed collection of individual pieces. Working night after night for audiences who demanded music that would keep them dancing for hours at a stretch, DJs rediscovered the single, expanded it to fill the time-frame offered by the twelve-inch long-playing vinyl disc, and developed techniques for blending one record into the next without interruption. (These turntable techniques paved the way for the use of recordings in popular genres of the eighties and nineties, such as hip-hop, house, and techno.)

"Disco" was derived from "discotheque," a term first used in Europe during the 1960s to refer to nightclubs devoted to the playing of recorded music for dancing. By the mid-1970s clubs featuring an uninterrupted stream of dance music were increasingly common in the United States, particularly in urban black and Latino communities, where going out to dance on a weekend night was a well-established tradition, and in the increasingly visible gay communities of cities such as New York and San Francisco. The rise of disco and its invasion of the Top 40 pop music mainstream were driven by several factors: the inspiration of black popular music, particularly Motown, soul, and funk; the rise in popularity of social dancing among middle-class Americans; new technologies, including synthesizers, drum machines, and synchronized turntables; the role of the Hollywood film industry in promoting musical trends; and the economic recession of the late 1970s, which encouraged many nightclub owners to hire disc jockeys rather than live musicians.

By the late 1970s disco had taken over the popular mainstream, owing in large part to the success of the film *Saturday Night Fever* (1977), the story of a working-class Italian kid from New York who rises to become a championship dancer. *Saturday Night Fever*—shot on location at a Brooklyn discotheque— strengthened interest in disco stars like Donna Summer and Gloria Gaynor. The film also launched the second career of the Bee Gees, an Australian group known theretofore mainly for sentimental pop songs like "Lonely Days" (a Number 3 Pop hit from 1970) and "How Can You Mend a Broken Heart" (Number 1 in 1971). The Bee Gees reinvented themselves by combining their polished Beatle-derived vocal harmonies with strong, repetitive rhythms, played by Miami studio musicians, and created a mix that appealed both to committed disco fans and a broader pop audience; their songs from the *Saturday Night Fever* soundtrack, such as "Stayin' Alive" and "Night Fever," were among the most popular singles of the late 1970s. At a more general level, *Saturday Night Fever* also helped to link disco music and dancing to a traditional American cultural theme, that of upward mobility. Spreading from the urban communities where it first took flower, disco dancing offered millions of working-class and middle-class Americans, from the most varied of cultural and economic backgrounds, access to glamour that hadn't been experienced widely since the days of the grand ballrooms.

The strict dress codes employed by the most famous discotheques implied a rejection of the torn T-shirt and jeans regalia of rock music, and the reinstatement of notions of hierarchy and classiness—if you (and your clothes) could pass muster at the velvet rope, you were allowed access to the inner sanctum. Walking through the front door of a disco in full swing was like entering a sensory maelstrom, with thundering music driven by an incessant bass pulse; flashing lights and mirrors on the ceiling, walls, and floor; and—most important—a mass of sweaty and beautifully adorned bodies packed onto the always limited space of a dance floor. For its adepts, the discotheque was a shrine to hedonism, an escape from the drudgery of everyday life, and a fountain of youth. (The death throes of this scene are evocatively rendered in the 1998 film *The Last Days of Disco*.)

A few examples must suffice here to give a sense of how thoroughly disco had penetrated popular musical taste by the late 1970s. One important stream of influence involved a continuation of the old category of novelty records, done up in disco style. A band called Rick Dees and His Gang of Idiots came out of nowhere to score a Number 1 hit with the goofy "Disco Duck" (1976), followed by the less successful zoo-disco song "Dis-Gorilla" (1977). The Village People—a group built from scratch by the French record producer Jacques Morali and promoted by Casablanca Records—specialized in over-the-top burlesques of gay life and scored Top 40 hits with songs like "Macho Man" (Number 25, 1978), "YMCA" (Number 2, 1978), and "In the Navy" (Number 3, 1979). For those who caught the inside references to gay culture, the Village People's recordings were charming, if simple-minded parodies; for many in disco's new mass audience, they were simply novelty records with a disco beat. Morali's double-entendre strategy paid off—for a short while in the late 1970s, the Village People were the bestselling pop group in North America.

For a few years everyone seemed to be jumping on the disco bandwagon. Barbra Streisand teamed up with disco artists, including the Bee Gees' Barry Gibb, who produced her multiplatinum 1980 album *Guilty*, and Donna Summer for the single "No More Tears" (Number 1 in 1979). Disco met the surf sound when Bruce Johnston of the Beach Boys produced a disco arrangement of "Pipeline," which had been a Number 4 instrumental hit for the Chantays back in 1963. Even hard rock musicians like the Rolling Stones released disco singles (such as "Miss You," Number 1 in 1978). On the other side of the Atlantic a genre called Eurodisco developed, featuring prominent use of electronic synthesizers and long compositions with repetitive rhythm tracks, designed to fill the entire side of an LP. (This sound, as developed by bands like Germany's Kraftwerk, was to become one important root of techno.) And black musicians, who had provided the basic material of which disco was constructed, were presented with new audiences, opportunities, and challenges. Motown diva Diana Ross scored several disco-influenced hits (e.g., "Love Hangover," Number 1 in 1976, and "Upside Down," Number 1 in 1980). And James Brown, who was knocked off the pop charts by disco music, responded in the late 1970s by promoting himself as the "Original Disco Man." (His R&B hit "It's Too Funky in Here," released in 1979, is a clear gesture in this direction.)

Few styles of popular music have inspired such passionate loyalty, or such utter revulsion, as disco music, and it is worth taking a few moments to consider the negative side of this equation. If you were a loyal fan of Led Zeppelin, Pink Floyd, and other album-oriented rock groups of the 1970s, disco was likely to represent a self-indulgent, pretentious, and vaguely suspect musical orientation. The rejection of disco by rock fans reached its peak during a 1979 baseball

The Village People performing in Germany in 1979. ©Jazz Archiv Hamburg/ullstein bild/ The Image Works.

game in Chicago, where several hundred disco records were blown up and a riot ensued. (This mass passion is reminiscent of the Beatles record burnings organized during the 1960s by fundamentalist Christian preachers.) After all, disco is only music—what on earth could inspire such a violent reaction?

Some critics connect the anti-disco reaction of the 1970s with the genre's links to gay culture. The disco movement initially emerged in Manhattan nightclubs such as the Loft and the Tenth Floor, which served as social gathering spots for homosexual men. According to this interpretation, gays found it difficult to get live acts to perform for them. The disc jockeys who worked these clubs responded to the demands of customers by rummaging through the bins of record stores for good dance records, often coming up with singles that had been successful some years earlier in the black and Puerto Rican communities of New York.

That disco was to some degree associated in the public imagination with homosexuality has suggested to some observers that the phrase "Disco Sucks!"— the rallying cry of the anti-disco movement—evinces a strain of homophobia among the core audience for album-oriented rock: young, middle- and working-class, and presumably heterosexual white men. Certainly disco's associations with a contemporary version of ballroom dancing did not conform to contemporary models of masculine behavior. The tradition of dancing to prefigured steps, or to music specifically designed to support dancing, which had found its last expression in the early 1960s with dance crazes like the twist, had fallen out of favor during the rock era. It may therefore have seemed to many rock fans that there was something suspect—even effeminate—about men who engaged in ballroom dancing.

Still, it can safely be assumed that the audience for album-oriented rock wasn't entirely straight, and that heterosexuals did patronize discos with large homosexual clienteles, at least in the big cities. The initial rejection of disco by many rock fans may have had as much to do with racism as with homophobia, since the genre's roots lay predominantly in black dance music. Another consideration is that the musical values predominant among rock fans—including an appreciation of instrumental virtuosity, as represented in the guitar playing of Jimi Hendrix, Eric Clapton, or Jimmy Page—would not have inclined them toward a positive regard of disco, which relied heavily on studio overdubbing and consisted mainly of fairly predictable patterns designed for dancing. The fact that millions of sports fans of all descriptions today enthusiastically mimic the movements of a popular—and, for some listeners, explicitly gay—disco record like the Village People's multimillion-selling single "YMCA" complicates the picture even further. Although disco cannot simply be identified as "gay music," there is no doubt that the genre's mixed reception during the late 1970s provides additional evidence of the transformative effect of marginalized musical styles and communities on the commercial mainstream of American popular music.

MIXING AND SCRATCHING: THE ORIGINS OF RAP MUSIC

Rap has been characterized as a vital link in the centuries-old chain of cultural and musical connections between Africa and the Americas; as the authentic voice of an oppressed urban underclass; and as a form that exploits long-standing stereotypes of black people. In fact, each of these perspectives has something to tell us about the history and significance of rap music. Rap is indeed based on principles ultimately derived from African musical and verbal traditions. Evidence of these deep continuities may be found in features familiar throughout the history of African American music: an emphasis on rhythmic momentum and creativity; a preference for complex tone colors and dense textures; a keen appreciation of improvisational skill (in words and music); and an incorporative, innovative approach to musical technologies. Much rap music does constitute a cultural response to oppression and racism, a system for communication among black communities throughout the United States ("black America's CNN," as rapper Chuck D once put it), and a source of insight into the values, perceptions, and conditions of people living in America's beleaguered urban communities. And finally, although rap music's origins and inspirations flow from black culture, the genre's audience has become decidedly multiracial, multicultural, and transnational. As rap has been transformed from a local phenomenon, located in a few neighborhoods in New York City, to a multimillion-dollar industry and a global cultural phenomenon, it has grown ever more complex and multifaceted.

Rap initially emerged during the 1970s as one part of a cultural complex called hip-hop. Hip-hop culture, forged by African American, Puerto Rican, and Caribbean American youth in New York City, included distinctive styles of visual art (graffiti), dance (an acrobatic solo style called b-boying, widely—though incorrectly—known as "breakdancing"), music, dress, and speech. Hip-hop was at first a local phenomenon, centered in certain neighborhoods in the Bronx, the most economically devastated area of New York City. Federal budget cuts caused a severe decline in low-income housing and social services for the residents of America's inner cities during the mid-1970s. By 1977, when President Carter conducted a highly publicized motorcade tour through New York's most devastated neighborhoods, the South Bronx had become, as *The New York Times* put it, "a symbol of America's woes."

The youth culture that spawned hip-hop can on one level be interpreted as a response to the destruction of traditional family- and neighborhood-based institutions and the cutting of funding for public institutions such as community centers, and as an attempt to lay claim to—and, in a way, to "civilize"—an alienating and hostile urban environment. The young adults who pioneered hip-hop styles such as b-boying, graffiti art, and rap music at nightclubs, block parties and in city parks often belonged to informal social groups called "crews," each associated with a particular neighborhood or block. It is important to understand that hip-hop culture began as an expression of local identities. Even today's multiplatinum rap recordings, marketed worldwide, are filled with inside references to particular neighborhoods, features of the urban landscape, and social groups and networks.

If hip-hop music was a rejection of mainstream dance music by young black and Puerto Rican listeners, it was also profoundly shaped by the techniques of disco DJs. The first celebrities of hip-hop music—Kool Herc (Clive Campbell, b. 1955 in Jamaica), Grandmaster Flash (Joseph Saddler, b. 1958 in Barbados), and Afrika Bambaataa (a mysterious figure whose birthdate and birth name have never been conclusively established) were DJs who began their careers in the mid-1970s, spinning records at neighborhood block parties, gym dances, and dance clubs, and in public spaces such as community centers and parks. These three young men—and dozens of lesser-known DJs scattered throughout the Bronx, Harlem, and other areas of New York City and New Jersey—developed their personal styles within a grid of fierce competition for celebrity and neighborhood pride. As Fab Five Freddie, an early graffiti artist and rapper, put it:

You make a new style. That's what life on the street is all about. What's at stake is honor and position on the street. That's what makes it so important, that's what makes it feel so good—the pressure on you

to be the best . . . to develop a new style nobody can deal with.
(George 1985: 111)

The disco DJ's technique of "mixing" between two turntables to create smooth transitions between records was first adapted to the hip-hop aesthetic by Kool Herc, who had migrated from Kingston, Jamaica, to New York City at the age of twelve. Herc noticed that the young dancers in his audiences responded most energetically during the so-called breaks on funk and salsa records, brief sections where the melody was stripped away to feature the rhythm section. Herc responded by isolating the breaks of certain popular records—such as James Brown's "Get on the Good Foot" (1972)—and mixing them into the middle of other dance records. These rhythmic sound collages came to be known as "breakbeat" or "b-beat" music, a term that was soon replaced by "hip-hop".

Another innovation helped to shape the sound and sensibility of early hip-hop: the transformation of the turntable from a medium for playing back recorded sound into a playable musical instrument. Sometime in the mid-1970s Kool Herc began to put two copies of the same record on his turntables. Switching back and forth between the turntables, Herc found that he could "backspin" one disc (i.e., turn it backward, or counterclockwise, with his hand) while the other continued to play over the loudspeakers. This allowed him to repeat a given break over and over, by switching back and forth between the two discs and backspinning to the beginning of the break. This technique was refined by Grandmaster Flash, who adopted the mixing techniques of disco DJs, particularly their use of headphones to synchronize the tempos of recordings and to create smooth transitions from one dance groove to the next. Using headphones, Flash could more precisely pinpoint the beginning of a break by listening to the sound of the disc being turned backward on the turntable. Flash spent many hours practicing this technique and gained local fame for his ability to "punch in" brief, machine gun–like segments of sound.

A new technique called "scratching" was developed by Flash's young protégé, GrandWizzard Theodore, who broke away and formed his own hip-hop crew at the tender age of thirteen. In 1978 Theodore debuted a new technique that quickly spread through the community of DJs. While practicing backspinning in his room, Theodore began to pay closer attention to the sounds created in his headphones as he turned the disc counterclockwise. He soon discovered that this technique yielded scratchy, percussive sound effects, which could be punched in to the dance groove. At first Theodore wasn't sure how people would react:

The Third Avenue Ballroom was packed, and I figured I might as well give it a try. So, I put on two copies of [James Brown's] "Sex Machine" and started scratching up one. The crowd loved it . . . they went wild. (Hager 1984: 38)

The distinctive sound of scratching became an important part of the sonic palette of hip-hop music—even in the 1990s, after digital sampling had largely displaced turntables as a means of creating the musical textures and grooves on rap records, producers frequently used these sounds as a way of signaling a connection to the "old school" origins of hip-hop.

Although all DJs used microphones to make announcements, Kool Herc was also one of the first DJs to recite rhyming phrases over the "breakbeats" produced on his turntables. Some of Herc's "raps" were based on a tradition of verbal performance called "toasting," a form of poetic storytelling with roots in the trickster tales of West Africa. The trickster—a sly character whose main goal in life is to defy authority and upset the normal order of things—became a common figure in the storytelling traditions of black slaves in the United States, where he took on additional significance as a symbol of cultural survival and covert resistance. After the Civil War the figure of the trickster was in part supplanted by more aggressive male figures, the focus of long, semi-improvised poetic stories called "toasts." The toasting tradition frequently focused on "bad men," hard, merciless bandits and spurned lovers who vanquished their enemies, sometimes by virtue of their wits, but more often through physical violence.

Although the toasting tradition had largely disappeared from black communities by the 1970s, it took root in prisons, where black inmates found that the old narrative form suited their life experiences and present circumstances. One of the main sources for the rhymes composed by early hip-hop DJs in the Bronx was the album *Hustler's Convention* (1973), by Lightnin' Rod, a pseudonym of Jalal Mansur Nuriddin, leader of a group of militant Black Nationalist performers known as the Last Poets. *Hustler's Convention* was a compelling portrait of "the life"—the urban underworld of gamblers, pimps, and hustlers—comprising prison toasts with titles like "Four Bitches Is What I Got" and "Sentenced to the Chair." The record, featuring musical accompaniment by an all-star lineup of funk, soul, and jazz musicians, became enormously popular in the Bronx and inspired Kool Herc and other DJs to compose their own rhymes. Soon DJs were recruiting members of their crews to serve as verbal performers, or "MCs" (an abbreviation of the term "master of ceremonies"). MCs played an important role in controlling crowd behavior at the increasingly large dances where DJs performed and soon became more important celebrities than the DJs themselves. If the DJs of the South Bronx were the predecessors of today's rap producers—responsible for shaping musical texture and groove—the MCs were the ancestors of today's superstar rappers, whose story we pick up in Chapter 10.

CONCLUSION

Although the seventies are often portrayed as a time of corporate consolidation and conservatism in popular music, that was only one dimension of a more complex story. The creativity and energy of genres such as punk, new wave, reggae, funk, disco, and early hip-hop extend a pattern we have discerned in earlier periods in the history of rock music: the periodic emergence of performers and styles situated at the margins of the commercial mainstream. In them, we find affirmation both of burgeoning changes in the production and consumption of music—changes that were to have a profound impact on popular taste in the decades to follow—and of deep continuities underlying the history of rock.

9

ROCK SUPERSTARS OF THE
1980s

From the viewpoint of the American music industry, the eighties began on a sour note. Following a period of rapid expansion in the mid-seventies, 1979 saw an 11 percent drop in annual record sales nationwide, the first major recession in the industry in thirty years. Profits from the sale of recorded music hit rock bottom in 1982 ($4.6 billion), down half a billion dollars from the peak year of 1978 ($5.1 billion). The major record companies—now subdivisions of huge transnational conglomerates—trimmed their staffs, cut back expenses, signed fewer new acts, raised the prices of LPs and cassette tapes, and searched for new promotional and audience-targeting techniques. The pattern of relying on a small number of multiplatinum artists to create profits became more pronounced in the 1980s. By the mid-1980s, when the industry began to climb out of its hole, it was clear that the recovery was due more to the mega-success of a few recordings by superstar musicians—Michael Jackson, Madonna, Prince, Bruce Springsteen, Whitney Houston, Phil Collins, Janet Jackson, and others—than to any across-the-board improvement in record sales.

A number of reasons have been adduced for the crash of the early eighties—the onset of a national recession brought on by the laissez-faire economic policies of the Reagan administration; competition from new forms of entertainment, including home video, cable television, and video games; the decline of disco, which had driven the rapid expansion of the record business in the late seventies; and an increase in illegal copying ("pirating") of commercial recordings by consumers with cassette tape decks. In 1984 sales of prerecorded cassettes, boosted by the popularity of the Sony Walkman personal tape player and larger portable tape players called "boomboxes," surpassed those of vinyl discs for the first time in history. (The introduction of digital audio tape, or DAT, in the early nineties, and of writable compact discs, or CD-Rs, at the turn of the millennium, provided consumers with the ability to make near-perfect copies of commercial recordings, a development that prompted the music industry to respond with new anti-copying technologies.)

Deregulation of the entertainment industry led to an explosion in the growth of cable television, one by-product of which was the launching of *Music Television* (MTV) in 1981. MTV changed the way the industry operated, rapidly becoming the preferred method for launching a new act or promoting the latest release of a major superstar. (The advent of videos designed to promote rock recordings is often traced to the band Queen's mock-operatic hard rock extravaganza "Bohemian Rhapsody," released in 1975. However, such early music videos were essentially advertisements for the sound recordings and not viewed as products that might be sold on their own merits.) Although the first song broadcast on MTV bore the title "Video Killed the Radio Star," it is more accurate to say that MTV—and its spin-off VH-1, aimed at an older, twenty-five- to thirty-five-year-old audience—worked synergistically with radio and other media to boost record sales and create a new generation of rock superstars. It also strongly influenced the direction of popular music in the early 1980s, sparking what has been called a second British Invasion by promoting English artists such as Eurythmics, Flock of Seagulls, Adam Ant, Billy Idol, and Thomas Dolby. (In July 1983 eighteen of the singles in *Billboard*'s Top 40 chart were by English artists, topping the previous record of fourteen set in 1965 during the first British Invasion.) By the mid-1980s the impact of MTV had been felt throughout the music industry.

The rise of MTV was facilitated by many social and cultural changes that were emerging in the early eighties. The election of President Ronald Reagan in 1980 ushered in a new era of social and political conservatism. One result of this new attitude was the raising of drinking ages in all states back to twenty-one, a change that had a devastating effect on live rock music, which in turn created new opportunities for televised music. As baby boomers moved into their thirties—a shift documented by movies such as *The Big Chill*, and television series like *Thirtysomething*—they naturally became more likely to prefer to experience music on television during the day than in a loud, smoky nightclub at midnight.

These demographic and social changes also affected the radio landscape. Throughout the seventies, the album-oriented rock (AOR) format had dominated FM radio. At that time, it represented a perfect marriage of artistic and commercial intent: AOR brought innovative new music to a coveted audience, the baby boomers. And their purchasing power was the economic fuel that powered the developing rock culture. By the eighties, however, this equation could no longer hold, if only because the first generation of rock listeners was steadily aging, and a new generation was coming up to replace them. Older listeners were less interested in new rock styles, and new rock styles were less interested in appealing to older listeners. At the same time, however, the rock industry didn't want to simply leave the baby boomers behind. So how could the industry appeal to the new listeners without alienating the old ones? Much of the eighties was spent trying to answer that question.

One solution was the development of a new radio format called "classic rock" to appeal to older listeners while reserving the AOR format for new rock, and preserving a large overlap in repertoire between the two. The name "classic rock" alone bespeaks a fundamental change in American culture: The idea that *any* form of rock could be old enough and acceptable enough to be considered "classic" would have been unthinkable even a few years earlier. But that was the whole point; the radio industry was highly interested in an audience that was infused with a rock sensibility, but also old and wealthy enough to have the disposable income to spend on advertisers' increasingly upscale products. There was also a specific practical motivation to shifting from AOR to classic rock. In the days before digital sound files, radio stations had to physically obtain the records they wanted to play. In that environment, changing the format of a radio station often involved seeking out, purchasing, filing, and storing thousands of new vinyl records. But AOR and classic rock were basically the same music, just presented in a different way, so very few new records needed to be purchased. In the early eighties, the low cost of shifting from one to the other made many stations much more open to making the change, and as digital technology came into the picture, the whole issue became moot.

It was taken for granted by MTV executives that a music video channel should be the television equivalent of an AOR radio station. What else could it possibly be? What they overlooked—or chose to ignore—was that an AOR station was only one of many choices available to radio listeners, while MTV was, at that time, the *only* significant music video channel. In other words, to viewers (and record companies), MTV was not the equivalent of *a* radio station, but the equivalent of *all* radio. This brought to the surface racial issues involved in radio that went back to the birth of rock itself. Out of more than 750 videos shown on MTV during the channel's first eighteen months, only about twenty featured black musicians (a figure that includes racially mixed bands). At a time when black artists such as Michael Jackson and Rick James were making multiplatinum LPs, they could not break into MTV; while MTV put Phil Collins's cover version of the Supremes' "You Can't Hurry Love" into heavy rotation, it played no videos by Motown artists themselves. Executives at

MTV responded to widespread criticism of their policy with the argument that their format focused on rock, a style now played by few black artists. Of course, this was a tautological argument—the restrictive format of MTV was the cause, and not merely a by-product, of the problem.

The mammoth success of Michael Jackson's *Thriller,* released by Columbia Records in 1982, forced a change in MTV's essentially all-white rock music format. The three videos made to promote the *Thriller* LP through three of its hit singles— "Billie Jean," "Beat It," and "Thriller"—set new standards for production quality, creativity, and cost, and established the video medium as the primary means of promoting popular music. "Thriller"—a horror movie *cum* musical directed by John Landis, who had previously made the feature film *An American Werewolf in London*—metamorphosed into a sixty-minute home video entitled *The Making of Michael Jackson's Thriller,* with the original fifteen-minute video and lots of filler material, including interviews with the star. *The Making of Michael Jackson's Thriller* sold 350,000 copies in the first six months, yet MTV still refused to air Jackson's videos. Finally, after Columbia Records threatened to ban its white rock groups from performing on MTV, the channel relented, putting Jackson's videos into heavy rotation. (It is notable that Jackson did not share the segregationist sentiments of MTV executives, going out of his way to include white rock stars such as Paul McCartney and Eddie Van Halen on his LP.)

The process of corporate consolidation (sometimes called "horizontal integration"), which has emerged at intervals throughout the history of American popular music, once again reared its head during the late 1980s and early 1990s.

Michael Jackson (and company) from the "Thriller" video. The Kobal Collection.

To a greater extent than ever before, record labels could no longer be considered stand-alone institutions but rather subdepartments of huge transnational corporations. By 1990 six corporations collectively controlled over two-thirds of global sales of recorded music: the Dutch *Polygram* conglomerate (owner of Mercury, Polydor, Island, A&M, and other labels); the Japanese corporations *Sony* (Columbia Records) and *Matsushita* (MCA and Geffen Records); the British firm *Thorn* (EMI, Virgin, Capitol); the German *Bertelsmann* conglomerate (BMG and RCA Records); and *Time-Warner,* the only American-based corporation in this list (Warner, Elektra, and Atlantic Records). Similarly, the American market for recorded music now had to be seen as part of a wider global market that transcended national borders. In 1990 the largest market for recorded music in the world remained the United States, which, at $7.5 billion, accounted for approximately 31 percent of world trade, followed at some distance by Japan (12 percent), the United Kingdom and Germany (9 percent each), and France (7 percent). Even in the United States, however, the record company executives concerned themselves to an unprecedented degree with global sales and promotion.

MTV AS HIT MAKER: PETER GABRIEL'S "SLEDGEHAMMER"

Peter Gabriel (b. 1950 in England) first achieved celebrity as a member of the art rock group Genesis. After leaving Genesis in 1975, Gabriel released four solo albums, all of them titled *Peter Gabriel.* Partly in an effort to clear up the consumer confusion that followed in the wake of this unusual strategy, he gave his next album a distinctive-if-brief title: *So. So* was an interesting and accessible amalgam of various musical styles, reflecting Gabriel's knowledge of the new digital technologies (see the following section), his budding interest in world music (see Chapter 10), and his indebtedness to black music, particularly R&B and soul music of the 1960s. The album peaked at Number 2 on the Top LPs chart, sold four million copies, and produced Gabriel's bestselling single, "Sledgehammer" (Number 1 Pop, Number 61 R&B in 1986), which we analyze in detail on page 254.

THE IMPACT OF DIGITAL TECHNOLOGIES

The 1980s saw the rise of technologies that would revolutionize musical culture. The new technologies—including digital tape recorders, compact discs, synthesizers, samplers, and sequencers—became central to the production, promotion, and consumption of popular music. These devices were the fruit of a long history of interactions between the electronics and music industries and between individual inventors and musicians.

Analog recording—the norm since the introduction of recording in the nineteenth century—transforms the energy of sound waves into physical imprints (as in pre-1925 acoustic recordings) or into electronic waveforms that closely follow (and can be used to reproduce) the shape of the sound waves

🎧 LISTENING TO "SLEDGEHAMMER"

"Sledgehammer" features a horn section led by the trumpet player Wayne Jackson, who, as a member of the Memphis Horns, had played on many of the biggest soul music hits of the 1960s ("Knock on Wood," "Soul Man," etc.). Jackson had deeply impressed sixteen-year-old Peter Gabriel during an appearance with the Otis Redding Soul Revue at a London R&B club in 1966. Gabriel described "Sledgehammer" as

> an attempt to recreate some of the spirit and style of the music that most excited me as a teenager—60s soul. The lyrics of many of those songs were full of playful sexual innuendo and this is my contribution to that songwriting tradition. It is also about the use of sex as a means of getting through a breakdown in communication. (Bright 1999: 267)

The lyrics to "Sledgehammer"—packed with double-entendre references to sledgehammers, big dippers, steam trains, the female "fruitcake" and the male "honeybee"—are in fact a G-rated variant of the sexual metaphors that have long been a part of the blues tradition. Gabriel's attempt to "recreate some of the spirit and style" of 1960s soul music may be successful precisely because he does not try to produce an exact copy of the African American musical styles that inspired him. Rather, he uses fundamental elements such as the twelve-bar blues form, call-and-response singing, strong funk-derived polyrhythms, and an R&B-style horn section as the basis for a performance that reflects his own musical experience and taste, including references to world music and harmonies that take the blues in new directions.

The success of "Sledgehammer" was in no small part due to the massive exposure it received on MTV in the mid-1980s. The video version of "Sledgehammer" was an eye-catching, witty, and technically innovative work that pushed the frontiers of the medium. It won nine MTV Awards (more than any video in history), including Best Video and the prestigious Video Vanguard Award for career achievement in 1987, and was ranked the fourth best video of all time in a 1999 retrospective aired on MTV.

The making of the video, which combined stop-motion techniques and live action, required Gabriel to spend eight painful sixteen-hour days lying under glass with his head supported by a steel pole. (Aardman Animations, the outfit that produced the "Sledgehammer" video, went on to work on the *Wallace and Gromit* videos and the talking car ads aired by Chevron in the late 1990s.)

One key to the success of any music video is the relationship it establishes between the sound of the original recording (which, except in the case of live concert videos, is always made first) and the flow of visual images. The video of "Sledgehammer"—directed by Steven Johnston—opens with enlarged microscopic images of human sperm cells impregnating an egg, which develops into a fetus, accompanied by the exotic sound of the synthesized flute. As the groove is established, we see Gabriel's face in close-up, moving to the groove, wiggling his eyebrows, ears, and mouth in time to the music. The stop-motion technique—in which the camera is halted and restarted in order to create the illusion of inanimate objects moving under their own power—creates a jerky stop-start effect that establishes a kind of parallel reality, carefully coordinated to match the rhythms of the music. The lyrics of the song are also reflected in the video images: When Gabriel sings "You could have a steam train," a toy locomotive circles his head on miniature tracks; when he sings "You could have a bumper car bumping, this amusement never ends," two smiling (and singing) bumper cars appear next to his ears, mountains of popcorn pile up behind him, and his hair turns to pink cotton candy. After a series of stop-motion sequences featuring everything from singing fruits and vegetables to dancing furniture, Gabriel is transformed into a "starman" and walks off into the night sky. Thus the video takes us from the microscopic origins of life to the vastness of the galaxy, with many diverting stops in between. As Gabriel himself admitted some years later, although the recording of "Sledgehammer" would probably have done well on its own, the ambitious and highly creative video of the song, played endlessly on MTV, introduced the song to millions of Americans who might otherwise never have purchased a Peter Gabriel record.

themselves. *Digital recording,* on the other hand, samples the sound waves and breaks them down into a stream of numbers (0s and 1s). A device called an *analog-to-digital converter* does the conversion. To play back the music, the stream of numbers is converted back to an analog wave by a *digital-to-analog converter* (DAC). The analog wave produced by the DAC is amplified and fed to speakers to produce the sound. There have been many arguments among musicians and audiophiles over the relative quality of the two technologies: Initially, many musicians found digital recording too "cold" (perhaps a metaphor for the process itself, which disassembles a sound into millions of constituent bits). Today, however, almost all popular recordings are digitally recorded.

The development of digital sound recording led to the introduction of the five-inch compact disc (CD), and the rapid decline of the vinyl disc. The sounds encoded on a compact disc are read by a laser beam and not by a diamond needle, meaning that CDs are not subject to the same wear and tear as vinyl discs. The first compact discs went on sale in 1983, and by 1988 sales of CDs surpassed those of vinyl discs for the first time. Although CDs cost about the same as vinyl LPs to manufacture, the demand for the new medium allowed record companies to generate higher profits by pricing them at thirteen dollars or more, rather than the eight or nine dollars charged for LPs. Digital technology also spawned new and more affordable devices for producing and manipulating sound—such as drum machines and sequencers, and samplers for digital sampling—and the musical instrument digital interface (MIDI) specification, which standardized these technologies, allowing devices produced by different manufacturers to "communicate" with one another. Digital technology—portable and relatively cheap—and the rapid expansion of the personal computer (PC) market in the early 1990s allowed musicians to set up their own home studios and stimulated the growth of genres like hip-hop and techno, both of which rely heavily on digitally constructed sound samples, loops, and grooves. For the first time, satellite technology allowed the worldwide simultaneous broadcast of live concerts, and the development of fiber optics allowed musicians in recording studios thousands of miles apart to work together in real time.

Synthesizers—devices that allow musicians to create or "synthesize" musical sounds—began to appear on rock records during the early 1970s, but their history begins much earlier. One important predecessor of the synthesizer was the *theremin,* a sound generator named after the Russian inventor who developed it in 1919. This instrument used electronic oscillators to produce sound, and its pitch was controlled by the player's waving his or her hands in front of two antennae. The theremin was never used much in popular music, although its familiar sound can be heard in the soundtracks of 1950s science fiction films such as *The Day the Earth Stood Still,* and on the Beach Boys' 1966 hit "Good Vibrations."

Another important stage in the interaction between scientific invention and musical technology was the *Hammond organ,* introduced in 1935 by the inventor

Laurens Hammond. The sound of the Hammond B-3 organ was common on jazz, R&B, and rock records (e.g., Santana's "Oye Como Va"), and its rich, fat sound is frequently sampled in contemporary popular music. The player could alter the timbre of the organ through control devices called "tone bars," and a variety of rhythm patterns and percussive effects were added later. Although the Hammond organ was not a true synthesizer, it is certainly a close ancestor.

In the early 1970s the first synthesizers aimed at a mass consumer market were introduced. These devices, which used electronic oscillators to produce musical tones, were clumsy and limited by today's standards, yet their characteristic sounds are viewed with some nostalgia and are often sampled in contemporary recordings. The first synthesizers to be sold in music stores alongside guitars and pianos were the *Minimoog,* which had the limitation of being able to play only one pitch at a time, and the *Arp* synthesizer, which could play simple chords. The *Synclavier,* a high-end (and expensive) digital synthesizer, was introduced to the market in 1976. The more affordable *Prophet-5,* introduced in 1978, was an analog synthesizer that incorporated aspects of digital technology, including the ability to store a limited number of sampled sounds.

The 1980s saw the introduction of the first completely digital synthesizers— including the widely popular Yamaha *DX-7*—capable of playing dozens of "voices" at the same time. The MIDI (musical instrument digital interface) specification, introduced in 1983, allowed synthesizers built by different manufacturers to be connected with and communicate with one another, introducing compatibility into a highly competitive marketplace. *Digital samplers*—for example, the *Mirage* keyboard sampler, introduced by Ensoniq in 1984—were capable of storing both prerecorded and synthesized sounds. (The latter were often called "patches," a nostalgic reference to the wires or "patch cords" that were used to connect the various components of early synthesizers.) *Digital sequencers,* introduced to the marketplace at around the same time, are devices that record musical data rather than musical sound and allow the creation of repeated sound sequences (loops), the manipulation of rhythmic grooves, and the transmission of recorded data from one program or device to another. *Drum machines* such as the *Roland TR 808* and the *Linn LM-1*—almost ubiquitous on 1980s dance music and rap recordings—rely on "drum pads" that can be struck and activated by the performer, and which act as a trigger for the production of sampled sounds (including not only conventional percussion instruments but also glass smashing, cars screeching, and guns firing).

Digital technology has given musicians the ability to create complex 128-voice textures, to create sophisticated synthesized sounds that exist nowhere in nature, and to sample and manipulate any sound source, creating sound loops that can be controlled with great precision. With compact, highly portable, and increasingly affordable music equipment and software, a recording studio can be set up literally anywhere—in a basement, or on a roof. As the individual musician gains more and more control over the production of a complete musical recording, distinctions between the composer, the performer, and the producer sometimes melt down entirely.

Certain contemporary genres make particularly frequent and effective use of digital technologies, particularly rap/hip-hop and various genres of electronic dance music. The technology of digital sampling allows musicians to assemble preexisting sound sources and to cite performers and music from various styles and historical eras. During the 1980s, musicians began to reach back into their record collections for sounds from the 1960s and 1970s. It has been suggested that this reflects a more general cultural shift toward a "cut-and-paste" approach to history, in which pop music cannibalizes its own past. However, it is worth remembering that, while the technology is new, the idea of recycling old materials (and thereby selectively reinventing the past) is probably as old as music itself.

Some interesting legal dilemmas are connected with the widespread use of digital sampling. American intellectual property law has always made it difficult to claim ownership of a groove, style, or sound—precisely those things that are most distinctive about popular music, like the timbre of James Brown's voice, the electric bass sound of Parliament/Funkadelic's Bootsy Collins, or the distinctive snare drum sound used on many of Phil Collins's hit recordings (a sound constructed in the studio out of a combination of sampled and synthesized sources). In recent years many lawsuits have centered on these issues, in which musicians and producers claim that their sound has been stolen by means of digital sampling. In 1993, George Clinton responded to the wholesale sampling of his albums by rap musicians by releasing a collection of sounds and previously unreleased recordings called *Sample Some of Disc, Sample Some of D.A.T.* The collection comes with a copyright clearance guide and a guarantee that users will only be "charged per record sold, so if your single flops, you won't be in the red."

THRILLER AND *BORN IN THE U.S.A.*

A brief look at two multimillion-selling albums of the 1980s will help document the variety of styles that characterized this period. Both of these albums represent the biggest commercial success in their respective artist's solo career. *Thriller*, in fact, ranks as the top-selling album in history as of this writing, having achieved worldwide sales that have reasonably been estimated to exceed 100 million copies, 30 million of them in the United States alone[1]; it was the Number 1 album in the United States for thirty-seven weeks during 1983. *Born in the U.S.A.* sold 15 million copies, and, like *Thriller*, spawned a record-breaking seven Top 10 singles, reinforcing the importance of the singles market in the golden age of the rock album.

---

1. Anderson, Kyle (2009). "Michael Jackson's *Thriller* Set to Become Top-Selling Album of All Time." MTV.com. *http://www.mtv.com/news/articles/1616537/thriller-set-overtake-eagles-topselling-lp.jhtml*

In the case of Michael Jackson, *Thriller* was the zenith of a career as a solo artist that had been gathering momentum throughout the 1970s, even while Jackson continued to be a pivotal member of the tremendously successful group the Jackson Five (which changed its name to the Jacksons with its departure from the Motown organization in 1976, a departure that caused no substantial interruption in its long-running success story). *Thriller* was state-of-the-art pop music, an album dedicated not so much to breaking new ground as to consolidating Michael Jackson's dominance of the contemporary pop scene by showcasing his versatility as a performer of a stylistically wide range of up-to-date material.

Bruce Springsteen's *Born in the U.S.A.* seemed more concerned with this country's past in its depiction of adult working-class Americans whose better days are behind them, and the album's music is drenched appropriately in Springsteen's typical roots-based rock sound. The glitzy, consciously "modern" sound and production values of *Thriller* clearly were not for Springsteen. In *Born in the U.S.A.* Springsteen was simply continuing to make the kind of music, and to voice the kinds of concerns, that had characterized his career from its beginning in the 1970s. The unexpected mega-success of the album (the best-selling album among Springsteen's previous efforts—*Born to Run* from 1975—had sold less than five million) took the artist himself somewhat by surprise and left him anxious to ascertain whether his newly enlarged audience was truly understanding the less-than-cheerful messages he wished to convey, as we shall see.

Thriller (Michael Jackson, 1982)

In fashioning *Thriller*, Michael Jackson (1958–2009) worked with the veteran producer Quincy Jones to create an album that achieved boundary-crossing popularity to an unprecedented degree. At a time when the pop music audience seemed to be fragmenting to a greater extent perhaps than ever before, *Thriller* demonstrated a kind of across-the-board appeal that established new and still unduplicated heights of commercial success. In a sense, Jackson here revived the goal that had animated his old boss at Motown, Berry Gordy Jr. (see Chapter 4): to create an African American-based pop music that was aimed squarely at the mainstream center of the market. That Jackson met his goal in such a mind-boggling fashion proved conclusively that there indeed still was a mainstream in the pop music of the early 1980s, and that Jackson had positioned himself unquestionably in the center of it.

To do this, Jackson had to be more than just "the sound of young America" (to quote Motown's memorable phrase from the 1960s). It is of course true that teenagers, pre-teenagers, and young adults made up a substantial portion of the 1980s market. But members of the baby boom generation, along with the many who came to maturity during the 1970s, were also still major consumers of pop music. And age was far from the only basis on which segmentation of

Michael Jackson performing during the Bad Tour in 1987. Dave Hogan/Getty Images.

the audience seemed to be taking place; fans of soft rock, heavy metal, funk, and new wave music, for instance, appeared to want less and less to do with one another. A disturbing subtext of all this was a tendency toward increasing resegregation along racial lines of the various audiences for pop. Heavy metal and new wave fans—and bands—were overwhelmingly white, while funk and the emerging genre of rap were associated with black performers and listeners.

Thriller represented an effort to find ways to mediate among the various genres of early 1980s pop music, to create points of effective synthesis from the welter of apparently competing styles, and to bridge the divides—actual or potential—separating different segments of the pop music audience. Jackson confronted the racial divide head-on by collaborating with two very popular, and very different, white artists: ex-Beatle Paul McCartney joined Jackson for a lyrical vocal duet on "The Girl Is Mine," while Eddie Van Halen of the heavy metal group Van Halen (see Chapter 10) contributed the stinging guitar solo on the intense "Beat It." Both of these radically different songs, along with two others on *Thriller,* were written by Jackson himself; his versatility and his gift for crossing genres extended also into the domain of songwriting. It is also clear that "The Girl Is Mine" and "Beat It" were fashioned to attract different segments of the white audience. The mere presence of Paul McCartney was a draw for many listeners who had been fans of the Beatles in the 1960s, as well as for those who admired McCartney's 1970s band Wings; as a song, "The Girl Is Mine" combines a gentle melodic flow with a feeling of rhythmic vitality, effectively echoing the virtues of the best Beatles and Wings ballads. "The Girl Is Mine" captured this essentially soft rock ambience—and its audience—especially well: The single release of this song held the Number 1 spot on *Billboard*'s Top Adult Contemporary chart for four weeks. Moreover, "The Girl Is Mine" had sufficient crossover appeal to top the R&B chart (now called "Hot Black Singles") for three weeks as well. As the first single to come out of the *Thriller* album, "The Girl Is Mine" demonstrated immediately how well Michael Jackson's new music could break down preconceptions about marketability.

"Beat It," on the other hand, has nothing to do with soft rock and was a gesture obviously extended to "metal-heads," who must have been struck by the novelty of a collaboration between a celebrated heavy metal guitarist and an African American pop icon. But this door also could, and did, swing both ways. "Beat It" joined "The Girl Is Mine" on the list of Number 1 Black Singles in 1983.

Much of *Thriller* consists of up-tempo, synthesizer- and bass-driven, danceable music that occupies a (probably conscious) middle ground between the heavy funk of an artist like George Clinton and the brighter but still beat-obsessed sound that characterized many new wave bands (of which Blondie would be a good example). Perhaps the outstanding—and, in this case, unexpected and highly original—example of the album's successful synthesis of diverse stylistic elements may be found in the title song. "Thriller" starts out depicting a horror-movie scene, which eventually turns out to be on the television screen being watched by two lovers, providing them with an excuse for cuddling "close together" and creating their own kind of thrills. In a conclusion that pairs an old white voice with a new black style, horror-movie star Vincent Price comes from out of nowhere to perform a "rap" about the terrors of the night. (This "rap" describes some typical horror-film situations, but its language is occasionally spiced up with current pop-oriented slang—as when Price refers to "the funk of forty thousand years.")

In the early years of long-playing records, the pop music album was typically a collection of individual songs, several (and sometimes all) of which had previously been released as singles. In our discussions of the 1960s and 1970s, we have remarked on the steadily increasing importance of the album over the single, as pop artists began more and more to conceive of the album as their principal creative medium. *Thriller* is a unique landmark in this evolutionary process. *Thriller* is not a concept album—unless the "concept" was to demonstrate that an album could be made to engender hit singles, rather than vice versa. For out of the nine songs on *Thriller,* seven were released as singles, one by one, starting with "The Girl Is Mine" (the only one to be released prior to the album itself), and all seven were Top 10 hits. (Both "Billie Jean" and "Beat It" were Number 1 pop hits; these two and "Thriller" sold over two million copies each as singles, while "The Girl Is Mine" was a million-selling single. The only songs from *Thriller* that were not turned into hit singles are "Baby Be Mine" and "The Lady in My Life.")

Visual media both old and new played a significant role in the *Thriller* saga. In May 1983 Jackson appeared on the television special *25 Years of Motown* and introduced what came to be known as his "moonwalk" dance while performing "Billie Jean" from *Thriller;* the performance was a sensation and doubtless added to the continuing popularity of the album. By this time, the videos for *Thriller* songs that Jackson had made were being shown regularly on MTV. Jackson's embrace of the relatively new medium of music video reflected his foresight in realizing its potential. While bringing his work to the attention of yet another segment of the music public, his videos in turn helped boost the power and prestige of MTV itself, because they were so carefully, creatively, and elaborately produced. Since Jackson was the first African American artist to be programmed with any degree of frequency on MTV, *Thriller* thus contributed to the breakdown of yet another emerging color line in pop culture. (Significantly, in the video of "Beat It," Jackson is seen breaking up a racially charged gang fight.)

Born in the U.S.A. (Bruce Springsteen, 1984)

By the seventies and eighties, many artists had begun to use rock's own history as an inspiration for their music. Perhaps the best example of this approach was Bruce Springsteen (b. 1949), whose work used elements drawn from different periods of rock's evolution to create a sophisticated, and often heart-wrenching, image

Bruce Springsteen. Getty Images.

of America's changing cultural landscape. In his music, lyrics, and performances, Springsteen often evoked a more innocent era of rock 'n' roll as a symbol of a more innocent America.

The instrumentation of Springsteen's band, prominently featuring acoustic piano and saxophone in an era of synthesizers and guitar heroes, was more consistent with that of a fifties rhythm & blues band than a late-seventies rock band. Springsteen himself even played a Fender Esquire guitar, one of the earliest production models of electric guitar, first produced in 1950 (though his was of a slightly later vintage). And Springsteen's overall sound intentionally recalled the "wall of sound" production aesthetic pioneered by Phil Spector in the early sixties, despite the fact that this sound had been out of fashion for over a decade by the time Springsteen embraced it. Even the band's name—Bruce Springsteen and the E Street Band—mimicked the old-fashioned, pre-Beatles, "X and the Y" band names of the late fifties. But Springsteen was no retro act. His intention was always clearly to *evoke* the youthful energy of early sixties rock, not *replicate* it. This was especially true of his lyrics, which often addressed the discrepancy between youthful dreams and adult realities in a complex poetic language that could only have emerged in the post-Dylan era (in fact, early in his career, Springsteen was promoted as "the new Dylan").

This approach won him a devoted following in the seventies that exploded into superstardom in the eighties. His work throughout this period extends the theme of longing for lost innocence to a variety of personal and political topics, relating the stories of still young but aging men and women with dead-end jobs (or no jobs at all), who are looking for romance and excitement in the face of repeated disappointments and seeking meaningful outlets for their seething energies and hopes in an America that seems to have no pieces of the American dream left to offer them. Some of the song titles from his first few albums are indicative: "Born to Run," "Darkness on the Edge of Town," "Hungry Heart," "Racing in the Street," "Wreck on the Highway," and so on.

The album immediately preceding *Born in the U.S.A.* represented a departure for Springsteen: *Nebraska* (1982) featured him in a solo, "unplugged" setting that underlined the particular bleakness of this collection of songs. Consequently, many fans may have celebrated *Born in the U.S.A.*, which brought back the E Street Band with an actual as well as a symbolic bang, as a kind of "return to form" for Springsteen. Certainly the album is dominated by up-tempo, rocking songs, with Springsteen shouting away in full voice and grand style, and the band playing full tilt behind him. Nevertheless, listening to the record (or tape or CD) with the album's lyric sheet in hand, it is hard to see how anybody could have regarded *Born in the U.S.A.* as anything other than a typically dire commentary by Springsteen on the current state of the union. Indeed, the very first lyrics of the title song, which opens the album, set the tone decisively:

Born down in a dead man's town,
The first kick I took was when I hit the ground.
You end up like a dog that's been beat too much
Till you spend half your life just covering up.

"Born in the U.S.A." tells the story of a returning Vietnam veteran unable to get a job or to rebuild his life, and its despairing message is characteristic of most of the songs on the album.

But maybe many people weren't listening to the words. In the wake of this album's rapid and enormous popularity, Springsteen found himself and his band on tour playing to huge, sold-out stadiums where—given the amplification levels and the crowd noise—most people probably couldn't even *hear* the words. Confronted with hordes of fans waving American flags, and the exploitation of his image in the presidential election year of 1984 by political forces for which he had little sympathy, Springsteen periodically found himself having to explain that he was not associated with "feel-good" politics or uncritical "America first" boosterism. Was Springsteen a victim of his own success, forced into a stadium rock culture that ill served the purpose and meaning of his songs? (Had rock music gained the world, so to speak, only to lose its soul?) Or was there actually some fundamental dichotomy between Springsteen's message and the energetic, crowd-pleasing music in which he was couching it?

There is, of course, no objectively "correct" answer to such questions. But when listening to *Born in the U.S.A.* as a recording, and as a whole, Springsteen's sincerity seems as apparent as his intensity, and it is hard not to sense, and hard not to be affected by, the prevailing dark ambience. In a general way, *Born in the U.S.A.* is a concept album: a series of musical snapshots of working-class Americans, all of whom seem to be somewhere around Springsteen's age (he turned thirty-five the year he released this album, the same age as his protagonist in the song "My Hometown"), many of whom are having economic or personal difficulties, and all of whom sense the better times of their lives slipping into the past. In the album's original LP form, each of the two sides starts out with a strong, aggressive song and winds down to a final cut that is softer in sound but, if anything, even darker in mood. The first side ends with the low-key but eerie "I'm on Fire," whose protagonist seems about to explode from the weight and pain of his own "bad desire"; in terms of the listening experience, the spooky urgency of this song appears to speak to the cumulative hard luck and frustration of all the different characters described in the songs of side one. Side two starts off with an extroverted rebound in musical energy and a cry of "No Surrender." But disillusionment and resignation come to characterize the songs on this side of the record as well, until the "fire" image reappears strikingly in the penultimate song, "Dancing in the Dark." Finally comes "My Hometown"; Springsteen, his voice drained of energy, sings of the decay of his place of birth and of possibly "getting out" with his wife and child, heading toward—it isn't clear what. In this poignant finale, Springsteen comes as close as any pop artist ever has to embracing and conveying an authentically tragic vision.

Amazingly, "My Hometown" was a major hit as a single recording, reaching Number 6 on the pop chart in early 1986 (and Number 1 on the Adult Contemporary chart). It was the last of seven consecutive singles to be culled from the album, all of which were Top 10 pop hits; in this respect, *Born in the U.S.A.* followed in the footsteps of *Thriller* as an album that spawned a parade of hit singles. The album itself sold over fifteen million copies, as we have already noted, and stayed on the album charts for over two years. Like Michael Jackson, Springsteen produced a series of music videos to go with several of the songs released as singles from *Born in the U.S.A.*; these videos proved popular in their own right and further enhanced the popularity of the album. Thus Springsteen stayed abreast of the changing music scene at the same time that he tried to speak, through his songs, to the values and attitudes that for him lay at the core of all that was worthwhile and enduring in rock.

NEW WAVE GOES DANCING: "SWEET DREAMS"

"Sweet Dreams (Are Made of This)," a Number 1 single from the early 1980s, is a good example of commercial new wave music of the early 1980s, an outgrowth of the 1970s new wave/punk scene promoted by major record labels. (We analyze this recording in greater detail on page 266.) It also exemplifies a more specific genre label that began to be used about this time: "synth-pop," the first type of popular music explicitly defined by its use of electronic sound synthesis. With its heavy reliance on electronically synthesized sounds, sequenced loops, and what has been described as a cool or austere emotional tone, Eurythmics' "Sweet Dreams" points the way toward later technology-centered music styles. Eurythmics consisted of a core of only two musicians—the singer Annie Lennox (b. 1954 in Scotland) and keyboardist and technical whiz Dave Stewart (b. 1952 in England).

Eurythmics. Lester Cohen/WireImage.

Eurythmics' first chart appearance in the United States came with the release of their second album, *Sweet Dreams (Are Made of This),* in 1983. The title track was released as a single soon after the album, rocketed to Number 2 on the English charts, and shortly afterward climbed to Number 1 on the American charts. The popularity of "Sweet Dreams (Are Made of This)" in the United States was boosted enormously by a video produced to promote the record, which was placed into heavy rotation by MTV. In particular, the stylishly androgynous image of Annie Lennox—a female David Bowie, in a business suit and with close-cropped orange hair—is often identified as an important ingredient in Eurythmics' success.

"BABY I'M A STAR": MADONNA, PRINCE, AND THE PRODUCTION OF CELEBRITY

The production of celebrity may be as central to the workings of the American music industry as the production of music itself. In the 1930s and 1940s, crooners such as Frank Sinatra were turned into media stars through increasingly sophisticated promotional techniques involving sound film, network radio, and the print media. In the years following World War Two,

🎧 LISTENING TO "SWEET DREAMS"

"Sweet Dreams" is built around a hypnotic digital loop: a repeated pattern established abruptly at the beginning of the record, as though the listener were dropped into the flow of a synthetic river of sound. A booming steady pulse, synthesized on a digital drum machine and reminiscent of disco music, underlies the melodic portion of the loop. Annie Lennox's singing alternates between an R&B- and soul-influenced melismatic style and the flatter, more deadpan tone that she adopts on the verses. The verses themselves consist of two four-line blocks of text, sung by Lennox in overdubbed harmonies. The singer seems to be expressing an unsettling—and titillating—combination of cynicism, sensuality, and—in the chorus—hope for the future. Some lines of the text ("some of them want . . .") hint darkly at sadomasochistic relationships, suggesting that the singer's sophistication has perhaps been won at some emotional cost. In the call-and-response chorus—which uses multitracking technology to alternate Lennox as lead singer with Lennox as choir—the mood changes, and the listener is exhorted to "hold your head up," while the multitracked voices urge us to keep "movin' on." Combined with Lennox's carefully cultivated sexual ambiguity—in a subsequent music video, "Who's That Girl," she plays male and female characters, and ends up kissing herself/himself—the lyrics and musical textures of "Sweet Dreams" suggest a sophisticated, even world-weary take on the nature of love.

Finally, although "Sweet Dreams" is sometimes regarded as an example of the emerging technological sophistication of the early eighties, the recording was made under less than optimum conditions. The studio rented by Stewart was a dingy, V-shaped warehouse attic, without any of the amenities of a professional studio (such as acoustical tiles or isolation booths for recording separate instrumental tracks). The equipment was rudimentary—an eight-track tape recorder and a cheap mixer, two microphones, an early version of a digital drum machine available in England at the time, and a handful of old sound-effects devices. "It sounded so sophisticated," reported Stewart in a 1983 feature in *Billboard*, "but often we had to wait for the timber factory downstairs to turn off their machinery before we could record the vocals." In fact, not all of the instrumental sounds on the recording are electronic in origin: the clinking counterpoint under the chorus of "Sweet Dreams" was played on milk bottles pitched to the right notes by filling them with different levels of water. In this sense "Sweet Dreams" both hearkens back to the "do it yourself" ethic of seventies punk and new wave music and points forward to the experiments of contemporary studio musicians, who sometimes introduce natural environmental sounds into their recordings.

network television became an indispensable tool for the promotion of popular music and the production of celebrity—it is, for example, hard to imagine the careers of Elvis Presley or the Beatles without the initial boost provided by network television appearances.

By the 1980s the "star maker machinery behind the popular song" (to quote a lyric by singer-songwriter Joni Mitchell) had grown to unprecedented proportions. Since the profitability of the music industry depended on the sales generated by a relatively limited number of multiplatinum recordings, the coordination of publicity surrounding the release of such recordings was crucial. The release of a potential hit album—and of those individual tracks on the album thought to have potential as hit singles—was cross-promoted in music videos, television talk show appearances, Hollywood films, and newspaper, magazine, and radio interviews, creating the overall appearance of a multifront military campaign run by a staff of corporate generals.

The power of mass-mediated charisma is rooted in the idea that an individual fan can enter into a personal relationship with a superstar via images and sounds that are simultaneously disseminated to millions of people. The space between the public image of the star and the private life and personality of the musician who fills this role is where the contemporary industry of celebrity magazines, television exposés, "unauthorized" biographies, and paparazzi flourishes, providing fans with provocative tidbits of information concerning the glamour, habits, and character traits of their favorite celebrities. This field of popular discourse is dominated by certain well-worn narratives. In what is perhaps the most common of these storylines, the artist, born into humble circumstances, rises to fame, is overtaken by the triple demons of greed, power lust, and self-indulgence, falls into a deep pit (of despair, depression, drug addiction, alcoholism), and then repents his or her sins and is accepted (in a newly humbled status) by the media and millions of fans. Other celebrities manage to flout convention and maintain their "bad boy" or "bad girl" image throughout their careers, while still others are portrayed as good-hearted and generous (if a bit bland) from the get-go. Of course, these story lines are as much about the fans themselves—and the combination of admiration and envy they feel toward their favorite celebrities—as about the particular musicians in question.

While stars such as the Beatles and Bob Dylan had played an important role in shaping their own public image, the 1980s saw the rise of a new breed of music superstar particularly adept at manipulating the mass media, and at stimulating public fascination with their personal characteristics, as well as with their music. Certainly, no analysis of celebrity in late twentieth-century America would be complete without a discussion of <u>Madonna</u> and <u>Prince</u>. Like their contemporary, Michael Jackson, Madonna Louise Veronica Ciccone and Prince Rogers Nelson were born in the industrial north-midwestern United States during the summer of 1958. (All three of these 1980s superstars were only six years old in 1964, when the Beatles stormed America, and not yet in their teens during the first Woodstock festival.) Despite the proximity of their geographical origins, Ciccone and Nelson followed quite distinctive career paths. To begin with, Ciccone was a dancer and photographic model who moved into music almost by accident, while Nelson had been making music professionally since the age of thirteen, as an occasional member of his father's jazz trio. Madonna first emerged out of New York's thriving dance club scene, while Prince's career developed in the regional metropolis of Minneapolis, Minnesota. Madonna's hit recordings—like most pop recordings—depended on a high degree of collaborative interaction between the singer, the songwriter(s), the producer, the recording engineers, studio session musicians, and others. But many of Prince's hit recordings, inspired by the early 1970s example of Stevie Wonder,

Superstars of the 1980s: **Prince** and **Madonna**. Frank Micelotta/Getty Images; Dave Hogan/ Getty Images.

were composed, produced, engineered, and performed solely by Nelson himself, many at his own studio in Minneapolis (Paisley Park, Inc.).

Despite these obvious differences, however, Madonna and Prince have much in common. Both are self-conscious authors of their own celebrity, creators of multiple artistic alter egos, and highly skilled manipulators of the mass media. Both experienced a meteoric rise to fame during the early 1980s and were dependent on mass media such as cable television and film. And both Madonna and Prince have sought to blur the conventional boundaries of race, religion, and sexuality and periodically sought to rekindle their fans' interest by shifting shape, changing strategy, and coming up with new and controversial songs and images. Early, sexually explicit recordings by Madonna and Prince played a primary role in stimulating the formation of the Parents' Music Resource Center (PMRC), a watchdog organization founded in 1985. During the second half of the 1980s, the PMRC—bolstered by its alliance with the Parent/Teachers Association (PTA)—pressured the recording industry to institute a rating system parallel to that used in the film industry. Although popular musicians ranging from Frank Zappa to sweet-voiced singer-songwriter John Denver argued against the adoption of a ratings system, the industry began to place parental warning labels on recordings during the late 1980s.

Madonna

From the late eighties through the nineties, Madonna's popularity was second only to that of Michael Jackson. Between 1984 and 1994 Madonna scored twenty-eight Top 10 singles, eleven of which reached the top spot on the charts. During the same ten-year period she recorded eight Top 10 albums, including the Number 1 hits *Like a Virgin* (1984), *True Blue* (1986), and *Like a Prayer* (1989). Over the course of her career, Madonna has sold in excess of sixty million albums in the United States (and more than 300 million worldwide) and is classified by the RIAA as the best-selling female rock artist in history. She paved the way for female dance music superstars of the nineties such as Paula Abdul, and for the public persona, performance style, and career strategy of contemporary pop star Lady Gaga.

As a purposefully controversial figure, Madonna has tended to elicit strongly polarized reactions. The 1987 *Rolling Stone* readers' poll awarded her second place for Best Female Singer and first place for Worst Female Singer. (In the same poll she also scored third place for Best-Dressed Female and first place for Worst-Dressed Female.) Jacques Chirac, the president of France, once described Madonna as "a great and beautiful artist," while the political philosopher Camille Paglia asserted that she represented "the future of feminism." The author Luc Sante's distaste for Madonna (as articulated in his article, "Unlike a Virgin," published in *The New Republic,* 8/20/90) was based largely on aesthetic criteria:

> Madonna . . . is a bad actress, a barely adequate singer, a graceless dancer, a boring interview subject, a workmanlike but uninspired (co-)songwriter, and a dynamo of hard work and ferocious ambition.

Other observers are ambivalent about Madonna, perhaps feeling—as the satirist Merrill Markoe once put it—"I keep trying to like her, but she keeps pissing me off!" (Sexton 1993: 14). In the academic field of popular culture studies, scholars have created a veritable cottage industry out of analyzing Madonna's social significance, variously interpreting her as a reactionary committed to turning back the advances of feminism, a postmodern performance artist, a politically savvy cultural subversive, and a "container for multiple images." Whatever one's view of these various characterizations is, the fact that it is difficult to find anyone who (a) has never heard of Madonna, or (b) harbors no opinion of her at all, is an indication that her career strategy has, by and large, been most effective.

Madonna Louise Veronica Ciccone was born into an Italian American family in Bay City, Michigan. She moved to New York City in 1977, worked as a photographic model, studied dance, and became a presence at Manhattan discotheques such as Danceteria, where the DJ, Mark Kamins, played her demo tapes. (It was Kamins who introduced Madonna to executives at Sire Records, the label of the Ramones and Talking Heads, and who in 1982 produced her first dance club hit, "Everybody.") In 1983 Madonna's breakthrough single "Holiday" (Number 16 Pop, Number 25 R&B) established certain elements of a distinctive studio sound, rooted in the synth-pop dance music of the early 1980s (see the discussion of "Sweet Dreams (Are Made of This)" on page 266). In addition, Madonna took a page from Michael Jackson's book, enlisting the services of manager Freddie DeMann, who had guided Jackson's career in the years leading up to the mega-success of *Thriller* in 1982. DeMann oversaw the production of Madonna's first two music videos, "Borderline" and "Lucky Star," the latter of which featured glimpses of the young star's navel, setting a precedent for subsequent, ever more explicit sexual provocations. The choice of Freddie DeMann also points toward an important aspect of Madonna's modus operandi—the ability to enlist a collaborative network of talented professionals, including producers, recording engineers, designers, and videographers.

In 1984 her second album—*Like a Virgin*, produced by Nile Rodgers, who was involved with the writing and production of a number of disco-era hits—shot to the top of the album charts, eventually selling more than ten million copies. The album spawned a series of hit singles: "Like a Virgin" (Number 1 for six weeks in 1984 and early 1985), "Material Girl" (Number 2 in 1985), "Angel," and "Dress You Up" (both Number 5 in 1985). *Like a Virgin* was promoted on MTV with a series of videos and formed the basis for an elaborately staged concert tour (the "Virgin Tour"), all carefully coordinated as part of a campaign to establish Madonna as a national celebrity. In 1985 Madonna also played a leading role in the film *Desperately Seeking Susan,* receiving generally positive reviews. In an industry where women are often treated as attractive but essentially noncreative "objects," Madonna began early on in her career to exert an unusual degree of control, not only over her music (writing or co-writing many of the songs on her early albums and playing an active role in the production process), but also over the creation and promulgation of her media image. Even seemingly uncontrollable events—like the ubiquitous tabloid accounts of her tempestuous and short-lived marriage to actor Sean Penn—seemed only to feed Madonna's growing notoriety.

During the second half of the 1980s Madonna began to write and record songs with deeper—and more controversial—lyric content. These included "Papa Don't Preach" (1986), in which a pregnant young woman declares her determination to keep her baby and urges her father to lend his moral support; "Open Your Heart" (1986), the video version of which portrays Madonna on display at a sleazy peep-show attended by dozens of men; "Express Yourself" (1989), in which she appears alternatively as a cross-dressing figure, dominating a tableau of male industrial workers, and as a submissive female stereotype, crawling under a table with a collar around her neck; and "Like a Prayer" (1989), the video of which included images of group and interracial sex, burning crosses, and an eroticized black Jesus. (This last video was censured by the Vatican and caused the Pepsi-Cola Corporation to cancel a lucrative endorsement deal with Madonna.)

🎧 LISTENING TO "LIKE A VIRGIN"

The core dichotomy of Madonna's public persona—the innocent, emotionally vulnerable, cheerful girl versus the tough-minded, sexually experienced, self-directed woman—was established in the hit single that propelled her to superstar status: "Like a Virgin" (Number 1 Pop and Number 9 R&B in 1984). "Like a Virgin" was not written by Madonna herself but by a pair of male songwriters, Billy Steinberg and Tom Kelly. As Steinberg himself put it, this is not a song about a virgin in any narrowly technical sense—rather, it is about the feeling that someone who has grown pessimistic about love gets from a new relationship. "Like a Virgin" is a good example of the mileage that Madonna and her producer, Nile Rodgers, were able to get out of a fairly simple set of musical elements.

The form of "Like a Virgin" is straightforward. After a four-bar instrumental introduction that establishes the dance groove, there is an eight-bar verse, which we are calling A^1 ("I made it through the wilderness . . . "); a ten-bar version of the verse with somewhat different harmonies, which we call A^2 ("I was beat, incomplete . . . "); and a chorus featuring the hook of the song, which we call B ("Like a virgin . . . "). The only additional structural element is an eight-bar interlude near the middle of the arrangement. The basic structure of the recording is thus

A^1A^2B

A^1A^2B

Eight-bar interlude

A^2BBB (etc., with a gradual fade-out)

As in much popular music, the timbre, texture, and rhythmic momentum of "Like a Virgin" are more important to the listener's experience than the song's structure. The studio mix—overseen by Madonna's longtime collaborator Shep Pettibone—is clean, with clear stereo separation, heavy reliance on synthesized sound textures, and the singer's voice strongly foregrounded over the instruments. (As on many dance-oriented hit singles of the 1980s, the characteristic lead guitar sound of rock music is absent here.) Synthesizers are indispensable to the overall effect of this recording—this is a studio sound that simply could not have been created ten years before. Throughout the recording, however, the producer and engineers are careful not to make the instrumental parts too busy or complex, so that Madonna's voice remains the undisputed center of the listener's attention.

As we have discussed, Madonna's persona on recordings and videos and in concert depends on the ironic manipulation of long-standing stereotypes about females. Her vocal style in "Like a Virgin" reflects this aspect of her persona clearly and deliberately, ranging from the soft, intimate breathiness associated with Hollywood sex symbols like Marilyn Monroe to the throaty, tougher sound of 1960s singers like Ronnie Spector, the lead singer on the Ronettes' "Be My Baby." (The contrast between these two vocal personas is reinforced in the video version of "Like a Virgin" by an alternation between images of one Madonna as a bride dressed in white, about to be taken to bed by her groom, and another Madonna dressed in a tight black skirt and top and blue tights, dancing sexily in a gondola moving along the canals of Venice.) During the verses Madonna uses a breathy, somewhat reedy "little girl" voice, occasionally interspersing little squeals, sighs, and intakes of breath at the ends of phrases. Throughout the recording, Madonna shifts back and forth between the two personas, the innocent virgin and the experienced, worldly wise woman, each signified by a distinctive set of vocal timbres.

Of course, how a song's lyrics are interpreted is strongly influenced by their musical setting and by the visual images that accompany the words and music in a video or live concert. When Madonna revived "Like a Virgin" for her 1990 *Blonde Ambition* tour, the song was placed in a more complex and provocative context, with Madonna clad like an ancient Egyptian princess, reclining on a huge bed, and framed on either side by black male dancers wearing cone-shaped brassieres. Whatever one's interpretation of the sexual and religious symbolism of Madonna's performances and its relationship to her own experience growing up as a Catholic, it is clear that she has a talent for recycling her repertoire in controversial and thought-provoking ways.

Madonna has frequently challenged the accusation—leveled at her by critics on both the left and the right—that her recordings, videos, and concert productions reinforce old, negative stereotypes of women. In a 1991 interview Madonna responded to these criticisms:

> I may be dressing like the typical bimbo, whatever, but I'm in charge. You know. I'm in charge of my fantasies. I put myself in these situations with men, you know, and everybody knows, in terms of my image in the public, people don't think of me as a person who's not in charge of my career or my life, okay? And isn't that what feminism is all about, you know, equality for men and women? And aren't I in charge of my life, doing the things I want to do? Making my own decisions? (Sexton 1993: 286)

Madonna's rhetorical question pulls us into the middle space between the public image and the private life: between the international superstar, Madonna, and Madonna Louise Veronica Ciccone, a talented and ambitious Italian American woman from the suburbs of industrial Detroit. Throughout her career, Madonna Ciccone has released tidbits of information about her private life, attitudes, and values that invite her fans (and her detractors) to imagine what the woman behind the "star maker machinery" is "really" like.

Prince

Between 1982 and 1992 Prince (a.k.a. the Artist) placed nine albums in the Top 10, reaching the top of the charts with three of them (*Purple Rain* in 1984, *Around the World in a Day* in 1985, and *Batman* in 1989). During the same decade he placed twenty-six singles in the Top 40 and produced five Number 1 hits. Over the course of his career, Prince has sold over eighty million albums, making him one of the most popular music superstars of the last three decades. More importantly, Prince is one of the most talented musicians ever to achieve mass commercial success in the field of popular music.

Prince Rogers Nelson was born in Minneapolis, Minnesota, the child of parents who migrated from Louisiana to the North and identify themselves as African Americans while acknowledging a mixed-race heritage that includes Italian and Native American ancestry. Prince has stated that growing up in a middle-class Minneapolis neighborhood exposed him to a wide range of music, and that his early influences included everything from James Brown and Santana to Joni Mitchell. As he testified in a 1985 interview on MTV (also transcribed in *Rock & Soul,* 4/86):

> I was brought up in a black-and-white world and, yes, black and white, night and day, rich and poor. I listened to all kinds of music when I was young, and when I was younger, I always said that one day

I would play all kinds of music and not be judged for the color of my skin but the quality of my work.

When he was seven his mother and father separated, and Prince spent much of his adolescence being shunted from one home to another. Various statements by Prince suggest that the instability of that period in his life, and the ambivalence of his relationships with his estranged parents, have formed the source material for some of his best-known songs.

One of the first things that strikes one about Prince's career is his amazing productivity. Throughout the 1980s and 1990s, when most superstars released an album every two or three years, Prince's output averaged over an album per year. During the 1980s he composed, performed, and recorded more than seventy-five songs each year. Only about three hundred of these songs have been released; the studio vault at Paisley Park is said to contain more than one thousand unreleased songs, more than ten thousand hours of material. Prince's compositions have been recorded by a wide range of artists, including George Clinton, Miles Davis, Joni Mitchell, Madonna, Bonnie Raitt, Celine Dion, and the Irish alternative singer Sinéad O'Connor, who had a massive international hit in 1990 with her cover version of Prince's "Nothing Compares 2 U." (The single reached Number 1 in the United States, England, France, Germany, and seven other countries.) In addition to recordings released under his own name, Prince has developed a variety of satellite projects, groups, or artists who have served in part as outlets for his music (for example, the Time, Apollonia 6, and Sheila E).

In stylistic terms, Prince's recorded output has encompassed a wide range of musical inspirations, from funk music and guitar-based rock 'n' roll to urban folk songs, new wave, jazz, and psychedelic rock. While the dominant impression of Prince's musical approach is that of a thoroughgoing open-mindedness, he has also from the very beginning of his career sought to exert tight control over his music, its marketing, and its distribution. Prince owns his own studio (Paisley Park Studios, in Minneapolis) and produces his own recordings, plays most of the instruments on his recordings, and has worked for years to maintain control over the master tapes recorded in his studio.

Prince's musical and commercial breakthrough came with his third album, *Dirty Mind*, which reached Number 7 on the R&B album charts in 1980. Recorded in his home studio, with Prince himself playing almost all of the instruments, *Dirty Mind* introduced a captivating new fusion of soul, synth-pop, and new wave sensibilities juxtaposed with a hard-edged rock sound centered on Prince's virtuoso guitar work. A number of the tracks were explicitly sexual in content, establishing Prince's controversial public image as an exuberant, and graphic, eroticist. He followed with a double album titled *1999* (1982), which demonstrated his musical range even more clearly, from pop ("Little Red Corvette") and rock 'n' roll ("Delirious") to apocalyptic dance-club funk—"Everybody's got a bomb, we could all die any day. But before I'll let that happen, I'll dance my life away"—embodied in the album's eponymous title track (Number 12 Pop in 1983).

During the mid-1980s, it was an album track (never released as a single) that did the most to reinforce Prince's reputation for controversy. "Darling Nikki," from the *Purple Rain* album, was the first recording ever to receive a Parental Advisory warning from the Parents' Music Resource Center, founded by Tipper Gore in 1985, and the song was attacked by the Trinity Broadcasting Network and preacher Jimmy Swaggart as "pornographic" and "satanic."

Prince's commercial success was accompanied by an increasing frustration with Warner Brothers, the corporation that had produced and promoted his early albums. By the early 1990s, he had entered into a protracted struggle with the company, going so far as to appear in public with the word "slave" written on his cheek. (During this period he is reported to have coined the deathless credo, "If you don't own your masters, your masters own you.") In 1993 Prince changed his name to a visual symbol (the Love Symbol) that combined male and female elements, leading wags in the press to dub him "The Artist Formerly Known as Prince" or, simply, "The Artist." A 1993 press release explained his motivations:

> Prince is the name that my mother gave me at birth. Warner Bros. took the name, trademarked it, and used it as the main marketing tool to promote all of the music that I wrote. The company owns the name Prince and all related music marketed under Prince. I became merely a pawn used to produce more money for Warner Bros. . . . I was born Prince and did not want to adopt another conventional name. The only acceptable replacement for my name, and my identity, was the Love Symbol, a symbol with no pronunciation, that is a representation of me and what my music is about.

Descriptions of Prince's personality in the popular press have presented a series of opposed images: He is portrayed as a flower child and as a dictator; a male chauvinist who can form close personal relationships only with women; an intensely private person and a shrewd self-promoter; a sexual satyr and a steadfastly pious man, who has dedicated many of his albums to God. These discussions of Prince draw many comparisons with earlier figures in the history of popular music: the extroverted and sexually ambiguous rock 'n' roll star Little Richard; the guitar virtuoso Jimi Hendrix; the groundbreaking and idiosyncratic bandleader Sly Stone; and the brilliant songwriter and multi-instrumentalist Stevie Wonder. Prince has been critical of the tendency of journalists and record company publicists to identify him only with black artists. In response to the question "What do you think about the comparisons between you and Jimi Hendrix?" he responded, "It's only because he's black. That's really the only thing we have in common. He plays different guitar than I do. If they really listened to my stuff, they'd hear more of a Santana influence than Jimi Hendrix" (Karlen 1985: 25).

Prince's British biographer Barney Hoskyns christened Prince "the Imp of the Perverse," referring to his apparent delight in confounding the expectations and assumptions of his audience, music critics, and the record industry. Certainly, Prince's relationship to the "star maker machinery" of the entertainment industry is as complex as his racial identity, sexual orientation, and musical style. As a public celebrity, Prince occupies a middle ground between the hermitlike reclusiveness that characterized Michael Jackson and the exuberant exhibitionism of Madonna. Throughout his career, Prince has granted few press interviews yet has for the most part managed to keep himself in the limelight.

Perhaps the best example of Prince's skill at manipulating the boundary between the public and the private are the film and soundtrack album *Purple Rain* (1984), which established him as a pop superstar. *Purple Rain* was the bestselling album of 1984, bumping Bruce Springsteen's *Born in the U.S.A.* out of the top position on *Billboard*'s pop album chart, holding the Number 1 position for twenty-four weeks, and producing five hit singles, including "When Doves Cry," "Let's Go Crazy," and "Purple Rain." Since 1984 the album has sold more than twenty million copies worldwide, making it one of the bestselling albums of all time. The film did reasonably well at the box office, although it did not succeed in establishing Prince as a matinee idol. Reviews varied widely, some critics regarding the film as a self-indulgent, poorly written, badly acted attempt to promote a music album, while *Rolling Stone* numbered it among the best rock movies ever made. The film and the album were cross-promoted by Warner Entertainment, which spent $3.5 million for television ads, and by MTV, which ran footage from the celebrity-packed premiere party in Hollywood. The single of "When Doves Cry" was released a few weeks before *Purple Rain* appeared in theaters and helped to boost the film's popularity, which in turn helped several other songs on the soundtrack to reach the Top 40.

The plot and characters of *Purple Rain* draw heavily on the details of Prince's life, both personal and professional. Prince stars as "the Kid," a young, gifted musician struggling to establish himself in the nightclub scene of Minneapolis. His main competition in the musical arena is Morris Day, the real-life leader of one of Prince's "satellite" projects, the Time. The Kid is attracted to a beautiful young singer named Apollonia (another of Prince's real-life protégés), who in the film is also being pursued by Morris Day. The Kid's parents—the only characters in the film portrayed by professional actors—are to some degree based on Prince's mother and father. Another subplot has to do with the Kid's inability to accept creative input from the musicians in his band, the Revolution. The film concludes on a relatively upbeat note as the Kid adopts one of his father's compositions, incorporating a rhythm track created by members of the Revolution, and creates the song "Purple Rain," which wins over his audience, the band, Apollonia, and even Morris Day.

LISTENING TO "WHEN DOVES CRY" (ALBUM VERSION)

"When Doves Cry"—a last-minute addition to the *Purple Rain* soundtrack—is an unusual pop recording in a number of regards. To begin with, the album track runs almost six minutes, a length that, although not without precedent, was much longer than the typical Top 40 hit of the 1980s. (A shortened version was released as a single.) Pop music recordings of the 1980s—such as Madonna's "Like a Virgin"—were typically the product of collaboration among the singer, songwriter(s), producer, studio engineers, session musicians, and others. "When Doves Cry," on the other hand, is essentially the work of a single person— Prince wrote the song, produced the recording, sang all of the vocal parts, and played all of the instruments, including electric guitar, keyboard synthesizers, and the Linn LM-1 digital drum machine. The lyric of "When Doves Cry," with its striking imagery and psychoanalytical implications, certainly does not conform to the usual formulas of romantic pop song. In addition, this recording crosses over the boundaries of established pop genres, fusing a funk rhythm with the lead guitar sound of heavy metal, the digitally synthesized and sampled textures of post-disco dance music, and the aesthetic focus and control of progressive rock and the singer-songwriter tradition. In this sense it is a good example both of Prince's desire to avoid being typecast as a traditional R&B artist and of the creative eclecticism that led music critics to come up with labels such as "dance rock," "funk rock," or "new wave funk" to describe his music.

The instrumentation of "When Doves Cry" is also somewhat unusual, as it lacks a bass part. Usually the bass helps to establish the tonality (or key) of a given piece of music and combines with the drums to provide the rhythmic bedrock of a recording. Prince's decision to "punch out" (exclude) the bass track that he had already recorded—apparently a spur-of-the-moment experiment during the process of mixing—gives the recording an unusually open feeling. In addition, Prince's composition

LISTENING CHART "WHEN DOVES CRY" (ALBUM VERSION)
Composed, performed, and produced by Prince; recorded 1984

FORM	LYRICS	DESCRIPTIVE COMMENTS
Intro		Lead guitar solo, no accompaniment.
Section One	0.03–3.19	
Groove (8)		Dance tempo established on drum machine; guitar stops at end of bar 5; digitized loop of Prince's voice enters in bar 6 (L side).
Groove (8)		Keyboard synthesizer enters, playing main riff; Prince's voice loop moves [L to R], then fades (bars 1–4).
A (8)	*Dig if you will . . .*	Keyboard drops out; solo voice and drum machine only.
A (8)	*Dream if you can . . .*	Second solo voice enters (overlaps with first voice); two voices combined (overdubbed), bars 5–8; vocal harmony in bars 7–8 ("They feel the heat").
B: (8)	*How can you . . .*	New vocal timbre added (growling bass voice); solo voice responds in bar 4 ("So cold"); new synthesizer pattern added (offbeats).
+		
(8)	*Maybe you're . . .*	More overdubbed voices added; four-part vocal harmony; solo voice responds in bar 4 ("She's never satisfied").

Groove (8)	1.34		Drum machine and keyboard synthesizer.
A (8)	1.50	*Touch . . .*	Vocal sounds in background (groans, sighs).
B: (8)	2.05	*How can you . . .*	New vocal timbre added (bass voice, growling); vocal responses in harmony.
+			
(8)	2.20	*Maybe you're . . .*	More overdubbed voices added; four-part vocal harmony.
Groove (8)	2.35		Drum machine and keyboard synthesizer; voices drift in and out (high falsetto timbre); vocal harmony riff (bars 6–7).
B: (8)	2.50	*How can you . . .*	Synthesized string sounds added in background; four-part vocal harmony with solo voice responses.
+			
(8)	3.05	*Maybe you're . . .*	Four-part vocal harmony with solo voice responses.
Section Two	3.20–5.51		
Interlude (8)			Synthesizer riff drops out; drum machine plus synthesized string sounds; Prince's "voices" overlap ("When doves cry").
Groove (8)			Groove reestablished; lead guitar solo begins; solo and duet voices drift in and out.
[NOTE: The single version of the song fades out and ends at this point.]			
Groove (8)			Guitar solo; solo and duet voices drift in and out.
Groove (8)	4:06		Guitar solo; solo and duet voices drift in and out; James Brown–style scream begins bar 5.
Groove (8)			Guitar solo ends; vocal sounds float over the groove (breathing, sighs, screams, groans).
Groove (8)	4.37		Vocal sounds float over groove.
Groove (8)			Stoptime in rhythm section with vocal harmony response; keyboard solo begins bar 5.
Groove (8)			Keyboard solo continues with vocal riff background; groove reestablished in bar 5.
Groove (8)			Prince's "voices" overlap ("When doves cry"); synthesized strings.
Groove (4)			Prince's "voices" overlap ("Don't cry").
Coda			Rising melodic pattern on keyboard; synthesized strings in background.

avoids the tendency, pronounced in many rock and pop recordings, to establish a clear distinction between a verse and a chorus, each having its own distinctive melody and harmonies. "When Doves Cry" does use the verse-and-chorus form, but the melody and supporting harmonies are almost identical in the two sections, making the distinction between them much less fixed. While many pop recordings use the verse-chorus structure to build to a final climax, followed by a relatively rapid fade-out, the musical intensity of "When Doves Cry" rises and falls continuously, creating a complex succession of peaks and valleys. (One critic has interpreted this "ebbing and flowing of pleasure" as embodying a female rather than male pattern of sexual excitement and has connected this musical approach to Prince's embracing of female qualities in his own personality.) Finally, the studio mix is also unusual, relatively spare and dry, and quite unlike the lush, reverb-laden studio sound of most 1980s dance music recordings (including Madonna's hit singles). Prince does use studio effects such as echo and digital processing, but they are tightly controlled and focused.

The arrangement of "When Doves Cry" can be divided into two major sections. Section One, about three and a half minutes in length, is basically a presentation of the song, with its alternation of verse (A) and chorus (B). Section Two consists of a series of eight-bar phrases in which the background texture is subtly varied while instrumental solos (guitar and keyboard synthesizer), sung phrases (both solo and overdubbed in harmony), and other vocal effects (breathing, screaming, sighing, groaning) are sometimes juxtaposed or layered on top of one another, and sometimes alternated one after the other. Perhaps the best analogy for the overall effect of this recording is that of a weaving, made up of patches of subtly shifting textural effects and tone colors, held together by the strong threads of a funk-derived dance groove, and strung on a formal loom made up of eight-bar sections. This is a recording that rewards repeated listening, not least because one musician has created every sound that you hear throughout.

"When Doves Cry" opens abruptly with a virtuoso burst of lead guitar, establishing from the very first moment Prince's mastery of the hard rock idiom. (We could say that Prince was able to do for himself what Michael Jackson needed Eddie Van Halen's help to accomplish on his *Thriller* album.) As the main dance groove is established on the Linn LM-1 digital drum machine, the guitar plays five more bars. We then hear a strange yet recognizably human sound, a pattern created by running Prince's voice through a digital processor and turning it into a repeating loop. As the keyboard synthesizer introduces a chord pattern that interlocks rhythmically with the drum machine (completing the basic groove that will carry us through most of the recording), Prince's voice moves across the stereo space of the recording from left to right and then fades out. Only sixteen bars into the recording, it is clear that this is not your normal pop single.

The first half of the arrangement (Section One) begins by placing equal weight on the verse and the chorus material (sixteen bars each) and then gradually de-emphasizes the verse (A), which finally disappears altogether (see the listening chart). The chorus is always followed by an eight-bar groove section, in which the underlying drum machine-and-synthesizer dance rhythm is brought to the fore. The presentation of the song, with its weakly contrasted verse-chorus structure, makes full use of studio technology and of Prince's remarkable abilities as a singer. In the first verse he sings alone, in a middle-register voice. The second verse introduces a second copy of Prince, another middle-register voice that overlaps slightly with the first one; as this concludes, the two Princes sing together, first in unison, then in overdubbed harmony. In the chorus ("How can you . . .") these two voices are joined by a third, low-register, growling voice; eventually ("Maybe you're . . . "), we are presented with four Princes singing in harmony with one another, plus a fifth Prince who interjects solo responses.

The second half of "When Doves Cry" (Section Two) presents an even more complex palette of timbral and textural variations, playing with combinations of the drum machine-plus-synthesizer groove, sustained orchestral sounds, instrumental solos (including a keyboard solo that resembles eighteenth-century music), and an astonishing variety of vocal timbres. If you listen closely you should be able to distinguish as many as a dozen unique voices in the studio mix, positioned to the left, right, and center, some heavily modified by digital technology, and others closer to the natural sound of Prince's singing voice. In addition to the complex patterns of harmony and call-and-response singing, Prince uses a variety of vocal effects, including a James Brown–like scream, rhythmic breathing, sighs, and groans. These sounds lend a sense of physical intimacy to the recording and enhance its aura of sexuality.

If "Like a Virgin" can be interpreted as a musical analogue to Madonna's "split personality," "When Doves Cry" may represent an even more complex set of psychological relations between the public persona and private personality of a pop superstar. In a 1996 television interview, Prince Rogers Nelson revealed that he, like millions of other children, had created an alternative personality, an imaginary companion who had not only helped him through the dislocations of his youth but also continued to offer him guidance as an adult. It may not be too much of a reach to suggest that the "multiple Princes" of "When Doves Cry"—a song that wears its Oedipal heart on its sleeve, so to speak—are not only an experiment in musical polyphony but also a conscious representation of the continuous inner dialogue that has shaped Prince's career. (In interviews, Prince has described how his "spirit" has advised him to change course, abandon projects, and even alter his name.) In its rich layering of instrumental textures and vocal personalities, "When Doves Cry" imparted to the public image of Prince a complexity and psychological depth that is in fact not typical of mass-media celebrities. And, in the process, it established his reputation as one of the most creative and influential musicians of the 1980s.

As with any semiautobiographical work, it is not easy to draw boundaries between the fictional character (the Kid), the celebrity persona (Prince), and the private individual (Prince Rogers Nelson). The character of the Kid—talented, self-absorbed, obsessed with exerting control over his music and his career, troubled by family conflicts and an inability to sustain intimate relationships— seems consonant with the accounts offered by Prince's family and professional associates. Apart from the Academy Award–winning soundtrack, a major source of the film's attraction for Prince's fans no doubt lay in the idea that this was a form of public psychoanalysis, a tantalizing opportunity to catch a glimpse of the "man behind the curtain." If *Purple Rain* is a film with genuinely confessional aspects, it is also a product of the increasingly sophisticated marketing strategies applied by entertainment corporations during the 1980s.

CONCLUSION

The eighties saw the flowering of tendencies that had shaped the production and consumption of rock music in the United States during the previous decade, including the rock-star-as-artist ideology; the music business's increasing reliance on multimillion-selling albums and international concert tours; the impact of new technologies on how people make and experience music; and the development of historical consciousness on the part of many musicians and fans about rock music and its roots. At the same time, the rise of alternative forms of music that either elaborated on or reacted against corporate rock—exemplified in the seventies by punk, reggae, funk, disco, and early hip-hop—continued apace in the eighties. In the next chapter we trace the movement of some of these alternative genres toward the center of the music industry, a process that both diversified and injected new energy into rock music.

1980s ROCK: NEW ALTERNATIVES, NEW ACCENTS

10

The mainstream of rock music in the eighties was dominated by the multiplatinum sales of recordings by a new generation of MTV superstars who extended and elaborated the ideology of the rock star as charismatic, iconoclastic artist. While the biggest stars of the eighties—Michael Jackson, Bruce Springsteen, Madonna, and Prince—dominated the mass media, including the new medium of cable television, a number of new streams of popular music, each in a particular kind of dialog or argument with mainstream rock, emerged into the limelight during the eighties. A subset of these diverse genres—heavy metal, hardcore punk, hip-hop, and worldbeat—forms the focus of our attention in this chapter.

HEAVY METAL

MTV had started out as a televised version of an AOR radio station, and by the mid-eighties its programmers were looking for music that combined the demographic appeal of classic rock with the flash and visual glamour necessary to win television viewers. The genre they stumbled upon was an offshoot of a scene that had roots in the early seventies: heavy metal.

One of the genre's early influences was Led Zeppelin, whose song "Stairway to Heaven" we discussed in Chapter 7. In the seventies, Led Zeppelin had mapped out a sound that provided the roots of the metal aesthetic: heavy— almost plodding drums, combined with distorted, riff-based guitar parts (interspersed with virtuosic solos) and a powerful vocal style which often used a high falsetto tone. Lyrically, their songs tended toward abstract poetry with a distinctly medieval bent, conjuring up a mythical past that was part Woodstock, part Mississippi juke joint, and part *Lord of the Rings* (Led Zeppelin actually made explicit reference to the J. R. R. Tolkien novels in several songs). Variations on this theme would later become an important part of heavy metal, as bands added faux-German umlauts (Mötley Crüe, Motörhead) to their names and created album covers with dark castles, swords, and armor. Led Zeppelin was also an early "stadium rock" band, one of the first to play larger venues in the seventies. This led to an emphasis on the kinds of flashy stage antics that—ten years later—would be taken up by rock musicians on MTV.

The band generally considered to be the first real metal group, <u>Black Sabbath</u>, further refined this approach. Formed in 1968 in the working-class industrial town of Birmingham, U.K., Black Sabbath (Ozzy Osbourne, vocals; Tony Iommi, guitar; Terry "Geezer" Butler, bass; Bill Ward, drums) was the first group to use metal to explicitly address feelings of social and economic powerlessness and frustration. This connection became increasingly central in the eighties, and in many ways has been the backbone of metal ever since. In the case of Black Sabbath and other bands that followed their lead, this attitude was often expressed in escapist lyrics and imagery that took up where Led Zeppelin had left off, even venturing into a not-so-serious brand of occultism that was designed to provide a kind of scary thrill, much like a roller coaster or horror movie. Black Sabbath opened the door for a new generation of British metal bands during the mid-seventies, including Iron Maiden, Saxon, and another band that was central to defining the metal aesthetic, Judas Priest.

Judas Priest performing in 1990. © Steve Jennings/Corbis.

Building on the gothic imagery of Black Sabbath, <u>Judas Priest</u> is credited with defining a distinctive visual culture for metal that exists to the present day, one that combined a blue-collar industrial experience with gothic imagery into a single aesthetic of black leather, chains, spikes, motorcycles, and more leather. Judas Priest was distinctive among metal bands at the time for their use of two guitar players, which allowed them to play riffs and solos at the same time, or—in what was to become true metal fashion—powerful unison riffs.

Judas Priest is also representative of metal in the eighties and nineties in that they were victims of an anti-metal hysteria that echoed the earlier reception of rock 'n' roll itself. In 1990, they were sued in a high-profile case in which the parents of two teens argued that their sons' 1985 suicide attempts (one successful, one not) were instigated by subliminal messages in the band's music. Judas Priest eventually won the lawsuit, but it was part of a larger movement in the United States to paint metal music as the cause of significant teen problems. As many fans and musicians pointed out, in most cases it was more likely that the relationship was the reverse of how it was presented: teens who were *already* troubled often turned to metal for comfort. Metal's role as a haven for those who felt like outsiders to mainstream society was also reflected in what for many

Van Halen in 1984. © Andy Freeberg/Retna Ltd.

remains the band's most surprising contribution to metal culture: In 1998, lead singer Rob Halford became the first major metal musician to come out as a gay man. For most fans, this was a nonissue: The solidarity that metal promoted—and its resistance to the perceived judgmentalism of the mainstream world—far outweighed any homophobia the fans may have been harboring.

Throughout the late seventies and early eighties, metal bands received very little radio play and even less critical acclaim. The music was associated with working-class life, limited musical skills, and musicians whose personal charisma was—at best—an acquired taste. That all changed with the rise of Van Halen.

Van Halen (David Lee Roth, vocals, Eddie Van Halen, guitar, Alex Van Halen, drums, Michael Anthony, bass) brought a new approach to heavy metal music. For one thing, rather than hailing from a dreary English industrial town or small midwestern city, they came from Southern California, home of surf, sand, and—not coincidentally—the record industry. Moreover, their appearance reflected that background, emphasizing youthful, smiling, athletic musicians with feathered hair, who preferred spandex (at the time associated with exercise-wear) to leather. Their lyrics reinforced this attitude as well; their songs were less about dissatisfaction and angst and more about partying and continuing to party. But by far the most distinctive and influential aspect of Van Halen's appeal was the unique guitar style of Eddie Van Halen.

Eddie Van Halen's approach to playing is characterized first and foremost by its emphasis on technical virtuosity. Up to that point, heavy metal guitar—and, in most cases, rock guitar in general—was associated with ragged-but-right soulfulness. Even widely praised guitarists like Eric Clapton and Jimi Hendrix were mainly appreciated for the way their technical skills facilitated emotional expression more than for the technical skills themselves. Eddie Van Halen, by contrast, ushered in an era in which a guitarist's notes-per-second rate was viewed as a good guide to the person's value as a musician. But although Van Halen was one of the fastest guitarists in rock history up to that point, his skills went far beyond simple speed. His solos showed a great deal of melodic and harmonic sophistication, and he also pioneered specific playing techniques that extended these skills even further. He was particularly noted for his use of "tapping," a technique whereby a guitarist quickly "taps" a note with the index finger of his or her right hand while still playing normally with the left hand. By alternating notes played the conventional way with tapped notes, a guitarist can play twice as fast as would otherwise be possible, while also making huge melodic leaps between notes. Tapping, then, allowed Eddie Van Halen to construct guitar solos that were almost inhumanly fast and melodically complex, a style of guitar playing that would later come to be known as "shredding."

Van Halen's musical credibility, combined with their affable attitude and Hollywood good looks—all of which were considered rarities in the metal world—made them naturals for MTV. One of the most important moments in the mainstreaming of heavy metal was the release of Van Halen's album *1984,* which featured the Number 1 pop single "Jump."

"Jump," which we discuss in more detail on page 285, was in some ways a remarkable departure from standard heavy metal practice. To begin with, its main instrumental melody was played on a synthesizer rather than an electric guitar. This may seem like a minor detail, but it was an important symbolic and aesthetic issue for hardcore metal fans, many of whom focus closely on the technical virtuosity of guitarists like Eddie Van Halen. From this perspective, the keyboard synthesizer (like disco music) is viewed as a somewhat questionable, perhaps even effeminate instrument. As Philip Bashe, an expert on heavy metal music, has put it, the fact that Eddie Van Halen played the bombastic opening theme of "Jump" on a synthesizer rather than a guitar was "a brave test of the Van Halen audience's loyalty" (Bashe 1985: 137). The success of the single was boosted by its corresponding music video, which was shot in home-movie style and featured the athletic prowess and oddball sense of humor of David Lee Roth—at that time Van Halen's lead singer.

Although some hardcore metal fans criticized Van Halen for moving away from the guitar-centered model of heavy metal musicianship, the band succeeded in introducing synthesizers into the genre, and in helping to spread metal's popularity to a larger and more diverse audience. In 1983 only 8 percent of records sold in the United States were heavy metal; a year later that total had risen to 20 percent, making metal one of the most popular genres of popular music. This process continued in 1986 when the pop metal band Bon Jovi released the album *Slippery When Wet,* which held the Number 1 spot for eight weeks and went on to sell over twelve million copies worldwide. By the end of 1986 MTV had launched *Headbangers' Ball,* a show designed specifically for metal fans, which soon became the most-watched show on the channel. In the late 1980s heavy metal music accounted for around half of the Top 20 albums on the *Billboard* charts on any given week.

Van Halen's popularity opened the door for other musicians that shared their musical vision, their charismatic visual appeal, or both. In the first category were musicians such as Yngwie Malmsteen, Joe Satriani, and Steve Vai, who pioneered a style of guitar-centric, primarily instrumental metal that was sometimes referred to as "neo-classical"—due to its emphasis on virtuosity and technical sophistication, and to the fact that many of the guitarists actually took European classical musicians and composers as influences. At the same time, other Southern California metal bands such as Mötley Crüe, Ratt, and Poison pushed the MTV-friendly stage craft of Van Halen to its limit, resulting in a subgenre called "hair metal" or "glam metal" due to its emphasis on the flashy physical appearance—embodied in their teased hair—of its practitioners.

In response to the explosive growth of what they saw as an overly accessible form of heavy metal, many fans and musicians went in another direction, emphasizing metal's uncompromising attitude, bass frequencies, and riffs. The

🎧 LISTENING TO "JUMP"

Written and performed by Van Halen; recorded 1984

On "Jump," the song itself, in the conventional sense of words-plus-melody, is not a core focus of attention for the musicians or their listeners. (Eddie Van Halen, when asked by an interviewer what his mother would think of the lyrics to his band's songs, said that he had no idea at all what they were!) The lyrics of "Jump"—a casual come-on to a girl from a guy leaning against a jukebox—seem almost an afterthought, apart, perhaps, from the clever "go ahead and jump!" hook phrase, which sounds rather as though David Lee Roth were counseling the object of his affections to jump off a high ledge, rather than into his arms.

The chief significance of a recording like "Jump," then, lies not in the song per se but in the musical textures created by the band and the studio engineer, and in the sensibility that they evoke. Although "Jump" relies heavily on the keyboard synthesizer for its effect, the sounds generated by Eddie Van Halen are in fact closely analogous to his guitar style. In particular, he uses the synthesizer to create something akin to "power chords," two-note combinations that, when played at high volume on an electric guitar, create the massive, distorted, bone-crunching sound associated with heavy metal bands. "Jump" opens with a synthesized power chord, as if to announce right from the beginning that the sheer sound of the music is more important than the specific instruments used to produce it. Thick textures and a strong pulse, played on keyboards, bass, and drums, propel us through the first two verses of the song. The arrival of the chorus is marked by a sudden opening up, in which the synthesizer plays long-sustained chords, the electric guitar plays a sizzling counterpoint to the vocal melody, and the drums and bass play an interesting irregular rhythmic pattern that first suspends the beat and then, after four bars, unleashes it with even greater energy. After another verse-and-chorus section, we are transported into the midst of a virtuoso guitar solo that uses Eddie Van Halen's famed techniques. The guitar solo is followed by a longer synthesizer solo, which develops an elaborate melodic improvisation that closely parallels the style of Van Halen's guitar playing.

undisputed leaders of this movement, known as speed metal, were Metallica (James Hetfield, vocals & guitar; Lars Ulrich, drums; Kirk Hammett, guitar; Robert Trujillo, bass). Rejecting the pop image of the Los Angeles–based bands, Metallica drew inspiration from both heavy metal and punk rock.

While to some degree Metallica retained the virtuosic approach of the neo-classical guitarists, they focused their efforts less on melody and more on achieving an almost military rhythmic precision, often changing tempos and meters abruptly in the middle of a song. This new rhythmic approach was emphasized by new playing techniques that use the guitar's low E string (played open, but dampened by the guitarist's fingers) almost as a percussion instrument, often playing in time with the bass drum. This, in turn, led to new developments in guitar construction, including seven-string guitars (with another string added below the low E string), and baritone guitars, which were built to allow the entire instrument to be tuned down to a lower pitch.

The emphasis on deep bass frequencies was partially a result of new technologies in sound reproduction that affected popular music across the board. Before the advent of digital recording, it was very difficult to record very low bass frequencies, since they could overwhelm the technology and cause the recording to be distorted. With the rise of compact discs, however, these frequencies could not only be captured in the studio with less trouble, but also reproduced for home listening. At the same time, improvements in home and car stereo systems rushed to take advantage of this new opportunity. In the nineties, it became common for both home and car stereo systems to include a subwoofer, a speaker that was designed specifically to reproduce extremely low frequencies. The influence of this change can be heard across the spectrum of popular music, from metal's new emphasis on deep guitar tones to hip-hop's uses of the Roland TR-808 drum machine, which allowed the producer to control the deep, resounding pitches of the bass drum.

Although much of Metallica's appeal during the 1980s had been based on a symbiotic relationship with the tightly knit underground metal community, their 1991 album *Metallica* was the ultimate confirmation of heavy metal's mass popularity and newfound importance to the music industry: It streaked to Number 1 on the album charts, sold over five million copies, and stayed on the charts for an incredible 266 weeks. The sudden mass appeal of underground metal led to new debates about authenticity and commitment. What—if anything—did Metallica owe the community that had supported them, now that they had outgrown it? Though it may seem strange, one of the most controversial moves made by Metallica in this period was entirely symbolic. In 1994, the members simultaneously cut off their long hair, a move that was widely viewed as an attempt by the band to align themselves with new trends in rock, and (by implication) distance themselves from the metal underground. Many older fans thus perceived it as a betrayal. It is interesting to note that the issues here—community, authenticity and commercialism—are almost exactly the same as those involved when Bob Dylan "went electric" in 1965.

Metallica in concert, 1984. ©Corbis.

Metallica also developed a large international following in the late eighties, presumably due to the universality of its message of dissatisfaction, and the fact that the music's aggressive sound made that message apparent regardless of whether one could understand the lyrics. By the 1990s, a Brazilian metal group like Sepultura could gain worldwide fame by combining the aggressiveness of metal with the sounds of traditional Brazilian music. (Another example of Metallica's international appeal is discussed on page 362.)

HARDCORE PUNK

In the early eighties, the original punk rock movement essentially split off into three separate subgenres: "hardcore" punk, a new iteration of the punk idea that was more intense (both musically and ideologically); a melodic post-punk movement that came to be known as "alternative" or "college rock," due to its main home on noncommercial college radio; and a commercialized version of New Wave that took much of the fashion and attitude of punk and combined it with a more radio- and TV-friendly sound.

Hardcore was an extreme variation of punk, pioneered during the early 1980s by bands in Washington, D.C. (Bad Brains and Minor Threat), San Francisco (the Dead Kennedys), and Los Angeles (the Germs, Black Flag, X, and the Circle Jerks). These groups—and others in other parts of the country—took the frenzied energy of the Ramones and the Sex Pistols and pushed it to the limit, playing simple riff-based songs at impossibly fast tempos and screaming nihilistic lyrics over a chaotic wall of guitar chords. Audiences at hardcore

Dead Kennedys, 1981. Photo by Peter Noble/Redferns.

clubs—typically adorned in tattoos, buzz cuts, and combat boots—developed the practice of *slam dancing* or *moshing,* in which members of the audience pushed their way up to a *mosh pit,* an area situated directly in front of the stage, and smashed into one another, sometimes climbing onto the stage and diving off into the crowd.

Hardcore punk was associated with small, local "scenes." This was largely a result of its guiding philosophy, DIY: "Do it yourself." At its root, this simply meant that attitude and commitment were more important than virtuosity, training, or institutional status. The idea was applied to everything from concert promotion to making records to media (especially so-called zines, or self-produced magazines) to musicianship itself, ultimately creating an almost entirely separate alternative to the dominant rock system. The idea was that one should not wait around for professionals to create what you wanted—just do it yourself. The prevalence of this attitude resulted in a series of mutually supportive local communities that soon linked themselves into a larger nationwide underground scene during the eighties. These connections, in turn, laid the groundwork for much of the rock music of the nineties. Two of the most influential hardcore scenes of the eighties were located in Washington, D.C., and in California, both centered around artist-owned independent record labels.

The "DC Hardcore" scene was an urban, intense, and somewhat doctrinaire community in which lifestyle politics were as important as music. Two of the most prominent groups to emerge from this scene, both of which are considered pioneers of the hardcore style, are <u>Minor Threat</u> and <u>Bad Brains</u>. Minor Threat—whose lead singer, Ian McKaye, was also the co-founder of one of punk's most important independent record companies, Dischord—helped to develop the early hardcore aesthetic. Generally speaking, this approach emphasized extremely fast, short songs that featured intensely distorted guitars, aggressive, high-speed drums, and a vocal style that focused more on plaintive sincerity than melodic sophistication (the entire chorus of their self-titled song "Minor Threat" consists of only two notes repeated over and over). Minor Threat and their fans were also committed to a somewhat severe politics of personal responsibility. This philosophy, as described in the song "Straight Edge," later evolved into a movement of the same name that rejected drinking, drugs, smoking, meat-eating, and casual sex. Another important band to emerge from this scene was Bad Brains, whose members were all African American Rastafarians, and who were the inheritors of a relationship between reggae and punk rock that began in England in the seventies, when the children of Jamaican immigrants found they had much in common with working class Anglos. By bringing this relationship into an American context and drawing on African American and Caribbean traditions in both their music and their lyrics, Bad Brains boldly proclaimed the relationship between rock and African American culture in an era when that connection had been all but lost. Although their music was not widely known outside the small hardcore scene of the eighties, they would later be cited as a

🎧 LISTENING TO "HOLIDAY IN CAMBODIA"

Written and performed by the Dead Kennedys; recorded 1980

"Holiday in Cambodia" by the Dead Kennedys, released on the independent label Alternative Tentacles in 1981, is a good example of the sensibility of early 1980s hardcore. The lyrics—written by the band's lead singer, Jello Biafra (Eric Boucher, b. 1959 in Boulder, Colorado)—brim with merciless sarcasm. The song is directed at the spoiled children of suburban yuppies, who, Biafra suggests, ought to be sent to forced labor camps in Cambodia—then in the grip of Pol Pot's genocidal regime—to gain some perspective on the magnitude of their own problems. The recording opens with a nightmarish display of guitar pyrotechnics, a series of Hendrix-inspired whoops, slides, scratches, and feedback, evocative of a war zone. The band—guitar, electric bass, and drums—gradually builds to an extremely fast tempo (around 208 beats per minute). Over this chaotic din, Jello Biafra's quavering voice sneers out the caustic lyrics:

> So you been to school for a year or
> two
> And you know you've seen it all
> In daddy's car, thinkin' you'll go far
> Back east your type don't crawl
> Play ethnicky jazz to parade your
> snazz [coolness]
> On your five grand stereo
> Braggin' that you know how the
> niggers feel cold

> And the slums got so much soul . . .

> Well you'll work harder with a gun in
> your back
> For a bowl of rice a day
> Slave for soldiers till you starve
> Then your head is skewered on a
> stake . . .

> Pol Pot, Pol Pot, Pol Pot, Pol Pot . . .

> And it's a holiday in Cambodia
> Where you'll do what you're told
> A holiday in Cambodia
> Where the slums got so much soul . . .

The Dead Kennedys' variant of hardcore was lent focus by the band's political stance, which opposed American imperialism overseas, attacks on human rights and the environment, and what the band saw as a hypocritical and soulless suburban lifestyle. Jello Biafra composed songs with titles like "California über Alles," "Kill the Poor" (a Jonathan Swift–like suggestion for the practical application of neutron bombs), and "Chemical Warfare." As the hardcore scene began to attract right-wing racial supremacists—a problem that the genre shared with 1970s punk rock—Biafra penned a song entitled "Nazi Punks F——Off" (1981), in an attempt to distance the progressive hardcore skinheads from their fascist counterparts.

fundamental inspiration for generations of African American rock musicians in the 1990s and 2000s. In the case of both Minor Threat and Bad Brains, the general rebelliousness of early punk had evolved into a more focused energy that was applied to specific programs and philosophies.

A similar evolution was taking place on the West Coast, particularly in Los Angeles and San Francisco. As with the DC hardcore scene, the West Coast hardcore scene combined a more intense musical approach with diverse cultural influences. In this case, this included such quintessentially California phenomena as skateboarding, Los Angeles gang culture, and leftist radical politics. Groups such as Suicidal Tendencies, Black Flag (who ran an independent record company called SST Records), and the <u>Dead Kennedys</u> (who ran an independent record company called Alternative Tentacles) embodied the DIY mentality on the West Coast.

HIP-HOP BREAKS THROUGH

In many ways, hip-hop's relationship to rock is similar to that of other forms of African American popular music over the last four decades: Though few would consider hip-hop to be rock music as such, there is a deeper mutual influence between the two styles than many people realize. Musically, hip-hop is based on the idea of the breakbeat, a section of a song where most of the instruments drop out, leaving only the drums. Early hip-hop deejays used two turntables, each with a copy of the same record, to repeat and thus extend these break beats, which soon gave the first hip-hop MCs (later known as rappers) something to rhyme over. As deejays competed with each other to find the most interesting breakbeats, they quickly turned to rock music. Many of hip-hop's earliest breaks came from such rock artists as Led Zeppelin, Black Sabbath, and the Rolling Stones. As hip-hop developed, it was deeply influenced by the New York punk rock scene of the late seventies and early eighties. Hip-hop pioneer Afrika Bambaataa even made a record in 1984 with John Lydon of the Sex Pistols, called "World Destruction." In the eighties, as hip-hop became more suburban, groups like Run-D.M.C. (from Hollis, Queens) and Public Enemy (from Roosevelt, Long Island) also began to bring an overt rock influence into their musical style, using everything from rock samples to rock attitude to actually collaborating with rock artists such as Aerosmith and Anthrax.

Until 1979 hip-hop music remained primarily a local phenomenon. The first indication of the genre's broader commercial potential was the twelve-inch dance single "Rapper's Delight," recorded by the <u>Sugarhill Gang</u>, a crew based in Harlem. This record, which popularized the use of the term "rapper" as an equivalent for MC, established Sugar Hill Records—a black-owned independent label based in New Jersey—as the predominant institutional force in rap music during the early 1980s. The recording recycled the rhythm section track from Chic's disco hit "Good Times," played in the studio by session musicians usually hired by Sugar Hill to back R&B singers. The three rappers—Michael "Wonder Mike" Wright, Guy "Master Gee" O'Brien, and Henry "Big Bank Hank" Jackson—recited a rapid-fire succession of rhymes, typical of the performances of MCs at hip-hop dances.

> *Well it's on-n-on-n-on-on-n-on*
> *The beat don't stop until the break of dawn*
> *I said M-A-S, T-E-R, a G with a double E*
> *I said I go by the unforgettable name*
> *Of the man they call the Master Gee*

Well, my name is known all over the world
By all the foxy ladies and the pretty girls
I'm goin' down in history
As the baddest rapper there could ever be

The text of "Rapper's Delight" alternates the braggadocio of the three MCs with descriptions of dance movements, exhortations to the audience, and humorous stories and references. One particularly memorable segment describes the consternation of a guest who is served rotting food by his friend's mother, seeks a polite way to refuse it, and finally escapes by crashing through the apartment door. The record reached Number 4 on the R&B chart and Number 36 on the pop chart and introduced hip-hop to millions of people throughout the United States and abroad. The unexpected success of "Rapper's Delight" ushered in a series of million-selling twelve-inch singles by New York rappers, including Kurtis Blow's "The Breaks" (Number 4 R&B, Number 87 Pop in 1980), "Planet Rock," by Afrika Bambaataa and the Soul Sonic Force (Number 4 R&B, Number 48 Pop in 1982), and "The Message," by Grandmaster Flash and the Furious Five (Number 4 R&B, Number 62 Pop in 1982).

By the early eighties, million-selling records like "Rapper's Delight" (1979) and "The Message" (1982) had created opportunities for New York rappers to perform at venues outside their own neighborhoods and thereby widen their audiences. They also alerted the major record companies to the commercial potential of hip-hop, eventually leading to the transition from the twelve-inch dance single as the primary medium for recorded rap (an inheritance from disco) to the rap album.

The mid-eighties witnessed a rapid acceleration of rap's movement into the popular mainstream. In 1983 the jazz fusion musician Herbie Hancock collaborated with DJ Grandmixer DST on "Rockit," which made the R&B Top 10 and was played on the still-young MTV channel. The following year, the popular soul singer Chaka Khan invited Melle Mel to provide a rap introduction for her hit single "I Feel for You," an adaptation of a Prince song that went to Number 1 R&B and Number 3 Pop. The year 1986 saw the release of the first two multiplatinum rap albums, *Raising Hell* by Run-D.M.C. (which reached Number 3 on *Billboard*'s Top Pop Albums chart and sold over three million copies) and *Licensed to Ill* by the Beastie Boys (Number 1 for seven weeks, with over seven million copies sold). That neither Run-D.M.C. nor the Beastie Boys hailed from the Bronx indicates the expanding appeal of rap music in the New York area. The key to the commercial success of these albums, however, was the expansion of the audience for hip-hop music, which now included millions of young white fans, attracted by the transgressive, rebellious sensibility of the genre. Both *Raising Hell* and *Licensed to Ill* were released on a new independent label called Def Jam, cofounded in 1984 by the hip-hop promoter Russell Simmons and the musician-producer Rick Rubin. During the 1980s Def Jam

🎧 LISTENING TO "THE MESSAGE"

Written by Sylvia Robinson, Duke Bootee, Ed Fletcher, and Melle Mel; performed by Grandmaster Flash and the Furious Five; recorded 1982

While most of the early hip-hop crossover hits featured relatively predictable party-oriented raps, "The Message" established a new (and, in the end, profoundly influential) trend in rap music: social realism. In a recording that links the rhythmic intensity of funk music with the toast-derived images of ghetto life in *Hustler's Convention*, "The Message" is a grim, almost cinematic portrait of life in the South Bronx. The rap on the first half of the recording was cowritten by Sylvia Robinson, a former R&B singer and co-owner of Sugar Hill Records, and Duke Bootee, a sometime member of the Furious Five. (Resident Sugar Hill percussionist Ed Fletcher composed the musical track, using a Roland TR-808 digital drum machine and keyboard synthesizer, embellished with various studio effects.) On top of the stark, cold electronic groove, Ed "Duke Bootee" Fletcher (a studio musician who helped write the song) intones the rap's grim opening hook, beginning "It's like a jungle sometimes..."

The sudden sound of glass shattering (produced on the drum machine) introduces a rhythmically complex and carefully articulated performance that alternates the smooth, slyly humorous style of Duke Bootee with the edgy, frustrated tone of MC Melle Mel who begins "Don't push me..."

The two MCs—Melle Mel in particular—time their performances with great precision, speeding up and slowing down, compressing and stretching the spaces between words, and creating polyrhythms against the steady musical pulse. The lyric alternates between the humorous wordplay typical of hip-hop MC performances and various images of desperation—threatening bill collectors, a homeless woman "living in a bag," violent encounters in Central Park, a young child alienated by deteriorating public schools. The relationship between the grim reality of ghetto life and the tough-minded humor that is its essential antidote is summed up by Melle Mel's humorless quasi-laugh.

The second half of "The Message"—a *Hustler's Convention*–style toast written and performed by Melle Mel—paints an even more chilling picture, an account of the life and death of a child born into poverty in the South Bronx, who gets sucked into the rackets of pimping and pushing drugs, ending up serving an 8-year prison term and eventually taking his own life.

This recitation is followed by the sound of the Furious Five—MCs Cowboy, Kidd Creole, Rahiem, Scorpio, and Mel—meeting and greeting on a street corner and discussing the evening's plans. Suddenly a police car screeches up and officers emerge, barking orders at the young black men. "What are you, a gang?," one of the policemen shouts. "Nah, man, we're with Grandmaster Flash and the Furious Five." Flash enters from one side to defend his friends: "Officer, officer, what's the problem?" "You're the problem," the cop shouts back, "get in the car!" We hear the car driving away with the Furious Five in custody, arrested evidently for the crime of assembling on a street corner, and the track quickly "fades to black."

A whole stream within the subsequent history of rap music can be traced from this gritty record, ranging from the explicitly political raps of KRS-One and Public Enemy to the "gangsta" style of Los Angeles MCs like N.W.A., Snoop Doggy Dogg, and 2Pac Shakur. As the first honest description of life on the streets of the nation's urban ghettos in the 1980s to achieve wide commercial circulation, "The Message" helped to establish canons of realness and street credibility that are still vitally important to rap musicians and audiences.

took up where Sugar Hill Records left off, cross-promoting a new generation of artists, expanding and diversifying the national audience for hip-hop, and in 1986 becoming the first rap-oriented independent label to sign a distribution deal with one of the "Big Five" record companies, Columbia Records.

Run-D.M.C.—a trio consisting of the MCs Run (Joseph Simmons, b. 1964) and D.M.C. (Darryl McDaniels, b. 1964), and the DJ Jam Master Jay (Jason Mizell, 1965–2002)—was perhaps the most influential act in the history of rap music. Simmons, McDaniels, and Mizell were college-educated black men, raised in a middle-class neighborhood in the borough of Queens. Working with Russell Simmons (Run's older brother) and producer Rick Rubin, they established a hard-edged, rock-influenced style that was to influence profoundly the sound and sensibility of later rap music. Their raps were literate and rhythmically skilled, with Run and D.M.C. weaving their phrases together and sometimes even completing the last few words of one another's lines. The "beats" produced by Rubin and Jam Master Jay were stark and powerful, mixing digitized loops of hard rock drumming with searing guitar sounds from heavy metal. Run-D.M.C. was the first rap group to headline a national tour and the first to appear on MTV. They popularized rap among the young, predominantly white audience for rock music; gave the genre a more rebellious image; and introduced hip-hop sartorial style—hats, gold chains, and untied Adidas sports shoes with fat laces—to millions of young Americans. The now familiar connection between rap music and athletic wear was established in 1986 when the Adidas corporation and Run-D.M.C. signed a $1.5 million promotional deal.

The Beastie Boys, the rap trio whose album *Licensed to Ill* topped the pop charts a few months after the release of *Raising Hell,* were the first commercially successful white act in hip-hop. Like Run-D.M.C., their recordings were produced by Rick Rubin, released on Def Jam Records, and benefited greatly from the distribution deal signed by Russell Simmons with industry giant Columbia Records. Although they received a great deal of criticism for ripping off a black style, it is perhaps more accurate to suggest that their early recordings represent a fusion of the youth-oriented rebelliousness of hardcore punk rock—the style that they began playing in 1981—with the sensibility and techniques of hip-hop. In 1985 the Beastie Boys were signed by Def Jam Records, appeared in *Krush Groove*—one of the first films to deal with hip-hop culture—and toured as the opening act for both Madonna and Run-D.M.C. The following year *Licensed to Ill,* their first album, sold 720,000 copies in six weeks and thereby became Columbia Records' fastest-selling debut album up to that point. The most popular track on the album, the Top 10 frat-boy anthem "(You Gotta) Fight for Your Right (to Party)" (a hit in 1987), established the Beastie Boys' appeal for the most rapidly expanding segment of the rap audience, young white males. After leaving Def Jam Records in 1988, the Beastie Boys continued to experiment with combinations of rap, heavy metal, punk, and psychedelic

Run-D.M.C. and **Steven Tyler.** Boston Herald/Rex USA.

rock, and they scored a series of critical and commercial successes in the 1990s, culminating with the release of their 1998 album *Hello Nasty.*

By 1987 a series of million-selling singles had proven rap's commercial potential on the pop and R&B charts; the hits included rap ballads (L.L. Cool J's "I Need Love," Number 1 R&B, Number 9 Pop in 1987), women's rap (Salt-N-Pepa's "Push It," Number 19 Pop, Number 28 R&B in 1987), humorous party records (Tone-Lōc's "Wild Thing," Number 2 Pop, Number 3 R&B in 1987), and rap specifically targeted at a young adolescent audience ("Parents Just Don't Understand" by D.J. Jazzy Jeff and the Fresh Prince, the single that established the career of actor Will Smith, which reached Number 12 Pop and Number 10 R&B in 1988). A number of the small independent labels that had sprung up to feed the growing demand for hip-hop music—Jive Records, Cold Chillin' Records, Tommy Boy Records, and Priority Records—followed the lead of Def Jam, signing distribution deals with the multinational entertainment conglomerates.

If 1986 and 1987 saw the emergence of new markets for hip-hop music, 1988 brought possibly an even more important milestone: the launching of

🎧 LISTENING TO "WALK THIS WAY"

Written by Joe Perry and Steven Tyler; performed by Run-D.M.C. with Perry and Tyler (from Aerosmith); recorded 1986

The creative and commercially successful synergy between rock music and hip-hop pioneered by Def Jam Records and Run-D.M.C. is well illustrated in "Walk This Way" (Number 4 Pop, Number 8 R&B in 1986), the million-selling single that propelled *Raising Hell* nearly to the top of the album charts. "Walk This Way," a collaboration between Run-D.M.C. and the popular hard rock group Aerosmith, was a cover version of a song written and previously recorded by Aerosmith. (Aerosmith brought a large portion of the hard rock audience to the table, having sold over twenty-five million albums since the early 1970s.) The recording opens with a sample of rock drumming from the original recording, interrupted by the sound of a turntable scratching, and the main riff of the song, played by Aerosmith's guitarist Joe Perry. Run and D.M.C. trade lines of the song's verses in an aggressive, shouted style that matches the intensity of the rock rhythm section. The chorus ("Walk this way, talk this way . . .") is performed by Aerosmith's Steven Tyler, who sings the lyrics in a high, strained voice, a timbre associated with heavy metal music. As the track progresses, Run, D.M.C., and Tyler combine vocal forces in the interest of collective mayhem, and the recording ends with a virtuoso guitar solo by Joe Perry.

The video version of "Walk This Way"—the first rap video to be put into heavy rotation by MTV—gives visual substance to the musical image of a tense conversation between the worlds of hard rock and rap, unified by the sizzling textures of hip-hop scratching and hard rock guitar, the contrasting but similarly aggressive vocal timbres of Run-D.M.C. and Steven Tyler, and the over-the-top male braggadocio of the song's text. (The lyrics to "Walk This Way," with references to horny cheerleaders and high school locker room voyeurism, suggest that one of the few things shared by the predominantly male audiences for rap and rock was a decidedly adolescent approach to sex.) The video opens with Run-D.M.C. performing in a small sound studio. The amplified sound of turntable scratching penetrates a wall that separates this intimate but restricted musical world from that of a hard rock concert, held on the stage of a huge arena. Disturbed by the noise, Steven Tyler uses his microphone stand to punch a hole in the wall, through which Run-D.M.C. run onto the stage of the concert and basically take over the show. Initially met with scowls from Tyler and Perry, the rappers succeed in winning them over, and the video ends in discordant harmony, with the huge, largely white crowd cheering. It is difficult to think of a more explicit (or more calculated) acting out of the process of black–white crossover in the history of American popular music, and the video of "Walk This Way" doubtless played a pivotal role in the mainstreaming of rap music.

MTV's first show dedicated entirely to hip-hop music. Hosted by hip-hop raconteur Fab Five Freddie Braithwaite, *Yo! MTV Raps* immediately attracted the largest audience in the network's history and was soon being broadcast on a daily basis. The mass popularity of rap was also reflected in the appearance of *The Source*, the first periodical devoted solely to hip-hop music and fashion. Over the subsequent decade *The Source* became the largest-selling music periodical in America, surpassing by a wide margin even such long-established publications as *Rolling Stone.* In 1988 the National Academy of Recording Arts and Sciences added a rap category to the Grammy Awards, and *Billboard*

Beastie Boys performing in 1996. Photo by Tim Mosenfelder/Getty Images.

added a rap singles chart. This mainstreaming of rap music had a number of interesting consequences. While some rappers and producers focused their energies on creating multiplatinum crossover hits, others reacted against the commercialism of "pop rap," reanimating the tradition of social realism that had informed recordings like "The Message" and creating a more hardcore sound that paradoxically ended up generating some of the biggest crossover hits of all.

The tradition of socially engaged rap, chronicling the declining fortunes of urban black communities, received its strongest new impetus from the New York–based group <u>Public Enemy</u>. Founded in 1982, Public Enemy was organized around a core set of members who met as college students, drawn together by their interest in hip-hop culture and political activism. The standard hip-hop configuration of two MCs—<u>Chuck D</u> (a.k.a. Carlton Ridenhour, b. 1960) and <u>Flavor Flav</u> (William Drayton, b. 1959)—plus a DJ—<u>Terminator X</u> (Norman Lee Rogers, b. 1966)—was augmented by a "Minister of Information" (<u>Professor Griff</u>, a.k.a. Richard Griffin) and by the Security of the First World (S1W), a cohort of dancers who dressed in paramilitary uniforms, carried Uzi submachine guns, and performed martial arts–inspired choreography.

The release of Public Enemy's second album in 1988—*It Takes a Nation of Millions to Hold Us Back*—was a breakthrough event for rap music. The album fused the trenchant social and political analyses of Chuck D—delivered in a deep, authoritative voice—with the streetwise interjections of his sidekick Flavor Flav, who wore comical glasses and an oversized clock around his neck. Their complex verbal interplay was situated within a dense, multilayered sonic web

Public Enemy projects the message live in 1991 (Chuck D is in the foreground, second from left). Lynn Goldsmith/ Corbis.

created by the group's production team, the Bomb Squad (Hank Shocklee, Keith Shocklee, and Eric "Vietnam" Sadler). Tracks like "Countdown to Armageddon" (an apocalyptic opening instrumental track, taped at a live concert in London), "Don't Believe the Hype" (a critique of white-dominated mass media), and "Party for Your Right to Fight" (a parody of the Beastie Boys' hit "Fight for Your Right (to Party)" from the previous year) turned the technology of digital sampling to new artistic purposes and insisted in effect that rap music continue to engage with the real-life conditions of urban black communities.

Keith Shocklee, one of Public Enemy's producers, openly cited rock as a major influence on their musical approach, noting that they were "basically a thrash group, a group that was very much rock 'n' roll oriented . . . the parallel that we wanted to draw was Public Enemy and Led Zeppelin. Public Enemy and the Grateful Dead" (Jeff Mao 1997: 113–114).

THE RISE OF "WORLD MUSIC"

During the eighties the boundary between mainstream and marginal styles of music became ever fuzzier, and the twin pressures to expand the global market

LISTENING TO "NIGHT OF THE LIVING BASEHEADS"

Written by Hank Shocklee, Eric Sadler, and Chuck D; performed by Public Enemy; recorded 1988

"Night of the Living Baseheads" is an instructive example of the moral authority and musical complexity of many of Public Enemy's recordings. The lyrics for "Night of the Living Baseheads" combine images of corpselike zombies with a commentary on the crack cocaine epidemic that was sweeping through America's inner cities during the 1980s. The track opens with the voice of black nationalist leader Khalid Abdul Muhammad, sampled from one of his speeches:

> *Have you forgotten that once we*
> *were brought here, we were robbed*
> *of our names, robbed of our language,*
> *we lost our religion, our culture, our*
> *God? And many of us, by the way we*
> *act, we even lost our minds.*

With these words still ringing in our ears, we are suddenly dropped into the middle of a complexly textured groove. The lead MC of Public Enemy, Chuck D, opens with a verbal explosion, a play on words derived from hip-hop slang:

> *Here it is*
> *BAMMM*
> *And you say, Goddamn*
> *This is the dope jam*
> *But let's define the term called dope*
> *And you think it mean funky now, no*

In hip-hop argot the term "dope" carries a double meaning: It can function as a positive adjective, broadly equivalent to older terms such as "cool," "hip," or "funky"; or as a reference to psychoactive drugs, ranging from marijuana to the new, more devastating drug being critiqued by Chuck D in "Night of the Living Baseheads," crack cocaine. The rhetorical tactic of announcing the arrival of a compelling performance (a "dope jam"), and thereby laying claim to the listener's attention, is common in rap recordings. Chuck D takes this opening gambit and plays with it, redefining the term "dope jam" as a message

about drug use and its effects on the black community. At the end of each stanza of his rap, Chuck D uses another pun, based on the homonyms "bass" (the deep, booming tones favored by rap producers) and "base" (a shorthand reference to "freebase," or crack cocaine).

> *Sellin', smellin'*
> *Sniffin', riffin'*
> *And brothers try to get swift an'*
> *Sell to their own, rob a home*
> *While some shrivel to bone*
> *Like comatose walkin' around*
> *Please don't confuse this with the*
> *   sound*
> *I'm talking about . . . BASE*

Chuck D presents here a chilling snapshot of the effects of crack on the human body ("Some shrivel to bone, like comatose walkin' around"), and uses the bass/base pun to draw a contrast between the aesthetics of hip-hop and the devastating scourge of crack cocaine ("please don't confuse this [base] with the sound [bass]"). After this first occurrence, the bass/base homonym returns periodically in a syncopated, digitally sampled loop that punctuates the thickly layered sonic texture created by the Bomb Squad. Chuck D goes on to scold black drug dealers for victimizing members of their own community ("Shame on a brother when he dealin' [drugs on] the same block where my [Oldsmobile] 98 be wheelin'"). A sampled verbal phrase ("How low can you go?") is used as a rhythmic and rhetorical device to set up the final sequence of Chuck D's rap, which concludes with the story of a crack addict, a former hip-hop MC fallen on bad times:

> *Daddy-O once said to me*
> *He knew a brother who stayed all day*
> *   in his jeep*
> *And at night he went to sleep*
> *And in the mornin' all he had was*
> *The sneakers on his feet*
> *The culprit used to jam and rock the*
> *   mike, yo*

He stripped the jeep to fill his pipe
And wander around to find a place
Where they rocked to a different kind
*   of . . .   come on, y'all*
[Samples of voices]
I'm talkin' 'bout BASE

The grim message of "Night" is enveloped in a jagged, stark sonic landscape, layered with fractured words and vocal noises, bits and pieces of music and other sounds sewn together like a crazy quilt. The producers incorporated digital samples from no fewer than thirteen different recorded sources, among them an early twelve-inch rap single, several soul music records, a gospel music group, a glam rock record, and the sound of drums and air-raid sirens. In musical terms, "Night of the Living Baseheads" is like a complex archeological dig, a site richly layered with sonic objects, the cumulative meaning of which depends on the cultural and musical expertise of the listener.

Although rap is often regarded primarily as a verbal genre, a recording like "Night of the Living Baseheads," with its carefully constructed pastiche of sampled sound sources, compels us to consider rap as music. Hank Shocklee has argued vociferously for a broader conception of music and musicianship:

Music is nothing but organized noise. You can take anything—street sounds, us talking, whatever you want—and make it music by organizing it. That's still our philosophy, to show people that this thing you call music is a lot broader than you think it is. (Rose 1994: 82)

This philosophy is similar to that expressed by certain art music composers throughout the twentieth century who have used tape recorders, digital technology, and elements of noise in their works. But it could be argued that the most extensive and creative use of the technology of digital sampling has been made in dance music—hip-hop, R&B, and other genres such as house music and techno—rather than in contemporary art music composition. Instead of creating a cold, disembodied form of self-expression—as many critics of the new technologies had feared—digital technology in pop music has often been used to create communal experiences on the dance floor. On the other hand, some critics bemoan what they see as a lack of creativity in much contemporary rap music, referring to the practice of sampling as "artistic necrophilia" and the end product as "Memorex music." Whatever one's position on these matters, Public Enemy's "Night of the Living Baseheads" stands as a pioneering example of the creative and social potential of digital sound technologies.

for American popular music and to create new alternative genres and audiences within the American market grew ever stronger. One of the most interesting results of these processes was the emergence of a category called *world music*. The term was first systematically adopted in the late 1980s by independent record label owners and concert promoters, and it entered the popular music marketplace as a replacement for longer-standing categories such as "traditional music," "international music," and "ethnic music." These sorts of records were traditionally positioned in the very back of record stores, in bins containing low-turnover items such as Irish folk song collections, Scottish bagpipe samplers, German polka records, recordings by tourist bands from the Caribbean and Hawai'i, and perhaps a few scholarly recordings of so-called primitive music from Africa, Native America, or Asia. International records were generally purchased by immigrants hungry for a taste of home, by cross-cultural music scholars such as ethnomusicologists, and by a handful of aficionados. In general, while transnational entertainment corporations became ever more successful at marketing American pop music around the globe, most of the world's music continued to have little or no direct influence on the American marketplace.

To be fair, we can point to some examples of international influence on the American pop mainstream before the eighties—Cuban rumba, Hawai'ian guitar, and Mexican marimba records of the 1920s and 1930s; Indian classical musician Ravi Shankar's album *Live at the Monterey Pop Festival,* which reached Number 43 in 1967, as the counterculture was at its peak; "Grazing in the Grass" (1968), a Number 1 hit by the South African jazz musician Hugh Masekela; or "Soul Makossa" (1973), the Top 40 dance club single by the Cameroonian pop musician Manu Dibango, often cited as a primary influence on disco music; and, of course, reggae. But these cosmopolitan influences were typically filtered through the sensibilities of Western musicians and channeled by the strategies of American and European record companies and publishing firms. A quintessential example of this is the Tokens' rock 'n' roll hit "The Lion Sleeps Tonight" (Number 1 in 1961), an adaptation of a hit single by urban folk group the Weavers, entitled "Wimoweh" (a Number 14 Pop single in 1952). "Wimoweh" had, in turn, been an adaptation of a 1939 South African recording by a vocal group made up of Zulu mine workers, Solomon Linda and the Evening Birds. By the time the Evening Birds' song reached the ears of Americans, it had undergone several bouts of invasive surgery, including the insertion of a pop-friendly melodic hook and English lyrics, and removal of all royalty rights pertaining to the original performers.

In the 1980s musicians from Africa, South Asia, the Near East, Eastern Europe, and Latin America began to tour the United States with increasing frequency. The first indication that musicians from the so-called Third World might gain increased access to the American market was the release in 1982 of the album *Juju Music,* by a Nigerian group called the African Beats, led by the guitarist King Sunny Adé. Featuring an infectious brand of urban African dance music that blended electric guitars, Christian church hymns, and Afro-Caribbean rhythms with the pulsating sound of the Yoruba "talking drum," *Juju Music* sold over 100,000 copies and rose to Number 111 on *Billboard's* album chart. The African Beats' next album, *Synchro System,* reached as high as Number 91 on the chart; however, the group was soon thereafter dropped by Island Records and never again appeared on the American pop charts.

In an article published in 1982 in the *Village Voice* by the popular-music critic Greg Tate, entitled "Are You Ready for Juju?" the author explicitly identified King Sunny Adé as a potential replacement for Bob Marley, the Jamaican reggae superstar who had very recently died. On one level, this seems perfectly logical, and it probably reflects the strategic thinking of Island Records, the label that released the Adé albums. Adé might well have had a shot at equaling Marley's success, but the fact that he sang in Yoruba—a language spoken by precious few American listeners—rather than Marley's richly spiced version of Jamaican English doomed him to failure from the beginning. (Very few American Top 40 hits have not featured English lyrics. This is an insurmountable barrier for many international musicians, although this may change as the linguistic makeup of the United States continues to diversify.)

By 1990, when the heading "world music" first appeared above a *Billboard* record chart, it was as a subcategory of the broader heading "adult alternative albums." Interestingly, this latter category also included New Age music, a genre of instrumental music designed to facilitate

The African Beats with guitarist **King Sunny Adé** performing in 1984. © Corbis.

contemplative and mystical moods, and sometimes loosely linked with the religious and healing practices of Native American, African, and Asian cultures. The larger category "adult alternative albums" suggests an effort on the industry's part to identify forms of alternative music that would appeal to an affluent baby boomer audience, rather than to the younger audience attracted by rock bands such as Nirvana. (Since 1991 the National Academy of Recording Arts and Sciences [NARAS] has limited its Grammy awards for world music, New Age, folk, Latin, reggae, blues, polka, and various other alternative genres to albums only, presumably on the assumption that such genres are unlikely to generate hit singles.) The world music sections of most record stores usually do not include Latin dance music (salsa) or reggae, genres that sell enough records to justify their own discrete territories.

What, then, is world music? In a strictly musical sense, it is a pseudo-genre, taking into its sweep styles as diverse as African urban pop (juju), Pakistani dance club music (bhangara), Australian Aboriginal rock music (the band Yothu Yindi), and even the Bulgarian State Radio and Television Female Vocal Choir, whose evocatively titled 1987 release *Le Mystère des Voix Bulgares* (*The Mystery of the Bulgarian Voices*) reached Number 165 on the *Billboard* album chart in 1988. Bestselling albums on *Billboard*'s world music chart have featured the Celtic group Clannad (whose popularity was boosted in the United States by their appearance in the soundtrack for a Volkswagen advertisement), Spanish flamenco music (played by the Gypsy Kings, a hotel band from France), Tibetan Buddhist chant (presented by Mickey Hart, one of the drummers for the Grateful Dead), and diverse collaborations between American and English rock stars and musicians from Africa, Latin America, and South Asia. The overlap among various types of "adult alternative" music—including New Age, world music, and certain forms of European sacred music—is reflected in the commercial success of albums like *Vision* (1994), a mélange of "12th-century chant, world beat rhythms, and electronic soundscapes," as one press release put it. (It's hard to imagine better confirmation of the historical saw that "the past is another country.") The attraction of world music for its contemporary American audience is bound up with stereotyped images of the "exotic," whether these be discovered on imaginary pilgrimages to Africa and the Himalayas, or in time travel back to the monastic Christianity of medieval Europe. Nonetheless, there are limits to the degree of musical exoticism most listeners are willing to tolerate. This may explain the almost total absence on the *Billboard* charts of music from East Asia, which many American listeners find particularly challenging.

We are all familiar with the assertion that music is a universal language, by which people usually mean to suggest that music can transcend the boundaries separating diverse nations, cultures, or languages. This statement, however comforting, does not stand up to close scrutiny—even within American culture, one person's music may be another person's noise. Nonetheless, the music industry has wasted no time in chaining the rhetoric of musical universalism to the profit motive, as for example in this mid-1990s advertisement for the E-mu Proteus/3 World, a digital device programmed with hundreds of samples of world music:

> **Enrich Your Music with a Global Texture.** As borders dissolve, traditions are shared. And this sharing of cultures is most powerful in the richness of music. . . . E-mu has gathered these sounds and more—192 in all. Use them to emulate traditional world instruments or as raw material for creating one-of-a-kind synthesized sounds of your own. (Théberge 1997: 201)

Music, with its ability to flow over the boundaries of society and the borders of nations, holds open the possibility that we may glimpse something familiar and sympathetic in people strange to us—that the inequalities of the world in which we live may for a moment be suspended, or even undermined, in the act of making or listening to music. Still, the suggestion that installing a digital device in your home studio in order to emulate the "gathered sounds" of faraway people has anything to do with "sharing cultures" reveals a critically impoverished vision of cross-cultural communication. There is no denying that music has the potential to traverse the boundaries of culture and language and thereby add to our understanding of people very different from us. But the ultimate responsibility for interpreting its meanings, and determining its impact, lies with us.

PAUL SIMON'S *GRACELAND* AND THE POLITICS OF "WORLDBEAT"

In the mid-1980s, as the general term "world music" began to gain a foothold in the music industry and popular music press, a more specific subcategory of the genre "worldbeat" also entered the lexicon of popular music. Worldbeat artists of the 1980s included cross-culturally adventurous rock musicians such as Peter Gabriel, David Byrne, Ry Cooder, Mickey Hart, and Paul Simon (see the following discussion), who experimented with the fusion of disparate musical styles in an attempt to bring various world music styles to a wider audience. The majority of international worldbeat artists who achieved a measure of popularity in the West during the 1980s came from Africa, a continent whose music had already exerted a centuries-deep influence on the development of music in the Americas. Musicians such as King Sunny Adé, Youssou N'Dour (Senegal), Salif Keita (Mali), Thomas Mapfumo (Zimbabwe), Papa Wemba (Congo), and Ladysmith Black Mambazo and Johnny Clegg (both from South Africa) took the hybridized styles of popular music that had developed in cities across Africa, and, to varying degrees, leavened them with Western influences—particularly rock instrumentation and technology—to appeal to a broad and cosmopolitan audience. (The audience for worldbeat music overlapped to a significant degree with the demographic that had supported reggae music since its arrival in the United States in the 1970s.) While it has never played a dominant role in the American music market, worldbeat has continued to provide inspiration for musicians seeking creative alternatives outside the mainstream. In an era where many formerly "marginal" musical styles in the United States have been thoroughly co-opted by the music business, the diversity of world music is seen by some as providing a kind of reservoir of creative possibility. On the other hand, the appropriation of non-Western music by wealthy rock stars seeking to reinvent themselves has also sometimes been viewed as a form of cultural imperialism not entirely dissimilar from the fashion industry's exploitation of cheap labor in Asia and Latin America. It is worth noting that the tension between these two perspectives—narratives of creativity and openness versus exploitation and rip-off—echoes rather precisely the rhetoric that has grown up around the role of white artists and record companies in making "cover versions" of recordings by black musicians since the early history of rock music (see Chapter 2). In both cases, of course, the reality is always more complicated than the rhetoric.

A supporting case for both points of view is provided by Paul Simon's album *Graceland* (1986), which revived a career that had seemed to be in decline in the early 1980s (Simon's two preceding albums had neither the critical nor the commercial success that greeted most of his work of the 1970s) and—with its employment of African musicians, African music, and (occasionally) African subject matter, along with other "exotic" touches—suddenly thrust Simon into

The *Graceland* concert in Harare, Zimbabwe, with **Paul Simon** front and center, flanked by (from left) South African musicians Joseph Shabalala, Miriam Makeba, Hugh Masekela (partially obscured), and Ray Phiri (1987). Camera Press/Retna, Ltd./Retna, Ltd.

the forefront of the new category called world music and helped to open up new vistas for other rock musicians.

Paul Simon's interest in music that was not indigenous to the United States manifested itself long before he recorded *Graceland*. When he was still singing with Art Garfunkel, Simon recorded "El Condor Pasa," a song that paired his own lyrics with a backing instrumental track based on an old Peruvian folk melody, performed in "native" style by a group called Los Incas. "El Condor Pasa" appeared on the 1970 Simon and Garfunkel album *Bridge Over Troubled Water* and was released as a single that same year. The song was indicative of the path Simon would later pursue much more systematically and thoroughly in *Graceland,* in which many of the songs present Simon's vocals and lyrics over an accompaniment performed in South African style by South African musicians.

A considerable portion of the music for *Graceland* was actually recorded in South Africa, and that resulted in some awkward political issues for Simon. Like Bruce Springsteen's *Born in the U.S.A.,* this album became a focus of political attention for fans, skeptics, and, with reluctance, its creator. At the time, a United Nations boycott on performing and recording in South Africa was in effect as part of an international attempt to isolate and ostracize the government of that country, which was still enforcing the widely despised policy of apartheid (separation of the races). Simon could not deny that he broke the boycott, but he claimed that he was in no sense supporting the ideology of the South African government by making music with black South Africans on their native soil. In fact, the success of *Graceland* helped bring black South African musicians and styles to a much wider and racially more diverse audience than they had ever been able to reach before; this proved to be true within South Africa itself, as well as in America and many other parts of the world. It could well be argued that Simon ultimately made, through his racially integrated music, a forceful statement about the virtues of free intermingling and cultural exchange. In any case, Simon came to a mutual understanding with the United Nations and the opponents of apartheid in relatively short order, and he stopped performing in South Africa until apartheid was dismantled several years later.

A truly "global" album from a geographical point of view, *Graceland* was recorded in five different locations on three different continents: In addition to Johannesburg, South Africa, tracks were cut in London, England; New York City; Los Angeles; and Crowley, Louisiana. Many of the selections on the album combine elements that were recorded at different times in different places, but others were the result of sessions where all the participants were present in the same place at the same time. While Simon flew to South Africa to work on several songs with musicians there, at another time he brought South African musicians to New York to work with him, and on yet another occasion Simon and the South African vocal group Ladysmith Black Mambazo recorded together in London.

What ultimately distinguishes *Graceland* from earlier forays into world music, whether by Simon or by other pop musicians, is the extent to which the album explores the concept of collaboration—collaboration among artists of different races, regions, nationalities, and ethnicities, which produced in turn collaboration among diverse musical styles and approaches to songwriting. This provides a conceptual basis for *Graceland*, to be sure, but Simon's album is quite different from the usual concept album. There is certainly no explicit or implicit story line that connects the songs, nor is there any single, central subject that links them all together—unless one is willing to view collaboration itself (primarily musical collaboration but also, in two instances, collaboration on lyrics as well) as the album's "subject matter." But the idea of an album designed to explore collaboration seems a perfectly logical, if unusual, concept to embrace in understanding *Graceland*.

The various approaches to the concept of collaboration that are found among the songs on Graceland run a gamut from "Homeless," in which both the words (in Zulu and English) and the music were cowritten by Simon and

Joseph Shabalala of Ladysmith Black Mambazo, to a cut like "I Know What I Know," in which Simon added his own lyrics and vocal melody to preexisting music (originally not written for Simon) by General M. D. Shirinda and the Gaza Sisters. In the case of "Homeless," the song makes a unified and gently poignant impression; the images of poor people could refer to South Africa or to America, or to both, and the slow-moving, harmonious vocal music encourages us to take their plight seriously. In "I Know What I Know," on the other hand, Simon deliberately makes no attempt to match the tone of his lyrics to the culture or to the implied locale of the original South African music. Instead, the lyrics seem to portray an encounter between two worldly wise and cynical people at an upper-crust cocktail party (or some such gathering), and their mood and subject both stand in remarkable, ironic contrast to the jubilant, uninhibited sound of the danceable South African instrumental music and to the Gaza Sisters' voices. The result is a virtual embodiment, in words and sounds, of a profound clash of cultures—as if some characters typical of Simon's earlier, sophisticated urban songs of late twentieth-century anxiety (such as those found on an album like *Still Crazy after All These Years,* from 1975) were suddenly dropped into the middle of a busy South African village on a day of celebration.

That the uneasy mismatch of music and lyrics in "I Know What I Know" is neither accidental nor careless on Simon's part is signaled by the presence on the album of songs that, occupying a middle ground between "Homeless" and "I Know What I Know," make cultural diversity an aspect of their stated subject matter and of their music. The third verse of "You Can Call Me Al" describes a man who is uncomfortable in a foreign culture, unable to speak the language of this "strange world" and surrounded by its "sound." The "sound" here is being produced by a group of black South African musicians playing with Simon and American session musicians in New York City; significantly, the multicultural group is joined on this cut by Morris Goldberg, who (Simon's liner notes pointedly inform us) is a white South African emigrant based in New York, and who contributes a striking pennywhistle solo. Members of this same diverse ensemble also play on "Under African Skies," the verses of which actually shift location from Africa to Tucson, Arizona, and back again. Here Simon is joined in vocal duet by Linda Ronstadt—from Tucson, Arizona.

In both the music and the words of *Graceland,* the meanings and implications can be allusive and elusive, often seeming to change color or to shift in midphrase. Yet the lilt of Simon's melodies and the dynamic rhythms provided by his diverse collaborators keep the album from ever sounding "difficult" or arcane. It is to Simon's credit that he never attempts to sound like anybody but himself, nor does he require his fellow musicians to adapt their style perforce to his; this is why the songs on *Graceland* are true collaborations, and such unusually successful ones. In the largest sense, one might say that *Graceland* is "about" the joys, complexities, and perplexities of living in an increasingly diverse, multicultural world. (This is a subject that also informs the words and music of Simon's next album, *The Rhythm of the Saints,* from 1990.)

That one need not venture to other continents, or even to other countries, to find "other" cultures is a point made, in effect, by the last two cuts on *Graceland*: "That Was Your Mother," in which Simon is joined by the zydeco band Good Rockin' Dopsie and the Twisters, from Louisiana; and "All Around the World, or The Myth of Fingerprints," in which Simon plays with Los Lobos, the well-known Mexican American band from Los Angeles. On both of these selections, the prominent employment of accordion and saxophone creates aural links with the sounds of South African ensembles on other songs from *Graceland*, demonstrating musically that the world is indeed a shrinking place. (Conversely, Simon remarks in his liner notes how the South African instrumentalists he recorded in Johannesburg for the title song produced a sound that reminded him in certain ways of American country music.) At the end, then, Paul Simon comes home, only to find himself still, and always, a musical "citizen of the world."

Graceland eventually sold over five million copies. As the Grammy Award winner for Album of the Year in 1986, it spectacularly revived Simon's then-flagging career and garnered a great deal of attention, not only for Simon himself, but also for many of the musicians who played on the album with him. In South Africa the album quickly rose to Number 1 on the charts, the best-selling international release since Michael Jackson's *Thriller*. *Graceland* did not prove to be a major source of hit singles, but a concert video featuring much of its music, taped in Africa with African musicians, was very popular. It is the album responsible, more than any other, for introducing a wide audience to the idea of world music, and for this reason alone the importance and influence of *Graceland* should not be underestimated.

As for the cultural politics of *Graceland*, there is, as usual, no easy answer. On one hand, the white-controlled apartheid government of South Africa used *Graceland*, without any hint of irony or embarrassment, to argue that cultural sanctions against the regime were unnecessary, since the album offered proof that blacks and whites was already getting along so well. On the other side of the argument, Ray Phiri, the guitarist and arranger on *Graceland*, labeled the album "the best thing that ever happened to South African musicians. . . . Paul Simon worked with people who believe in their music and who needed to let the world know that we also have something to say" (Mgxashe 1997, p. 169). Whatever stance one chooses to adopt, it is clear that the engagement of rock music and musicians with diverse musical traditions from around the globe is likely to be a continuing source of creative inspiration and political ferment.

CONCLUSION

Music Television was clearly the most important factor in the development of rock in the eighties. Some artists and genres—particularly those with visual appeal—were able to achieve tremendous popularity very quickly through the exposure that MTV provided, while others were almost entirely shut out. The split between the two became increasingly pronounced during this era, leading to the emergence of alternative streams and countermovements such as punk, alternative rock, underground metal, and worldbeat. Eventually, these movements—along with hip-hop—began to spill over into the world of MTV, setting the stage for the rock of the nineties.

11

ROCK IN THE 1990s: ALTERNATIVE BECOMES THE MAINSTREAM

The nineties were a time of adjustment for rock and for the music industry generally. A new generation—soon to be tagged "Generation X"—had come on the scene to displace the baby boomers. Raised on classic rock and punk, they had imbibed the rock culture of their elders and were poised to create their own styles. As the first generation to have grown up with MTV, their worldview was shaped by it in many ways. First and foremost, the idea of a single central media outlet for rock, as opposed to many competing radio stations in different cities, seemed normal. The days of a song "breaking" (becoming a hit) in one city and then gradually spreading to the rest of the country were over. A song was either on MTV—and thus successful—or it wasn't. This led initially to a sharp split between artists who were MTV-friendly—mainly "hair metal" bands and pop artists like Madonna and Prince—and artists who were not, primarily those working in such genres as alternative and hip-hop. As a result, the idea of *not* being on MTV, whether by choice or not, became a sign of artistic integrity.

As "non-MTV" musical genres became popular, however, they were slowly brought into the fold, at first through specially designated shows (*120 Minutes* for alternative rock and *Yo! MTV Raps* for hip-hop), and later as part of the regular rotation. This, in turn, created something of a crisis for these genres: Having defined themselves in opposition to MTV, could they now become part of it without losing an essential part of their *raison d'être*? The various strategies they developed to deal with the apparent contradictions of being rebellious anti-establishment figures that were suddenly embraced by the mainstream would come to define both rock and hip-hop in the nineties. Other important subgenres that defined themselves largely in opposition to MTV in the nineties included a growing "jam band" scene that followed the lead of the Grateful Dead in emphasizing the live performance experience over recordings as well as in its specific culture, and an established scene of women-identified music that rejected the imagery of women on MTV and in many of the economic institutions that supported it.

HOME RECORDING

One way that many of these subgenres rejected what they saw as the "slickness" of MTV was through a growing reliance on home recording studios, rather than the professional studios that had been prevalent up to that point. This reflected a number of changes in both technology and attitude. Most important was the growing availability of inexpensive home recording equipment. In particular, the cassette-based four-track recorder, introduced by Tascam in 1979, had become a staple in many home studios by the early nineties. This was a relatively inexpensive machine that combined simplified versions of the studio's mixing board and tape recorder into a single, easy-to-use unit, allowing musicians to record four separate musical tracks and then mix them down to a stereo or mono recording. While this didn't make professional studios obsolete, it did open many new opportunities for musicians. At a minimum, it gave them the opportunity to experiment with different musical ideas and recording techniques before spending the money to go into a professional studio. At maximum, it allowed them to actually record their music at home without going into the studio at all. That possibility was important for two reasons.

First, since studios and the personnel needed to run them were so expensive, few if any musicians could afford to pay for substantial studio time out of their own pockets. Rather, studio expenses were paid by the record company and then deducted from the musicians' profits after the record came out. For the vast majority of musicians, this meant that the only way to make a professional recording in the first place was to go into debt to a record company. This, in turn, meant that an important step in the process of becoming a professional musician was convincing a record company that your music was likely to be a profitable investment.

One only needs to imagine a committee of executives attempting to determine which young rock musicians were likely to turn a profit—and which were not—to see the effect that this would have on rock overall. In an earlier era, this kind of conservatism had been mitigated by the fact that most record labels were run by passionate (and sometimes flat-out crazy) individuals who were willing to invest in artists that they felt had commercial potential despite all evidence to the contrary. In fact, the ability to spot such musicians—known as having a "good ear"—was considered an essential qualification for a music business executive in the fifties, sixties, and seventies. By the eighties, however, record companies were increasingly being bought by major international corporations whose executives had far less patience for that kind of risk. Home recording allowed musicians who made music with less obvious commercial appeal to record it without having to be concerned with how it would affect a corporate record company's balance sheet.

The second effect of home recording was related to the first. The idea that self-produced music was the hallmark of musicians who wouldn't (or couldn't) deal with major labels made the mediocre sound quality of home recording *itself* an indicator of artistic integrity. This dovetailed perfectly with a larger anti-commercial philosophy becoming associated with young rock fans in the early nineties. Many members of Generation X, who had been influenced by punk rock's DIY approach (see previous chapter), intentionally showed their rejection of commercialism through an embrace of home-made and low-quality products, whether that meant a used flannel shirt bought for two dollars at a thrift store, a "zine" that you had photocopied at Kinkos, or a song that you had recorded in a home studio and copied to give to your friends.

ON THE TERM "ALTERNATIVE"

In the 1990s the marketplace for popular music continued to metastasize into hundreds of named genres, each correlated with a particular segment of the audience. From jangle pop to trip hop, psychobilly to thrashcore, the decade saw a splintering of genres that exceeded anything previously experienced in the history of American popular music. While many of these styles sprang from the ground up, as it were, nurtured by local audiences, regional networks of clubs, and low-profit independent labels, the entertainment industry had refined its ability to identify such "alternative" genres and their specialized audiences.

By the end of the 1990s, almost every major genre had sprouted an alternative subcategory. According to the *All Music Guide* (www.allmusic.com), a widely consulted Internet guide to popular music, the range of alternative genres included alternative dance (including techno, which often forms its own category, and groups such as Pop Will Eat Itself and Everything but the Girl), alternative country (k.d. lang, Dwight Yoakam, Lyle Lovett), alternative country rock (Uncle Tupelo, the Jayhawks), alternative contemporary Christian music (Sixpence None the Richer, Jars of Clay), alternative metal (Rage against the Machine, Korn, Limp Bizkit), alternative hip-hop (De La Soul, Arrested Development, Lauryn Hill), and a variety of styles lumped under the general heading of alternative rock (R.E.M., Sonic Youth, Nirvana, Pearl Jam, Nine Inch Nails, Green Day, Red Hot Chili Peppers, Phish, Alanis Morissette, Dave

Matthews Band, and many other artists). Some artists classified under the alternative rock rubric sound similar, while others seem to have come from different musical planets entirely. Some record for small independent labels, while others sign contracts with major record companies. Some have a strong social, moral, or political outlook—right-wing or left-wing—that shapes their music, and others do not. And to all these subcategories, still others could be added, such as "alternative female singer-songwriters" (Sinéad O'Connor, Ani DiFranco, Tracy Chapman, Alanis Morissette). What, then, defines them all as "alternative" musicians?

Our difficulty in coming up with a one-size-fits-all definition of alternative music stems partly from the use of this term to advance two different and often conflicting agendas. On one hand, the term "alternative"—like the broadly equivalent terms "underground" and "independent"—is used to describe (and to positively valorize) music that, in one regard or another, challenges the status quo. From this perspective alternative music is fiercely iconoclastic, anti-commercial, and anti-mainstream; it is thought by its supporters to be local as opposed to corporate, homemade as opposed to mass-produced, and genuine as opposed to artificial.

However, an entirely different sense of the term underlies the music industry's use of "alternative" to denote the choices available to consumers via record stores, radio, cable and satellite television, and the Internet. This sense of the term is bound up with the need of the music business to identify and exploit new trends, styles, and audiences. In an interview conducted during the late 1980s, a senior executive for a major record company revealed that

> There's a whole indie section [of our company. There are] kids that
> will only buy records that are on an indie label . . . which is why we
> sometimes concoct labels to try and fool them. (Negus 1992: 16)

The notion of a huge entertainment corporation cooking up a fake independent record label to satisfy an audience hungry for musical expressions of authenticity and rebellion may seem a bizarre contradiction at first glance. From an historical perspective, however, we can see this institutional development as the culmination of a decades-old trend within the music business. In the days before rock 'n' roll, genres such as blues, rhythm & blues, country music, and ethnic music were predominantly the bailiwick of small independently owned and operated record labels. By the nineties, however, the major record companies had fully internalized the hard lesson of rock 'n' roll and had come to view independent labels as the functional equivalent of baseball farm teams: small, specialized, close-to-the-ground operations perfectly situated to sniff out the next big thing. In an era when most so-called independent labels are distributed, promoted, and even owned outright by huge entertainment corporations, it became difficult to sustain a purely economic definition of alternative music as music that doesn't make money. To put it another way, the fact that a band's music, song lyrics, appearance, and ideological stance are anti-commercial doesn't mean that they can't sell millions of records and thereby help to generate huge corporate profits.

"SMELLS LIKE TEEN SPIRIT": ALTERNATIVE ROCK HITS THE CHARTS

Although underground bands began to appear on the charts during the late 1980s, the commercial breakthrough for alternative rock—and the occasion of its enshrinement as a category in the pop music marketplace—was achieved in 1992 by Nirvana, a band from the Pacific Northwest (see Box on the "Seattle Sound" on page 316). Between 1992 and 1994, Nirvana—a trio centered on singer and guitarist Kurt Cobain (b. 1967 in Hoquiam, Washington; d. 1994) and bassist Krist Novoselic (b. 1965 in Compton, California)—released two multiplatinum albums that moved alternative rock's blend of hardcore punk and heavy metal out of the back corners of specialty record stores and into the commercial mainstream. The rise of so-called *grunge rock*—and the tragic demise of Kurt Cobain, who committed suicide in 1994 at the age of twenty-

Kurt Cobain, in a pensive moment. Kevin Mazur Archive 1/WireImage.

🎧 LISTENING TO "SMELLS LIKE TEEN SPIRIT"

One source of *Nevermind's* success was the platinum single "Smells Like Teen Spirit," a Number 6 Pop hit. One of the most striking aspects of "Teen Spirit" is its combination of heavy metal instrumental textures and pop songwriting techniques, including a number of memorable verbal and melodic hooks. The band's sound, which had been thick and plodding on its Sub Pop recordings, is sleek and well focused (thanks in part to the production of Butch Vig and the mixing of engineer Andy Wallace). The song itself combines a four-chord harmonic progression with a somewhat conventional formal structure, made up of four-, eight-, and twelve-bar sections. The overall structure of the song includes a verse of eight bars ("Load up on guns . . . "), which we are calling A, and two repeated sections, or choruses, which we have labeled B (eight bars in length) and C (twelve bars).

LISTENING CHART "SMELLS LIKE TEEN SPIRIT"
Music by Nirvana; lyrics by Kurt Cobain; performed by Nirvana; recorded 1991

FORM		LYRICS	DESCRIPTIVE COMMENTS
Intro			
(16 = 4 + 8 + 4)			Bars 1-4: solo guitar plays progression (quiet); bars 5-12: whole band plays progression (loud, intense); bars 13-16: bass plays progression with guitar chimes (soft).
A (8)	0.34	*Load up . . .*	Lead vocal enters; quiet, somewhat depressed tone; gentle instrumental texture.
B (8)	0.50	*Hello, hello . . .*	Spacey one-word vocal, backed with continuous guitar chords; gradual crescendo.
C (12)	1.06	*With the lights out*	Vocal angry, growling; heavy metal power chords, loud and distorted.
Interlude (4)	1.31		Stoptime effect with guitar response.
Intro (4)	1.39		Last four bars of Introduction; bass plays progression with guitar chimes (soft).
A (8)	1.47	*I'm worse . . .*	
B (8)	2.04	*Hello, hello . . .*	Dreamy vocal (like Beatles); continuous bed of distorted guitar chords.
C (12)	2.20	*With the lights out*	Vocal angry, growling; heavy metal power chords, loud and distorted.
Interlude (4)	2.45		Stoptime effect, answered by guitar.
Guitar solo (16)	2.53		Guitar plays melody of sections A and B (little if any improvisation).
Intro (4)	3.25		Last four bars of Introduction.
A (8)	3.33	*And I forget . . .*	
B (8)	3.50	*Hello, hello . . .*	Crescendo, spacey one-word vocal.
C (20 = 12 + 8)	4.05	*With the lights out . . .*	Vocal angry, growling; heavy metal power chords, loud and distorted.

These sections are marked off by distinctive instrumental textures, shifting from the quiet, reflective, even somewhat depressed quality of A, through the crescendo of B, with its spacey one-word mantra and continuous carpet of thick guitar chords, into the C section, where Cobain bellows his unfocused feelings of discontent and the group slams out heavy metal–style power chords. This ABC structure is repeated three times in the course of the five-minute recording, with room created between the second and final iterations for a sixteen-bar guitar solo.

Nirvana's "Smells Like Teen Spirit," the first alternative rock single of the 1990s to enter the Top 10, is a carefully crafted pop record. The sleek, glistening studio sound; Cobain's liberal use of melodic and verbal hooks; the trio's careful attention to textural shifts as a means of marking off formal sections of the song; and the fact that Cobain's guitar solo consists of an almost note-for-note restatement of the melodies of the A and B sections, driving these hooks even deeper into the listener's memory, all serve to remind us that the Beatles were as profound an influence on 1990s alternative rock as were bands like the Velvet Underground.

seven—provide some insight into the opportunities and the pressures facing alternative rock musicians in the early nineties.

Cobain and Novoselic met in 1985 in the town of Aberdeen, an economically depressed logging town some one hundred miles from Seattle. (Cobain's parents had divorced when he was eight years old, an event that by his own account troubled him deeply and left him shy and introspective.) Inspired by the records of underground rock and hardcore bands and the creativity of the Beatles, and frustrated with the limitations of small-town working-class life, they formed Nirvana in 1987 and began playing gigs at local colleges and clubs. The following year they were signed by the independent label Sub Pop Records, formed in 1987 by the entrepreneurs Bruce Pavitt and Jonathan Poneman. (Sub Pop started out as a mimeographed fanzine for local bands before mutating into a record label.)

Nirvana's debut album, *Bleach* (1989), cost slightly over six hundred dollars to record—less than the cost of thirty minutes of recording time at a major New York or Los Angeles recording studio—and sold thirty-five thousand copies, an impressive amount for a regional indie rock release. In 1991 the group signed with major label DGC. (By this time, Ohio-born drummer Dave Grohl had become a steady member of the group.) Following a European tour with punk rock pioneers Sonic Youth, Nirvana released the album *Nevermind* in September 1991, quickly selling out its initial shipment of fifty thousand copies and creating a shortage in record stores across America. By the beginning of 1992 *Nevermind* had reached Number 1, displacing Michael Jackson's highly publicized comeback album *Dangerous*. The album stayed on the charts for almost five years, eventually selling more than ten million copies.

Although alternative bands like R.E.M. and Sonic Youth handled their rise to fame with relative aplomb, success destroyed Nirvana. The group's attitude toward the music industry appears to have crystallized early on, as this 1989 Sub Pop press release (reproduced at Sub Pop Records' website) indicates:

> NIRVANA sees the underground scene as becoming stagnant and more accessible to big league capitalist pig major record labels. But does NIRVANA feel a moral duty to fight this cancerous evil? NO WAY! We want to cash in and suck up to the big wigs in hopes that we too can GET HIGH AND F—— . . . SOON we will need groupie repellant. SOON we will be coming to your town and asking if we can stay over at your house and use the stove. SOON we will do encores of "GLORIA" and "LOUIE LOUIE" at benefit concerts with all our celebrity friends.

The sardonic humor of this public relations document only partially masks the band's intensely ambivalent attitude toward rock celebrity, a kind of "listen to us, don't listen to us" stance. As *Nevermind* rose up the charts, Nirvana had begun to attract a mass audience that included millions of fans of hard rock and

THE "SEATTLE SOUND"

Regional styles or "sounds" have played an important part in the history of rock music, from the Chicago blues of Muddy Waters to the Memphis rockabilly style of Elvis Presley and the Southern California inflections of surf rock and gangsta rap. Seattle, where Nirvana honed their sound and built a local fan base, was already home to a thriving alternative rock scene by the late 1980s. (The Pacific Northwest, while at somewhat of a remove from the main centers of the recording industry, had twenty-five years earlier played a role in the development of garage band rock, an important predecessor of punk rock.) The group often singled out as an originator of the "Seattle sound" was Green River (formed in 1983), whose 1988 album *Rehab Doll*, released on Sub Pop, helped to popularize grunge rock, blending heavy metal guitar textures with hardcore punk. Green River was also the training ground for members of later, more widely known Northwest bands such as Mudhoney (formed 1988), which was Sub Pop's biggest act until Nirvana came along, and Pearl Jam (formed 1990), who went on to become one of the most popular rock bands of the 1990s (see the next section in this chapter). One of the first bands signed to the fledgling Sub Pop label was Soundgarden (formed 1984), a heavy metal band that many insiders expected to be the first group to break the Seattle grunge sound on the national market. However, Soundgarden's first across-the-boards success—the album *Superunknown*, which reached Number 1 on the charts and sold five million copies—was not released until 1994.

Today, the push to define a regional style often comes as much from the promotion departments of record companies as from the local artists and fans themselves. The documentary video *Hype!* (1996), a revealing portrait of the role of Sub Pop Records in the Seattle alternative rock scene, suggests that many Seattle-based musicians and fans rejected the grunge label as a commercial gimmick, especially when it was adopted by advertising agencies and upscale fashion designers. This tension between commercialism and authenticity continues to play a central role in the creation and promotion of alternative rock music.

commercial heavy metal music, genres to which their own music was explicitly opposed. This realization impelled the group to ever more outrageous behavior, including baiting their audiences, wearing women's clothing, and kissing one another onstage. In 1992 Cobain married Courtney Love, the leader of an all-female alternative rock (a.k.a. "foxcore") group called Hole. Rumors concerning the couple's use of heroin began to circulate, and an article in *Vanity Fair* charged that Love had used the narcotic while pregnant with the couple's child, leading to a public struggle with the Los Angeles child services bureau over custody of the baby. In the midst of this adverse publicity, Nirvana released the album *In Utero,* a return to the raw sound of Nirvana's early Sub Pop recordings, which shot to Number 1 in 1993 and sold four million copies.

In 1994, after the band had interrupted a concert tour of Europe, Kurt Cobain overdosed on champagne and tranquilizers, remaining in a coma for twenty hours. Although the event was initially described as an accident, a suicide note was later discovered. He returned to Seattle and entered a detoxification program, only to check out two days later. On April 8, 1994, Cobain's body was discovered in his home; he had died three days earlier of a self-inflicted shotgun wound. While there is a diversity of opinion concerning the ultimate meaning of Cobain's suicide—he is viewed on one hand as a martyr of alternative rock, and on the other as a self-indulgent, hypocritical rock star—his death has widely come to be viewed as evidence of the pressures faced by alternative musicians who are pulled into the mainstream.

THE 1990S ROCK MAINSTREAM

A brief overview of the biggest selling rock albums of the nineties will give us a sense of how thoroughly genres and styles that were formerly excluded from the commercial mainstream were coming to dominate the music business during this period. Alternative rock bands like Nirvana, Pearl Jam, Green Day, and the Red Hot Chili Peppers recorded multiplatinum albums that combined the hard-driving, thick textures of hardcore punk and heavy metal with an approach to songwriting that could be traced back to the Beatles and Bob Dylan, and lyrics that often explored the darker aspects of human psychology.

"Jeremy," from Pearl Jam's breakthrough album *Ten* (1991), is a case in point. The song, composed by lead singer Eddie Vedder and bassist Jeff Ament, takes its inspiration from a newspaper article about a fifteen-year-old boy in Texas who committed suicide in front of his classmates. In a March 2009 interview with Clint Brownlee in *Seattle Sound Magazine*, Vedder said that he felt "the need to take that small article and make something of it—to give that action, to give it reaction, to give it more importance." In fact, the lyrics fuse together the story of adolescent suicide with an incident closer to Vedder's personal experience:

I actually knew somebody in junior high school, in San Diego, California, that did the same thing, just about, didn't take his life but

Pearl Jam in 1991 (Eddie Vedder, second from left). © Joe Giron/Corbis.

ended up shooting up an oceanography room. I remember being in the halls and hearing it and I had actually had altercations with this kid in the past. . . . So it's a bit about this kid Jeremy and it's also a bit about a kid named Brian that I knew and I don't know.

"Jeremy" includes two sequences of narrative text, the first beginning with a description of the disturbed boy at home, drawing pictures "of mountain tops with him on top, lemon yellow sun, arms raised in a V," and then invoking a horrific classroom scene. The second narrative sequence implicitly compares Jeremy with Vedder's schoolmate, Brian, who responds to his classmates' bullying by fighting back, rather than turning his anger inward ("and he hit me with a surprise left, my jaw left hurtin', dropped wide open"). These verses are separated by a refrain that describes the emptiness of Jeremy's relationship with his parents ("Daddy didn't give affection...") and his resulting self-involvement ("King Jeremy the Wicked ruled his world"), and concludes by suggesting that the only way for the emotionally disturbed young man to "speak" to his classmates was through an act of violence against himself ("Jeremy spoke in class today").

The musical texture of "Jeremy" supports the brooding tone of the lyrics while also creating a powerful rhythmic flow that propels the song forward. The track opens in a contemplative mood, with the distinctive sound of Ament's twelve-string electric bass guitar playing the song's signature riff, interspersed with harmonics (bell-like tones produced by lightly touching and releasing the strings with the left hand while plucking with the right). The structure of the song—essentially a verse-and-chorus form—is not strikingly unconventional, and the chords are relatively static, apart from the second refrain ("Jeremy spoke in class today"), where the idea of suicide as a form of self-expression when all other channels of communication are closed off is highlighted by a shift in key. Pearl Jam's fusion of thick instrumental textures and riffs derived from 1970s rock music with a relatively uncluttered song structure bristling with memorable "hooks," and gritty subject matter derived from punk rock, helped to move alternative rock onto the Top 10 album and singles charts.

Though it is hard to imagine an album like *Ten* selling a million copies in the previous decade, it was one of the most commercially successful rock albums of the nineties, peaking at Number 2 and eventually selling over twelve million copies. Although *Ten* didn't begin selling in significant numbers until 1992, after Nirvana had paved the way for alternative rock bands on mainstream rock radio, Pearl Jam was soon outselling Nirvana.

The commercial success of "Jeremy" (which reached Number 7 on the singles chart when it was re-released in 1995) was due in no small part to a controversial video version of the song that was aired on MTV beginning in 1992. The psychological focus of "Jeremy" is intensified by the almost constant presence of Eddie Vedder's darkly textured, expressive voice throughout the recording, and almost half of the duration of the music video is focused on the singer, who functions as a more or less continuous narrator. The video opens with a rapid-fire montage of newspaper clippings and phrases extracted from them ("an affluent suburb," "3:30 in the afternoon," "64 degrees and cloudy," "no note was found," "the White House declined comment"), presented in a stark white, childlike font against a black background. As the music begins, we experience a sequence of rapidly alternated, nightmarish images—first, a boy's anguished face lit crudely from underneath, as if by a flashlight; then the same young man scrawling intensely on a notepad, running wild through the woods, standing before images of an empty dress and an empty suit (the emotionally absent parents), and taunted by classmates, with a blackboard inscribed with clinical phrases like "Anxiety Disorder," "Environmental Stress," and "Hereditary Factors" hanging in the background.

Interspersed with these arresting images are intermittent textual fragments, including a reference to the book of Genesis and, by extension, the Christian concept of Original Sin. The phrase "because I say so" flashes onscreen, and Jeremy is shown arguing with his parents, who are completely unresponsive. As the musical texture becomes more richly layered and the performance gains intensity, Jeremy's behavior becomes correspondingly more agitated. He is shown surrounded by flames, wrapped in an American flag, and in the final scene, walks out of the woods into the classroom, puts a gun into his mouth and pulls the trigger, spattering his classmates with blood.

The music video of "Jeremy" generated considerable controversy, despite the fact that it was aired in a bowdlerized version that did not explicitly depict the act of suicide. (This strategy inadvertently led many viewers to believe that Jeremy had shot his classmates, rather than himself.) In 1996, a shooting occurred at Frontier Junior High School in Moses Lake, Washington, that left a teacher and two students dead. At the trial, the legal defense team for the shooter stated that he had been influenced in his actions by the music video of "Jeremy." After the Columbine High School shootings in 1999 the MTV and VH1 cable networks withdrew "Jeremy" from airplay completely, and subsequently omitted the video from several retrospective documentaries on rock music of the nineties.

In an October 18, 1993, "Rockline Interview" on KISW-FM in Seattle, Vedder offered his interpretation of the video's ultimate message:

> It came from a small paragraph in a paper which means you kill yourself and you make a big old sacrifice and try to get your revenge. That all you're gonna end up with is a paragraph in a newspaper. Sixty-three degrees and cloudy in a suburban neighborhood. That's the beginning of the video and that's the same thing, is, that in the end, it does nothing . . . nothing changes. The world goes on and you're gone. The best revenge is to live on and prove yourself. Be stronger than those people. And then you can come back.

Whatever one's interpretation of the style, content, and impact of the MTV version of "Jeremy," the video certainly reinforced the association of alternative rock with complex, real-world social issues, and with a tradition of psychologically oriented songwriting that reaches back through Prince and the Doors to the Beatles and Bob Dylan.

A sense of the musical diversity contained within the category alternative rock can be gained by surveying some of the best-selling acts of the nineties. R.E.M., who had helped to spark the underground/college rock movement back in the early eighties, reached a peak of popularity in the now more alternative-friendly environment with the albums *Out of Time* and *Automatic for the People* (Number 1 and Number 2, respectively, in 1991 and 1992). Metallica, the "thrash metal" trio who had taken heavy metal back from the spandex-and-hair bands during the late eighties, scored a massive hit with their eponymous 1991 album, and were soon featured as headliners on the alternative rock Lollapalooza tour. The Red Hot Chili Peppers, a Los Angeles band, fused punk rock with funk music, a mix that propelled their 1991 album *Blood Sugar Sex Magik* to Number 3 on the album charts and generated their first Top Ten single, "Under the Bridge" (Number 2, 1992). Hootie & the Blowfish, a band formed by college classmates from the University of South Carolina, specialized in an easy-going blend of folk rock and the alternative southern rock style of R.E.M. Their album *Cracked*

Hootie & the Blowfish performing in 1995. Photo by Jeff Kravitz/FilmMagic, Inc.

Rear View (Number One, 1994) sold over twelve million copies in the United States, spawning four Top 40 singles.

Green Day came out of the northern California punk scene and specialized in stripped-down, up-tempo punk-revival songs like "Basket Case" (1994), a tongue-in-cheek homage to the Ramones' mid-seventies song "I Wanna Be Sedated":

> *Do you have the time to listen to me whine*
> *About nothing and everything, all at once?*
> *I am one of those melodramatic fools*
> *Neurotic to the bone, no doubt about it.*

Green Day's breakthrough album, *Dookie* (1994), paralleled Nirvana's *Nevermind* in that it was the first big-budget, major label recording by a promising underground band. *Dookie* went on to sell sixteen million copies worldwide, and won the Grammy for Best Alternative Music Album in 1995, amid claims by some in the punk community that the band had "sold out" (a not uncommon response to the mainstreaming of underground rock bands).

The Canadian-born singer-songwriter Alanis Morissette scored the best-selling rock album of the nineties with *Jagged Little Pill* (1995), which held the Number 1 position on the charts for twelve weeks and is the best-selling debut album ever by a female artist, having sold over thirty million copies worldwide. *Jagged Little Pill* is an intensely personal album, hearkening back thematically to Joni Mitchell's *Blue* (1971, see page 189) as a portrait of a young woman's psyche, but more emotionally direct and forceful, decidedly a rock album in both style and sensibility. Morissette, who began her recording career as a dance-pop diva, reinvented herself as part of a women's movement within alternative rock that also included artists such as Sinéad O'Connor (who won the first Alternative Music Grammy in 1991) and Tori Amos, and the songs on *Jagged Little Pill* are strongly informed by a feminist perspective. The darkness and anguish of the autobiographical lyrics and the use of rock instrumentation juxtaposed with a pop-friendly, even slick approach to studio production, place *Jagged Little Pill* firmly within the alternative rock category.

The sales of *Jagged Little Pill* were buoyed by five Number 1 singles which received heavy airplay on alternative rock radio stations and MTV, including "You Oughta Know," a bitter rebuke of a former lover, which conveys a mood of barely controlled fury.

> . . . *the love that you gave, that we made, wasn't able*
> *To make it enough for you to be open wide, no*
> *And every time you speak her name*
> *Does she know how you told me you'd hold me*
> *Until you died, 'til you died?*
> *But you're still alive*
> *And I'm here to remind you*
> *Of the mess you left when you went away*
> *It's not fair to deny me*
> *Of the cross I bear that you gave to me*
> *You, you, you ought'a know*

The scathing, sexually explicit lyrics of "You Oughta Know"—censored for the MTV video version of the song—were doubtless part of its attraction for a large segment of the alternative rock audience. The song's frank expression of jealousy and anger functioned as a sign of emotional authenticity, and speculation about the identity of the song's intended target only added to the buzz. (Precedents for the "who is getting slammed?" song-marketing strategy include Carly Simon's 1973 hit "You're So Vain," the subject of which remains a matter of fan speculation nearly four decades later.)

Even with the sexual references edited out, the music video of "You Oughta Know" played an important role in popularizing both the single and the album. Scenes of Morissette wandering through an arid wasteland, carrying only a beat-up suitcase, and of the band performing in a deserted, dilapidated building, reinforced visually the song's themes of abandonment and desolation. In musical terms, the track begins sparsely, with sustained tones on an electric bass guitar, a snare drum played with wire brushes, and the faint, whispering sound of a flute. Red Hot Chili Peppers band members Flea and Dave Navarro played bass and guitar, respectively, on the song, and the texture and bouncing rhythmic feel of "You Oughta Know" are influenced by that band's fusion of alternative rock and funk music. The track alternates between the gentle mood of the introduction

Alanis Morissette performing in 1995. Photo by Jeff Kravitz/FilmMagic, Inc.

and bone-crushing textures dominated by guitar, bass, and drums, following the emotional arc of the lyrics. Interestingly, *Jagged Little Pill*'s producer, Glen Ballard, also cowrote Michael Jackson's hit single "Man in the Mirror" (Number 1, 1988), and there are hints of Jackson's influence in the style and phrasing of Morissette's vocal performance. It is perhaps worth noting that this is alternative rock you can dance to, and that this may have had the intent (and the effect) of expanding the album's audience by millions of listeners.

JAM BANDS

Although the term "alternative rock" is most often used to describe bands like R.E.M., Nirvana, Pearl Jam, and Green Day—ultimately inspired by the seventies punk rock movement—some forms of alternative rock found their inspiration elsewhere. The band <u>Phish</u> created a loyal following by extending the approach of the quintessential 1960s concert band, the Grateful Dead (see pages 154–157). Like the Dead, the members of Phish embraced eclectic tastes

Phish performing in 1994. Photo by Tim Mosenfelder/Getty Images.

and influences. A typical Phish concert would weave together strands of rock, folk, jazz, country, bluegrass, and pop. A band devoted to improvisation, Phish required a live performance environment to be fully appreciated. There are some obvious differences between Phish and the Dead—Phish being a smaller and in some regards a more technically adept band, with a range of stylistic references arguably even broader than that of the Grateful Dead. Be that as it may, bands like Phish, Blues Traveler, and Dave Matthews Band, inspired by the counterculture of the 1960s and by the improvisational work of jazz musicians such as Miles Davis (see pages 205–206) and Sun Ra, provided an optimistic, energetic, and open-minded alternative to the nihilism and relentless self-absorption of many alternative rock bands. The fact that Phish was often dismissed by rock critics—in part because their music doesn't make sense in terms of the rock-as-rebellion scenario that dominates such criticism—didn't impede their success as a live act. Unlike bands such as R.E.M., Nirvana, and Pearl Jam, however, their popularity as a touring act never translated into massive record sales. By the mid-1990s Phish was able to pack stadiums—selling out New York's Madison Square Garden in merely four hours—but none of their albums has sold as many as a million copies.

The twelve-and-a-half-minute track "Stash," from the concert album *Phish: A Live One* (1995), exemplifies the band's loose-jointed, freewheeling approach to collective improvisation. (This is, it must be admitted, a relatively brief selection. For an even better sense of the band's improvisational prowess, we would advise that you listen to one of the longer tracks, perhaps the half-hour-long "Tweezer.") The song—in the sense of a verse-chorus structure with a more or less fixed melody and lyrics—takes up only a small proportion of the track, which is an extended collective exploration of the improvisational possibilities of a minor-key chord progression, carried along on a rhythmic groove indebted to Latin American music. Certain relatively fixed elements create a sense of structure—for example, the tangolike melody played by guitarist Trey Anastasio at the beginning of the track and periodically throughout. (The audience's familiarity with these structural points is evidenced by the fact that they fill in one part of the melody with collective, and reasonably precise, clapping.) At some points these structural elements seem to melt away completely, as the guitar, acoustic piano, electric bass, and drums develop a subtle interplay, taking the performance in unexpected directions.

In an interview in *Addicted to Noise* (issue 1.07, June 1995), Anastasio talked about the fact that Phish has never, in over a decade of touring, had a hit album or single:

> Lately I've been thinking . . . the worst thing that could happen to a band is to have a hit single. . . . Because you weaken your fan base. People start coming in that aren't interested in the whole thing. And then they're expecting to hear that one song. . . .
> Kind of like life. You don't go from being 13 to being 30, you gotta go through everything in between. Music is life to a musician. Having a hit single is very similar to going up to someone in eighth grade and saying, "Wow, that thing you did in eighth grade was really great. We're going to skip you to college. Here you go! Good luck!" Take it slow. Life is long.

Life is long, but individual lives are sometimes short. It is in the end difficult to explain why musicians such as Ray Charles, Paul Simon, and the Grateful Dead managed to sustain a pattern of creative growth over several decades, while others—for instance, Hank Williams, Jimi Hendrix, Janis Joplin, Jim Morrison, and Kurt Cobain—burned out almost overnight, consumed by social pressures or personal demons. Anastasio's quote suggests that the key to musical longevity may be the ability to balance the passionate involvement of music making with a philosophical, even somewhat distanced perspective on the business of making a living from music.

HIP-HOP IN THE 1990s

As hip-hop became more commercially dominant in the nineties, rock itself even began to be defined by its relationship to hip-hop. In some cases that relationship was antagonistic, as in the case of rock radio stations that proudly proclaimed that they played "no rap." In other cases it was more collaborative, as in the case of rock groups that were influenced by hip-hop, such as Limp Bizkit. On a deeper level, by the end of the nineties, even many rock musicians who were not overtly borrowing from hip-hop were still serious fans of the music, and thus were shaped by its sensibility in various ways, particularly with regard to the use of digital sampling in their music. This, in turn, circled back to influence hip-hop artists such as Jay-Z and Kanye West, who engaged in more prolonged collaborations with rock musicians.

The expanding nationwide appeal of rap music during the late 1980s and early 1990s followed a familiar pattern. At the same time that some artists moved toward the pop mainstream, developing styles that blended the verbal cadences of rap and the techniques of digital sampling with R&B-derived dance rhythms and vocal styles, a variety of alternative rap styles emerged, reflecting the attitudes, experiences, and dialects of particular segments of the hip-hop audience. Interestingly, these marginal variants of hip-hop—especially so-called *gangsta rap*—ended up generating millions and millions of dollars in profits for the record industry.

The year 1990 was a watershed year for the mainstreaming of hip-hop. MC Hammer (Stanley Kirk Burrell, b. 1962), a rapper from Oakland, California, hit the charts in March of that year with *Please Hammer Don't Hurt 'Em,* which held the Number 1 position for twenty-one weeks and sold over ten million copies, becoming the bestselling rap album of all time. Hammer's celebrity was boosted by music videos that highlighted his impressive abilities as a dancer, by his appearances in corporate soft drink advertisements, and even by a short-lived children's cartoon show, called *Hammerman.* At the height of his popularity, Hammer was attacked by many in the hip-hop community for his lack of skill as a rapper and for pandering to a mass audience. There can be no denying that Hammer's success pushed rap fully into the mainstream, continuing a trend started in the mid-1980s by Run-D.M.C. and the Beastie Boys. At the same time, Hammer's pop-friendly rap style opened the door for an artist widely considered hip-hop's icon of "wackness" (weakness), the white rapper Vanilla Ice (Robert Van Winkle, b. 1968 in Florida). Ice's first album, *To the Extreme* (1990), monopolized the Number 1 position for sixteen weeks in early 1991, selling seven million copies. In hip-hop culture, a performer's credibility is correlated by fans not only with musical and verbal skill but also with the degree to which the artist in question possesses "street knowledge," that is, firsthand experience of the urban culture that spawned rap music. When it was discovered that Van Winkle, raised in reasonably comfortable circumstances in a middle-class neighborhood, had essentially invented a gangster persona for himself—a form of misrepresentation known in hip-hop parlance as "perpetrating"—many fans turned their backs on him. It is undeniable that race was also a factor in the rejection of Vanilla Ice, for he was widely regarded as being merely the latest in a long line of untalented white artists seeking to make a living off

the fruits of black creativity. Yet some white rappers and producers—for example, the Beastie Boys—have managed to gain acceptance as legitimate hip-hop artists, largely by virtue of their ability to forge a distinctive style within the parameters of an African American tradition.

By the late 1980s a number of distinctive regional variations on the formula of hip-hop music were well established in cities such as Philadelphia, Cleveland, Miami, Atlanta, Houston, Seattle, Oakland, and Los Angeles. The music critic Nelson George noted this process of regionalization:

> The rap that'll flow from down South, the Midwest and the West Coast will not, and should not, feel beholden to what came before. Just as hip-hop spit in the face of disco (and funk too), non–New York hip-hop will have its own accent, its own version of b-boy wisdom, if it's to mean anything. (George 1998: 132)

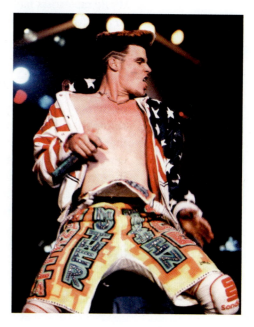

M.C. Hammer and **Vanilla Ice** performing in 1991. © Reuters/Corbis; Photo by Mick Hutson/ Redferns.

During this period Southern California became a primary center of hip-hop innovation, supported by a handful of independent labels and one of the few commercial AM stations nationwide to feature hip-hop programming (KDAY).

The sound of "new school" West Coast rap differed from "old school" New York hip-hop in a number of regards. The edgy, rapid-fire delivery of Melle Mel and Run-D.M.C. remained influential but was augmented by a smoother, more laid-back style of rapping. The dialects of southern California rappers, many of them the offspring of migrants from Louisiana and Texas, also contributed to the distinctive flavor of West Coast rap. And if the verbal delivery of West Coast rap was sometimes cooler, the content of the MCs' recitations themselves became angrier, darker, and more menacing, the social commitment of Public Enemy supplanted by the outlaw swagger of artists such as Ice-T (Tracy Marrow), who in 1987 recorded the theme song for *Colors,* Dennis Hopper's violent film about gang-versus-police warfare in South Central Los Angeles. Both the film and Ice-T's raps reflected ongoing changes in Southern California's urban communities, including a decline in industrial production and rising rates of joblessness, the continuing effects of crack cocaine, and a concomitant growth of drug-related gang violence.

The Rise of Gangsta Rap

The emergence of West Coast gangsta rap was heralded nationwide by the release of the album *Straight Outta Compton* by N.W.A. (Niggaz with Attitude). While rap artists had previously dealt with aspects of urban street life in brutally straightforward terms, N.W.A. upped the ante with recordings that expressed the gangsta lifestyle, saturated with images of sex and violence straight out of the prison toast tradition. The nucleus of the group was formed in 1986, when O'Shea "Ice Cube" Jackson (b. 1969), the product of a middle-class home in South Central Los Angeles, met Andre "Dr. Dre" Young (b. 1965), a sometime member of a local funk group called the World Class Wreckin' Cru. Jackson and Young shared an interest in writing rap songs, an ambition that was realized when they teamed up with Eric "Eazy-E" Wright (1973–95), a former drug dealer who was using the proceeds of his occupation to fund a record label, Ruthless Records. Soon, the three began working together as N.W.A., eventually adding D.J. Yella (Antoine Carraby) and MC Ren (Lorenzo Patterson) to the group.

When the group started work on their second album, *Straight Outta Compton,* the idea of establishing a distinctive West Coast identity within hip-hop was clearly in their minds. As MC Ren put it in a 1994 interview in *The Source*:

> When we did N.W.A . . . New York had all'a the bomb groups. New York was on the map and all we was thinking, man—I ain't gonna lie, no matter what nobody in the group say—I think we was all thinking about making a name for Compton and L.A. (George 1998: 135)

Released in 1989, the album was more than a local success, selling 750,000 copies nationwide even before N.W.A. started a promotional tour. The album's attitude, sound, and sensibility were clearly indebted to earlier hip-hop recordings—particularly Public Enemy's *It Takes a Nation of Millions to Hold Us Back,* released the year before—but were in some ways unlike anything heard before, featuring tracks with titles like "F——the Police" and "Gangsta Gangsta," underlain by a soundtrack that mixed the sound of automatic weapon fire and police sirens with samples from funk masters such as George Clinton and James Brown, a bouncy drum machine–generated dance groove called new jack swing, and high-pitched, thin-sounding synthesizer lines. The raps themselves were harrowing egocentric accounts of gang life, hearkening back to the bleakest aspects of the prison toast tradition. The cover of the CD—with the posse staring implacably down at, and holding a gun to the head of, the prospective purchaser—reinforced the aura of danger, one of the main appeals of the group for the young suburban audience that pushed the album to multiplatinum sales.

Snoop Doggy Dogg. UPI Photo/Michael Bush/Landov.

The acrimonious breakup of N.W.A., beginning in 1989, had the effect of disseminating the group's influence over a wider territory. During the 1990s Ice Cube went on to make a series of platinum albums totaling almost six million in sales, including the brilliant *AmeriKKKa's Most Wanted* (Number 19 in 1990), a more explicitly political album recorded in New York with Public Enemy and the Bomb Squad; and *The Predator,* which reached Number 1 in 1992. Eazy-E sold over five million albums in the 1990s, all released on his Ruthless Records label, and MC Ren sold one million copies of his *Kizz My Black Azz* (Number 12 in 1992). But the most influential and economically successful member of N.W.A. turned out to be Andre Young (Dr. Dre), who founded an independent record label (Death Row/Interscope), cultivated a number of younger rappers, and continued to develop a distinctive hip-hop production style, christened "G-Funk" in homage to the P-funk style developed in the 1970s by George Clinton, often sampled on Dre's productions. Dr. Dre's 1992 album *The Chronic*— named after a particularly potent strain of marijuana—sold over three million copies and introduced his protégé, <u>Snoop Doggy Dogg</u> (Calvin Broadus, born in Long Beach in 1972).

Hip-Hop, Digital Sampling, and the Law

As we have seen, the tradition of incorporating beats from secondary sources is as old as hip-hop itself. However, the increasing sophistication and affordability of digital sampling technology had, by the late 1980s, made it possible for rap producers to go much farther, weaving entire sound textures out of prerecorded

🎧 LISTENING TO "WHAT'S MY NAME?"

Written by George Clinton, Gary Shider, Snoop Dogg, and David Spradley; produced by Dr. Dre; performed by Snoop Doggy Dogg; recorded 1993

Snoop's soft drawl and laid-back-but-lethal gangster persona were featured on *Doggystyle* (1993), which made its debut at the top of the album charts. The million-selling single—"What's My Name?" a so-called clean remix of the opening track on the *Doggystyle* album—will give us a sense of Snoop Doggy Dogg's prowess as a rapper and of Dr. Dre's distinctive G-funk production style. (Like many rap recordings intended to cross over to the pop charts, "What's My Name?" was released on the album in its original, unexpurgated version and in a "clean" version on a single designed for radio airplay and mass distribution. We will analyze the remix here, which reached Number 8 on the *Billboard* Hot 100 singles chart in 1993.) Although the track opens with a dense, scratchy sample reminiscent of a Public Enemy/Bomb Squad recording— actually a brief sequence from an old Parliament track, looped to create a syncopated pattern—the texture soon shifts to a smoother, more dance-oriented sound. A relaxed, medium-tempo dance groove is established by drum machine and keyboard synthesizers (including a weighty and sinuous keyboard bass part), over which a digitally processed, nasal-sounding human voice floats, singing a melismatic phrase:

> *Eee-yi-yi-yi-yi-yah, the Dogg Pound's in the hou-ouse*

A female choir enters, repeating the phrase "Snoop Doggy Dogg" in soul music style, and is answered by the sampled voice of George Clinton, intoning "Da Bomb" (a phrase commonly used to describe compelling grooves and other pleasurable experiences). After this brief mood-setting introduction, Snoop's drawling, laconic voice enters:

> *From the depths of the sea, back to the block [the neighborhood]*
> *Snoop Doggy Dogg, funky as the, the, the Doc [Dr. Dre]*
> *Went solo on that ass, but it's still the same*

> *Long Beach is the spot where I served my cane [sold my cocaine]*

These two stanzas immediately establish Snoop's local identity, his indebtedness to his mentor Dr. Dre, and his street credibility.

He then explodes into a rapid-fire, percussively articulated sequence of tongue-twisting wordplay:

> *Follow me, follow me, follow me, follow me, but you betta not slip*
> *'Cause Nine-trizzay's the yizzear [1993's the year] for me to f—up sh—[make an impact]*
> *So I ain't holdin nuttin back*
> *And once again I got five on the twenty sack [put five dollars down on a twenty-dollar bag of marijuana, i.e., I'm back in the game]*

Snoop declares his arrival in no uncertain terms, asserting that 1993 is the year for him to make a major impact on the scene, musically and otherwise. He then shifts to a more threatening posture—aided by Dr. Dre's interjection of an automatic weapon–like sound effect:

> *It's like that and as a matter of fact (Dr. Dre: rat-tat-tat-tat)*
> *'Cause I never hesitate to put a fool on his back [imitating Muhammad Ali]*
> *(Dr. Dre: Yeah, so peep out the manuscript [pay close attention to the words]*
> *You see that it's a must we drop gangsta sh——[talk gangster talk])*
> *Hold on, wha's my name?*

The female choir re-enters, introducing a bit of hip-hop history, a melodic line from Parliament's "Give Up the Funk (Tear the Roof off the Sucker)" (see the discussion of this recording in Chapter 8). Then Snoop continues to add verbal layers to his gangsta persona, boasting about his potential for lethal violence, referring to himself as

"Mr. One Eight Seven"—a reference to the California penal code for homicide—and departing the scene of a bloody massacre by disappearing mysteriously into the night ("I step through the fog and I creep through the smog").

The following interlude between verses introduces a digitally processed voice chanting "Bow-wow-wow, yippie-yo-yippie-yay," a sly reference to country and western music and cowboy films. (References to cowboys and country music are not at all unknown in rap music; for example, Seattle-based rapper Sir Mix-A-Lot's "Buttermilk Biscuits," recorded in 1988, is a parody of square dance music.) In the third and final section, Snoop moves on to another favorite subject, his sexual potency. He begins with a catchphrase that goes back to the South Bronx origins of hip-hop and MCs like Kool Herc and Grandmaster Flash:

> Now just throw your hands way up in
> the air
> And wave them all around like ya just
> don't care

Read as words on a page, divorced of their musical context, "What's My Name?" is simply an updated version of "Stagger Lee," a traditional African American ballad about a powerful black desperado of prison toast fame. But the commercial success of "What's My Name?" had as much to do with the musical groove and texture of the recording as with the content and flow (rhyme and rhythm) of Snoop Doggy Dogg's verbal performance. "What's My Name?" is in fact a club dance record, more than half of which is taken up by instrumental music or singing. (It could be argued that most of the people that bought this record could not have interpreted portions of the text in any case, given the use of local references and gang jargon.) This recording is obviously less musically complex than Public Enemy's "Night of the Living Baseheads," judged from the viewpoints of textural complexity, tone color, or historical references. Dr. Dre's G-funk sound, while indebted to the innovations of Public Enemy's production team, the Bomb Squad, has an entirely different aesthetic and commercial goal. Dre's approach to the use of digital sampling is much less ambitious than Public Enemy's: He uses here only three prerecorded sources—George Clinton recordings from the 1970s and early 1980s—and generally seems to aim for a clean, crisp studio sound. (The less ambitious use of digital samples may have to do with the court cases that by the mid-1990s made it much more difficult for hip-hop producers to experiment with prerecorded sources.) Despite its controversial verbal content, "What's My Name?" is a quintessential pop record, bristling with hooks, catchy melodies, riffs, and verbal mottoes, organized around a medium-tempo groove, and carefully calibrated for dance club consumption.

materials. This development triggered some interesting court cases, as some of the artists being sampled sought to protect their rights.

In 1989 the Miami-based rap group 2 Live Crew released a song called "Pretty Woman," which borrowed from the rock 'n' roll hit "Oh, Pretty Woman" (Number 1 pop in 1964), written by Roy Orbison and William Dees. Although 2 Live Crew had tried to get permission from the music publisher of the song, Acuff-Rose Music, to make a rap version of the song, permission had been denied. A lawsuit ensued over rapper Luther R. Campbell's (a.k.a. Luke Skyywalker's) raunchy send-up of the tune, and Campbell took the position that his use of the song was a parody that was legally protected as a fair use. The Supreme Court recognized the satirical intent of Campbell's version and held that 2 Live Crew's copying of portions of the original lyric was not excessive in relation to the song's satirical purpose.

Although the 2 Live Crew decision upheld the rights of rap musicians and producers to parody preexisting recorded material, control over actual digital sampling tightened up during the 1990s, as a result of a few well-publicized court cases. In 1991 the 1960s folk-rock group the Turtles sued the hip-hop group De La Soul for using a snippet of the Turtles' song "You Showed Me" on a track called "Transmitting Live from Mars." The Turtles won a costly out-of-court settlement. That same year, an up-and-coming hip-hop artist named Biz Markie recorded a track that sampled the sentimental pop song "Alone Again (Naturally)," a Number 1 pop hit for the Irish songwriter Gilbert O'Sullivan in 1972. O'Sullivan was not pleased and pursued the case, eventually forcing Warner Brothers to remove Biz Markie's album from the market until the offending track was itself removed from the album. These decisions sent a chill through the rap music industry and encouraged producers to be less ambitious in their use of sampled materials. As the hip-hop historian Nelson George phrases it, "The high-intensity sound tapestries of Public Enemy have given way to often simpleminded loops of beats and vocal hooks from familiar songs—a formula that has grossed [MC] Hammer, Coolio, and Puff Daddy millions in sales and made old R&B song catalogs potential gold mines" (George 1998: 95).

Gangsta Rap Conflicts

While the conflation of gangsta rhetoric and reality at least temporarily boosted the sales of rap recordings, it also had terrible real-life consequences, as the matrix of conflict between posses—one source of the creative energy that gave birth to hip-hop in the 1970s—turned viciously in on itself during the mid-1990s. Such conflicts—evoked constantly in gangsta rap—can develop at many levels: between members of the same posse ("set trippin'"), among posses representing different 'hoods, between gangs of different ethnicity (as for example between Chicano and black gangs in Los Angeles), among larger organizations (for example, national gangs like the Crips, Hoods, and Black Gangster Disciples), and between entire cities or regions of the country.

The mid-1990s saw the violent eruption of conflicts between East and West Coast factions within the hip-hop business. Standing in one corner was Marion "Suge" Knight, CEO of Los Angeles–based Death Row Records, and Death Row's up-and-coming star Tupac (2Pac) Shakur (1971–96). In the other corner stood the producer and rapper Sean "Puffy" Combs (a.k.a. Puff Daddy, P. Diddy), CEO of the New York independent label Bad Boy Records, and the up-and-coming star the Notorious B.I.G. (Christopher Wallace, a.k.a. Biggie Smalls, 1972–97). By the time the stranger-than-fiction scenario played itself out at the end of the 1990s, Tupac Shakur and Christopher Wallace had been shot to death; Suge Knight, already on parole for a 1992 assault conviction, was reincarcerated after an attack on two rappers in a Las Vegas casino and had come under federal investigation for racketeering; Interscope, a subdivision of Time Warner Entertainment, had severed its formerly lucrative promotion and distribution deal with Death Row Records; Tupac Shakur's mother had sued Death Row for the rights to her dead son's tapes; and Dr. Dre and Snoop Doggy Dogg, Death Row's biggest stars, had severed ties with the label. In January 1998 Snoop told the *Long Beach Press-Telegram* (as quoted in RockOnTheNet.com) that he was leaving Death Row Records for fear of his life:

> I definitely feel my life is in danger if I stay in Death Row Records. That's part of the reason why I'm leaving . . . there's nothing over there. Suge Knight is in jail, the president; Dr. Dre left and 2Pac is dead. It's telling me that I'm either going to be dead or in jail or I'm going to be nothing.

Chillingly, both 2Pac and the Notorious B.I.G. had recorded prophetic raps that ended with the narrator speaking from the grave rather than standing in bloody triumph over his victims. True to the logic of the popular music business, these voices were manifested in highly profitable posthumous albums with titles like *Life after Death, Born Again, Still I Rise,* and *Here After.*

Since the late 1980s the highly stylized narratives of gangsta rap have provided a chronicle of the dilemmas faced by urban communities—poverty, drug addiction, and violence—from a first-person, present-tense viewpoint. The recordings of artists like Ice-T, N.W.A., Snoop Doggy Dogg, 2Pac Shakur, and the Notorious B.I.G. combine a grim, survivalist outlook on life with a gleeful celebration of the gangster lifestyle. This celebratory nihilism, propelled by funk-derived, digitally sampled grooves and surrounded in the video versions of rap recordings with a continual flow of images of hip-hop fashion, champagne, expensive cars, and sexy women (characterized as "bitches" and "whores"), provokes an understandable ambivalence toward gangsta rap on the part of observers genuinely sympathetic to the plight of people struggling for economic and cultural survival in America's cities. How, such critics ask, could a genre of music that presents itself as being committed to "keeping it real" so deeply indulge itself in the escapism of consumer capitalism and in the exploitation of women as sex objects?

Part of the answer may lie in the fact that rap music is a part not only of African American culture but also of American culture as a whole. Rap reflects the positive qualities of American culture—its creative energy, regional diversity, and technological acumen—just as it expresses American society's dark side: the obsession with guns and violence, material wealth and status symbols, and long-standing traditions of racism, homophobia, and sexism. (And, as a number of observers have pointed out, folk tales of black outlaws like Stagger Lee have always existed in a dialogue with popular images of white gangsters like Capone and Dillinger, and with violent Hollywood films like *Little Caesar, Scarface,* and *Natural Born Killers.*)

All Hail the Queen

Queen Latifah (b. 1970) was not the first nationally popular female hip-hop artist—that honor belongs to the all-female rap crew Salt-N-Pepa, who scored a string of hits in the late 1980s and reached the peak of their commercial success with the release of the album *Very Necessary* (Number 4 Pop in 1994). There can be no doubt, however, that Queen Latifah is the most important woman in the history of hip-hop, in terms of both her commercial success and her effectiveness in establishing a feminist beachhead on the male-dominated field of rap music. Latifah provided an alternative to the misogynist braggadocio of gangsta rappers like Snoop Doggy Dogg, while her strong R&B-influenced voice and assertive persona evoked earlier rhythm & blues and soul artists such as Big Mama Thornton and Tina Turner.

Born in inner-city Newark, New Jersey, Dana Elaine Owens received the nickname Latifah—an Arabic word signifying "gentle" or "pleasant"—from a cousin at the age of eight. She began rapping in high school, and in college participated in Afrika Bambaataa's Native Tongues collective, a group dedicated to raising the political consciousness of hip-hop. Her debut album on Tommy Boy Records, *All Hail the Queen* (1989), reached Number 6 on the R&B album chart and spawned the hit single "Ladies First" (Number 5 Rap, 1990), a direct challenge to the putative supremacy of male rappers:

The ladies will kick it, the rhyme that is wicked
Those that don't know how to be pros get evicted
A woman can bear you break you take you
Now it's time to rhyme, can you relate to
A sister dope enough to make you holler and scream?

All Hail the Queen, with its R&B and reggae influences, gave an early indication of Latifah's talent and musical range. However, her second album (*Nature of a Sista*, 1991) failed to crack the R&B Top 20, and Tommy Boy Records decided not to re-sign her contract. After a hiatus—motivated in part by the death of her brother in a motorcycle accident—she signed with Motown Records, and in 1993 released *Black Reign*, which earned a gold record. Dedicated to her brother and featuring her biggest hit single, "U.N.I.T.Y.," it reached Number 7 on the R&B charts, crossed over to the pop Top 40, and won a Grammy for Best Solo Rap Performance.

Queen Latifah. Neal Preston/Corbis.

🎧 LISTENING TO "U.N.I.T.Y."

The track opens with a sample of jazz tenor saxophone with guitar, string bass, and drum set accompaniment and then moves into a slow, sultry, reggae-influenced groove, anchored by a window-rattling bass riff and digitized snare drum backbeat. The reggae association is continued in the opening refrain, which Latifah performs in a languorous Jamaican *patois*, interrupted by more aggressive responses in an American dialect. The hypnotic flow of the music—with the "old school" jazz saxophone reappearing periodically—supports the refrain's idealistic message, that black men and women should treat one another with love and respect:

> *Uh, U.N.I.T.Y., U.N.I.T.Y. that's a unity*
> *U.N.I.T.Y., love a black man from infinity to*
> *infinity*
> *(Who you calling a bitch?)*
> *U.N.I.T.Y. (You gotta let him know)*
> *U.N.I.T.Y. that's a unity (You go, come on*
> *here we go)*
> *U.N.I.T.Y. (You got to let him know)*
> *Love a black woman from infinity to infinity*
> *(You ain't a bitch or a ho', here we go,*
> *here we go, uh)*

Then Queen Latifah launches into her rap, abandoning the Jamaican dialect entirely, squaring off and dropping rhythmic accents into her speech like a boxer jabbing at her opponent:

> *Instinct leads me to another flow*
> *Everytime I hear a brother call a girl a*
> *bitch or a ho' (music halts briefly)*
> *Trying to make a sister feel low*
> *You know all of that gots to go*
> *Now everybody knows there's exceptions to*
> *this rule*
> *I don't be getting mad when we playin', it's*
> *cool*
> *But don't you be callin me out my name*
> *I bring wrath to those who disrespect me*
> *like a dame*
> *That's why I'm talkin, one day I was walkin*
> *down the block*
> *I had my cutoff shorts on, right, cause it*
> *was crazy hot*

> *I walked past these dudes, when they*
> *passed me (uh)*
> *One of 'em felt my booty, he was nasty*
> *(yeah?)*
> *I turned around red, somebody was*
> *catching the wrath*
> *Then the little one said, "Come on, yeah me,*
> *bitch" [man's voice], and laughed*
> *Since he was with his boys he tried to*
> *break fly*
> *Huh, I punched him dead in his eye and*
> *said "Who you calling a bitch?"*

In her next verse, Latifah tightens the narrative focus, describing an abusive relationship with a man:

> *I guess I fell so deep in love I grew*
> *dependency*
> *I was too blind to see just how it was*
> *affecting me*
> *All that I knew was you was all the man I had*
> *And I was scared to let you go, even though*
> *you treated me bad*
> *But I don't wanna see my kids see me*
> *getting beaten*
> *By daddy smacking mommy all around*
> *You say I'm nothing without ya, but I'm*
> *nothing wit' ya*
> *A man don't really love you if he hits you*

The overall musical structure of the track is straightforward, alternating the "U.N.I.T.Y" refrain with a series of rapped verses. On this track, as in so many hip-hop recordings, the focus is on the verbal performance, and the music functions to set the mood, create a temporal flow, and (through digital sampling) evoke a range of associations. Queen Latifah's performance counterpoises her smoldering indignation over the abuse of women by men with a more empathetic and optimistic approach. (This dialectic is emphasized in the music, which plays off the assertive, even pugilistic quality of Latifah's rapping against the laid-back, sensuous feeling of the bass-heavy groove and the hauntingly mellow jazz saxophone, bathed in reverb.) If "U.N.I.T.Y." is a threat, delivered in the most straightforward terms, it is also a plea for civility and the healing power of love.

Queen Latifah established a precedent for sustainable hip-hop careers—an antithesis to the live-fast, die-young ethos of gangsta rap. Following her early success as a recording artist, she appeared on television and in films, including the acclaimed movie musical *Chicago* (2002), which garnered her Best Supporting Actress nominations from both the Screen Actors Guild and the Golden Globe awards. And in 2004 she demonstrated her musical versatility once again, releasing an album of Tin Pan Alley and soul standards backed with big band and strings. *The Dana Owens Album* broke the Top 20 on both the pop and R&B album charts and presaged a whole new set of commercial and artistic opportunities for the queen of hip-hop.

On one hand, rap has provided an unvarnished view of the dystopia that infects many urban communities—what Cornel West, the prominent African American cultural critic, has called "the lived experience of coping with a life of horrifying meaninglessness, hopelessness, and lovelessness . . . a numbing detachment from others and a self-destructive disposition toward the world" (West 1993, p. 14). On the other hand, it is also clear that gangsta recordings, promoted by huge entertainment corporations to a predominantly white mass audience, may have served inadvertently to reinforce some old and pernicious stereotypes of black masculinity, dating back to the knife-toting dandy of the nineteenth-century minstrel show. Perhaps this is what Chuck D was referring to when in 1998 he told an interviewer, "Ten years ago, I called rap music black America's CNN. My biggest concern now is keeping it from becoming the Cartoon Network."

WORLD MUSIC/ROCK COLLABORATIONS IN THE 1990S

By the nineties collaborations between American rock musicians and foreign artists—pioneered in the previous decade by rock stars like Paul Simon, David Byrne, and Peter Gabriel—had become more common, spurred on one hand by alternative music fans' search for a broader range of musical experiences, and on the other by the globalization of the music industry. Two particularly interesting examples of this sort of transnational collaboration are the album *Talking Timbuktu,* which won the Grammy Award for Best World Music Recording in 1994, and a sampler album inspired by the film *Dead Man Walking,* which reached Number 61 on the album charts in 1996.

Talking Timbuktu was produced by the singer and guitarist Ry Cooder (b. 1947 in Los Angeles), whose career as a session musician and bandleader had already encompassed a wide array of styles, including rock, blues, reggae, Tex-Mex music, urban folk song, Hawai'ian guitar music, Dixieland jazz, and gospel music. The sound and sensibility of *Talking Timbuktu* are derived from the music of Ali Farka Touré (1939–2006), a guitarist and traditional praise singer (*griot*) from the West African nation of Mali.

Encountering a track like "Diaraby," an American listener is likely to be struck by the music's close affinities with the blues. This is no accident. To begin with, the blues styles of Mississippi, Texas, and other southern states were strongly influenced by the traditions of African slaves, many of whom came precisely from the Sahel region of West Africa, homeland of Ali Farka Touré's people, the Bambara. The high-pitched, almost wailing sound of Touré's singing; the percussive, repetition-driven guitar patterns; and the use of song as a medium for social and personal commentary—all of these features represent an evolution of centuries-old links between the West African griot tradition and the blues created by black musicians in America's Deep South. In point of fact, it turns out that Ali Farka Touré's style was directly influenced by American blues musicians such as John Lee Hooker, whose records Touré discovered after his career was already well established in Africa.

Talking Timbuktu features contributions by the blues guitarist and fiddler Clarence "Gatemouth" Brown and various prominent session musicians. The result, as exemplified by "Diaraby," sung in the Bambara language, hews close to its African roots, with the American musicians playing in support of Touré. The lyric of the song is itself reminiscent of the bittersweet emotion of some American blues:

> *What is wrong my love? It is you I love*
> *Your mother has told you not to marry me, because I have nothing. But*
> *I love you.*
> *Your friends have told you not to marry me, because I have nothing. But*
> *I love you.*
> *Your father has told you not to marry me, because I have nothing. But I*
> *love you.*
> *What is wrong my love? It is you I love.*
> *Do not be angry, do not cry, do not be sad because of love.*

The sound and sensibility of "Diaraby" provide additional evidence, if any were needed, of the deep links between African and American music. This is not music functioning as a universal language, but rather a conversation between two dialects of a complexly unified Afro-Atlantic musical language.

The track "The Face of Love" is a different sort of collaboration, featuring the lead singer for Pearl Jam, Eddie Vedder, and the great Pakistani musician Nusrat Fateh Ali Khan (1948–97), and produced by Ry Cooder. Khan was a leading performer of *qawwali,* a genre of mystical singing practiced by Sufi Muslims in Pakistan and India. (Sufism was founded in Iran between the ninth and twelfth centuries C.E. A response to orthodox Islam, Sufism emphasizes the inner kinship between God and human beings and seeks to bridge the distance between them through the force of love.) *Qawwali* singing is traditionally accompanied by a double-headed drum called the *dholak* (or a *tabla,* used in Indian classical music) and a portable keyboard instrument called the harmonium, which creates a continuous drone under the singing. In traditional settings the lead singer (or *qawwal*) alternates stanzas of traditional poetic texts (sung in unison with a choir) with spectacular and elaborate melodic improvisations, in an attempt to spiritually arouse his listeners and move them into emotional proximity with the Divine.

During the 1990s Nusrat Fateh Ali Khan became the first *qawwali* artist to command a large international following, owing to his performances at the annual WOMAD (World Music and Dance) festivals curated by the rock star Peter Gabriel, and to a series of recordings released on Gabriel's Real World label. Khan began to experiment with nontraditional instruments and to work with musicians outside the *qawwali* tradition, leading some critics to charge that the music had moved away from its spiritual roots. "All these albums are experiments," Khan told the interviewer Ken Hunt in 1993. "There are some people who do not understand at all but just like my voice. I add new lyrics and modern instruments to attract the audience. This has been very successful." (See the web version of *All Music Guide*.)

Most American listeners first heard Khan in the soundtracks to *The Last Temptation of Christ* and *Natural Born Killers,* though without knowing it, since he was part of the overall blend. (Khan was unhappy about being included in the soundtrack for *Natural Born Killers,* since it did not reflect the spiritual goals of *qawwali*.) The 1996 film *Dead Man Walking*—the story of a nun's attempt to redeem the soul of a convicted murderer on the verge of execution—was the first to foreground Khan's contributions. Many reviews of *Dead Man Walking* stressed the contribution of Khan's voice to the haunting, mystical, and spiritual atmosphere of the film. The song "The Face of Love" is based on a simple melody, sung first by Khan with lyrics in the Urdu language, and then with English lyrics by Pearl Jam's lead singer Eddie Vedder.

In this case the sound of the music (particularly the drone of the harmonium) and the mysticism of the Sufi poetic text resonate with the transcendental atmosphere of the film—the contemplative mood of a man sentenced to die by lethal injection. The filmmaker does not make an explicit argument for or against the death penalty, and the music, with its subtly shifting textures, embodies the complexity and ambivalence of the film's subject. Although Eddie Vedder could not be expected to possess the formidable vocal improvisatory technique that Khan unleashes briefly in the middle of this track, he nonetheless manages to blend the timbre of his voice (and his acoustic guitar playing) with the mood and texture of the *qawwali* ensemble. In addition, Vedder's English lyrics do evoke the theme of mystical love so central to *qawwali* singing. This is not an example of music's functioning as a universal language, for most members of the film's American audience neither understood the words that Khan sang nor possessed any knowledge of the centuries-long history of Sufi mystical traditions. Nonetheless, it could be argued that this is a case where the well-meaning effort of artists to reach across cultural and musical boundaries does produce something like an aesthetic communion, a common purpose embodied in musical texture and poetry, provisional though it might be.

Khan's appearance on the soundtrack of *Dead Man Walking* led to his being signed by the indie label American Recordings, managed by Rick Rubin, formerly the mastermind behind the rappers Run-D.M.C. and the Beastie Boys. The American music industry's market positioning of world music as yet another variant of alternative music is indicated by that label's roster of artists, which included not only Nusrat Fateh Ali Khan but also the "death metal" band Slayer, the rap artist Sir Mix-A-Lot, and the late country music icon Johnny Cash.

CONCLUSION

In the nineties, the implications of MTV's dominance began to ripple out through the rock genre. In particular, the clear distinction between rock styles that embraced MTV and those that rejected it (or were rejected by it) began to break down. Some marginal subgenres of rock were absorbed into the world of MTV, while others developed their own infrastructures and chose to push forward without the help of mass media. At the same time, the baby boomer generation, simply by getting older, was moving from its former position at the center of rock innovation toward a new role as a more conservative element of the rock community. As the millennium turned, the changes in rock would accelerate, though now they would not primarily be driven by stylistic or social changes but by technology.

12

THE INTERNET ERA:
2000 –

As home recording and Internet distribution of music became more common, an unprecedented wave of change began to sweep through every aspect of rock. The seemingly solid relationship between music, commerce, and culture that had sustained the genre for most of its life was breaking down. At the same time, rock's longstanding dominance over other popular music genres also began to crumble: Of the twenty top-selling musical artists and groups of the first decade of the twenty-first century, only *four* were contemporary rock acts—two others were rock acts whose sales consisted primarily of older music. (See the "Chart Watch" blog by Paul Grein, May 29, 2009: http://new.music.yahoo.com/blogs/chart_watch/34074/chart-watch-extra-the-top-20-album-sellers-of-the-2000s/.) Rock and its culture were no longer at the center of American popular music. So where were they? In this chapter we explore rock's attempts to address that question.

As we have discussed, the music industry developed a coherent approach to the production of rock music in the late 1960s, and this approach remained essentially unchanged for more than three decades. Songs were performed by the same people who had written them, with both aspects being viewed as part of a larger artistic process. This process also included the recording of these songs, and their assembly into a larger album-length statement. Songs were recorded under the direction of a professional producer in an expensive studio that was paid for by a record company, establishing a well-defined relationship between the artists who made the music and the business people who turned the music into a product. This distinction served both to reinforce the idea of authenticity on the part of the artist and also frame that authenticity within an economic relationship with a record label. The record company would then physically produce the recordings and distribute them to stores. Radio and television stations would present the music (and its video) to consumers, who could then purchase the album in the form of a physical object (record, cassette, or CD), take it home, and listen to it on their stereo systems. The concept of rock music as an album-length artistic statement embodied in a physical object was reinforced at every stage of the process, from creation to distribution to advertisement to purchase to listening. At the turn of the millennium, however, every aspect of this system suddenly changed. It began with developments in technology.

MUSIC AND THE INTERNET: THE REVOLUTION WILL BE DOWNLOADED

The most profound transformations in the dissemination and consumption of popular music have been catalyzed by the Internet. The digital revolution in music production, distribution, and consumption was kicked off in the 1990s by the introduction of MPEG, a digital file compression algorithm that allows sound files to be squeezed to as little as one-twelfth of their original size. This, in turn, allowed for the first time the wide and rapid dissemination of sound recordings over the Internet, a technological precondition for the emergence of a huge market in downloaded music, and for the emergence of personal digital audio players such as the iPod. The introduction of MPEG technology—and its descendant, the **MP3** audio encoding format—spurred a series of bitter struggles between entertainment corporations and small-scale entrepreneurs, echoing past conflicts between major and indie record labels, though on an even larger scale. As with digital sampling, this new way of disseminating musical materials raised a host of thorny legal problems, centered on the issue of copyright. While MP3 files are not inherently illegal, the practice of digitally reproducing music and giving it away for free without the artist's or record company's permission arguably is illegal.

In 1999, an eighteen-year-old college dropout named Shawn Fanning developed Napster, an Internet-based software program that allowed computer users to share and swap files, specifically music, through a centralized file server. Soon thereafter, the Recording Industry Association of America (RIAA), the trade association whose corporate members—Universal, Sony, Warner Brothers, Arista, Atlantic, BMG, RCA, Capitol, Elektra, Interscope, and Sire Records—controlled the sale and distribution of approximately 90 percent of the offline music in the United States, filed suit against Napster, charging them with tributary copyright infringement. (This meant that the firm was accused not of violating copyright itself but of contributing to and facilitating other people's violation of the law.) In its countersuit the firm argued that because the actual files were not permanently stored on its servers but rather transferred from user to user, Napster was not acting illegally. A federal court injunction finally forced Napster to shut down operations in February 2001, and users exchanged some 2.79 billion files in the closing days of Napster's existence as a free service.

In the wake of Napster's closure a number of companies specializing in peer-to-peer (p2p) file-sharing networks were established. These services' claim to exemption from copyright law was based on the fact that in a peer-to-peer network there is no central server on which files are even temporarily stored, and thus no "place" in cyberspace to which the act of copyright violation can be traced, apart from the millions of computers of the network's users. From the viewpoint of these users—including many musicians attempting to promote their recordings outside the corporate framework—p2p was the ultimate realization of musical democracy, a decentralized system made up of millions of individuals expressing free choice. From the RIAA's viewpoint, peer-to-peer music sharing was a case of mass theft, a maddeningly complex cybernetwork that challenged the ability of corporations (and the courts) to apply traditional conceptions of music as a form of property. The MP3 file-sharing debates of the early years of the decade raised fundamental questions about American culture, some involving the not-always-harmonious relationship between representative democracy and corporate capitalism. In legal terms the matter was settled in 2005, when the U.S. Supreme Court ruled unanimously that online firms had violated copyright "on a massive scale," and within months all of them had stopped distributing their file-sharing software.

The development of new personal listening devices went hand in hand with the rise of file sharing on the Internet. In 2001 Apple Computer introduced the first-generation iPod player, which could store up to one thousand CD-quality tracks on its internal hard drive. The iPod and other MP3 players have come to dominate the market for portable listening devices, in part because they provide the listener with the ability to build a unique library of music reflecting his or her personal tastes. (This trend was initiated half a century earlier with the introduction of the 45 r.p.m. record changer, which allowed consumers to play their favorite songs in whatever order they chose). The ability of the iPod to "shuffle" music— that is, to play tracks in a random order, mixing genres, performers, and historical periods—has not only exerted an influence on personal listening habits but has also provided a metaphor for the contemporary (some would say postmodern) state of consumer culture. (In 2005 Apple introduced a device called the iPod Shuffle, promoted with the advertising slogans "Random is the New Order" and "Lose Control. Love It.") In October 2009, Apple announced that more than 220 million iPods had been sold worldwide, making it by far the most popular individual listening device in history.

In 2001 Steve Jobs, the president of Apple Computers, launched a fee-based music downloading service called iTunes, designed to supply content for the then-new iPod. The following year Jobs negotiated a deal with the five biggest music corporations (at that time EMI, Universal, Warner, Sony Music Entertainment, and BMG) to make the great majority of their recordings available for purchase and download. (Some of the major holdouts at the time, including the Beatles, Led Zeppelin, and Radiohead, have subsequently made their music available via iTunes.) In 2003 the iTunes Store was launched, making some 200,000 tracks available for download for 99 cents each; and within a couple of years iTunes commanded 70 percent of the online market, eventually becoming the top music retailer in the United States. In February 2010, Apple announced that over 10 billion tracks had been downloaded from the iTunes store worldwide since its inception. Internet music vendors such as iTunes led to a renewed emphasis on the individual song as opposed to the album, which was a serious challenge to the way rock had been conceptualized for the previous four decades.

Another major outlet for popular music is YouTube, an online video website that was launched in 2005. The first big YouTube hit was a quirky video called "A Million Ways," featuring the Chicago-based rock band OK Go dancing on treadmill machines. The video itself cost the band only $4.99 to make, and it was ultimately downloaded nine million times, transforming the band from locally popular musicians to international superstars. In 2006 Warner Music made a deal with YouTube to make its entire music video catalog available online; and soon thereafter Google bought YouTube for $1.65 billion in stock. Today the range of videos posted on YouTube is astounding, from the earliest sound films of the 1920s and 1930s to work by the latest alternative artists, and from slick professional productions to homemade low-tech efforts.

THERE'S NO PLACE LIKE HOME: DIGITAL RECORDING, PRO TOOLS, AND ROCK MUSIC

Developments in sound recording technology and software also had a profound impact on the music industry and on rock music in particular. Software programs such as Pro Tools, designed to run on personal computers, allowed musicians working on a limited budget to set up a basic home studio at relatively small expense, while industry professionals could use the same technology to build highly sophisticated digital sound facilities. This software allowed recording engineers and musicians to gain even more control over every parameter of musical sound, including not only the pitch and tempo of a performance, but also the quality of a singer's voice or an instrumentalist's timbre.

Pro Tools was a significant departure from most previous recording systems in two ways. First, previous recording technology, being based on the use of analog recording tape, imposed serious limitations on the kinds of changes that could be made after the music had been recorded. Pro Tools, by contrast, was a purely digital format that allowed virtually unlimited alteration of the music with no loss in sound quality. Second, that potential was reinforced by the fact that Pro Tools was based on a visual interface; the sound of the music was represented graphically on the computer screen. This led to new, more visual, ways of thinking about rock music production, particularly in terms of patterns, repetition, and consistency. It became a simple matter, for example, to simply cut-and-paste the same chorus of a song each time it came around rather than play it again. This led to a more modular approach to recording, with songs being *assembled* from constituent parts more than *performed* in the recording studio. While this approach was not entirely new, Pro Tools made the process much easier and more precise, allowing musicians and producers to move, change, or erase individual notes and phrases. It also allowed musicians to experiment with different changes, knowing that they could simply undo those that they didn't like, something that was much more difficult to do when using analog tape.

As with any increase in artistic options, this was a double-edged sword. On one hand, it gave musicians an unprecedented amount of control over every aspect of their sound. On the other, it also led to a new level of musical obsessiveness that could easily destroy the spontaneity that has so often been at the heart of rock. It is now common practice, for example, for a producer to quickly go through an entire song and erase the sound of the vocalist inhaling before each phrase they sing. Do such gestures serve to improve the sound of the recording or dehumanize it? Of course, the answer to this question is a matter of opinion, but from the perspective of many rockers, "imperfection" is a necessary part of music as a form of human expression.

As we have seen many times in the course of our study, rock music can become a sounding board for larger cultural issues, including the impact of new technologies on our daily lives. At one end of the spectrum stand musicians, including some practitioners of punk, rockabilly, ska, folk music, and alternative rock, who reject digital technology and celebrate hands-on, analog, low-fidelity approaches as a cornerstone of their aesthetic. At the other end are artists who have avidly incorporated digital synthesis, recording, and mixing techniques into the very heart of their work. Of course, these "back-to-basics" and futurist impulses in popular music are nothing new; we could easily count the late guitarist and musical technologist Les Paul among the latter camp, though he began his experiments as long ago as the 1930s!

"THE SYSTEM IS BROKEN": CHANGES IN THE MUSIC BUSINESS

During the first decade of the new millennium it became clear that online file-sharing, the emergence of portable technologies for reproducing and listening to music, and the widespread availability of music recording software had posed serious challenges to the record industry, which had not changed its essential structures, strategies, and modes of operation for well over half a century. At the time of this writing, the music business is still struggling to find a response, seemingly alternating aggressive policing tactics with an acceptance of the inevitable. Though it is still early in the process to speculate, two major trends have become apparent.

The first trend, somewhat surprisingly, is a renewed focus on the baby boom generation as a primary source of revenue. There are clearly several factors involved in that decision. For one thing, it is a generation whose culture and desires are well known to the music industry. There is little risk in releasing a new Eric Clapton or Jimi Hendrix compilation. Moreover, as they age, baby boomers have more income to spend on high-end rock offerings such as elaborately packaged boxed sets and expensive concert tickets. In the spring of 2011, for example, the Grateful Dead offered a 73-CD boxed set containing recordings of every show from their 1972 European tour. At a retail price of $450, the limited edition set sold out in three days. But perhaps the most significant factor in the baby boomers' appeal to the record industry is their perceived unwillingness (or inability!) to illegally download music files. In other words, they are an important market simply because they're the only ones who are still buying music at all. A secondary effect of this trend has been the establishment of rock culture of the sixties and seventies as the definitive model of rock in general, even for younger listeners. Just to take one rather startling example: If asked to name the top-selling rock group of 2000–2010, few people would guess that it was the Beatles, especially since they hadn't existed as a group since 1970. But that is, in fact, the case. And rock stars of the 1960s and 1970s, including Neil Young, Bob Dylan, and the Rolling Stones, continue as of this writing to score huge box office receipts on their international concert tours.

The second trend is a search on the part of record companies for sources of income that do not rely on actually selling records. On the sales end, this often involves placing songs in movies, television shows, commercials, and as cell phone ring tones. On the business end, there is an increased emphasis on making so-called "360-degree deals" with artists. A "360-degree deal" is one in which a record company (and their affiliated businesses) handle every aspect of an artist's career, not the just the recording aspect. For most of the history of rock, such things as live performances, T-shirt and poster sales, and even sheet music were handled separately from the artist's recording career. This made sense at the time, because the record companies neither wanted to, nor were equipped to, handle these other areas. At the turn of the millennium, however, the different parts of the music business were increasingly being consolidated under large corporate umbrellas, which left companies much better equipped to address *all* of the artists' business needs. At the same time—by coincidence—record income happened to be diminishing, which made these other aspects of the music business more attractive to record companies. In short, the record industry is slowly adjusting itself to an era in which music is no longer disseminated as a physical object.

The cumulative impact of these and other recent technological developments—including the rise of cellular telephone ringtones, with their own specialized *Billboard* sales chart and half-billion-dollar U.S. market—has transformed the music industry forever. The "music business" is no longer synonymous with the "record business." Following several public relations debacles, the major labels now offer most of their music for download without copy protection. The compact disc is virtually dead; from 2004 on, the best-selling CD in the United States every year has been a blank, recordable disc. Media convergence—the ever-closer interactions among digital technologies—is a major force, with hit songs finding their initial release not only on the radio and online, but also via cellular ringtones and video games. Music is seemingly everywhere, all the time, in hitherto unimaginable variety and quantity.

If the new, mobile digital technologies are the fundamental drivers of change in the music business, one of the most important outcomes of this process has been a transformation in the relationship between musicians and music corporations. In essence, a new generation of artists has moved to cut out the middleman, in an effort to reach their audience directly without mediation of record companies.

Touring has become an increasingly important component of the total profits generated by the music business, rather than a sideline designed to promote record sales. By 2006, concert tour revenues from popular music (including the sale of merchandise) exceeded $3.5 billion worldwide, and the shift toward vertical integration of aspects of the music business—recording, media dissemination, artist management, promotion, ticketing, merchandising, and so on—had intensified. The clearest indication of this trend was provided in 2008, when the world's largest ticket outlet, Ticketmaster, bought the artist-management company Frontline for $123 million. Frontline, owned by Irving Azoff, represented a roster of popular music stars that included the Eagles, Jimmy Buffett, Neil Diamond, Christina Aguilera, and Miley Cyrus, and the deal installed Azoff as CEO of the new, combined company. The plot thickened further when in February 2009 Live Nation and Ticketmaster Entertainment announced that the two corporations would merge, combining the biggest concert promoter in the world with the leading ticketing and artist-management company, and adding Madonna, U2, and Nickelback to the company's combined roster of artists. Though the merger raised serious antitrust concerns, it was approved by the U.S. Department of Justice in January of 2010, opening the door for the combined company, with almost $6 billion in sales, to permeate virtually every aspect of the concert business. In an interview in the *Los Angeles Times* (February 12, 2009), Irving Azoff said:

> The system is broken. This is about being in the music business—not
> just the record business, not just touring, not just ticketing. With the

almost complete collapse of the ability to monetize recorded music, we think this model will allow artists to control their fate along several product lines within the music business.

As might have been predicted, this development has generated a variety of responses, ranging from horror to eager anticipation. On the positive side, those involved in the prospective merger claim that one of their aims is to drive down ticket prices and to better control the secondary ticket market, where fans pay exorbitant prices for tickets bought up by speculators. On the negative side lurk familiar demons: corporate monopoly, conflicts of interest, and sheer avarice. Caught in the middle, and fading fast, is the record industry, which once sat astride the world of popular music like a colossus.

In his insightful book on the decline of the record business, *Appetite for Self-Destruction*, Steve Knopper (music business contributing editor for *Rolling Stone*) quotes Mark Williams, longtime A&R man for Interscope Records:

> People at the majors for some time have been looking for an answer. The obvious answer is "there is no answer." . . . It's like, drop a globe and it shatters into a million pieces. It's going to be like in the 50s and 60s, when you had hundreds and hundreds of small labels. It's going to be a lot of trial and error. None of us know whether it'll work right. I laugh when people say, "We're going to try to fix it." They can try, but there's no real answer. It's over. It's just done. (Knopper 2009: 248)

Given the uncertainty of the global economic situation, what lies ahead for the music industry? Revenues from the sale of recorded music in the United States dropped from a high of $14.6 billion in 1999 to $10.4 billion in 2008, and there have been authoritative predictions that they could sink as low as $9.2 billion by 2013. Overall sales in all popular music genres were down by 2010, even in genres that had enjoyed growth in recent years, and it is clear that online sales of popular music are not replacing CD sales, dollar for dollar. The four major music corporations, already under stress, are in the process of downsizing, laying off employees, and evaluating the way forward. "Big box" stores like Wal-Mart and Best Buy sell more recorded music than specialized music outlets, and they have driven even formerly powerful retail chains like Tower Records and Virgin Megastores out of business. The record business appears to be dying; however, it could be argued that the music business is simply changing shape as it adapts to new conditions.

Digital music futurists have argued that music now plays a role something like the role of water in the developed world—a resource that was historically the source of intense political struggle, social conflict, and profit seeking, but is now regarded by citizens as a virtually ever-present, constantly flowing common good (Kusek and Leonhard 2005). We are living through profound transformations in the way that music is made, consumed, and experienced, changes that would have been hard to imagine even a decade ago. The convergence of technological and social forces—the rise of the Internet and mobile technologies; the shifting relationships among artists, corporations, and audiences; and the ongoing turmoil in the global economy—will lead to outcomes that cannot be predicted accurately from our present perspective. But it seems inevitable that the role of music in our daily lives will continue to be shaped by new technologies, new business strategies, and the evolving, always complex relationship between musicians and their audiences.

ROCK MUSIC IN THE AGE OF DIGITAL REPRODUCTION

The changes in the evolving relationship between musicians, their audiences, and the music business have affected rock in several ways. First and foremost, the rise of digital production and distribution has irrevocably altered the *process* of creating rock music. Under the old system, almost every practical aspect of creating a commercially viable product was beyond the means of the average musician. The recording process required a specially designed studio staffed with a variety of professionals. Production required pressing plants to physically create the record, designers to make the album cover, and commercial printers to print it. And distribution (actually delivering the record to stores) required elaborate commercial networks, warehouses, trucks, truck drivers, and so on. The expense and organizational difficulties of these processes made it so that musicians almost always had to rely on a record company to facilitate them. Now, by contrast, virtually anyone can create music with inexpensive recording software (the "GarageBand" music production application actually comes pre-installed on every Apple Mac computer sold), and then distribute it as digital sound files via the Internet. In other words, a recording is no longer a physical object, and thus no longer requires the whole chain of materials and labor associated with producing physical products. After all, you don't need a truck driver to deliver an MP3! This may seem like a minor change, but as we've discussed, the entire context in which rock music was made was shaped by the imperatives and limitations of the music business. As that context changed, musicians' entire sense of what they were supposed to be doing changed as well.

To take one very basic example, for most of rock's history, artists were expected to release about one album per year, then spend about six months touring to promote it. This would be followed by about six months of preparing the next album, after which the whole process would begin again. This schedule made equal sense from the perspectives of the artist, the record company, and the consumer. The amount of time it took for a musician to write and record an album's worth of material was aligned with the time required for the record company to physically produce and distribute the record, the time it took for magazines to review it, and the time it took for fans and radio stations to get tired of the previous album and begin to demand a new one. The idea that each album would constitute the artist's musical statement for that year deeply affected the album's content, style, and overall approach, as well as the way these things were understood by fans. Which songs should be included, which songs should *not* be included, how the album fit into the band's history and image, how the music would be interpreted relative to what other artists were doing that year . . . all of these questions were influenced by the established timetable of rock releases.

But high-quality digital home recording made it possible for artists to record songs whenever the mood struck them. And the Internet made it possible to deliver this music to fans instantaneously, at little or no cost, in collections of any length, from single songs to hours-long collections. In such an atmosphere, the idea that a band should create exactly one hour's worth of music per year suddenly made very little sense. But if they were no longer supposed to do that, what *were* they supposed to do? And how were the media and fans supposed to interpret it? Such a seemingly simple change—the length and frequency of rock releases—affected the whole approach of the music. And that was only one of many changes happening in the first decade of the new millennium.

In essence, the music business as it had existed for almost a half-century had become obsolete almost overnight. On the surface, this would seem to be very liberating for rock: freed of its business concerns, rock could now be pure artistic expression. But as we have discussed, the culture and music of rock were intimately associated with the practical and economic concerns of the business that supported it. It is no surprise, then, that rock itself is changing profoundly even as we write. The nature of the product has changed from a physical object to a stream of data, and from albums to single songs. The timetable of releases has become more open, the distribution and publicity machines have become decentralized, and rock music has become more fragmented in response. The "gatekeeper" functions of record companies and radio are all but gone. And with no central outlet for rock like MTV or AOR radio, the genre is more fragmented than ever.

Initially, most musicians simply shifted their focus to fit the new circumstances, but it soon became clear that many of the deeper connections between commerce and art that sat at rock's foundation were wearing away. In an earlier era, the boundaries of rock had often been defined by record companies, radio stations, and MTV to suit their needs. Music had to fit into certain categories in order to be eligible for certain economic opportunities. In the Internet era, however, this no longer applied to anywhere near the same degree. But if there is no longer a compelling commercial need to define the boundaries of rock, is there still a compelling social or artistic need? If so, how will those boundaries be defined? If not, does it still make sense to speak of "rock" as a distinctive genre? And if the old model for balancing art and commerce is no longer serviceable, what—if anything—will replace it? At this writing, it is still too early to see how these questions will be answered, but several trends seem to be emerging.

Some artists, such as <u>Nickelback</u>, have continued to embrace a traditional approach to the music and business of rock. Formed in 1995 in Vancouver, Canada, Nickelback came to prominence in the United States in 2000 with their album, *The State*. Mixing a mid-tempo post-grunge sound with country influences, particularly in their vocals and intermittent use of acoustic guitars, Nickelback was well suited to appeal to America. In 2005, they released their fifth album, *The Right Reasons*, which sold over seven million copies. While this would have been an extraordinary accomplishment in any era, in the era of Internet downloading, it was nothing short of miraculous. The success of Nickelback demonstrates that the traditional approach to rock music (albums promoted and sold to rock audiences via radio and television) is far from dead. At the same time, while this approach is clearly still viable for some artists, it is available to fewer of them every year. The trend toward increasing conservatism on the part of record labels—a process that had started in the early eighties—accelerated rapidly in the new millennium. Major labels increasingly directed their resources toward a smaller number of bands that they felt sure about, rather than spreading their investment out over a broad range of artists, in hopes that some of them would be successful. While such conservative investing strategies on the part of the industry may make sense from an economic standpoint, by definition they tend to discourage innovation and experimentation. This does not mean that creativity is dead in rock, it simply means that the system no longer encourages it in the same way. The traditional rock star system established in the seventies—in which the musician's artistic vision is considered an almost mystical force to be supported through record company patronage—is available to fewer and fewer artists.

Some groups, such as <u>Linkin Park</u>, have worked within a framework that is fundamentally rock-based, but which integrates other influences, such as hip-hop. Blending traditional rock instrumentation with turntables and other electronic instruments, Linkin Park exemplifies the decreasing significance of genre boundaries in the new millennium. Rather than take two clear-cut genres and melding them (as might be suggested by a term like "rap-rock"), their music is more a reflection of individuals with diverse musical influences bringing them together into a whole that collectively represents their wide-ranging musical sensibilities. While musicians have always done this to some degree, in the past such endeavors required crossing not only musical and cultural boundaries but also the infrastructural boundaries of the music industry itself. Musicians that blended genres had to navigate difficult practical realities: On which radio format would they try to get their records played? In which part of the record store would their records be filed? In which magazines would they seek coverage? The success of a band like Linkin Park reflects the diminishing relevance of these kinds of questions, as changes in technology and media have given artists more freedom to operate in multiple genres simultaneously. For example, despite being seen primarily as a rock musician, Linkin Park guitarist Mike Shinoda collaborated in 2006 with the well-respected hip-hop deejays Roc Raida and DJ

Linkin Park performing in 2001. Photo by KMazur/WireImage.

Vlad to produce *Rock Phenomenon*, an underground mixtape that featured the vocals from well-known hip-hop songs layered over the music from classic rock songs. The "tape" (actually a CD) was sold via underground hip-hop channels for over a year before receiving a wider general release, and it was ultimately acclaimed by both hip-hop and rock audiences.

The members of Linkin Park are also an example of how contemporary rock reflects the changing demographics of youth in the United States, in that the band notably features two Asian American members: Shinoda, whose father is Japanese; and Joe Hahn, who is Korean American. Until the late nineties, the Asian American presence in rock had been limited, but as the population of U.S.-born Asian American adults increased in the 1990s (partially as a delayed result of the Immigration and Nationality Act of 1965, which made it easier to immigrate to the U.S. from Asian countries), their perspectives have increasingly become part of the rock landscape. Other important Asian American rock musicians of this era include James Iha of Smashing Pumpkins, Kirk Hammett of Metallica, Karen O of the Yeah Yeah Yeahs, Sean Ono Lennon, the son of Yoko Ono and John Lennon, and Kim Thayil of Soundgarden.

Creed performing at the My VH-1 Music Awards 2001. Photo by KMazur/WireImage.

As bands became less economically reliant on the mass media and record stores, they faced less pressure to respect the categories that these businesses were based on. In fact, many artists have taken the opportunity offered by the diminishing practical significance of genre boundaries to develop styles that bring together entire audiences that previously would have been separated by the demands of the marketplace.

Christian (or Christian-influenced) rock—at one time viewed as an entirely separate genre from mainstream rock—has come to exert a larger influence on the mainstream in the form of bands such as Creed. Historically, Christian rock had been considered a subcategory of the genre of Contemporary Christian Music, directed primarily toward followers of American evangelical Protestantism. For this reason, Christian rock had often operated as the "rock" aspect of Christian music rather than the "Christian" aspect of rock music, a distinction that served to define the music in two ways.

First, the music was specifically marketed by and to the evangelical community along with other aspects of Christian culture, as a component of a comprehensive lifestyle. Designed specifically to replace mainstream rock in the lives of its listeners, it actively sought to avoid overlapping with it. (One notable historical exception to this trend was Stryper, a Christian metal band whose 1986 album *To Hell With The Devil*, was a crossover hit, selling over two million copies.) Second, since the main purpose of Christian rock was to express or reinforce a religious doctrine, the genre tended to be defined more by its lyrical content than by its musical characteristics. "Christian rock" was essentially *any* rock music that promoted a Christian message.

In contrast to this model, Creed aimed to spread their message through mainstream channels, promoting themselves as a rock band that *dealt with*

Christian themes, rather than a "Christian Rock" band *per se*. Formed in 1993, Creed released their first album, *My Own Prison*, in 1997, before achieving their greatest success in 1999 with the album *Human Clay*, which sold over eleven million copies, largely on the strength of their hit single, "Higher." They released another album, *Weathered* (2001), before breaking up in 2004, largely due to personal problems on the part of lead singer Scott Stapp. In 2009, the band reunited for a new album and tour, though its future remains unclear.

Another strategy for rock musicians in the new millennium has been to take a more experimental approach to both the sound *and* the economics of rock. Perhaps the best example of this approach is <u>Radiohead</u>, who began their career firmly within the

Radiohead performing at the Lollapalooza music festival in Chicago, August 2008. Kevin Mazur/WireImage.

boundaries of alternative rock, but subsequently experimented not only with diverse musical influences but also with varied approaches to the marketing and distribution of their music.

Though they had been recording since 1992, Radiohead came to prominence in the United States in 1997, with their third album, *OK Computer*. Over their next two albums, *Kid A* (2000) and *Amnesiac* (2001), they increasingly integrated sampling and other electronic music techniques and approaches. In 2007, Radiohead extended their experimentation to distribution as well, releasing their Number 1 album *In Rainbows* as a digital download and allowing fans to set their own price. Several months later, for those that wanted the more traditional experience of purchasing a physical CD, they offered an expensive boxed set featuring many extras and souvenirs. Rather than choose between the traditional rock business model and the new culture of downloading, Radiohead chose both. Moreover, in the context of the changes that were happening in popular music during this era, it is not difficult to see Radiohead's artistic and economic experimentation as being related to each other.

But as that ideology—and its associated musical approach—becomes increasingly mainstream, the very concepts of "mainstream" and "alternative" themselves have begun to lose their meaning. Most alternative music fans do not regard the Grammys, awarded each year by the National Academy of Recording Arts and Sciences (NARAS), as a bastion of rebellious individualism and musical authenticity. Nonetheless, there was a good deal of online fist pumping among fans when the Canadian band <u>Arcade Fire</u> came from the back of the field to win the 2011 Grammy Award for Best Album of the Year over the pop music

🎧 LISTENING TO RADIOHEAD'S "BODYSNATCHERS"

I t could be argued that the eclecticism of Radiohead's business strategy has been echoed in the sensibility of their music. The track "Bodysnatchers" (Number 8 on the Rock Tracks chart in 2008) will serve as an example of Radiohead's creative extension of the basic formula of alternative rock. Like other "alt rock" bands, Radiohead has drawn upon the nihilistic sensibility of hardcore punk rock and the thick, guitar-dominated textures of arena rock and heavy metal. (Radiohead even upped the ante by using three, rather than the usual one or two, electric guitars!) At the same time, they have also brought into play a wide range of musical influences, from progressive rock and electronic dance music to orchestral music, flamenco, jazz, and the singer-songwriter tradition.

Although *In Rainbows* has been described as Radiohead's "gentlest" album in musical terms—with tracks such as "House of Cards," "Nude," "All I Need," and "Jigsaw Falling into Place" featuring acoustic guitar and piano, falsetto singing, and moody electronic textures—"Bodysnatchers" evokes the trademark edginess and sonic power of Radiohead's earlier recordings. The track begins abruptly with a distorted, "bone-crunching" electric guitar riff, performed with the guitar's lowest string tuned down and left open as a more or less continuous drone. The upper part of the opening guitar riff outlines the song's melody, which is then picked up and developed by lead singer Thom Yorke. The song's lyric describes the alienation of a person incarcerated within his own body, a theme expressed quite explicitly in the opening verse:

> I do not understand
> What it is I've done wrong
> Full of holes, check for pulse, blink
>   your eyes
> One for yes, two for no
> I have no idea what I am talking about
> I am trapped in this body and can't
>   get out

Like an etherized-yet-conscious patient, the first-person subject of the song is confined within the limitations of his physical body, unable to connect directly to the world around him.

The scale used in the main melody of "Bodysnatchers" is reminiscent of the song "Within You Without You" (from the Beatles' 1967 album *Sgt. Pepper's Lonely Hearts Club Band*), a self-consciously philosophical ode that featured instruments and sounds derived from Indian classical music (including the *tambura*, a drone instrument). The vaguely exotic quality of the instrumental and vocal melodies in "Bodysnatcher" combines eerily with the lyric's exploration of a metaphor from 1950s science fiction, rooted in Cold War fears over the loss of free will in society (whether to Communists or extraterrestrials). While the original "pod people" in the 1956 film *Invasion of the Body Snatchers* were interstellar spores that replaced sleeping people with perfect physical duplicates, the alienated narrator of Thom Yorke's song remains fully and ineffectually conscious within his own body. It is not too much of a stretch to connect this sensation of helplessness with the constant demand that musicians harness their creativity to the goal of generating profits:

> After fulfilling its contract in 2003 with its last album for EMI, "Hail to the Thief," Radiohead turned down multimillion-dollar offers for a new major-label deal, preferring to stay independent. "It was tough to do anything else," Mr. Yorke said during Radiohead's first extensive interviews since the release of [In Rainbows]. "The worst-case scenario would have been: Sign another deal, take a load of money, and then have the machinery waiting semi-patiently for you to deliver your product, which they can add to the list of products that make up the myth, la-la-la-la." (Pareles 2007)

This theme—the struggle to retain control over one's creative voice in a profit-driven industry—is driven home even more explicitly in the second verse of "Bodysnatchers":

> You killed the sound, removed
>   backbone

A pale imitation, with the edges . . .
   sawn off

A little more than halfway through the track (2:07), the instrumental texture opens up and a solo guitar takes the lead, enhanced by reverb that creates the sense of a great, wide-open space. Thom Yorke then re-enters, a solitary voice in a vast sonic expanse, singing a series of six couplets:

Has the light gone out for you?
   Because the light's gone out for me
It is the 21st century (2x)
They got a skin and they put me in
   (2x)
All the lines wrapped around my face
   (2x)
And for anyone else to see (2x)
I'm a lie . . .

Another minute into the track (3:09), and the electric guitars take over once again, playing a riff related to, though distinct from, the opening pattern. Yorke sings a wordless, slowly descending line ("la-la-la-la"), doubling it in unison with his guitar. This sequence is repeated, and

(at 3:32) the guitars move in with a vengeance, tripling the riff in unison and creating a massively rocking wall of sound. This three-guitar "rave-up" concludes the track, as we hear the final line "I seen it coming"— a prophecy in the past tense, too late—shouted four times over the chaotic tumult.

Toward the middle of "Bodysnatchers," Thom Yorke sings "I have no idea what you are talking about, your mouth moves only with someone's hand up your ass." It's certainly hard to think of a more evocative metaphor than a hollow, soulless ventriloquist's dummy for the frustration and fears of artistic infertility that appear to have haunted Radiohead's members during the four-year gap between albums that was broken, triumphantly, by the release of *In Rainbows* across several media platforms. Although the emotional angst of rock superstars and the melodrama of the music business may not seem the most lofty or compelling subject matter, it can be argued that the subtext of "Bodysnatchers"—that is, the role of free will and creativity in a business traditionally dominated by corporate concerns—is both an essential theme in the history of rock music and a key component of the ideology of contemporary alternative rock.

diva Lady Gaga and the rapper Eminem, making them the first alternative rock band to achieve that recognition. The unexpected victory of their album, *The Suburbs*, seemed to some fans to signal the "arrival" of alternative rock at the center of popular music, a kind of culmination of the work of bands such as R.E.M. and Nirvana. (The fact that the band members themselves were not expecting to win the Grammy was revealed by the first words uttered when they came back onstage to accept the award: "What the hell?!?")

Arcade Fire, based in Montreal, Canada, is a seven-piece band centered on the married duo of Win Butler, a Texas-raised guitarist and singer, and Régine Chassagne, a Canadian vocalist and keyboardist of Haitian descent. Each member of Arcade Fire plays more than one instrument, and a typical concert by the band features an almost constant switching around of guitars, drums, bass guitar, piano, violin, viola, cello, double bass, xylophone, glockenspiel, keyboard, French horn, accordion, harp, mandolin, and hurdy-gurdy (a mechanically bowed string instrument popular during the Renaissance).

Arcade Fire performing at the 2011 Grammy Awards. Photo by Jeff Kravitz/ FilmMagic.

The band's stylistic influences are equally diverse, including arena rock, punk, synth-pop, Brazilian *bossa nova*, French *chanson*, Cajun music, and classically tinged pop music. Their performances are self-consciously theatrical, a sort of cross between cabaret and arena rock.

Arcade Fire's debut album—2004's *Funeral*—explored the value of community and family in the face of death, while their next effort, *Neon Bible* (Number 2 in 2007), was more somber and spiritually questioning, using traditionalist musical elements such as pipe organ, a military choir, and string orchestra. The album *The Suburbs* (Number 1, 2011) evokes the experiences of kids born and raised in the vast stretches of recession-impoverished suburban sprawl that surround most North American cities (including Houston, Texas, where Win Butler grew up).

This theme is captured evocatively by the song "Sprawl II (Mountains beyond Mountains)," a meditation on suburban emptiness carried along on an ironically sprightly, synth-pop rhythm:

> *Living in the sprawl,*
> *Dead shopping malls rise like mountains beyond mountains, and there's*
> *no end in sight. . .*

The hard-rocking, Ramones-inspired song "The Month of May"— performed by Arcade Fire at the 2011 Grammy concert with teens on street bikes zooming around and through the band—is even more directly focused on the isolation and desperation of suburban youth. The song's lyric features verbal images of cars driving "around and around and around and around" in a bleak neighborhood decimated by a violent storm (evoked by a roar of digitally generated "white noise" at the beginning of the track), and groups of teens "all standing with their arms folded tight":

So young, so young
So much pain for someone so young
Well, I know it's heavy, I know it ain't light
But how you gonna lift it with your arms folded tight?

A third song, "The Suburbs," takes yet another musical approach to the theme of suburban decline, beginning with a folksy, lighthearted groove with acoustic guitars and piano, reminiscent of some country-rock recordings of the 1970s. The initial charm of the "good ol' days," skip-along-the-sidewalk soundtrack begins to fade, however, as the singer narrates a dream of his childhood, with his friends "still screamin' and runnin' through the yard," and moves on to the subsequent collapse of "all of the houses they built in the seventies," capped with the bleak refrain "it meant nothin' at all." Trapped in the suburbs and seeking a way out, the singer asks if we can understand

Why I want a daughter while I'm still young
I wanna hold her hand
And show her some beauty
Before this damage is done

By the time "The Suburbs" segues into the following track, the texture of the music has gradually become more complex and layered, with the falsetto chorus singing a refrain over a continuous bed of strings— "Sometimes I can't believe it, I'm movin' past the feeling . . . in my dreams we're still screaming." Toward the very end we hear a melancholy guitar riff and some virtuoso *Sgt. Pepper*–style melodic runs on the violins, half-buried in the texture, and bathed in studio reverb that gives the impression of a vast, desolated space, a dying community.

Whatever the future of alternative rock—and of the whole concept of the "alternative" within the music industry—Arcade Fire's heady mix of rock concert theatrics and musical versatility, and their drive to explore both the diversity of music and the social and philosophical dilemmas faced by their generation, support the prediction that new voices and perspectives will continue to enrich rock music in the years to come.

ROCK AROUND THE WORLD

A final change in the rock landscape that is worth noting is the diminishing significance of national boundaries. For most of rock's history, the music, culture, and business of rock traditions have been clearly associated with specific countries, unless a special effort was being made to embrace an international audience. But in the twenty-first century several factors arose that changed that landscape substantially. First and most obviously, the rise of the Internet allowed music to travel around the world (and back!) instantaneously. Music hosted on websites in Ghana, Japan, and the United States is now equally accessible to anyone in the world. At the same time, as transnational corporations continued to buy and consolidate record companies, it became increasingly common for record companies themselves to be transnational. For a record company executive, introducing a musician to a new country could now be as easy as cc'ing one more person on their corporate emails. Finally, and largely as a result of the increase in transnational media and business, governments were motivated to see that their copyright and intellectual property laws were consistent with each other. While rock has been international since its inception, the changes of the first decade of the new millennium allowed the rock traditions of different countries to mix, blend, and reach new audiences at an unprecedented pace.

This story goes back to the very beginnings of rock 'n' roll, as the recordings of Bill Haley, Elvis Presley, and Chuck Berry found their way into record collections and radio broadcasts all around the world. Just as young musicians in Liverpool were listening intently to the Everly Brothers and Buddy Holly's Crickets, and Jamaican musicians in Kingston were making their own cover versions of Louis Jordan and Fats Domino songs, so, too, musicians in Eastern Europe, Asia, Oceania, Africa, and Latin America imitated and experimented with aspects of rock 'n' roll. The global distribution of American recordings and films—including *Blackboard Jungle*, the 1955 movie that forever associated rock 'n' roll with teenage delinquency, and Elvis Presley vehicles such as *Love Me Tender* (1956) and *Jailhouse Rock* (1957)—catalyzed the appearance of "cover bands" and imitation Elvii in cities all around the globe.

Perhaps the best-known example of an early rock 'n' roll star outside the Anglo-American orbit is Johnny Hallyday (1943–), the "French Elvis," who was a huge star both in France and in its former colonies in Africa, the Caribbean, and Southeast Asia, but who never made a serious dent on the American market. In Mexico, the reaction to Elvis-mania was double-edged—debuts of his films were publicly protested and attacked by the press and government as a symptom of cultural imperialism and the prospective "feminizing" of young Mexican men; while, at the same time, the Mexican record industry moved quickly to record local groups singing Spanish-language cover versions of *norteamericano* rock 'n' roll hits and marketed them under the heading *Rocanrol* (a business strategy encouraged by the high price of imports).

Johnny Laboriel, a member of the early *rocanrol* group Los Rebeldes del Rock (The Rebels of Rock, formed in 1958), has described his first encounter with rock 'n' roll records in Mexico City:

> The first time I heard rock 'n' roll was on the jukebox. We used to go to this ice-cream café, and it was there that we started to hear what

it was all about. I remember the first word I heard was "darling," but shouted out like this! . . . I started to sing rock 'n' roll. But I didn't know any English . . . [so] I used to sing to the girls, making up the words as I went along. (Zolov 1999: 66)

This process of translation involved making sense of the original lyrics—however well or poorly understood—in terms of local values and mores. A Spanish-language cover version of Little Richard's 1958 hit "Good Golly Miss Molly" by the Mexican *rocanrol* band <u>Los Teen Tops</u> (1959) featured both a new title (*La Plaga*, or "The Plague," evoking the infectious nature of rock 'n' roll) and toned-down lyrics:

Little Richard (1958)	Los Teen Tops (1959) [English translation]
Mama, Papa told me,	*My parents told me*
"Son, you better watch yourself,"	*To quit that rock 'n' roll*
If they knew about Miss Molly,	*"If we see you with that girl*
Have to watch my Pa myself!	*Your allowance is finished!"*

From the very beginning, then, young people in various parts of the world sought to make sense of rock 'n' roll in their own, culturally specific terms and to adapt the music (and the images and behaviors that accompanied it) to their own identities and aspirations.

Today the field of international rock music is vast and variegated, and we can only provide the briefest sketch of its dimensions. (All of the tracks discussed here are available at iTunes.com.) One thing that is readily apparent, no matter where you go, is the sheer range of musical expressions that comprise the category "rock." Fans overseas often develop a sense of the history of rock music and its many specialized subgenres that rivals or even surpasses that of aficionados in the United States and Europe, the *loci classici* of rock. Some of these distinctions among genres should be familiar: In Japan, for example, a stark ideological and stylistic distinction is drawn between artists working in the slick, commercial area of J-Pop, which dominates the Japanese market for mainstream popular music; and alternative rock groups like <u>Guitar Wolf</u>, whose track "Fujiyama Attack" (on the 2003 album *Jet Generation*) exemplifies the quintessence of punk attitude and sound, in the manner of the Sex Pistols and Los Angeles hardcore bands like X and the Black Flags. The issue of musical authenticity or "realness," so important in today's alternative music genres, is also ever-present on the global rock-scape. Take the case of <u>Panda</u> (also known as PXNDX), a Mexican alternative rock band who have been accused by critics of plagiarizing the music of North American bands like Green Day and Smashing Pumpkins. Former fans turned off by the group's appropriation of ideas from *norteamericano* alternative bands have even formed a self-styled "Anti-Panda" movement, creating web pages on Facebook and YouTube and showing up to jeer the band at concerts.

As we have seen, American rock musicians like Paul Simon have found inspiration in the rich musical traditions of South Africa; but this is only one side of a more complex story of interchange and influence. The South African progressive rock band BLK JKS ("Black Jacks"), for example, has created a style that incorporates the influences of Jimi Hendrix, Led Zeppelin, Jamaican dub, and local urban genres like *mbaqanga* and *maskanda* street guitar music. (Both of these genres, alongside the choral singing of Ladysmith Black Mambazo, were critical to the sensibility and success of the *Graceland* album.) Having signed with an American indie rock label in 2007, the BLK JKS' 2009 album, *After Robots,* reached Number 4 on *Billboard's* Top World Albums chart, led by the evocative song "Lakeside," which blends Hendrix-style lead guitar with the thumping dance groove of *mbaqanga* music.

Some international variants of rock music have resulted from the efforts of musicians to triangulate their love of rock with local musical roots that they either grew up with or are eager to recover from neglect. The recasting of rock instrumentation, style, and attitude within the framework of local traditions and cultural commitments takes myriad forms around the world. In Australia, for example, the band Yothu Yindi was among the first indigenous Australian

Yothu Yindi in 1998. AP Photo/Handout.

groups to play and record rock music. Yothu Yindi use traditional songs, instruments, and dances from Yirkalla, their natal community in northern Australia, and combine them with rock instrumentation, rhythmic patterns, and harmonies. Some of their compositions deal with traditional concerns and beliefs (including songs about the spirit figures that inhabit the Dreamtime, believed to be a kind of parallel universe that animates the everyday world), while others dwell on contemporary concerns, including racism, alcoholism, crime, and the politics of land ownership.

The song "Treaty," on the album *Tribal Voices* (1992), is a good example of this last theme, and of the powerful combination of traditional songs and texts with the style and sensibility of rock music. The structure of the main song, based upon regular four-measure phrases, is derived from rock music, while the text deals with a legal matter of enormous importance to Australian aboriginals, indigenous land rights:

> *Well, I heard it on the radio, and I saw it on the television*
> *Back in 1988, all those talking politicians*
> *Words are easy, words are cheap, much cheaper than our priceless land*
> *But promises can disappear, just like writing in the sand*

The song "Treaty" was composed by Yothu Yindi in collaboration with members of the white Australian band Midnight Oil—political activists in their own right—to protest the government's failure to honor its promises to indigenous Australians. While the basic form, chords, and rhythm of the song's verses and refrain ("Treaty yeah, treaty now!") are derived from rock music, the musicians in Yothu Yindi also created musical interludes that incorporate a musical genre they had grown up with as young men, called *djatpangarri*. The distinctive vocal timbre of the singing, the use of the *dijeridu*, a long wooden trumpet that has become a potent symbol of aboriginal identity, and the incorporation of lyrics in the Yolngu language, come together in "Treaty" to create a powerful fusion of the emotional drive and intensity of rock 'n' roll with the deep cultural resonances of traditional aboriginal music. This potent mix made "Treaty" an anthem for indigenous land rights activists and their allies and pushed both the song and the album *Tribal Voices* onto the Australian charts. (See http://www.yothuyindi.com/music/treaty.html.)

The international influence of rock sometimes runs much deeper than a simple engagement with the stylistic surfaces of the music itself. In particular, the relationship between rock and politics, which emerged so strongly in the United States during the 1960s, has made itself manifest in many international contexts. The so-called Mexican Woodstock, a festival held in Avándaro, a suburb of Mexico City, attracted some 300,000 fans in 1971. This demonstration of mass support for young musicians who were exploring themes of personal freedom analogous to those being explored by their North American counterparts led authorities to ban these musicians' music from the airways in Mexico for the next fifteen years. In East Germany, rock bands (including groups specializing in a unique blend of punk and cabaret music) played a critical role in articulating popular opposition to the communist regime before the fall of the Berlin Wall in 1989, and rockers played analogous and equally important roles in countries from Poland to Brazil.

Indonesia, the world's fourth most populous country, provides another interesting case study of the political associations and impacts of rock music. In 1964, the pioneering Indonesian rock 'n' roll band Koes Plus—six of whose albums have been ranked among the Top 40 of all time by *Rolling Stone Indonesia*—was jailed by the regime of then-President Sukarno for playing American-style music. When Sukarno's successor, General Suharto, seized power in 1967 his regime took the opposite tack, allowing an emerging rock music scene to flourish in Indonesia, part of an effort to improve relations with the United States government. By the 1970s, recordings of American and English artists such as the Beatles, Jimi Hendrix, the Doors, Led Zeppelin, the Rolling Stones, and Black Sabbath flooded Indonesia's radio waves, inspiring a generation of local rock bands.

However, the attitude of the Suharto regime toward rock music had long since soured by 1993, when a riot took place at a Metallica concert in the Indonesian capital of Jakarta, and the disturbance spread to surrounding neighborhoods. The riot was sparked by the frustration of Indonesian metal fans—mainly young men from the impoverished neighborhoods of Jakarta—who could not afford tickets to the event and stormed the police barricades surrounding the stadium. But the Metallica riot soon came to represent a broader set of political issues under Suharto's New Order government, leading them to ban live rock concerts for three years (see Baulch 2007).

Even on the Indonesian island of Bali, long a center of the global tourist trade renowned for the "timeless" aesthetic and ecological balance of its culture, rock music has played a role in local cultural politics. Here is Bangkal Kusuma, a Balinese anthropologist and activist, talking about the popularity of heavy metal music among Balinese youth (as quoted in Baulch and Bangkal 1994):

> Another thing is the young people who are expressing their anger through their love of heavy metal music. In a way, this is a global phenomenon among youth, but in Bali it has a special meaning. Previously, the trance dance was very much a part of youth culture, and used by young people as a channel for venting anger. This is a part of youth culture which is no longer fulfilled because they feel so fed up and critical with constant ritualization, they need an alternative channel to express their anger. I think the popularity of Metallica for Balinese youth reveals a deep disillusionment with

> tourism development, and its failure to ensure them bright futures and jobs. Also they are angry at being told how to be Balinese: to fit in with the tourist image you should have a cute smile, be submissive and exotic. They don't want that!

This is an instructive example, in that it highlights the difficulty of predicting the meanings that rock may hold for listeners in different cultural contexts. Sometimes rock has been viewed negatively as the cultural vanguard of American (or Western) imperialism and a deadly threat to local traditions. In other cases, the revolutionary potential of rock music—an association forged in the United States during the 1960s—has supported the efforts of activists in various countries to protest political oppression and censorship. Sometimes rock music symbolizes teen rebellion, but the consumption of rock has also sometimes functioned as a mechanism for cultural conformity, like buying imported sneakers or cosmetics. The plain truth is that the meaning of rock— like the meaning of all music—is a matter of interpretation, a process that is itself influenced by the expectations and values one has formed growing up as a member of a particular society. In seeking to understand the global impact of rock music we should keep in mind that the meanings we may ascribe to a recording by Elvis Presley, Prince, Metallica, Jay-Z, or Pearl Jam may or may not be shared by people who have grown up in cultural settings different from our own. Whatever the specific meanings of the music for listeners and musicians worldwide, however, there is no denying rock's continuing global impact.

Finally, we should mention the important role that rock music has sometimes played in the experience of immigrants, both in the United States and abroad. Many migrants face a dual challenge—how to maintain a connection with deep cultural roots that may lie many thousands of miles away while at the same time adapting to one's new circumstances and creating a cosmopolitan, modern identity. Music is one way that we can publicly "broadcast" our identity to others, through our association with certain genres and performers. This process often involves blending or juxtapositioning of traditional and popular musical styles, texts, and performance techniques.

A case in point is <u>Gogol Bordello</u>, a self-styled "transcultural rock band" based in New York City. The band's leader and lead singer, Eugene Hütz, was born in Ukraine and lived as a refugee in Poland, Hungary, Austria, and Italy before moving to the United States in 1993. Hütz's cultural background and his experience of being an "outsider" shaped the hybrid sound of Gogol Bordello's music, which fuses aspects of punk rock, reggae, Slavic folk music, the music of the nomadic Rom people ("Gypsies"), an Arabic popular style called *rai* music, and Spanish *flamenco* guitar, all played on a mixture of rock instruments and Eastern European wedding band instruments. The band's concerts include wild stage shows influenced by the cabaret style of German playwright Bertolt Brecht and the Afro-futurist vision of George Clinton's Parliament-Funkadelic. (One

Gogol Bordello—shot of their home page (excluding tour info) www.gogolbordello.com.

typically surrealist Gogol Bordello concert portrayed the story of a band of super-powered immigrant Ukrainian vampires.)

As of this writing, the members of Gogol Bordello include immigrants from Russia, Israel, Ethiopia, Ecuador, and Hong Kong (via Scotland). This is quite literally a band that would not exist were it not for globalization. Originally called *Hütz and the Béla Bartóks*, in honor of the great Hungarian composer, they soon decided to change their name because (as Hütz himself put it) "nobody knows who the hell Béla Bartók is in the United States" (Elliott 2006). Gogol Bordello started their career in 1999 playing at immigrant weddings on the Lower East Side of Manhattan. The band soon developed a following among alternative music and punk fans, alongide the other segment of Gogol Bordello's loyal audience, Russian Ukrainian and Romanian immigrants, whose traditions of musical appreciation sometimes involved the smashing of plates. Their fifth album, *Trans-Continental Hustle* (2010), was produced by hip-hop pioneer Rick Rubin, who had helped to launch the careers of Run-D.M.C., the Beastie Boys, and Public Enemy. *Trans-Continental Hustle* reached Number 12 on *Billboard*'s Top Independent Albums chart and Number 19 on the Top Rock Albums chart in 2010, driven by politically charged, high-energy tracks like "Immigraniada (We Comin' Rougher)" (see discussion on pages 366–367).

HIP-HOP IN THE EARLY TWENTY-FIRST CENTURY

As rock's dominance of popular music declined, much of its previous audience was claimed by hip-hop. And as hip-hop became more mainstream and lucrative, the genre was faced with the same paradox that had challenged rock in the early seventies: How could the voice of the underdog become culturally dominant without losing the rebellious spirit that made it appealing in the first place? Hip-hop attempted to answer this question in three ways.

The first was to emphasize the character of the "hustler," a person who works hard to become successful in an underground economy (legal, illegal, or somewhere in between). The hustler concept combined the outlaw appeal and street credibility of the gangster with the materialism and work ethic of the self-made millionaire. Conveniently, it also made the issue of "selling out" moot. If the main theme of your music was entrepreneurialism, then getting rich was not a betrayal of your principles but a fulfillment of them. This theme soon became more than a subject for lyrics: As a philosophy, it opened the door for rappers to develop clothing lines, video games, energy drinks, and even signature brands of liquor at the exact moment when recording income was plummeting across the music industry. Leading proponents of this approach included Shawn "Jay-Z" Carter, and the previously mentioned Marion "Suge" Knight and Sean "P. Diddy" Combs.

A second answer to hip-hop's dilemma was to embrace the rock star paradigm in much the same way that the original rock stars had: to accept the idea that economic success was a key to artistic freedom. (See Chapter 7.) Eminem and Kanye West can be seen as exponents of this school of thought.

A third approach was essentially to ignore the boundary between hip-hop, rock, and pop music, an approach that became increasingly relevant as the previous economic and marketing pressures that had maintained those boundaries began to break down. Outkast is a good example of this approach.

Jay-Z

As one of the leading figures in hip-hop in the new millennium, it is not surprising that Shawn "Jay-Z" Carter (b. 1969) embodied the role of the "hustler" more thoroughly, and in more diverse venues, than any other figure. Jay-Z's first album, *Reasonable Doubt* (1996), painted a detailed picture of the life of a Brooklyn drug dealer, over hard-edged, jazz-influenced beats. The mere sound of Jay-Z's music sent an intrinsic message about both his roots in Brooklyn and his intention to leverage those experiences to rule the world of popular music. Following a traditionalist model of complex lyrics over sample-based beats,

🎧 LISTENING TO (AND WATCHING) "IMMIGRANIADA (WE COMIN' ROUGHER)"

The music video version of "Immigraniada" (available on YouTube), shot in the predominantly Mexican American neighborhood of East Los Angeles, opens with a quotation from President Franklin D. Roosevelt—"Remember always, that all of us, and you and I especially, are descended from immigrants"—which gradually fades into a grainy black-and-white image of two immigrant parents and a child standing with their backs to us, looking at the Statue of Liberty. We hear the plaintive sound of a ferry boat's horn, while blood-red pigment drips onto the image, forming a splatter-map of the United States. Next we see Eugene Hütz running into traffic to wash the windows of passing cars. The music track opens with an up-tempo reggae-derived rhythm played on acoustic guitar, electric bass, and drums, and then shifts abruptly into a fast groove perfectly designed to encourage listeners to pogo (a vigorous, up-and-down dance style that is most closely associated with punk rock).

Hütz sings the song's title phrase ("immigrada, immigradiana") over this groove while peering intently at us through the windshield, as his squeegee wipes away the grime. As he launches into the song's impassioned refrain ("We're coming rougher every time . . ."), we see a rapid-fire succession of old photographs and film footage of immigrants entering America. We then encounter a series of video portraits of contemporary immigrants from Germany, Puerto Rice, Denmark, and Ecuador, their countries of origin mapped in the blood-red pigment seen earlier.

The scene shifts to a Hispanic neighborhood, where Hütz greets the Ecuadorian immigrant worker (a member of the band), and then to a small office, where he asks the thuggish owner of a sub–minimum wage "sweat shop" clothing factory for a job. The first verse of the song is sung by Hütz as he unrolls and cuts huge bales of cloth:

> In corridors full of tear gas...
> Like deleted scenes from Kafka...

As the video continues, we see close-up portraits of more members of Gogol Bordello, immigrants from Mexico, Russia, China, and Ukraine, and the *mise-en-scène* suddenly switches from the sweat shop to a claustrophobic steam-filled restaurant kitchen, where Hütz and his colleagues sing as they bus and wash dishes and mop the floors:

> Frozen eyes, sweaty back...
> All my life I pack, unpack...

The scene shifts one final time, to a backyard party in an East Los Angeles neighborhood, the transition marked by a reverb-drenched surf-rock guitar solo, reminiscent of the music of "spaghetti westerns" from the mid-1960s. For the first time we see the band rocking out together, surrounded by an appreciative audience, and hear sinuous Eastern European violin and accordion melodies intertwining with the insistent beat of punk rock—a gray-bearded Russian fiddler, a young female musician of Asian descent, a pink-Mohawked American drummer, and a shaggy, pogoing Ukrainian singer joining forces to create a shared, visceral expression of the frustrations and dreams of immigrants in the United States.

It's a video we always wanted to make, because it completes our story. It's very autobiographical, and tells a story about eight people who are all immigrants, who came to pursue something in New York City. That's our biography. But on the other hand, like it coincides with the idealistic belief that people shall always be free to choose the place of their residence. This ties in to the whole movement of worldwide citizenship. . . .

All the scenes in the video, starting with me washing cars, are all autobiographical experiences. I was a car washer once. And when we shot the video, hey, I made some money that day, polishing my old skills. . . . We kind of wanted to take the viewer through a day of and the tasks of the immigrant community, exactly as it is, including all of the nitty-gritty side and including the solidarity of immigrants [at] the party . . . where we as representatives of the Russian community go to East LA, to the Latino neighborhoods there, and make a party for kids with our trans-cultural music. (http://boingboing .net/2010/09/ 16/gogol-bordello-immig .html)

It is difficult to think of a more evocative example of music's potential to create bridges between people distant in cultural background and experience. Whatever one's ultimate position on the issue of immigration, cosmopolitan rock musicians like Gogol Bordello, whose lives have been impacted for better and worse by the experience of mobility and the forces of globalization, enjoy a unique ability to connect their deep cultural *roots* to the transnational *routes* that have shaped their lives, alongside millions of other migrants.

Jay-Z presented himself as a narrator of street stories, often even inserting a distinctive chuckle into his rhymes, as if observing his characters' tribulations from a distance.

But Jay-Z didn't only draw upon his youthful underworld experiences as a source of true crime stories; he also used them as the foundation of a business paradigm. From his earliest days as a musician, his career was as much about making deals as it was about making records. In an earlier era of hip-hop, this may have been viewed as a contradiction. But since the pursuit of wealth was actually a central theme of his music, Jay-Z's business acumen was viewed by fans as a sign of authenticity, not compromise. In fact, that very first album, *Reasonable Doubt,* was released on Rocafella Records, an independent label that he had founded with partner Damon Dash. In 1997, he released his second album, *In My Lifetime, Vol. 1*, and quickly followed it with *Vol. 2 . . . Hard Knock Life* in 1998, also released on his own label. These albums kept him at the forefront of hip-hop music, continuing

Jay-Z performing in 2001. Photo by KMazur/WireImage.

to explore the relationship between the street and the boardroom at precisely the moment that hip-hop in general was being confronted with the apparent contradictions of its own success.

In 1999, Rocafella spawned its own clothing line, Rocawear, constituting Jay-Z's first serious nonmusical business enterprise. Jay-Z's move into the world of fashion was not unusual for hip-hop artists in this era, who increasingly drew on other elements of the culture to build alternative revenue streams to supplement their surprisingly meager recording income. (In addition to all of the normal economic pitfalls faced by pop musicians, hip-hop artists often had to give up a major portion of their royalties due to sample clearance.) But Jay-Z was among the first to see his business interests as more than an adjunct to his music career. He took them extremely seriously, as evidenced by the fact that Rocawear was ultimately sold in 2007 for $204 million. (See http:// www. nytimes.com/2007/03/07/business/07clothes.html.) Largely influenced by Jay-Z and the Wu-Tang Clan (who also had their own clothing line, Wu-Wear), this approach became increasingly typical of hip-hop, as artists began to view themselves as brands that could be leveraged in the worlds of clothing, sports drinks, and video games. After releasing four more albums in as many years, Jay-Z announced his retirement from recording in 2003 (though he would return in 2006). The following year, he became president and CEO of Def Jam Recordings (bringing Rocafella under their corporate umbrella), as well as part owner of the New Jersey Nets. In 2009, he left Def Jam to form his own label, Roc Nation. In both his music and his business dealings, Jay-Z continues to be an icon of the contemporary rap industry, forging new paths to economic and artistic success.

Kanye West

Kanye West (b. 1977) moved from Chicago to Brooklyn in 2000 to begin his career as a producer for Jay-Z's Rocafella Records. In that capacity, he developed a signature sound based largely on sampling soul hits of the sixties and seventies, an approach that had fallen out of favor in the mid-nineties. In that sense, West's style was itself an indicator of hip-hop's longevity; it was widely viewed as having a "retro" element in both its sound and its style. West produced many of the biggest hits of the early 2000s, including Jay-Z's "Takeover" and "Izzo," Alicia Keys's "You Don't Know My Name," Talib Kweli's "Get By," Beyoncé's "'03 Bonnie & Clyde," and Ludacris's "Stand Up."

In 2004, he emerged as an artist in his own right, releasing his acclaimed first solo album *College Dropout*. Although many at the time questioned his skills as an MC, he was eventually embraced both for the quality of his beats, which was expected, and the highly introspective nature of his lyrics, which was not. "We all self-conscious, I'm just the first to admit it," he rhymed on the song "All Fall Down," in a startling departure from typical rap braggadocio.

As the decade progressed, West established himself as a pop culture icon, becoming known for public outbursts and incidents that would make any seventies rock star envious, including going off-script to criticize then-president George Bush at a telethon for victims of Hurricane Katrina, and jumping onstage to interrupt Taylor Swift's acceptance speech for Best Female Video at the 2009 MTV Video Music Awards. But—in true rock star fashion—these incidents were presented as part of an overall grandiosity that was intimately linked to his artistic output. His fifth album, *My Beautiful Dark Twisted Fantasy* (2010)—a rock album title if ever there was one—explores themes of fame, alienation,

Kanye West in "The Truth Tour 2004." Photo by Frank Micelotta/Getty Images.

and self-doubt. As the online site AV Club noted: "The darkly funny, boldly introspective, and characteristically fame-obsessed *Fantasy* is . . . a rock album in spirit (and sometimes sound) with an unimpeachable commitment to sex, drugs, and electric guitars" (see the November 23, 2010 posting by Nathan Rabin).

Eminem

Another artist who embodied the increasingly blurred line between rock and hip-hop at this time was Marshall "Eminem" Mathers (b. 1972). Coming to prominence in 1999 with *The Slim Shady LP*, an expanded major-label re-release of an earlier independent album, Eminem was the first white rapper to enjoy substantial mainstream success while also being accepted by the hip-hop community. While initially this was largely due to the credibility he gained by being produced by Dr. Dre (of N.W.A.), it quickly became clear that Eminem was a skilled and dedicated hip-hop artist in his own right. Particularly impressive were Eminem's extraordinary rhythmic sensibility and ability to use the *sound* of his words as musical elements. He was also adept at the use of compound rhymes, a skill he attributed to the influence of underground

New York emcees such as Lord Finesse and Big L. In his lyrics, Eminem explored his own identity and experiences in a way that connected with multiple demographics simultaneously. Rather than renouncing his whiteness, he embraced it as a symbol of working-class mid-western anxiety. The reality of that equation for a huge segment of American society is something that had rarely, if ever, been addressed in hip-hop music.

Eminem's ability to be both a rap and rock star simultaneously was aided tremendously by the fact that he was one of the first—arguably *the* first—rapper to be consistently played on rock radio, a fact that would be hard to attribute to anything other than his race. At the same time, Eminem's music did embrace intensely personal themes that were unusual for hip-hop. The idea that pop music should serve in a sense as therapy for the artist, as a way to exorcise his most intimate demons, was something that was much more closely associated with rock music—and the "rock star" approach—than it was with hip-hop. In a larger sense, the question of the degree to which Eminem drew on hip-hop approaches as compared to rock is beside the point. What's important is that it seemed not to matter either to him or to his fans. His ability to ignore those genre boundaries yet still be

Eminem performing at the 2002 MTV Video Music Awards. Photo by Kevin Kane/WireImage.

successful is, of course, a reflection of his personal talent and skill in positioning himself culturally, but it is also reflective of the decreasing significance of these boundaries in the first place. In other words, at the start of the twenty-first century, the question is not "Is Eminem a rock artist or a rap artist?" The question is, "Who cares?"

Outkast

A similar ability to cross genre boundaries can be seen in the career of <u>Outkast</u>. As hip-hop continued to expand, the Southern United States—and particularly Atlanta, Georgia—became an increasingly important center for hip-hop music. Geographically removed from the music industry centers of New York and Los Angeles, Southern rappers tended to be signed to artist-owned independent labels, and they often created performance and promotional infrastructures to support their own local "scenes" as well, much in the same way that punk rock musicians had done in the eighties. In short, they knew how to be successful without the help of the mainstream music industry. This, somewhat ironically, made them very attractive to major labels in the late 1990s, since most of the groundwork had already been done. The labels simply had to buy in to a musical system that was already successful. Even as the music industry itself began to falter in the 2000s, these more independent groups remained relatively secure, since they were not dependent on the mainstream music industry in the first place.

For that reason—and also as a result of the diminishing significance of genre boundaries in the music industry generally—southern rap artists often expanded their stylistic approach beyond the conventional margins of what had previously been considered hip-hop. Southern hip-hop artists embraced over-the-top personas that seemed to recall seventies funk and stadium rock attitudes more than the "street reporter" authenticity of a previous generation of hip-hop MCs. Southern hip-hop also became increasingly reliant on the use of live instrumentation (as opposed to sampling) during this era. At the same time, it became common to combine singing and rapping in various ways on hip-hop recordings. Southern rappers embraced everything from duets between singers and rappers, to individual performers alternating between singing and rapping on the same song, to vocal styles that, in themselves, straddled the line between singing and rapping. Outkast, who released their first record in the nineties but achieved their greatest popularity at the turn of the century, is an example of this approach to hip-hop.

The duo of <u>Andre "Andre 3000" Benjamin</u> and <u>Antwan "Big Boi" Patton</u>—known collectively as Outkast—first came to public prominence in 1994, with the release of their first album, *Southernplayalisticadillacmuzik*. Part of the larger Dungeon Family collective, which included other Atlanta-based groups such as Goodie Mob, Joi, and the Organized Noize production team among others, Outkast forged a distinctive sound that combined social and political

Outkast performing in 2003. Photo by Frank Micelotta/Getty Images.

commentary with a freewheeling party feel and funk-influenced sound. On their subsequent albums *ATLiens* (1996*)*, *Aquemini* (1998), and *Stankonia* (2000), they continued to experiment with combining live instruments and samples, and they also mixed rhyming and singing. Their next album, *Speakerboxxx/The Love Below* (2003), was actually a pair of solo albums (one from each partner), packaged together as an Outkast double album. (It is worth noting that this strategy had been pioneered by the rock band Kiss, who released solo albums by all four of its members on the same day in 1978.) The album was Number 1 on the *Billboard* charts for seven weeks, ultimately sold over five million copies, and won the 2004 Grammy for Record of the Year. The fact that *Speakerboxxx/ The Love Below* was recognized by the Grammys outside of the rap category is significant, in that it demonstrates that rap artists were now seen as mainstream pop musicians.

The song begins with Andre 3000 "counting off" the rhythm, as one would do in a live situation to make sure that all members of the band start playing at the same time. Since the song is a studio creation made with multiple overdubs, this serves no practical purpose, other than to reference the *idea* of a live band. This gesture is followed by the first twenty-four-bar verse, and a series of lyrics

🎧 LISTENING TO (AND WATCHING) "HEY YA"

"**H**ey Ya" was the lead single from *The Love Below*, the Andre 3000 half of *Speakerboxxx/The Love Below*. Though credited to Outkast, it is essentially an Andre 3000 solo record. In spite of the fact that it was recorded by a hip-hop artist, "Hey Ya" is not a rap song by any reasonable definition of the term; for one thing, it contains no rapping. Stylistically, the song draws most clearly from the rock and pop of the mid-1960s in its instrumentation, chord structure, lyrics, and rhythmic feel. This interpretation is also supported by the song's video (see the following discussion), which directly references the sixties. On the other hand, the song's aesthetic approach does show deep influences from the hip-hop tradition, particularly in its juxtaposition of elements from different eras of pop history. As an indicator of how this song broke the boundaries between rock, hip-hop, and pop,

it is noteworthy that "Hey Ya" made appearances on no less than *six* different *Billboard* charts (Hot 100, R&B/Hip-Hop, Pop, Radio, Alternative, and Adult Pop) and also won a Grammy for Best Urban/Alternative single. The fact that the song had such tremendous success in spite of being basically unclassifiable in terms of genre is a testament both to its broad appeal and to the decreasing significance of genre boundaries in the music industry overall.

"Hey Ya" is based on an unusual six-measure line, comprising three measures of four beats each, followed by one measure with two beats, followed by another two measures of four beats. Each verse is twenty-four measures long, consisting of four of these six-measure lines. The choruses and break are also twenty-four measures long and are based on the same metric and chord structure.

LISTENING CHART "HEY YA"
Music and lyrics by Andre Benjamin; performed by Outkast; recorded 2003

FORM		LYRICS	DESCRIPTIVE COMMENTS
Introduction	0.00	*1-2-3-uh!*	Spoken count-off, suggestive of a live band.
A: a a a a	0.01	*My baby don't . . .* *But does she really . . .* *Don't try to . . .* *Thank God for Mom and Dad . . .*	Verse 1; same melody for all lines.
B: b b b b	0.34	*Hey Ya . . . (4 times)*	Chorus; same chords as verse, but different melody.
A: a a a a	1.07	*You think you've . . .* *We get together . . .* *If what they say . . .* *So why you . . .*	Verse 2: same melody as Verse 1.
B: b b b b	1.40	*Hey Ya . . . (4 times)*	Chorus.
A: c c c c	2.14	*Alright now fellas . . .* *I said what's cooler . . .* *OK now ladies . . .* *Now I want to . . .*	Same chords but lyrics are replaced by spoken call and response.
BREAK: d d d d	2.47	*Shake it . . . (4 times)*	(Instruments drop out except for drums and synthesized bass).
B: b b b b		*Hey Ya . . . (4 times)*	Chorus.
Fade-out . . .			

sung to a repeated melody. The lyrics, in true pop fashion, reflect a narrator questioning the stability of the relationship he is in. The chorus, based on the same chords, simply repeats the nonsense syllables "Hey Ya" over and over again. While the lyrics in this section may not mean much, they are clearly not meant to. The goal of the chorus—as with almost all pop music—is to be a catchy "hook," and to say that it succeeds at this would be a vast understatement. The second verse continues to articulate the narrator's angst. As with the first verse, the contrast between the anxiety of the lyrics and free-spirited joy of the melody creates a feeling of ambiguity in the song overall.

The second iteration of the chorus is followed by a section that might or might not be considered a third verse. It features the same chords and instrumentation, but the sung lyrics of the first two verses are replaced by a spoken call-and-response section, in which Andre 3000 interacts with the "band" (portrayed by overdubbed versions of himself) in a style that is evocative of sixties and seventies soul artists, particularly James Brown.

This leads into a new section that also features the same chords, but this time the instrumentation is reduced to drums and synthesized bass. Such sections are often referred to in soul music as "breaks," and it was the breaks of the soul songs emulated here that provided the foundation of hip-hop itself. (See Chapter 8.) The lyrics to this section—variations on the phrase "Shake it like a Polaroid picture"—fulfill several functions at once. On one level, they are simply an encouragement to the listener to dance, or to "shake it." But on another level they are referencing the hip-hop practice of using "metaphors" (which technically are often similes) for comedic effect. In this case, the comparison is to the use of old-fashioned Polaroid instant cameras; when the picture emerged from the camera, users would commonly shake it to dry the developing chemicals. In the era of digital cameras, this technology is completely obsolete, which added to its "retro" charm as a lyrical element.

The break section is followed by a return of the chorus, at the end of which the song fades. It is notable that, despite the clear intention to imitate rock and pop song structures, there are no solos of any kind in this song. In that sense, it is more like a hip-hop song.

The video that was released to promote "Hey Ya" presents a band—notably called "The Love Below" rather than Outkast—performing on what appears to be an early-sixties British television show, setting up the performance as a kind of reverse British Invasion. The band comprises a drummer, lead singer, keyboard player, acoustic guitar player, and three identically dressed backup singers, all of whom are played by Andre Benjamin via digital technology. This would be a slightly strange instrumentation for a real band, particularly the lack of electric guitar. On a more general level, the idea of a "one-man band" associates the performance with a hip-hop approach to music production.

The performance itself is presented anachronistically. In an early backstage scene, the band's manager is seen holding a huge, eighties-era cell phone, while the show itself is presented as being broadcast over mid-sixties style black-and-white television (sixties-style television cameras can be seen in wide shots). The band and audience (mainly screaming Beatles-style fans) are dressed in fashions associated with the late sixties and early seventies, with the exception of the three backup singers, who are inexplicably dressed as jockeys. A family, seen dancing together at home in front of the television, are also dressed in late-sixties fashions. Taken as a whole, the video paints a picture of Andre 3000 as living within a kind of genre-less pop music heaven in which the Beatles, Motown, James Brown, and early-eighties hip-hop coexist in an eternity beyond time, which is as good a metaphor as any for the general approach that Outkast has brought to popular music in the new millennium.

CONCLUSIONS

The artists and trends we've explored in this chapter demonstrate how profoundly rock has changed in last ten years. In the early twenty-first century, the Internet and other technological and cultural innovations presented the music business with challenges and with opportunities. As creative people always have, rock musicians embraced both. While there is no question that music and creativity will survive, the form in which they will be expressed remains in flux. As rock increasingly mixes with other genres, business models, and audiences, can it continue as a coherent genre? Or will it merge with other musical forms and approaches to create new, unforeseen musical styles and techniques? Only time will tell.

PATTERNS IN ROCK HISTORY

T he history of rock can be compared to a river with many tributaries, currents, and eddies. Its headwaters flow from the mid-1950s recordings of rock 'n' roll pioneers such as Bill Haley, Chuck Berry, and Elvis Presley; on through the musical and social experimentation of the late 1960s; emptying into the relatively sedate waters of corporate rock in the 1970s and '80s; and delivering us at last into the turbulent but exciting era of digital production, Internet distribution, economic transformation, and globalization.

In this survey of the history of rock music we have encountered visionary artists and brilliant promoters, copycats and charlatans, hustlers and saints. We have paid close attention to the development of the music business, including the continual struggle (and occasional collaboration) between huge entertainment corporations and the smaller, independent producers that have played such a critical role in introducing new styles and performers into the marketplace. We have traced the ways in which this complex relationship has been accompanied by a persistent tension between "mainstream" and "alternative" impulses in rock music and in popular musical taste. And we have been accompanied on our journey by the ever-changing audience for rock, beginning with the creation of the teenager-as-consumer in the 1950s; the transformation of that social category into the so-called baby boom generation that dominated popular taste and buying patterns beginning in the late 1960s; and the subsequent rise of Generations X, Y, and Z, the Internet generation.

At this point, rock's history is so long and diverse that it is virtually impossible to draw any conclusions about it that would be applicable to all of rock and yet also specific enough to be meaningful. It is, however, possible to trace the general shape of that history and make some generalizations about the *kinds* of forces that led the history to unfold the way it did.

Rock 'n' roll split off from rhythm and blues in the mid-1950s due to a unique combination of cultural, economic, and artistic factors. As it began to take on its own distinctive identity in the late fifties and early sixties, the mainstream music industry tried to reintegrate it into existing business models, particularly those that made a clear distinction between singers and songwriters. This, in turn, provoked a backlash from those who valued rock's estrangement from previous styles. As we have seen, those holding this belief had many different reasons for doing so, each of which forged a different path for rock in the sixties. As the sixties wore on, new cultural influences, new technologies, and new media opportunities led to an increasing tendency to view rock more as an artistic calling than as a job in the entertainment industry. In the early seventies this "art for art's sake" view was itself integrated into the music industry through the concept of the rock star. The system that developed in the seventies—arguably a perfect balance between art and commerce—came to define rock for more than three decades. In the new millennium, though, changes in technology made many aspects of the rock business obsolete, which in turn deeply altered the economic foundation on which its artistic principles rested. Whether rock will survive this latest challenge largely depends on how the idea of rock itself is defined. In any case, there are several generalizations we can draw from this history.

First, rock's artistic and economic history is deeply connected to the demographics of its audience. Generational identity, ethnicity, age, gender, class, and even country of origin have each deeply influenced the nature of rock culture in multiple ways. Generationally, rock has been largely associated with baby boomers. Since they were teenagers when rock 'n' roll emerged, this has led to a somewhat bifurcated approach to the genre's demographic identity, with one strain following the baby boomers' changing perspectives as they aged and the other catering to successive generations of teens and young adults as they came along. Ethnicity and race have also been important factors in the way rock was defined at various points in its history. It is significant, however, that the specific meanings that race and ethnicity have carried in rock have changed many times over the genre's history. In other words, rather than make a consistent argument about the nature of such identities, rock seems to serve more as a *venue* in which these arguments can be made. Similarly, while ideas of class and gender have been central to the way rock has been defined over the last half-century, there is little agreement as to the nature of the specific relationship that they each have to rock culture overall. As with race and ethnicity, many would argue that that is not a weakness on rock's part but a strength: It provides a space for artists and fans to explore their individual and collective identities.

A second generalization we may make is that, once the general principles of rock were established, many of the changes that came about over the years stemmed from a kind of pendulum swing between a philosophy that saw rock as art (where the artists' primary responsibility is to express their inner feelings) and one that saw rock as entertainment (where the artists' primary responsibility is to satisfy their fans). Throughout rock's history one view or the other has become dominant, only to be overturned by a swing back in the other direction. Since each moment of dominance spawned multiple rebellions (many of which were at odds with one another), each change resulted in a variety of new options. To offer one of many threads in this pattern: The commercialism of the early sixties' Brill Building approach was dethroned by the artistic experimentation of the late sixties and early seventies, which was then overtaken by the commercialism of stadium rock and disco in the seventies, which were in turn besieged by punk rock and hip-hop in the eighties, and so on.

Third, regardless of which end of the spectrum a given movement occupied, all were ultimately facilitated by some kind of relationship between art and commerce. There is a tendency within certain rock ideologies to see the music industry as a constraining and exploitative force that is almost by nature opposed to rock musicians' most innovative artistic impulses. While this is often true in specific cases, it should also be clear from the preceding pages that—for better or worse—many of rock's most important developments would not have happened without economic opportunities and cultural systems that were created in the service of business interests. This does not mean that musicians simply did what businesspeople wanted; in many cases they did the exact opposite. But they still used resources that were made available to them by those relationships.

Finally, part of what motivated rock's development over time was a tension between songwriting and performing that has remained in force to the present day. This tension was an outgrowth of the way the music business developed in the pre-rock era, combined with an unwillingness or inability of the business to change when rock culture emerged. For much of rock's history, as we have discussed, this tension was harnessed into a system that made a virtue of these discrepancies. At the time of this writing, however, that entire system seems to be falling apart. What—if anything—will replace it remains to be seen.

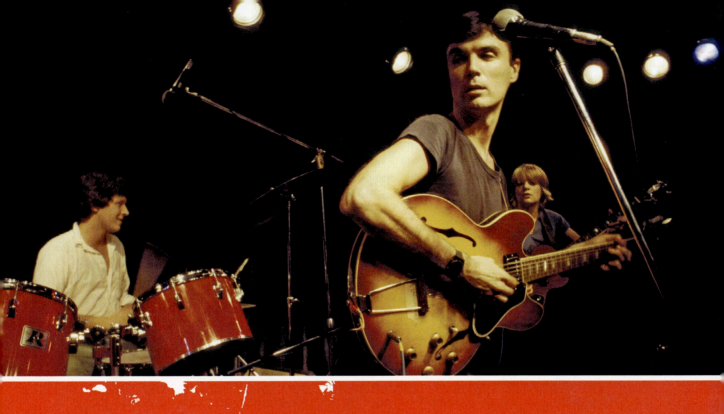

GLOSSARY

This glossary consists of terms requiring specialized definitions that recur throughout the book. Such terms appear in the text in **boldface** when they are first used.

a cappella Vocal singing that involves no instrumental accompaniment.

A&R Abbreviation for "artists and repertoire." This is the department of a record company whose responsibility it is to discover and cultivate new musical talent and to find material for the artists to perform—naturally, with an eye toward commercial potential. As many artists today write and record their own material, the latter function of A&R has atrophied to some extent.

arranger A person who adapts (or arranges) the melody and chords of a song to exploit the capabilities and instrumental resources of a particular musical ensemble. For example, a simple pop tune originally written for voice and piano may be arranged for a jazz "big band" with many horns and a rhythm section.

ballad A type of song consisting usually of verses set to a repeating melody (see **strophic** form) in which a story, often romantic, historic, or tragic, is sung in narrative fashion.

blue notes Expressive notes or scalar inflections found primarily in blues and jazz music. The blue notes derive from African musical practice; although they do not correspond exactly to the Western system of **major** and **minor** scales, it is helpful to imagine them as "flatter" or "lower" versions of the scale degrees to which they are related, and thus one speaks of "blue" thirds, fifths, and sevenths.

blues A genre of music originating principally from the field hollers and work songs of rural blacks in the southern United States during the latter half of the nineteenth century. Themes treated by blues lyrics included the oppressive conditions suffered by African Americans; love gone wrong; alienation; misery; and the supernatural. The lyrics are often obscured by a coded, metaphorical language. The music of the blues is rich in Africanisms and earthy rhythms. Originally an acoustic music, the blues moved to the urban north in the mid-twentieth century, becoming electrified in the process.

bridge A passage consisting of new, contrasting material that serves as a link between repeated sections of melodic material. A bridge is sometimes called a **release** (see discussion of Tin Pan Alley song form in Chapter 1).

cadence A melodic or harmonic event that signals the end of a musical line or section, or of the piece as a whole.

call and response A characteristic feature of much African American music, in which musical forces alternate with one another, usually in quick succession: a solo singer with a chorus or backing group; sung lines with guitar or band passages; an instrumental solo with a larger instrumental group; and so forth. This form of expression has spread to many musical styles and genres but is a characteristically African phenomenon in its origins and so is most associated in America with African American expression.

chord The simultaneous sounding of different pitches.

chorus A repeating section within a song consisting of a fixed melody *and* lyric that is repeated exactly each time it occurs, typically following one or more verses.

coda The "tail end" of a musical composition, typically a brief passage after the last complete section that serves to bring the piece to its conclusion.

composer A person who creates a piece of music. Although the term may be, and often is, used to describe the creators of popular songs, it is more commonly applied to those who create more extended, formally notated works of music.

conjunto Spanish term for a musical group or ensemble, used widely in Latin America (e.g., Cuba and Mexico).

counterculture A subculture existing in opposition to and espousing values contrary to that of the dominant culture. The term is most often used to describe the values and lifestyle of young people during the late 1960s and early 1970s (see Chapter 10).

counterpoint The sounding of two independent melodic lines or voices against one another.

cover version The term "cover" or "cover version" refers to a performance of a song other than that regarded as the "original" version ("original" usually because it preceded all others, and sometimes because of its direct association with the creator(s) of the song).

dissonance A harsh or grating sound. (The perception of dissonance is culturally conditioned. For example, the smaller intervals employed in certain Asian and Middle Eastern musics may sound "out of tune" and dissonant to Western ears; within their original context, however, they are regarded as perfectly consonant.)

distortion A buzzing, crunchy, or "fuzzy" tone color originally achieved by overdriving the vacuum tubes of a guitar amplifier. This effect can be simulated today by solid state and digital sound processors. Distortion is often heard in a hard rock or heavy metal context.

DJ Disc jockey (deejay); one who plays recordings (as on a radio program).

feedback Technically, an out-of-control sound oscillation that occurs when the output of a loudspeaker finds its way back into a microphone or electric instrument pickup and is reamplified, creating a sound loop that grows in intensity and continues until deliberately broken. Although feedback can be difficult to manage, it becomes a powerful expressive device in the hands of certain blues and rock musicians, most notably the guitarist Jimi Hendrix. Feedback can be recognized as a "screaming" or "crying" sound.

groove Term originally employed by jazz, rhythm & blues, and funk musicians to describe the channeled flow of swinging, "funky," or "phat" rhythms.

hook A "catchy" or otherwise memorable musical phrase or pattern.

lyricist A person who supplies a poetic text (lyrics) to a piece of vocal music; not necessarily the composer.

major Refers to one of the two scale systems central to Western music (see **minor**); a major scale is arranged in the following order of whole- and half-step intervals: 1-1-½-1-1-1-½ (This pattern is easy to see if one begins at the pitch C on the piano keyboard and plays the next seven white notes in succession, which yields the C major scale: CDEFGABC.) A song is said to be in a major tonality or key if it uses melodies and chords that are constructed from the major scale. Of course, a song may (and frequently does) "borrow" notes and chords from outside a particular major scale, and it may "modulate" or shift from key to key within the course of the song.

melisma One syllable of text spread out over many musical tones.

minor Refers to one of the two scale systems central to Western music (see **major**); a minor scale is arranged in the following order of whole- and half-step intervals: 1-½-1-1-½-1-1. (This pattern represents the so-called natural minor scale, often found in blues and blues-based popular music; it is easy to see if one begins at the pitch A on the piano keyboard and plays the next seven white notes in succession, which yields the A minor scale: ABCDEFGA. The two other minor scales in common usage—the melodic minor and harmonic minor scales—have ascending and descending forms that differ somewhat from the natural minor scale.) A song is said to be in a minor tonality or key if it uses melodies and chords that are constructed from the minor scale. Of course, a song may (and frequently does) "borrow" notes and chords from outside a particular minor scale, and it may "modulate" or shift from key to key within the course of the song. In comparison to the major scale, the minor scale is often described as having a "sad" or "melancholy" sound.

montuno Spanish term for a formal section within a performance of Afro-Cuban dance music (such as a rumba, mambo, or salsa). The montuno, generally the second half of a given piece, alternates a fixed vocal refrain (the *coro*) with a solo vocal improvisation (the **pregón**) and may also include instrumental solos.

MP3 A variant of the MPEG compression system, which allows sound files to be compressed to as little as one-twelfth of their original size.

payola The illegal and historically widespread practice of offering money or other inducements to a radio station or deejay in order to ensure the prominent airplay of a particular recording.

polyrhythm The simultaneous sounding of rhythms in two or more contrasting meters, such as three against two, or

five against four. Polyrhythms are found in abundance in African and Asian musics and their derivatives.

pregón Spanish term for "announcement." In Afro-Cuban music pregón refers to 1) an improvised vocal solo based on the cries of street vendors, or 2) the improvised solo part in call-and-response singing (as in the montuno form).

producer A person engaged either by a recording artist or, more often, a record company, who directs and assists the recording process. The producer's duties may include securing the services of session musicians; deciding on arrangements; making technical decisions; motivating the artist creatively; helping to realize the artistic vision in a commercially viable way; and not unimportantly, ensuring that the project comes in under budget. A good producer often develops a distinctive signature sound, and successful producers are always in great demand. They are often rewarded handsomely for their efforts, garnering a substantial share of a recording's earnings, in addition to a commission.

R&B Rhythm & blues. An African American musical genre emerging after World War II. It consisted of a loose cluster of styles derived from black musical traditions, characterized by energetic and hard-swinging rhythms. At first performed exclusively by black musicians and aimed at black audiences, R&B came to replace the older category of "race records" (see Chapter 7).

refrain In the verse-refrain song, the refrain is the "main part" of the song, usually constructed in AABA or ABAC form (see discussion of Tin Pan Alley song form in Chapter 1).

release *See* **bridge.**

reverb Short for "reverberation"—a prolongation of a sound by virtue of an ambient acoustical space created by hard, reflective surfaces. The sound bounces off these surfaces and recombines with the original sound, slightly delayed (reverb is measured in terms of seconds and fractions of seconds). Reverberation can occur naturally or be simulated either electronically or by digital sound processors.

riff A simple, repeating melodic idea or pattern that generates rhythmic momentum; typically played by the horns or the piano in a jazz ensemble, or by an electric guitar in a rock 'n' roll context.

rockabilly A vigorous form of country and western music ("hillbilly" music) informed by the rhythms of black R&B and electric blues. It is exemplified by such artists as Carl Perkins and the young Elvis Presley.

sampling A digital recording process wherein a sound source is recorded or "sampled" with a microphone, converted into a stream of binary numbers that represent the profile of the sound, quantized, and stored in computer memory. The digitized sound sample may then be retrieved in any number of ways, including "virtual recording studio" programs for the computer, or by activating the sound from an electronic keyboard or drum machine.

scat singing A technique that involves the use of nonsense syllables as a vehicle for wordless vocal improvisation. It is most often found in a jazz context.

slap-back A distinctive short reverberation with few repetitions, often heard in the recordings of rockabilly artists, such as the Sun Records recordings of Elvis Presley.

strophes Poetic stanzas; often, a pair of stanzas of alternating form that constitute the structure of a poem. These could become the **verse** and **chorus** of a **strophic** song.

strophic A song form that employs the same music for each poetic unit in the lyrics.

syncopation Rhythmic patterns in which the stresses occur on what are ordinarily weak beats, thus displacing or suspending the sense of metric regularity.

tempo Literally, "time" (from Italian). The rate at which a musical composition proceeds, regulated by the speed of the beat or pulse to which it is performed.

timbre The "tone color" or characteristic sound of an instrument or voice, determined by its frequency and overtone components. Timbre is the aspect of sound that allows us, for example, to differentiate between the sounds of a violin and a flute when both instruments are playing the same pitch.

tonic Refers to the central or "home" pitch, or chord, of a musical piece—or sometimes of just a section of the piece.

tremolo The rapid reiteration of a single pitch to create a vibrating sound texture. This effect can be produced by acoustic instruments or by electronic means.

verse In general usage, this term refers to a group of lines of poetic text, often rhyming, that usually exhibit regularly recurring metrical patterns. In the verse-refrain song, the verse refers to an introductory section that precedes the main body of the song, the **refrain** (see discussion of Tin Pan Alley song form in Chapter 1).

vibrato An expressive musical technique that involves minute wavering or fluctuation of a pitch.

waltz A dance in triple time with a strong emphasis on every third beat.

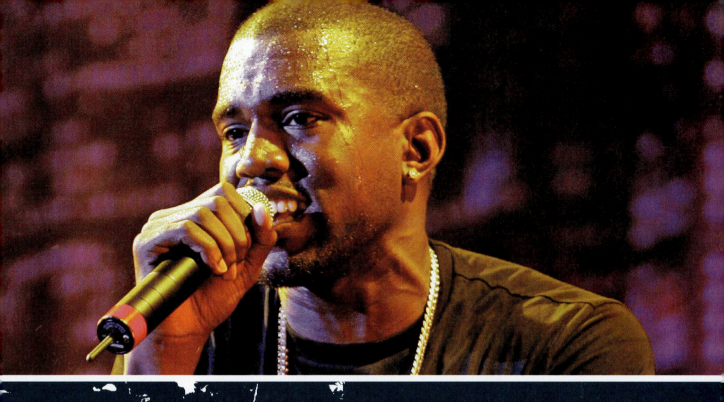

BIBLIOGRAPHY

This list includes all major works cited in the body of this book, along with a small number of others that may be recommended for further reading on individual topics and issues central to the material covered in the preceding pages. No attempt is made to offer a comprehensive bibliography here, or to list books of a general introductory nature in the area of American popular music.

Bashe, Philip. *Heavy Metal Thunder*. Garden City, NY, 1985.

Baulch, Emma. *Making Scenes: Reggae, Punk, and Death Metal in 1990s Bali*. Durham, NC, and London, 2007.

Baulch, Emma and Kusuma Bangkal. "The McDonaldisation of Bali." *Inside Indonesia*, December 1994.

Beatles, the. *Anthology*. San Francisco, 2000.

Berry, Chuck. *The Autobiography*. New York, 1987.

Brackett, David, ed. *The Pop, Rock, and Soul Reader: Histories and Debates*. New York, 2005.

Bright, Spencer. *Peter Gabriel: An Authorized Biography*. London, 1999.

Chapple, Steve, and Reebee Garofalo. *Rock 'n' Roll Is Here to Pay: The History and Politics of the Music Industry*. Chicago, 1977.

Charles, Ray, and David Ritz. *Brother Ray: Ray Charles' Own Story*. New York, 1978.

Chilton, John. *Let the Good Times Roll: The Story of Louis Jordan and His Music*. Ann Arbor, MI, 1994.

Clarke, Donald. *The Rise and Fall of Popular Music*. New York, 1995.

Cohen, Rich. *Machers and Rockers: Chess Records and the Business of Rock & Roll*. New York, 2004.

Collin, Matthew. *Altered State: The Story of Ecstasy Culture and Acid House*. London, 1997.

Deffaa, Chip. *Blue Rhythms: Six Lives in Rhythm and Blues*. Urbana, IL, 1996.

Douglas, Susan J. *Where the Girls Are: Growing Up Female with the Mass Media.* New York, 1994, 1995.

Elliott, Debbie. "Gogol Bordello: Music from 'Gypsy Punks.'" *All Things Considered*, National Public Radio, April 29, 2006.

Frith, Simon. *Sound Effects: Youth, Leisure, and the Politics of Rock 'n' Roll.* New York, 1981.

George, Nelson. *Hip Hop America.* New York, 1998.

George, Nelson, et al., eds. *Fresh: Hip Hop Don't Stop.* New York, 1985.

George-Warren, Holly, and Patricia Romanowski, eds. *The Rolling Stone Encyclopedia of Rock & Roll,* third edition. New York, 2001.

Gillett, Charlie. *The Sound of the City: The Rise of Rock and Roll.* New York, 1996.

Goodwin, Andrew. *Dancing in the Distraction Factory: Music Television and Popular Culture.* Minneapolis, 1992.

Graham, Bill, and Robert Greenfield. *Bill Graham Presents: My Life Inside Rock and Out.* New York: 1992.

Guralnick, Peter. *Sweet Soul Music: Rhythm and Blues and the Southern Dream of Freedom.* New York, 1986.

———. *Last Train to Memphis: The Rise of Elvis Presley.* Boston, 1994.

———. *Careless Love: The Unmaking of Elvis Presley.* Boston, 1999.

———. Liner notes for CD *Sam Cooke: Portrait of a Legend, 1951–1964.* ABKCO Records 92642. New York, 2003.

———. *Dream Boogie: The Triumph of Sam Cooke.* New York, 2005.

Hager, Steven. *Hip Hop: The Illustrated History of Break Dancing, Rap Music, and Graffiti.* New York, 1984.

Holden, Stephen. "The Pop Life: 25 Years of A & M." *The New York Times*, June 10 (p. 24, Section C), 1987.

Jones, Quincy. *Q—The Autobiography of Quincy Jones.* New York, 2002.

Karlen, Neal. "Prince Talks." *Rolling Stone,* September 12 (pp. 24-26), 1985.

Keil, Charles. *Urban Blues.* Chicago, 1966.

Keil, Charles, and Steven Feld. *Music Grooves.* Chicago, 1994.

Knopper, Steve. *Appetite for Self-Destruction: The Spectacular Crash of the Record Industry in the Digital Age.* New York, 2009.

Kusek, David, and Gerd Leonhard. *The Future of Music: Manifesto for the Digital Music Revolution.* Boston, 2005.

Laing, Dave. *One-Chord Wonders.* Philadelphia, 1985.

Lewis, Randy. "Is this merger just the ticket?" *Los Angeles Times*, February 12, 2009.

Malone, Bill C. *Country Music, U.S.A.* Revised edition, Austin, TX, 1985.

Mao, Jeff. "Behind the Boards with the Bomb Squad." *Ego Trip* 4:1, 1997.

Maslin, Janet. "Bob Dylan," in *The Rolling Stone Illustrated History of Rock & Roll*, Jim Miller, ed. New York, 1980.

Mgxashe, Mxolisi. "A conversation with Ray Phiri," in *The Paul Simon Companion*, Stacey Luftig, ed. New York, 1997.

Morse, Dave. *Motown and the Arrival of Black Music.* New York, 1971.

Negus, Keith. *Producing Pop: Culture and Conflict in the Popular Music Industry.* London, 1992.

O'Dair, Barbara, ed. *Trouble Girls: The Rolling Stone Book of Women in Rock.* New York, 1997.

Oliver, Paul. *Blues Fell This Morning: Meaning in the Blues.* Cambridge, England, 1990.

Palmer, Robert. *Deep Blues.* New York, 1981.

———. "The Cuban Connection." *Spin,* 4:8, 1988.

———. *Rock & Roll: An Unruly History.* New York, 1995.

Pareles, Jon. "Pay what you want for this article." *The New York Times*, December 9 (Arts Section p. 36), 2007.

Petkov, Steven, and Leonard Mustazza, eds. *The Frank Sinatra Reader.* New York, 1995.

Reynolds, Simon. *Generation Ecstasy: Into the World of Techno and Rave Culture.* New York, 1998.

Roberts, John Storm. *The Latin Tinge: The Impact of Latin American Music on the United States,* second edition. New York, 1998.

Rose, Tricia. *Black Noise: Rap Music and Black Culture in Contemporary America.* Middletown, CT, 1994.

Sante, Luc. "Unlike a Virgin." *The New Republic*, August 20 (pp. 25–29), 1990.

Schafer, R. Murray. *The Tuning of the World.* New York, 1977.

Sexton, Adam, ed. *Desperately Seeking Madonna.* New York, 1993.

Shaw, Arnold. *Honkers and Shouters: The Golden Years of Rhythm and Blues.* New York, 1986.

Sublette, Ned. *Cuba and its Music: From the First Drums to the Mambo.* Chicago, 2004.

———. "The Kingsmen and the Cha-Cha-Cha," in *Listen Again: A Momentary History of Pop Music.* Eric Weisbard, ed. Durham, NC, 2007.

Taylor, Timothy D. *Global Pop: World Music, World Markets.* New York, 1997.

Théberge, Paul. *Any Sound You Can Imagine: Making Music/Consuming Technology.* Middletown, CT, 1997.

Toop, David. *The Rap Attack 2: African Rap to Global Hip Hop.* London, 2000.

Wald, Elijah. *Escaping the Delta: Robert Johnson and the Invention of the Blues.* New York, 2004.

Walser, Robert. *Running with the Devil: Power, Gender, and Madness in Heavy Metal Music.* Middletown, CT, 1993.

West, Cornel. *Race Matters.* Boston, 1993.

Wynn, Ron. *Tina: The Tina Turner Story.* New York, 1985.

Zolov, Eric. *Refried Elvis: The Rise of the Mexican Counterculture.* Berkeley and Los Angeles, 1999.

CREDITS

INDEX